Daily Telegraph
CRICKET YEAR BOOK 84

Michael Melford
Bill Frindall

Consultant editor Michael Melford
Statistics Bill Frindall
Other contributors Michael Carey
(England Tests and World Cup), E.W. Swanton (special articles), George Abbott, Rajan Bala (India), Mike Beddow, Tony Cozier (West Indies), Rachael Flint, John Fogg, David Green, Neil Hallam, Derek Hodgson, Doug Ibbotson, Michael Owen-Smith (South Africa), S.S. Perera (Sri Lanka), Terry Power (New Zealand), Qamar Ahmed (Pakistan), D.J. Rutnagur, Alan Shiell (Australia), A.S.R. Winlaw.

Editor Norman Barrett
Designer Martin Bronkhorst
Illustrator Dennis Curran

Acknowledgements Thanks are due to David Armstrong and Mike Gear for supplying the statistics for the Minor Counties and Second XI championships, respectively, and to the TCCB for making the first-class fixtures available.

Most of the photographs appearing in this book are reproduced by permission of Adrian Murrell/All-Sport and Bill Smith. Other pictures were provided by Syndication International and Associated Sports Photography.

The editors particularly wish to thank Radford Barrett, Daily Telegraph Sports Editor, for his generous help.

Published by the Daily Telegraph
135 Fleet Street, London EC4P 4BL

First Published 1983
© Daily Telegraph 1983
Scorecharts © Bill Frindall 1983
ISBN 0 86367 000 8 paperback
ISBN 0 86367 001 6 hardback

Conditions of Sale:
This book is sold subject to the conditions that it shall not, by way of trade or otherwise, be lent, re-sold, hired out or otherwise circulated without the publisher's prior consent in any form of binding or cover other than that in which it is published.

Printed in Great Britain
by Biddles Limited, Guildford, Surrey
Typeset by Shanta Thawani, London

Contents

4	Foreword, by Sir Donald Bradman	130	Schweppes County Championship
7	**Looking Back**	134	Review of the Counties
8	India Bring a Touch of Romance, by Michael Melford		134 Derbyshire, 136 Essex, 138 Glamorgan, 140 Gloucestershire, 142 Hampshire, 144 Kent, 146 Lancashire, 148 Leicestershire, 150 Middlesex, 152 Northamptonshire, 154 Nottinghamshire, 156 Somerset, 158 Surrey, 160 Sussex, 162 Warwickshire, 164 Worcestershire, 166 Yorkshire
12	From Pitch to Press Box, by David Green		
14	Daily Telegraph 'Twin Hundreds', by E.W. Swanton		
15	Daily Telegraph Cricketers of the Year, by E.W. Swanton		
17	**England's Winter Tour 1982-83**	168	University Cricket
18	England in Australia	171	First Class Averages
32	Benson & Hedges World Series Cup	179	Benson & Hedges Cup
36	England in New Zealand	182	NatWest Bank Trophy
37	**Overseas Cricket 1982-83**	185	John Player League
38	India v Sri Lanka	187	Second XI County Championship and Under-25 Competition
40	Pakistan v Australia		
47	Pakistan v India	188	Minor Counties Championship
56	New Zealand v Sri Lanka	190	Village and Club Cricket
61	West Indies v India	191	Schools Cricket
69	Sri Lanka v Australia	192	Young Australians Tour
71	Cricket in Australia	193	Women's Cricket
75	Cricket in South Africa	**195**	**Extras**
79	Cricket in the West Indies	196	Test Career Averages
81	Cricket in New Zealand	203	Guide to Newcomers
83	Cricket in India	208	Obituary 1982-83
86	Cricket in Pakistan	**211**	**Looking Forward**
88	Cricket in Sri Lanka	212	England on Tour 1983-84
89	**Prudential World Cup 1983**	213	The 1984 Season
101	**New Zealand in England 1983**	214	Fixtures 1984
129	**English Season 1983**		

Foreword

Having retired from most things to do with cricket except watching, I thought perhaps my days of writing forewords were also over. But I agreed to Bill Frindall's personal invitation to do just one more, this time for the *Daily Telegraph Cricket Year Book,* primarily because it enabled me to pay a tribute to this relatively new but extremely valuable production and to the *Telegraph* for its tremendous support over the years for the game of cricket.

Cricket is notorious for the mass of literature it spawns. There are monthly magazines in both England and Australia. And each of the Australian States has been responsible for producing a year book, but their cost and the demands on staff have been causing problems, whilst their appearance is often understandably belated. Of course, Wisden's wonderful *Cricketers' Almanack* dominates them all, but it comes under a special category.

In 1983, however, it seems to me that the world is welcoming, in concise, readable form, more-or-less instant productions to fit the age of television, instant replays, and one-day cricket. At least, it is my assessment that this *Daily Telegraph* book splendidly meets a current need.

I am writing these lines shortly after the conclusion of an Australian summer that surely produced cricket of a quantity to satisfy the most avid supporter. Whether there was sufficient quality is another matter, and the division between the devotees and antagonists of one-day cricket remains.

There will, I think, however be unanimity that the new format, whereby the Test series was played to a conclusion in the first part of the season and the one-day matches took the spotlight in the second half, was a vast improvement on the former mishmash. One-day cricket has its deficiencies, and I have constantly deplored the departure in it from one of cricket's basic essentials, namely the need to dismiss your opponents. The quantity of wickets taken (if fewer than 10) has no relevance. It really does seem an absurdity that if each side completes its allotted number of overs, a score of 200 for 9 defeats a total of 199 for 0, bearing in mind that the latter score was probably held down by a more ruthless use of negative bowling and defensive field placing. On the other hand, I applaud a system which by its very nature gets rid of that unutterable bore who thinks occupancy of the crease is all that matters.

Public acceptance of the one-day game as entertainment plus was confirmed by the marvellous crowd of 84,153 people who swarmed into the Melbourne Cricket Ground to see England play Australia on January 23rd, 1983. The authorities so badly misjudged the attendance that a massive foul-up occurred when the manned turnstiles were quite unable to handle the volume of people seeking admission. Apart from this record, other matches also had an excellent response.

The splendid public support accorded the Test matches was also gratifying evidence that two such diverse types of cricket can exist, as it were, side by side. It would indeed be tragic if the excitement of the one-day game sounded the death knell of the more sedate but authoritative skills of the Test arena.

The 1982-83 Australian season undoubtedly produced a resurgence of genuine competition for batting spots in the Australian side. It highlighted New Zealand's development as a most worthy opponent at the highest level, but it must surely have presented England's selectors with a man-sized headache.

I am not conversant with the full range of talent available in English county cricket, but do not think it unfair to observe that an attack comprising nothing but medium-to-fastish and off-spin bowling is devoid of that variety which captains should have at their disposal. And it would also seem that they can no longer expect Ian Botham to go on winning matches off his own bat and/or arm. Clearly, there is much rebuilding to do.

More than usual prominence was given to doubtful umpiring decisions, and despite the visual proof on TV of an occasional error, my observations led me to believe that the umpiring as a whole stood up very well in comparison with that of previous years, when the modern proof of error did not exist. However, as the miracle of television is a fact of life, I would support the judicious use of it as an aid to umpires for such clearly observable events as run-outs. A simple procedure could be devised, and I would have thought umpires should welcome it. But I would not support its use for lbw's, where the umpire's unique positioning to exercise judgement and opinion should remain dominant.

A couple of other observations before I close. I have always opposed and deplored the change to calling no-balls off the front foot. The latter has now became so farcical and such a bore to spectators and players alike (more of an irritant perhaps to players) that I cannot understand the stubborn refusal of administrators to admit the cure is worse than the disease, especially when a remedy, given a modicum of common sense, could so easily be forthcoming and bring back to cricket an exciting moment that has been killed. The obvious attitude of bowlers today, knowing that the no-ball is most unlikely to be scored from, and sundries is the only sufferer, is one of detached disdain. Legislation that detracts from cricket as a spectacle should be discouraged at every turn. Perhaps the administrators don't bother to listen to the incessant, and in my view justifiable, adverse comments on this law by every knowledgeable radio and television commentator.

And on a technical note, I am disturbed and disappointed by a growing tendency for batsmen, misguidedly, to adopt the upright bat in the stance, a method so beloved by Mike Brearley. As an observer of almost every great batsman who has adorned the stage this century, and as one who can modestly claim some knowledge of the art and technique of batsmanship, I am positive the new idea is negative and regressive, and detracts greatly from the style and flow of batsmanship. The greatest golfer will tell you that the preliminary waggle is an essential part of a good golf swing. In the same way, there is a need for the truly great batsman (Sir Jack Hobbs comes vividly to mind) to make footwork and balance the cornerstone of his batting. To that end he must be on the move (like a golf waggle) as the ball is about to be delivered. He cannot do that standing like a sentinel with bat in mid air. Even though it may occasionally assist the defence of a very tall man, or one with an exaggerated backswing, it inhibits the versatility and mobility in attack, and therefore should not be embraced by those who aspire to the highest grade.

Looking back

India Bring a Touch of Romance
by Michael Melford

A review of cricket in the 1980s is likely to be an unglamorous tale of commercial successes and failures, political dissensions, and technical wrangles over disagreeable subjects such as short-pitched bowling. India's success in the Prudential Cup, therefore, brought a much needed touch of romance. Giant-killers appeared in a field wherein none seemed possible.

India had won occasional one-day victories, indeed had beaten England in a three-match series in India 18 months earlier. But their previous form in such events in England, and their relative disinterest in a form of cricket for which they were usually ill equipped, made them no better than sixth favourites in a field of eight. When they started their preparations in England with a defeat by the Minor Counties at Monks Risborough, it seemed no more than confirmation of their innocuousness in limited-over cricket abroad.

Their win only six days later over West Indies at Old Trafford could be easily dismissed as an isolated blemish on the formbook, especially when West Indies won the second match between them easily at The Oval and when only Kapil Dev's superb 175 not out kept them from defeat by Zimbabwe at Tunbridge Wells.

But fortified by what was probably a huge piece of luck, they rose to new heights in the semi-final and final, with victories over England and West Indies, showing that fast bowling is not everything, and demonstrating many of the major cricketing virtues.

The luck of which they took such brilliant advantage lay, I believe, in the English weather. The dry spell after the floods of May produced pitches, especially at Old Trafford, that were like many in India. At Old Trafford one might have been in Kanpur as England's fast bowlers thumped the ball in with the minimum of menace after the Indian bowlers of gentle medium pace, bowling straight and on a full length, had led batsmen trying to assault them into fatal errors on a pitch doing just enough to make nothing quite straightforward. It was a triumph for subtlety over power, and as such to be greatly applauded.

The limited-over influence I believe that, except for the surfeit of bouncers and no-balls that are common now to all forms of cricket, the three-day game is providing more entertainment than for many years. For this, players and captains earn full marks, but the influence of the limited-over game also probably has something to do with it.

In that batsmen have discovered that they can, with fair success, play strokes that they did not know were in their repertoire, the one-day game has been beneficial. But the sight of batsmen cutting off the leg-stump and bowlers angling the ball into the batsman's toes, wherever they are, must be a nightmare to coaches. The defensive bowling required in limited-over cricket has undoubtedly made it harder for many young bowlers to master their craft in the conventional game.

Thus, though the three-day game has greatly improved as a spectacle in the last twenty years, I believe that it is partly because the standard of bowling has fallen. Certainly most counties have imported fast bowlers, but not all are of the top class, and the best of them individually are less formidable than when they are assembled as a team.

Helmets Any topical review has to mention helmets and the argument that, by making batsmen and fielders foolhardy and bowlers less concerned, they create almost as many accidents as they prevent. But it is a far-reaching and involved argument and, as a ban on the unlovely things would lead to all sorts of recriminations as soon as a batsman or close fielder was hit, it has to be accepted that the helmet is here to stay.

Politics The game continued to be bedevilled by political issues in 1983. MCC members voted on whether they should send a team to South Africa, a motion that many interpreted as whether they should be free to send a team to South Africa (or anywhere else) if such a tour was considered useful by both sides at the non-first-class level at which it would have been undertaken. Out of a membership of some 18,000, 4,344 voted for the motion; 6,604 were against sending a team, because it would upset other member-countries of the ICC, weaken MCC's position in the counsels of cricket, lead to financial ruin if other countries refused to play Test matches at Lord's, the big money-earner, and lay Lord's open to vandalism of a high quality.

Most of the political action of the year involved West Indies, some of whose governments refused at the last minute to accept an English women's team because five players had been to South Africa on private cricket holidays. The West Indians preparing for the Prudential Cup were also refused permission by their Board to play Yorkshire if Yorkshire included players banned for taking part in the 1982 tour of South Africa. Yorkshire insisted on playing whom they wished, and the match to mark the 150th anniversary of the death of the great anti-slave-trader, William Wilberforce, which had seemed a good idea to the worthy organizers from Hull University, did not take place. However, the TCCB took up the matter of team selection on the West Indies 1984 tour of England, and the West Indies Board of Control eventually agreed that it was purely a matter for the counties whom they picked.

The most remarkable tour of the year was undoubtedly that to South Africa made by the West Indians captained by Lawrence Rowe. They followed a visit by a team of Sri Lankans who, though including several Test players, were not good enough to trouble South African sides, lost money for their hosts, and were banned for 25 years at home.

The West Indians were a huge success, were fêted everywhere, and contracted to return in 1984. The impact of their visit was felt immediately. Some of the English cricketers who annually spend their winters coaching in South Africa found that, whereas previously 25 African boys would turn up at the classes, now it was 250. Football has been the main game among Africans, who now would fill nearly all the places in a representative South African XI. The fervour for cricket was something new.

Those who list the sad, sometimes cruel, often absurd paradoxes caused by political intrusion into sport were thus given another item. One reason that South African sport was originally ostracized was because the outside world took exception to the fact that non-Whites did not have equal sporting opportunities in South Africa. Now those cricketers who are really doing something to help and enthuse young Africans – not only the West Indians, but Gooch, Emburey and others – are banned wholly or partially in their own countries.

The TCCB, in an effort to prevent more English players from taking part in unofficial tours of South Africa in the future, proposed a contract with what became known as a 'loyalty' clause. It was rejected by the Cricketers Association, who saw it as an interference with the players' freedom of choice. The word 'loyalty', wherever it sprang, seemed misplaced anyhow. In 1977, players could be called 'disloyal' because they chose to play Packer cricket rather than for England. Now there is no suggestion that they are not available for England at all times. They would be going to South Africa in their own time if not needed elsewhere.

Four-day matches The proposal of four-day matches in the County Championship, most strongly supported by Warwickshire, was not endorsed by other counties. As one who would have supported it twenty years ago in the hope that it would give spin bowlers more opportunity and provide a better training ground for Test cricket, I have to admit to a change of mind in view of the difficulties of finding good four-day pitches, of devising a suitable fixture list in these days of three limited-over competitions, and of persuading the public that longer matches would not necessarily produce slower, duller cricket.

These considerations seem to outweigh the advantages, which would be to encourage more attacking bowling and help not only the spinner but the middle-order batsman, who would in theory have more time to 'build' an innings.

Decision by toss of a coin There was widespread dismay that the Benson & Hedges quarter-final between Gloucestershire and the ultimate winners, Middlesex, at Bristol should by the rules have had to be decided by the toss of a coin after three days of rain. The difficulty of finding another day in a congested season is obvious. If it is not possible to find a less wet ground in the neighbourhood for a 10-over contest, as when Yorkshire and Cambridgeshire took themselves off to Castleford in the Gillette Cup of 1967, would it not be an idea to use a local leisure centre or indoor school for either a six-a-side match or a straight bowling competition. Five bowlers a-side to bowl an over each at the stumps would be rather more satisfactory, for example, than settling a long-drawn-out football competition by penalties. Whatever the choice, players and public seem to be agreed that anything is preferable to just spinning a coin.

Weak teams against tourists The tendency of counties to field weak sides against the touring teams was even more pronounced in 1983. It may be an opportunity to rest vital players – though so little cricket was played in May that exhaustion might have been expected to set in later than usual. It may be a chance to try young players. But it is a discourtesy to the tourists and no help to the prestige of county cricket.

I do not ordinarily favour touring sides who publicly criticize their hosts, but I thought that Sir Allan Wright, manager of a very popular New Zealand side, did a service by speaking out without rancour about the weakness of sides fielded against the New Zealanders. He excepted the reigning champions, Middlesex, who put out the strongest side available.

Apart from being a discourtesy to visitors seeking the strongest possible competition between Test matches, fielding a weak side is surely not appreciated by members of county clubs, who must want to see their best players in action, especially as they may not see some of them anyhow during Tests.

Memorable feats The outstanding 'feat' of the season, I suppose, was that of Surrey's being bowled out for 14 by Essex on an evening in May after Essex had made 287. The pitch by all accounts was far from impossible, for Surrey easily saved the game. And though the ball swung a lot and Essex bowled vastly better than Surrey batted, they were strange circumstances in which to achieve a score 'worsened', for want of an appropriate word, only four times in first-class cricket, most recently in 1907.

History was made by Robin Boyd-Moss, who became the first batsman to score a hundred in each innings in the University Match, which dates back to 1827. Admittedly, the match is now played in a less defensive spirit, avoiding defeat being no longer as powerful an influence, but it is still astonishing that none of the many fine Oxford and Cambridge batsmen of the past achieved the feat.

One other unusual accomplishment was that of Roland Butcher, whose 37 catches for Middlesex was still the highest in the country even though he suffered a serious injury on July 18 and did not play for the last eight weeks of the season. He took some brilliant slip catches, especially off the slow bowlers, but is reported to have had by no means a 100 per cent record – which says something for the regularity with which the Middlesex bowlers were finding the edge during their mid-season heyday.

From Pitch to Press Box
by David Green

As an ex-first-class cricketer who has laid down the Gray-Nicolls in favour of the felt-tip, I am sometimes asked what advantages, if any, my playing experience gives me in my new career.

The poacher-turned-gamekeeper has fewer trump cards in his hand than might be supposed. His technical knowledge, which ought to be deeper than that of writers without comparable background, is a double-edged sword. For a description for a daily paper of a two-hour century by Gooch or Vivian Richards gains little from an analysis of top-hand position, shoulder alignment, or degree of wrist-pronation in the backlift.

More important than such minutiae is an instinct for what is happening on the field. And it would be both ludicrous and arrogant to suggest that this is possessed only by former cricketers, many of whom have had highly successful careers without understanding what they were doing, let alone how or why. A number of fine cricket writers have a most accurate feel for the game while being indifferent performers themselves. But I know from talking to such luminaries as John Arlott that this has been gained from years of observation and deep discussion with cricketers. It is comforting to me as a journalistic tyro that I do not have to scratch my head to form judgements about the cricket I am watching.

An instance occurred last season in the Somerset v New Zealand match at Taunton. The tourists batted till lunch on the second day, scoring 544 for nine. By 12.30 on the last day, Somerset had been bowled out for 267 on a pitch taking spin. Though the New Zealanders had a lead of 277, Geoff Howarth did not enforce the follow-on. He batted again for 18 overs, in which 46 runs were scored without loss, and then declared, setting Somerset 324 to win in 3 hours and 40 minutes. Various reasons were advanced to support this peculiar piece of cricket. Perhaps Howarth wanted a heavy roller to break up the pitch (which was already turning and bouncing). Perhaps (Good grief!) he did not want to field all day under a hot sun. Perhaps he wished to set his opponents a target so as to lure them to a defeat that they might avoid through a stolid block-out.

To my mind his decision to bat again merely gave an unexpected respite to Somerset, who predictably saved the match with their last pair together, the New Zealanders having lost 70 minutes' bowling time and the opportunity of a morale-boosting win.

Though certain that a tactical error had been made, I did not think that the point should be laboured. Cricketers are human beings and prone to error, as I know all too well from my own career, which, though not without its times of prosperity, also encompassed seemingly interminable periods of palsied ineptitude. It may, then, be a little easier for a former player to be sympathetic towards the cricketers he is watching, for he ought to understand what they are trying to do and also be able to accept that at times they are unable to do it.

Lack of such sympathy can produce unbalanced reporting, as may be illustrated by the 1964 Gillette Cup Semi-Final between Lancashire and Warwickshire at Old Trafford, a match in which I played.

It should be made clear that, when the Gillette Cup started in 1963, cricketers were immediately aware that the limited-overs game lent itself to purely defensive tactics by the fielding side, for whom 240 for 0 was preferable to 241 all out. They felt, though, that the game would present a better spectacle (and it was obviously designed as such) if it was played to largely orthodox fields, and there was unspoken agreement to this effect.

Accordingly, Warwickshire, having won the toss on a purler of a pitch, nicked and slogged their way to 294, a big score in those days. We replied in kind and were 67 for 0 after 12 overs, at which point tea was taken. Our rate of progress evidently alarmed our opponents, for a brainstorming session during the interval produced field-settings now familiar but then distinctly shocking. For the first time there was an inner ring of four saving one and five boundary fielders, and there were bowlers of the calibre of Cartwright, Rudi Webster, Bannister, and Ibadulla in the attack.

The impact of this tactic may be gauged by the fact that Ken Grieves, our captain, suggested to our Chairman that if Warwickshire wanted to win the game that badly we should concede it. We were baffled. Some of us blocked in protest, and it is clear that we were wrong to do so. A few of the large crowd booed our opponents. Many more barracked us.

We did not expect a good Press, but we felt that the contrast in field placings and the fact that Bob Barber, an England leg-spinner, bowled eight overs of seam-up might constitute mitigating circumstances in the eyes of a Press box that habitually presented itself as being rather more idealistic about the game than ourselves. We were, however, almost universally condemned. One well-known writer fulminated to such an extent that one of our players, reading his piece next day, said 'He can't write this, can he?', to which another replied, 'Of course he can, he invented the game, didn't he?'

On reflection, perhaps the most important thing that playing first-class cricket has taught me is that it is no more complicated than any other sort of cricket. When a batsman, well set with 60 or 70 to his credit on a good pitch, suddenly has his stumps knocked over, explanations are sought and offered. The bowler, if consulted, will perhaps say that he moved in closer to the stumps, put a bit extra in and it nipped back a bit. The batsman will nod, adding that he thought it kept a bit low as well. But *he* knows (and *I* know, because I have been that soldier) that he simply missed the wretched thing.

Daily Telegraph 'Twin Hundreds'
by E.W. Swanton

It will be a pleasure, when the moment comes, to hand to John Emburey the award with which the *Daily Telegraph* have identified my name – for being the first bowler last summer to reach a hundred wickets. It was a keen race to the post, and any of at least four others looked at times the likeliest winner over the latter half of the season. The unluckiest man must be accounted John Lever, who missed seven first-class matches recovering from a serious operation yet reached the magic target by taking 11 wickets in the last match. Phillippe Edmonds must have cursed the suspect back that enabled his Middlesex spinning partner to catch up and pass his total of wickets. Derek Underwood, the old faithful, came on in the final straight and was pipped only by a day or two, while Norman Gifford at the age of 43 enjoyed an Indian summer with his best haul for many a year.

Since I believe intimidation and an overdue accent on speed to be the biggest twin evils of modern cricket, and the recovery of spin to its rightful place to be the blessing most to be wished for, I was naturally delighted that of these five bowlers four were spinners and all were English. Emburey, with his control of the arts of flight and off-spin and high, easy action, is a model for any aspiring bowler, and I trust we may see him back in the England XI in 1985.

As regards the fastest century-maker of the season, to whom is awarded the Lawrence Trophy, I can only express dismay that the traditional intentions of the donors to reward attacking batting with a prize dating back to 1934 should have been frustrated on the last day of the season for the sake of a fruitless plan whereby Leicestershire deemed it necessary to present Lancashire with 190 runs in 35 minutes by non-bowlers sending down full-pitches and long-hops. Steven O'Shaughnessy in these farcical circumstances equalled the genuine hundred made in a record 35 minutes by P.G.H. Fender at Northampton in 1920.

Young O'Shaughnessy is a promising cricketer who was unlucky to have found himself involved in what he himself described as a hollow achievement. I do not say that, after delays, circumstances may not occasionally make the offering of cheap runs over a short period a justifiable ploy. But there must be a close limit to such artificial cricket if the game is not to be brought into disrepute – and if the patron's intentions are not to be mocked.

It was particularly unfortunate that this accident occurred, since for the best part of three months the lead had been held by another young cricketer, Nigel Popplewell of Somerset. Against Gloucestershire at Bath, he had reached his hundred in 41 minutes – a time only three times bettered in history – when his side were forcing the pace against, if not a formidable attack, at least recognized bowlers.

LOOKING BACK/CRICKETERS OF THE YEAR
Daily Telegraph Cricketers of the Year
by E.W. Swanton

In 1981-82, the inaugural season of this Year Book, all-rounders took most of the honours bestowed by our correspondents in the seven Test-playing countries and South Africa. In 1982-83, the accent is on the art of batting as represented by the names of Gower, Lloyd, Amarnath, Duleep Mendis, and Cook. The only two cricketers to have been re-selected are the all-rounders Hadlee and Imran Khan, who so far as their bowling is concerned represent speed (though not just undiluted pace), as also does the eighth nomination, Lawson. The choices are only perhaps less than ideal in that this time spin bowling is not represented.

With Ian Botham's skills rather in eclipse over the twelve months from end to end of the English seasons of 1982-83, there can scarcely have been a rival to David Gower as the one batsman of world class born in this country, and in addition a marvellously good all-round fielder and a man who can still play Test cricket with a smile.

Tony Cozier names Clive Lloyd, 19 years after making his debut for Guyana, 'in every respect' the West Indian cricketer of the year. Apart from his leadership of the West Indies and Lancashire, he led his own country to success in the Shell Shield 'and remained the safest slip catcher' in Test matches. How Clive, with his large frame and suspect joints, manages to shrug off the wear and tear is a lesson in courage and determination to all his younger contemporaries.

Amarnath is picked (even above Kapil Dev!) by Rajan Bala for the same quality of courage with which in his mid-30s, and after having been dropped for three years from the Indian side, he returned with the utmost success against Pakistan and West Indies with their fast bowling array. 'The man dropped because experts said he could not play short-pitched bowling proved that against this sort of stuff he was India's best' – with five hundreds and two near-hundreds in eleven Tests.

Mendis, captain of Sri Lanka in this early period of their Test life, has brought them through with honour, and attracted the cricket world's attention by making 105 in each innings against India at Madras. Jimmy Cook, of the Transvaal, is inevitably little known outside South Africa. Michael Owen-Smith mentions that only five South Africans have ever made more in a season than his 755, with an average of 58 in the keenly contested Currie Cup of 1982-83, and describes him as a covers fielder little behind Peter Kirsten.

In Alan Shiell's opinion, Geoff Lawson just earns the vote over the much-harassed Kim Hughes (for whom many cricket-lovers outside Australia have both admiration and sympathy) as the leading Australian of 1982-83. Lawson, after being the most successful bowler in the short series in Pakistan, easily topped the list with 34 wickets in the Ashes series, and still had the stamina to bowl well in the protracted one-day tournament involving England and New Zealand.

The easiest of the eight to pick must have been the great all-rounders Richard Hadlee and Imran Khan. Terry Power points out that Hadlee has taken more Test wickets than the rest of the New Zealand touring team to England combined. After a decade of Test cricket during which he has been the mainstay of the side, his crowning moment perhaps came when at the end of the England tour this last summer he was named Man of the Series.

Hadlee is a whole-hearted cricketer if ever there was one, and so likewise is our remaining nomination, from Pakistan, Imran Khan (both of them, incidentally, have good cricket blood in their veins). At the age of 30, Imran has become the only one of his countrymen to take 200 Test wickets, while as forcing batsman and fielder he would be worth his place if he never bowled a ball. Added to this, Qamar Ahmed points out that, in leading Pakistan to victory in Test series against Australia and India, he has infused a new spirit into his team. All this, and for Imran as for most of these men further laurels should be in store.

England's winter tour 1982-83

England in Australia

While it was hardly a surprise that England, with an ill-balanced and below-strength party, should lose the Test series – and with it the Ashes – by two Tests to one in Australia last winter, there were times when the gulf between the sides did not look unbridgeable.

In the end, however, the supremacy of Australia's fast bowlers prevailed, notably the excellent Geoff Lawson, although it was reasonable to wonder what might have happened if England had not opted to bowl first on one of the best batting surfaces in the world at Adelaide, or suffered from a dreadful umpiring error – in the first over! – as they embarked on the task of trying to save the series at Sydney.

The fact that Australia's selectors hit upon their highly effective fast bowling combination only by chance also had a certain irony that would not be lost on the tourists. Terry Alderman, who dislocated his shoulder in a fracas with a spectator during the first Test at Perth, was not seen again in the series.

Nor was Dennis Lillee, who suffered a recurrence of a knee injury. In their absence, the selectors turned to Rodney Hogg and Jeff Thomson, who with Lawson comprised a formidable trio. At times, notably in the second Test at Brisbane, the dominance of Australia's fast bowlers led them to overstep the bounds of fairness with excessive short-pitched bowling, with only one, belated, warning (to Thomson) from the umpires.

They posed constant problems for England, who could never have ventured previously on such a demanding tour with such a lack of proven ability and Test experience among their opening batsmen. Geoff Cook had a miserable time and could never adjust to the extra bounce of Australian pitches, even though most encountered were not particularly noted for their pace.

Graeme Fowler, on his first tour, experienced wretched luck in the State games, finding various ways of getting out which severely damaged his self-confidence. Yet there were times when he made runs well, and no innings was more courageous than his, in the face of much short-pitched bowling, at Brisbane.

The frequent loss of an early wicket put additional pressure on Chris Tavaré, who was often quite happy to attempt little more than survival. But England nevertheless often overcame the problem of poor starts, and at various times David Gower and Derek Randall, the only two century-makers, and Allan Lamb all played well in the middle order. Indeed, more than once they established advantageous positions, only to squander them by lack of application or suspect methods against the fast bowlers.

All this, plus the known weaknesses in England's bowling, meant that the role of Ian Botham was even more important than usual. He made only one half-century in the series, and, although he took 18 wickets, they cost 40 runs each. Overall his form did much to confirm the theory that when Botham is successful, so are England. Unfortunately, he was rarely able to use the new ball with either penetration or accuracy, which merely increased the pressure on the rest of the England attack. Botham has yet to achieve in Australia anything to match the remarkable all-round feats he has produced elsewhere.

While no one expected miraculous deeds from him all the time (in the end, just one telling performance with either bat or ball might have swayed the series), Botham appeared to pay the price for what seemed to be an over-casual approach to the State matches preceding the Test series. This, alas, seemed to be condoned by both captain and tour management, and may well have had a disturbing influence on younger players. Time and again, when Botham's lack of form was queried, the pat answer came: 'He is a big-occasion player. He will be all right when the Test matches arrive.'

The renaissance never materialized, and it led to more than one moment when England's tactics were baffling. Not least of these occurred in the second Test, when Botham was allowed to continue with an erratic and expensive spell with the new ball, while Norman Cowans found himself removed after one costly over and subsequently, until his splendid match-winning performance at Melbourne, frequently found himself called upon to bowl at the wrong time and at the wrong batsman.

Consequently, until Cowans was at last allowed to use the new ball at Melbourne, responding by playing a leading role in a historic victory, no one was able to fill the gap. Derek Pringle often looked out of his depth at this level, and probably suffered from being chosen for England too soon on the evidence of what he had achieved for Cambridge University against below-strength county sides the previous season.

Robin Jackman bowled fewer than 100 overs on the entire tour, and although he enjoyed moments of success in the subsequent one-day series, never came into contention for a Test place. If his selection was perhaps a reward for his efforts the previous summer and his misfortune in the past, rather than what he might achieve on Australian pitches at his pace, it was also curious that his plan to retire from first-class cricket immediately afterwards (and announced during the tour) was not known to the selectors. The opportunity to give a younger cricketer valuable experience was thus sadly lost.

Predictably, the choice of three off-spinners was no more successful than it had been 20 years earlier, when David Allen, Fred Titmus, and Ray Illingworth – who lose little in comparison with their modern counterparts – were chosen. Indeed, England's last slender chance of saving the series disappeared when Geoff Miller and Eddie Hemmings bowled disappointingly on a dusting, turning pitch at Sydney. Of the trio, Miller, although not as prolific a wicket-taker as on his previous tour, was the most successful. Hemmings was a disappointment, and Vic Marks did well in one-day internationals, although his three first-class wickets on the tour cost 117 runs each.

ENGLAND'S WINTER TOUR 1982-83/IN AUSTRALIA

First Test: Perth, November 12, 13, 14, 16, 17.
Drawn.

An injury to Alderman, the Australia fast bowler, in a skirmish with a spectator not only weakened their attack but had a telling effect on the rest of the series. England, after being put in, made the first of many frail starts, but Tavaré, Gower, Lamb, and Randall sustained them, often against bowling that was lacking control.

England in turn, had their problems on a good pitch – not least in the balance of their attack – and Chappell, after a highly suspect start, batted with increasing brilliance for his hundred to give his side a slender lead.

At the start of the last day, England, only 150 ahead with 5 wickets down, were in some danger. But Randall followed his first innings success by again batting well to avoid the possibility of defeat.

Second Test: Brisbane, November 26, 27, 28, 30, December 1.
Australia won by 7 wickets.

England batted erratically after being put in on a pitch offering bounce and movement, and a disciplined century by Wessels on his first appearance steered Australia to a first innings lead of 122, latterly against some loose bowling.

By the end of the third day England had made 71 for 1, albeit with a great deal of discomfort against an excess of short-pitched bowling, which surprisingly brought only one bowler, Thomson, a caution from the umpires and was played by Fowler, especially, with much courage.

With Rackemann injured, there were hopes that England might develop a winning position. But Thomson undermined them, Lawson finished them off, and they contributed to their own downfall by missing chances as Australia completed a nervous victory.

Third Test: Adelaide, December 10, 11, 12, 14, 15.
Australia won by 8 wickets.

Opting to bowl first on what is widely regarded as the best pitch in Australia, England paid a high price, starting when Chappell made a brilliant hundred, joining Sir Donald Bradman and Clem Hill as the third Australian to make more than 2,500 runs against England.

Though Australia were contained later, they still made 438. Then, on the third day, England found themselves following on. After going through the morning with Gower and Lamb together, they lost their remaining eight wickets between lunch and tea.

On the fourth day, Gower and Botham held England together, but six wickets fell against the second new ball, leaving a second Australian win a formality.

ENGLAND'S WINTER TOUR 1982-83/IN AUSTRALIA

Fourth Test: Melbourne, December 26, 27, 28, 29, 30.
England won by 3 runs.

Inspired by the penetrative bowling of Cowans, England achieved a memorable win by one of the smallest margins in Ashes history. From first ball to last, the match swung one way then another on a pitch of variable bounce, England suffering a familiar collapse before a crowd of 64,051 after they had been put in. They lost their last seven wickets for 67 runs, their last five falling for only 25.

Australia's tail fared little better, their last five wickets falling for 26 runs. England had an incident-packed second innings, and then Cowans's splendid effort left Australia's last-wicket pair together with 74 runs needed.

The admirable Border, whose six previous innings in the series had yielded only 83 runs, batted with great composure and latterly scarcely played a false stroke. England opted to give him the single in order to attack the more impetuous Thomson, but the two took the game into a fifth day with half the required runs made. On a tense final morning, before a crowd of nearly 20,000 who had been admitted free, the score crept up, despite several singles declined by the batsmen in order to protect Thomson from the bowling.

With Australia only one firm stroke from victory and the field closing in to cut off the single, Thomson edged Botham to second slip, where the ball went in and out of Tavaré's hands before Miller snatched it out of the air to give England a famous victory – and the Kent captain peace of mind for the rest of his days.

Fifth Test: Sydney, January 2, 3, 4, 6, 7.
Drawn

Needing victory to save the series, England were frustrated from the first over when Dyson was given the benefit of the doubt in a clear-cut run-out episode. Dyson went on to make 79, and Australia 314, more than might have been the case. With England behind on first innings, despite the efforts of Gower and Randall, much depended on the spin of Hemmings and Miller when Australia began the fourth day with a lead of 167 and seven wickets left. As the pitch became slower, the hoped-for breakthrough never materialized. With 460 required for victory, England gained consolation only from avoiding defeat and an innings of 95 from nightwatchman Hemmings.

Australia v England 1982-83 1st Test
Match Drawn
Played at the WACA Ground, Perth, November 12, 13, 14, 16, 17 1982
Toss: Australia. Umpires: A.R. Crafter and M.W. Johnson
Debuts: England, N.G. Cowans (England's 500th player). Man of the Match: D.W. Randall

England

G. Cook	c Dyson b Lillee	1	c Border b Lawson	7
C.J. Tavaré	c Hughes b Yardley	89	c Chappell b Yardley	9
D.I. Gower	c Dyson b Alderman	72	lbw b Lillee	28
A.J. Lamb	c Marsh b Yardley	46	c Marsh b Lawson	56
I.T. Botham	c Marsh b Lawson	12	b Lawson	0
D.W. Randall	c Wood b Yardley	78	b Lawson	115
G. Miller	c Marsh b Lillee	30	(8) c Marsh b Yardley	0
D.R. Pringle	b Lillee	0	(9) not out	47
R.W. Taylor†	not out	29	(7) b Yardley	31
R.G.D. Willis*	c Lillee b Yardley	26	b Lawson	0
N.G. Cowans	b Yardley	4	lbw b Chappell	36
Extras	(B 7, LB 9, W 2, NB 6)	24	(B 5, LB 11, W 2, NB 11)	29
		411		**358**

Australia

G.M. Wood	c and b Willis	29
J. Dyson	lbw b Miller	52
A.R. Border	c Taylor b Botham	8
G.S. Chappell*	c Lamb b Willis	117
K.J. Hughes	c Willis b Miller	62
D.W. Hookes	lbw b Miller	56
R.W. Marsh†	c Cook b Botham	0
G.F. Lawson	b Miller	50
B. Yardley	c Lamb b Willis	17
D.K. Lillee	not out	2
T.M. Alderman	did not bat	
Extras	(B 4, LB 1, W 1, NB 25)	31
	(9 wickets declared)	**424**

	c Taylor b Willis	0	
	c Cowans b Willis	12	
	not out	32	
	not out	22	
	(2 wickets)	**73**	

Australia	O	M	R	W	O	M	R	W
Lillee	38	13	96	3	33	12	89	1
Alderman	43	15	84	1				
Lawson	29	6	89	1	32	5	108	5
Chappell	3	0	11	0	2.3	1	8	1
Yardley	42.4	15	107	5	41	10	101	3
Border					7	2	21	0
Hookes					1	0	2	0

England	O	M	R	W	O	M	R	W
Willis	31.5	4	95	3	6	1	23	2
Botham	40	10	121	2	6	1	17	0
Cowans	13	2	54	0	3	1	15	0
Pringle	10	1	37	0	2	0	3	0
Miller	33	11	70	4	4	3	8	0
Cook	4	2	16	0				
Lamb					1	1	0	0

Fall of Wickets

Wkt	E 1st	A 1st	E 2nd	A 2nd
1st	14	63	10	2
2nd	109	76	51	22
3rd	189	123	77	
4th	204	264	80	
5th	304	311	151	
6th	323	311	228	
7th	342	374	242	
8th	357	414	292	
9th	406	424	292	
10th	411		358	

*Captain †Wicket-keeper

Australia v England 1982-83 2nd Test
Australia won by 7 wickets
Played at Woolloongabba, Brisbane, November 26, 27, 28, 30, December 1 1982
Toss: Australia. Umpires: R.C. Bailhache and M.W. Johnson
Debuts: Australia, C.G. Rackemann, K.C. Wessels. Man of the Match: K.C. Wessels

England

C.J. Tavaré	c Hughes b Lawson	1	c Marsh b Lawson	13
G. Fowler	c Yardley b Lawson	7	c Marsh b Thomson	83
D.I. Gower	c Wessels b Lawson	18	c Marsh b Thomson	34
A.J. Lamb	c Marsh b Lawson	72	c Wessels b Thomson	12
I.T. Botham	c Rackemann b Yardley	40	(6) c Marsh b Thomson	15
D.W. Randall	c Lawson b Rackemann	37	(5) c Yardley b Thomson	4
G. Miller	c Marsh b Lawson	0	c Marsh b Lawson	60
R.W. Taylor†	c Lawson b Rackemann	1	c Hookes b Lawson	3
E.E. Hemmings	not out	15	b Lawson	18
R.G.D. Willis*	c Thomson b Yardley	1	not out	10
N.G. Cowans	c Marsh b Lawson	10	c Marsh b Lawson	5
Extras	(LB 2, W 1, NB 14)	17	(B 8, LB 8, W 1, NB 35)	52
		219		**309**

Australia

K.C. Wessels	b Willis	162	b Hemmings	46
J. Dyson	b Botham	1	retired hurt	4
A.R. Border	c Randall b Willis	0	c Botham b Hemmings	15
G.S. Chappell*	run out (Miller/Taylor)	53	c Lamb b Cowans	8
K.J. Hughes	c Taylor b Botham	0	not out	39
D.W. Hookes	c Taylor b Miller	28	not out	66
R.W. Marsh†	c Taylor b Botham	11		
B. Yardley	c Tavaré b Willis	53		
G.F. Lawson	c Hemmings b Willis	6		
C.G. Rackemann	b Willis	4		
J.R. Thomson	not out	5		
Extras	(B 2, LB 8, NB 8)	18	(B 2, LB 5, NB 5)	12
		341	(3 wickets)	**190**

Australia	O	M	R	W	O	M	R	W
Lawson	18.3	4	47	6	35.3	11	87	5
Rackemann	21	8	61	2	12.2	3	35	0
Thomson	8	0	43	0	31	6	73	5
Yardley	17	5	51	2	40.4	21	50	0
Chappell					6	2	8	0
Hookes					2	0	4	0

England	O	M	R	W	O	M	R	W
Willis	29.4	3	66	5	4	1	24	0
Botham	22	1	105	3	15.5	1	70	0
Cowans	6	0	36	0	9	1	31	1
Hemmings	33.3	6	81	0	29	9	43	2
Miller	19.3	4	35	1	3	0	10	0

Fall of Wickets

Wkt	E 1st	A 1st	E 2nd	A 2nd
1st	8	4	54	60
2nd	13	11	144	77
3rd	63	94	165	83
4th	141	99	169	
5th	152	130	194	
6th	152	171	201	
7th	178	271	226	
8th	191	310	285	
9th	195	332	295	
10th	219	341	309	

*Captain †Wicket-keeper
In the 2nd innings Dyson retired hurt at 20-0.

24 ENGLAND'S WINTER TOUR 1982-83/IN AUSTRALIA

Australia v England 1982-83 3rd Test
Australia won by 8 wickets
Played at the Adelaide Oval, December 10, 11, 12, 14, 15 1982
Toss: England. Umpires: R. A. French and M.W. Johnson
Debuts: Nil. Man of the Match: G.F. Lawson

Australia

K.C. Wessels	c Taylor b Botham	44	(2) c Taylor b Botham	1
J. Dyson	c Taylor b Botham	44	(1) not out	37
G.S. Chappell*	c Gower b Willis	115	(4) not out	26
K.J. Hughes	run out (Randall/Pringle)	88		
G.F. Lawson	c Botham b Willis	2	(3) c Randall b Willis	14
A.R. Border	c Taylor b Pringle	26		
D.W. Hookes	c Botham b Hemmings	37		
R.W. Marsh†	c Hemmings b Pringle	3		
B. Yardley	c Gower b Botham	38		
R.M. Hogg	not out	14		
J.R. Thomson	c and b Botham	3		
Extras	(LB 6, NB 18)	24	(NB 5)	5
		438	(2 wickets)	**83**

England

C.J. Tavaré	c Marsh b Hogg	1	c Wessels b Thomson	0
G. Fowler	c Marsh b Lawson	11	c Marsh b Lawson	37
D.I. Gower	c Marsh b Lawson	60	b Hogg	114
A.J. Lamb	c Marsh b Lawson	82	c Chappell b Yardley	8
I.T. Botham	c Wessels b Thomson	35	c Dyson b Yardley	58
D.W. Randall	b Lawson	0	c Marsh b Lawson	17
G. Miller	c Yardley b Hogg	7	lbw b Lawson	17
R.W. Taylor†	c Chappell b Yardley	2	(9) not out	3
D.R. Pringle	not out	1	(8) c Marsh b Thomson	9
E.E. Hemmings	b Thomson	0	c Wessels b Lawson	0
R.G.D. Willis*	b Thomson	1	c Marsh b Lawson	10
Extras	(LB 5, NB 11)	16	(B 7, LB 6, W 3, NB 15)	31
		216		**304**

England	O	M	R	W	O	M	R	W
Willis	25	8	76	2	8	1	17	1
Botham	36.5	5	112	4	10	2	45	1
Pringle	33	5	97	2	1.5	0	11	0
Miller	14	2	33	0				
Hemmings	48	17	96	1	4	1	5	0

Australia	O	M	R	W	O	M	R	W
Lawson	18	4	56	4	24	6	66	5
Hogg	14	2	41	2	19	5	53	1
Thomson	14.4	3	51	3	13	3	41	2
Yardley	21	7	52	1	37	12	90	2
Border					8	2	14	0
Hookes					3	1	9	0

Fall of Wickets

Wkt	A 1st	E 1st	E 2nd	A 2nd
1st	76	1	11	3
2nd	138	21	90	37
3rd	264	140	118	
4th	270	181	236	
5th	315	181	247	
6th	355	194	272	
7th	359	199	277	
8th	391	213	289	
9th	430	213	290	
10th	438	216	304	

*Captain †Wicket-keeper

ENGLAND'S WINTER TOUR 1982-83/IN AUSTRALIA

Australia v England 1982-83 4th Test
England won by 3 runs
Played at Melbourne Cricket Ground, December 26, 27, 28, 29, 30 1982
Toss: Australia. Umpires: A.R. Crafter and R.V. Whitehead
Debuts: Nil. Man of the Match: N.G. Cowans

England

Batsman	Dismissal	R	Dismissal (2nd)	R
G. Cook	c Chappell b Thomson	10	c Yardley b Thomson	26
G. Fowler	c Chappell b Hogg	4	b Hogg	65
C.J. Tavaré	c Yardley b Thomson	89	b Hogg	0
D.I. Gower	c Marsh b Hogg	18	c Marsh b Lawson	3
A.J. Lamb	c Dyson b Yardley	83	c Marsh b Hogg	26
I.T. Botham	c Wessels b Yardley	27	c Chappell b Thomson	46
G. Miller	c Border b Yardley	10	lbw b Lawson	14
D.R. Pringle	c Wessels b Hogg	9	c Marsh b Lawson	42
R.W. Taylor†	c Marsh b Yardley	1	lbw b Thomson	37
R.G.D. Willis*	not out	6	not out	8
N.G. Cowans	c Lawson b Hogg	3	b Lawson	10
Extras	(B 3, LB 6, W 3, NB 12)	24	(B 1, LB 9, NB 7)	17
		284		**294**

Australia

Batsman	Dismissal	R	Dismissal (2nd)	R
K.C. Wessels	b Willis	47	(2) b Cowans	14
J. Dyson	lbw b Cowans	21	(1) c Tavaré b Botham	31
G.S. Chappell*	c Lamb b Cowans	0	c sub (I.J. Gould) b Cowans	2
K.J. Hughes	b Willis	66	c Taylor b Miller	48
A.R. Border	b Botham	2	(6) not out	62
D.W. Hookes	c Taylor b Pringle	53	(5) c Willis b Cowans	68
R.W. Marsh†	b Willis	53	lbw b Cowans	13
B. Yardley	b Miller	9	b Cowans	0
G.F. Lawson	c Fowler b Miller	0	c Cowans b Pringle	7
R.M. Hogg	not out	8	lbw b Cowans	4
J.R. Thomson	b Miller	1	c Miller b Botham	21
Extras	(LB 8, NB 19)	27	(B5, LB 9, W 1, NB 3)	18
		287		**288**

Bowling

Australia	O	M	R	W	O	M	R	W
Lawson	17	6	48	0	21.4	6	66	4
Hogg	23.3	6	69	4	22	5	64	3
Yardley	27	9	89	4	15	2	67	0
Thomson	13	2	49	2	21	3	74	3
Chappell	1	0	5	0	1	0	6	0

England	O	M	R	W	O	M	R	W
Willis	15	2	38	3	17	0	57	0
Botham	18	3	69	1	25.1	4	80	2
Cowans	16	0	69	2	26	6	77	6
Pringle	15	2	40	1	12	4	26	1
Miller	15	5	44	3	16	6	30	1

Fall of Wickets

Wkt	E 1st	A 1st	E 2nd	A 2nd
1st	11	55	40	37
2nd	25	55	41	39
3rd	56	83	45	71
4th	217	89	128	171
5th	227	180	129	173
6th	259	261	160	190
7th	262	276	201	190
8th	268	276	262	202
9th	278	278	280	218
10th	284	287	294	288

*Captain †Wicket-keeper

Australia v England 1982-83 5th Test
Match drawn
Played at Sydney Cricket Ground, January 2, 3, 4, 6, 7 1983
Toss: Australia. Umpires: D.A. French and M.W. Johnson
Debuts: Nil. Man of the Match: K.J. Hughes. Man of the Series: G.F. Lawson

Australia

K.C. Wessels	c Willis b Botham	19	(2) lbw b Botham	53
J. Dyson	c Taylor b Hemmings	79	(1) c Gower b Willis	2
G.S. Chappell*	lbw b Willis	35	c Randall b Hemmings	11
K.J. Hughes	c Cowans b Botham	29	c Botham b Hemmings	137
D.W. Hookes	c Botham b Hemmings	17	lbw b Miller	19
A.R. Border	c Miller b Hemmings	89	c Botham b Cowans	83
R.W. Marsh†	c and b Miller	3	c Taylor b Miller	41
B. Yardley	b Cowans	24	c Botham b Hemmings	0
G.F. Lawson	c and b Botham	6	not out	13
J.R. Thomson	c Lamb b Botham	0	c Gower b Miller	12
R.M. Hogg	not out	0	run out (Lamb)	0
Extras	(B 3, LB 8, W 2)	13	(LB 7, NB 4)	11
		314		**382**

England

G. Cook	c Chappell b Hogg	8	lbw b Lawson	2
C.J. Tavaré	b Lawson	0	lbw b Yardley	16
D.I. Gower	c Chappell b Lawson	70	(4) c Hookes b Yardley	24
A.J. Lamb	b Lawson	0	(5) c and b Yardley	29
D.W. Randall	b Thomson	70	(6) b Thomson	44
I.T. Botham	c Wessels b Thomson	5	(7) lbw b Thomson	32
G. Miller	lbw b Thomson	34	(8) not out	21
R.W. Taylor†	lbw b Thomson	0	(9) not out	28
E.E. Hemmings	c Border b Yardley	29	(3) c Marsh b Yardley	95
R.G.D. Willis*	c Border b Thomson	1		
N.G. Cowans	not out	0		
Extras	(B 4, LB 4, NB 12)	20	(B 1, LB 10, W 1, NB 11)	23
		237	(7 wickets)	**314**

England Bowling

	O	M	R	W	O	M	R	W
Willis	20	6	57	1	10	2	33	1
Cowans	21	3	67	1	13	1	47	1
Botham	30	8	75	4	10	0	35	1
Hemmings	27	10	68	3	47	16	116	3
Miller	17	7	34	1	49.3	12	133	3
Cook					2	1	7	0

Australia Bowling

	O	M	R	W	O	M	R	W
Lawson	20	2	70	3	15	1	50	1
Hogg	16	2	50	1	13	6	25	0
Thomson	14.5	2	50	5	12	3	30	2
Yardley	14	4	47	1	37	6	139	4
Border					16	3	36	0
Hookes					2	1	5	0
Chappell					1	0	6	0

Fall of Wickets

Wkt	A 1st	E 1st	A 2nd	E 2nd
1st	39	8	23	3
2nd	96	23	38	55
3rd	150	24	82	104
4th	173	146	113	155
5th	210	163	262	196
6th	219	169	350	260
7th	262	170	357	261
8th	283	220	358	
9th	291	232	382	
10th	314	237	382	

*Captain †Wicket-keeper

ENGLAND'S WINTER TOUR 1982-83/IN AUSTRALIA 27

Statistical Survey: Australia v England 1982-83 – Australia

Australia – Batting/Fielding

	M	I	NO	Runs	HS	Avge	100s	50s	4s	Min	Balls	r/h	Ct	St
K.J. Hughes	5	8	1	469	137	67.00	1	3	42	1445	1159	40	2	–
D.W. Hookes	5	8	1	344	68	49.14	–	4	46	695	563	61	2	–
G.S. Chappell	5	10	2	389	117	48.62	2	1	49	820	624	62	8	–
K.C. Wessels	4	8	0	386	162	48.25	1	1	41	1015	729	53	8	–
A.R. Border	5	9	2	317	89	45.28	–	3	36	926	736	43	4	–
J. Dyson	5	10	2	283	79	35.37	–	2	26†	1050	707	40	4	–
B. Yardley	5	7	0	141	53	20.14	–	1	14	372	302	47	6	–
R.W. Marsh	5	7	0	124	53	17.71	–	1	11	364	300	41	28	–
G.M. Wood	1	2	0	29	29	14.50	–	–	3	97	78	37	1	–
G.F. Lawson	5	8	1	98	50	14.00	–	1	8	324	223	44	3	–
R.M. Hogg	3	5	3	26	14*	13.00	–	–	2	123	82	32	–	–
J.R. Thomson	4	6	1	42	21	8.40	–	–	3	204	137	31	1	–
C.G. Rackemann	1	1	0	4	4	4.00	–	–	–	34	30	13	1	–
D.K. Lillee	1	1	1	2	2*	–	–	–	–	27	19	11	1	–
T.M. Alderman	1	–	–	–	–	–	–	–	–	–	–	–	–	–
Totals	55	90	14	2654	(162)	34.92	4	17	281†	7496	5689	47	69	0

Australia – Bowling

	O	M	R	W	Avge	Best	5w/I	10w/M	b/w	r/h	NB	Wides
J.R. Thomson	127.4	22	411	22	18.68	5-50	2	–	35	54	45	3
G.F. Lawson	230.4	51	687	34	20.20	6-47	4	1	41	50	71	3
R.M. Hogg	107.3	26	302	11	27.45	4-69	–	–	59	47	17	2
B. Yardley	292.2	91	793	22	36.04	5-107	1	–	80	45	6	–
D.K. Lillee	71	25	185	4	46.25	3-96	–	–	107	43	9	2
Also bowled:												
T.M. Alderman	43	15	84	1	84.00	1-84	–	–	258	33	1	–
A.R. Border	31	7	71	0	–	–	–	–	–	38	–	–
G.S. Chappell	14.3	3	44	1	44.00	1-8	–	–	87	51	–	2
D.W. Hookes	8	2	20	0	–	–	–	–	–	42	–	–
C.G. Rackemann	33.2	11	96	2	48.00	2-61	–	–	100	48	15	1
Totals	959	253	2693	97	27.76	(6-47)	7	1	59	47	164	13

*not out. †plus one 5. r/h = runs per 100 balls. 5w/I = 5 wickets in an innings. 10w/M = 10 wickets in a match. b/w = balls per wicket.

28 ENGLAND'S WINTER TOUR 1982-83/IN AUSTRALIA

Statistical Survey: Australia v England 1982-83 – England

England – Batting/Fielding

	M	I	NO	HS	Runs	Avge	100s	50s	6s	4s	Min	Balls	r/h	Ct	St
D.W. Randall	4	8	0	115	365	45.62	1	2	–	39	860	635	57	3	–
D.I. Gower	5	10	0	114	441	44.10	1	3	–	49	1313	887	50	4	–
A.J. Lamb	5	10	0	83	414	41.40	–	4	2	56	1014	743	56	5	–
G. Fowler	3	6	0	83	207	34.50	–	3	–	23	738	515	40	1	–
E.E. Hemmings	3	6	1	95	157	31.40	–	1	–	9	451	389	40	2	–
I.T. Botham	5	10	0	58	270	27.00	–	1	1	39	640	440	61	9	–
D.R. Pringle	3	6	2	47*	108	27.00	–	–	–	15	445	318	34	–	–
C.J. Tavaré	5	10	0	89	218	21.80	–	2	–	27	1090	732	30	2	–
G. Miller	5	10	1	60	193	21.44	–	1	–	18	630	467	41	3	–
R.W. Taylor	5	10	3	37	135	19.28	–	–	–	16	497	325	42	13	–
N.G. Cowans	4	7	1	36	68	11.33	–	–	1	9	147	115	59	3	–
R.G.D. Willis	5	9	3	26	63	10.50	–	–	–	7	254	182	35	4	–
G. Cook	3	6	0	26	54	9.00	–	–	–	3	236	170	32	1	–
Totals	55	108	11	(115)	2693	27.76	2	17	4	310	8315	5918	46	50†	0

England – Bowling

	O	M	R	W	Avge	Best	5w/I	10w/M	b/w	r/h	NB	Wides
R.G.D. Willis	166.3	28	486	18	27.00	5-66	1	–	56	49	68	–
G. Miller	171	50	397	13	30.53	4-70	–	–	79	39	–	1
N.G. Cowans	107	14	396	11	36.00	6-77	1	–	58	62	5	1
I.T. Botham	213.5	35	729	18	40.50	4-75	–	–	71	57	–	3
E.E. Hemmings	188.3	59	409	9	45.44	3-68	–	–	126	36	1	–
D.R. Pringle	73.5	12	214	4	53.50	2-97	–	–	111	48	49	–
Also bowled:												
G. Cook	6	3	23	0	–	–	–	–	–	64	–	–
A.J. Lamb	1	1	0	0	–	–	–	–	–	0	–	–
Totals	927.4	202	2654	73	36.35	(6-77)	2	–	76	48	123	4

*not out. †plus 1 ct by substitute (I.J. Gould). r/h = runs per 100 balls. 5w/I = 5 wickets in an innings. 10w/M = 10 wickets in a match. b/w = balls per wicket.

Statistical Highlights of Tests

1st Test, Perth. Norman Cowans became the 500th cricketer to represent England in 586 official Tests, and the 8th to gain a first England cap in 1982. Ian Botham scored his 3,000th run and took his 250th wicket to achieve a unique Test double. Other personal Test career aggregates achieved in this match were: Bruce Yardley 100 wickets in 28 Tests; John Dyson 1,000 runs in 23 Tests; Geoff Miller 1,000 runs and 50 wickets in 28 Tests. David Gower scored his 10,000th run in the 288th innings of a career begun in 1975. Chris Tavaré spent 90 minutes with his score on 66 in the first innings, and took 63 minutes to score his first run in the second. England (358) achieved their highest second innings total at Perth. The match produced only the second draw in 10 Test matches at the WACA ground.

2nd Test, Brisbane. Queensland, who have still to win a Sheffield Shield title after 50 attempts since entering the competition in 1926-27, contributed five of Australia's team for the first time. Rodney Marsh became the first to hold 300 catches in Test cricket when he caught Lamb. His six catches in the second innings set a new Ashes record, while his total of nine in the match equalled the Australian record set by Gil Langley at Lord's in 1956. All England's first innings wickets fell to catches for only the second time in Ashes Tests (Melbourne 1958-59, 5th Test). They became the first team in Test history to lose 19 wickets in a match to catches. Kepler Christoffel Wessels (162 and 46), the first South African-born player to represent Australia, set a new record aggregate for a first appearance for that country. He became the 13th to score a century in his first Test for Australia. David Gower (3,000 runs in 46 Tests), Allan Border (1,000 runs in 15 Tests against England), and Derek Randall (1,000 runs in 16 Tests against Australia) all achieved notable aggregates. Geoff Lawson (11-134) became the first bowler to take 11 wickets in an Ashes Test in Brisbane. The 52 extras conceded by Australia in the second innings constitutes a record for Tests in Australia, while the 35 no-balls not scored off equals the world Test record.

3rd Test, Adelaide. Willis became the third England captain, after P.B.H. May (1958-59) and M.H. Denness (1974-75), to elect to field first at Adelaide. All three decisions resulted in defeat. Bob Taylor made his 50th dismissal against Australia when he caught Wessels in the first innings, and joined the select company of A.F.A. Lilley, T.G. Evans, and A.P.E. Knott. Greg Chappell's hundred was his first in Tests at his birthplace, his 22nd for Australia and his 9th against England. He became the third Australian after C. Hill and D.G. Bradman to score 2,500 runs against England. Ian Botham and David Gower each completed 1,000 runs in Test cricket during 1982. Botham also reached his 1,000 against Australia in 21 matches.

4th Test, Melbourne. The first Test match to be contested on the relaid portion of the MCG square was the 250th played between Australia (95 wins) and England (83 wins). Three other matches have been abandoned. Melbourne became the first ground to stage 75 Tests. England's victory equalled the narrowest runs margin established (also in the fourth Test of an Ashes series), at Manchester in 1902. (Playing in his only Test, last man Fred Tate, father of

Maurice, joined Wilfred Rhodes with eight runs wanted for victory. To his eternal sorrow he was bowled by Jack Saunders for 4.) For the first time in any series, the side winning the toss elected to field in each of the first four Tests. Their dividend: one win, two defeats, and one draw. For the first time in any Test in which all 40 wickets fell, the four innings totals fell within a range of 10 runs. On the same ground in 1974-75, England (242 and 244) drew with Australia (241 and 238-8). Ian Botham's vital last wicket gave him the fastest double of 100 wickets and 1,000 runs in Tests between England and Australia, in 22 matches. Monty Noble (29 matches) and George Giffen (30) are the only Australians to achieve this feat, while Wilfred Rhodes (37 Tests) is the only other Englishman. Marsh, who became the first Australian to appear in 90 Tests, took his total of dismissals for the series to 27, and so broke the Test record set in South Africa in 1961-62 by John Waite in five matches against New Zealand. All of Marsh's wickets in this series have fallen to catches, and only 12 of his 333 dismissals in Test cricket have been stumped. During their heroic last-wicket partnership of 70 in 128 minutes, Border and Thomson declined to run 29 comfortable singles.

5th Test, Sydney. Taylor made his 150th Test match dismissal when he caught Dyson, and completed his 1,000 runs and the wicket-keeper's double on the final evening of the series. Marsh extended his record series aggregate to 28 dismissals, all caught. This was only the fourth drawn Test in 46 matches at Sydney.

England Tour of Australia 1982-83
First-Class Match Statistics
Results: Played 11; Won 4, Lost 3, Drawn 4.

Batting/Fielding	M	I	NO	HS	R	Avge	100	50	Ct	St
A.J. Lamb	9	18	0	117	852	47.33	2	5	6	-
D.W. Randall	9	17	1	115	732	45.75	1	4	11	-
D.I. Gower	10	19	1	114	821	45.61	2	6	9	-
E.E. Hemmings	5	9	3	95	228	38.00	-	2	3	-
G. Cook	7	14	1	99	428	32.92	-	4	4	-
I.J. Gould	4	5	0	73	164	32.80	-	1	8	2
G. Miller	10	19	4	83	465	31.00	-	2	5	-
R.D. Jackman	4	5	2	50*	88	29.33	-	1	2	-
C.J. Tavaré	10	19	0	147	489	25.73	1	2	4	-
G. Fowler	9	18	0	83	445	24.72	-	4	6	-
I.T. Botham	9	18	0	65	434	24.11	-	2	17	-
R.W. Taylor	7	14	5	37	188	20.88	-	-	16	1
D.R. Pringle	9	16	5	47*	207	18.81	-	-	6	-
R.G.D. Willis	7	13	5	26	65	8.12	-	-	7	-
V.J. Marks	4	6	0	13	41	6.83	-	-	4	-
N.G. Cowans	8	13	2	36	70	6.36	-	-	5	-

Bowling	O	M	R	W	Avge	Best	5w/I	10w/M
G. Cook	56	12	178	8	22.25	3-47	-	-
R.G.D. Willis	225	41	656	28	23.42	5-66	1	-
G. Miller	325	96	761	27	28.18	4-63	-	-
N.G. Cowans	223.4	38	745	26	28.65	6-77	1	-
D.R. Pringle	263.3	53	739	22	33.59	4-66	-	-
E.E. Hemmings	323	84	789	23	34.30	5-101	1	-
I.T. Botham	319.4	63	1033	29	35.62	4-43	-	-
R.D. Jackman	88.5	15	272	3	90.66	2-37	-	-
V.J. Marks	107	26	351	3	117.00	1-39	-	-

Also bowled: G. Fowler 6-0-43-2; A.J. Lamb 1-1-0-0.
*not out

Benson & Hedges World Series Cup

For a team with such a wealth of experience in one-day cricket, England were woefully inconsistent in the Benson & Hedges World Series Cup, played in Australia in January and February. Even so, they might have contested the final but for encountering unseasonal rain and a poor pitch at Perth, on which they lost to New Zealand in their last, crucial match.

Victory would have sufficed, but England, after being put in, not only struggled on a pitch from which the ball darted about awkwardly off the seam – making contact, let alone stroke-play difficult – but were also cruelly interrupted by the heaviest rainfall seen in Western Australia for five years. When the rain arrived, England, after being put in, had struggled to 45 for 3 from 18 overs, of which Botham had made 19 in 7 overs, largely from powerful legside blows against Cairns's inswing. Yet although this proved briefly feasible for a man of his strength, the most telling comment on the conditions lay in the way they restricted David Gower.

Gower had some 500 runs behind him at an average of 60, such had been his brilliant form in the series. Yet with Richard Hadlee bowling what amounted to virtually unplayable fast leg-breaks on a pitch that had started curiously damp, the England vice-captain needed 38 deliveries to make his first 3 runs. After the stoppage, he improvised effectively, enabling his side to make 43 from the 5½ overs remaining, and his innings of 35 proved to be the highest made in both matches played in Perth – on the same pitch – that weekend.

England were thus restricted to a highly inadequate 88 for 7, and New Zealand triumphed by 7 wickets, despite some whole-hearted bowling by Norman Cowans and Bob Willis; England's last hope of reaching the final lay in Australia losing to New Zealand for the fourth time in five matches the next day, but here again they were out of luck.

Australia, who were also put in, were spared interference from the weather and reached a total of 191 for 9, which owed much to the positive efforts of their new opening pair, Graeme Wood and Steve Smith, who scored 65 from 16 over, and perhaps the fact that Hadlee went off with a strained hamstring after conceding only seven runs in 5 overs.

New Zealand were on terms with their task at times, but Dennis Lillee, exploiting the conditions well, dismissed Glenn Turner and Jeff Crowe with successive balls, and after Hadlee and Lance Cairns had both fallen in the same over, they were all out 27 runs short.

The match, sadly, also produced one or two examples of the ill feeling that had developed between the two sides during the series. Glenn Turner, who had complained in a newspaper article that his side had been subject to much abuse both on and off the field, was the recipient of a good deal of short-pitched bowling, mainly from Jeff Thomson, which went unchecked by the umpires.

Curiously, they also took no action when Rodney Marsh was seen to kick the ball away when running between the wickets and batting against

John Morrison. The act looked wilful enough and clearly prevented Morrison from fielding the ball and possibly from attempting a run-out, but New Zealand's appeals brought no response.

Before the finals began, a meeting was held between captains, umpires, and the match referee, a member of the Australian Board of Control, at which several matters, including short-pitched bowling and swearing were discussed. They did not manifest themselves again, although the rain did when Australia won the first final in Sydney by 6 wickets with 29 balls to spare.

The second, at Melbourne, which was watched by a crowd of 71,393, was won emphatically by Australia, who made 302 for 8, a record for the competition, and triumphed by 149 runs. Their openers, Smith and Wood, put on 140 together, and New Zealand, swiftly reduced to 92 for 7, had only the consolation of 52 from 25 balls by Cairns.

England had started the series by squandering favourable positions in their opening two games. First, at Sydney, they dismissed Australia for 180, and reached 131 for 4 with 20 overs left. At that point, the dismissal of Lamb (49) led to the loss of 6 wickets for 18 runs, 3 to the medium pace of Greg Chappell in 5 balls. In the next game, at Melbourne, New Zealand were contained to 239 for 8 on a mild pitch and Gower's accomplished century looked like seeing England home. They reached 190, with Botham and Gower together, but at a time when only ones and twos were needed, Botham was caught trying unnecessarily to hit over the top, and when Gower was out with only 17 required from three overs, New Zealand squeezed home.

England redeemed themselves in Brisbane by beating New Zealand by 54 runs, their first win, which owed much to a superlative innings of 158 by Gower. This enabled them to make 267 for 6, which always looked out of reach.

The story was different on the same ground the following day, however, when Australia's fast bowlers, despite some erratic moments, forced England into errors, and they made only 182 after being put in. Randall's valuable, if flawed, half-century was England's only innings of substance, and though Willis and Cowans bowled well, an unbeaten half-century by Hookes saw Australia comfortably home by 7 wickets.

An unbeaten 108 in 106 balls by Allan Lamb enabled England to beat Australia by 8 wickets in their fifth game, but their inconsistency continued to haunt them. There were few games in which both batting and bowling functioned efficiently, and the nadir came at Adelaide where, after making 296 for 5, a record for the competition, they bowled and fielded so badly that New Zealand achieved a memorable, if unexpected, win, by 4 wickets with 7 balls to spare.

ENGLAND'S WINTER TOUR 1982-83/B & H WORLD SERIES

The Benson & Hedges World Series Cup was played in Australia after the Ashes Test series had been completed. New Zealand, who had made a brief pre-Christmas tour of the Eastern States, returned to compete in a tournament of fifteen 50-overs matches (ten per country), which culminated in a 3-match final, England surprisingly being the eliminated team.

Qualifying Rounds

9 January at Melbourne. AUSTRALIA beat NEW ZEALAND by 8 wickets. New Zealand 181 (44.5 overs) (J.G. Wright 54, C.G. Rackemann 10-1-39-4). Australia 182-2 (46.4 overs) (K.C. Wessels 79, J. Dyson 78*).

11 January at Sydney. AUSTRALIA beat ENGLAND by 31 runs. Australia 180 (46.4 overs). England 149 (41.1 overs).

13 January at Melbourne. NEW ZEALAND beat ENGLAND by 2 runs. New Zealand 239-8 (50 overs) (J.G. Wright 55). England 237-8 (50 overs) (D.I. Gower 122).

15 January at Brisbane. ENGLAND beat NEW ZEALAND by 54 runs. England 267-6 (50 overs) (D.I. Gower 158). New Zealand 213 (48.2 overs).

16 January at Brisbane. AUSTRALIA beat ENGLAND by 7 wickets. England 182 (46.4 overs) (D.W. Randall 57). Australia 184-3 (41 overs) (D.W. Hookes 54*).

18 January at Sydney. NEW ZEALAND beat AUSTRALIA by 47 runs. New Zealand 226-8 (50 overs) (G.M. Turner 55, J.J. Crowe 56). Australia 179 (45.3 overs) (K.C. Wessels 58, D.W. Hookes 68; B.L. Cairns 10-4-16-4).

20 January at Sydney. ENGLAND beat NEW ZEALAND by 8 wickets. New Zealand 199 (47.2 overs) (B.A. Edgar 74; R.G.D. Willis 9-0-23-4). England 200-2 (42.4 overs) (C.J. Tavaré 83*, A.J. Lamb 108*).

22 January at Melbourne. NEW ZEALAND beat AUSTRALIA by 58 runs. New Zealand 246-6 (50 overs) (J.G. Wright 84). Australia 188 (44.1 overs) (K.C. Wessels 62; G.B. Troup 10-0-54-4).

23 January at Melbourne. AUSTRALIA beat ENGLAND by 5 wickets. England 213-5 (37 overs) (A.J. Lamb 94, D.W. Randall 51*). Australia 217-5 (34.4 overs) (A.R. Border 54, J. Dyson 54, D.W. Hookes 50).

26 January at Sydney. ENGLAND beat AUSTRALIA by 98 runs. England 207 (41 overs). Australia 109 (27.3 overs).

29 January at Adelaide. NEW ZEALAND beat ENGLAND by 4 wickets. England 296-5 (50 overs) (I.T. Botham 65, D.I. Gower 109, T.E. Jesty 52*). New Zealand 297-6 (48.5 overs) (J.J. Crowe 50, R.J. Hadlee 79).

30 January at Adelaide. ENGLAND beat AUSTRALIA by 14 runs. England 228-6 (47 overs) (D.I. Gower 77). Australia 214-7 (47 overs) (D.W. Hookes 76).

31 January at Adelaide. NEW ZEALAND beat AUSTRALIA by 46 runs. New Zealand 199-9 (50 overs) (G.M. Turner 84). Australia 153 (44 overs).

5 February at Perth. NEW ZEALAND beat ENGLAND by 7 wickets – match reduced to 23 overs because of rain. England 88-7 (23 overs). New Zealand 89-3 (20.3 overs).

6 February at Perth. AUSTRALIA beat NEW ZEALAND by 27 runs. Australia 191-9 (50 overs). New Zealand 164 (44.5 overs).

ENGLAND'S WINTER TOUR 1982-83/B & H WORLD SERIES

Qualifying Table

	P	W	L	Points
NEW ZEALAND	10	6	4	12
AUSTRALIA	10	5	5	10
England	10	4	6	8

Final Round Results

9 February at Sydney. AUSTRALIA beat NEW ZEALAND by a faster scoring rate in a rain-interrupted match. New Zealand 193-7 (49 overs) (J.V. Coney 58*). Australia 155-4 (33.1 overs) (K.J. Hughes 63).

13 February at Melbourne. AUSTRALIA beat NEW ZEALAND by 149 runs. Australia 302-8 (50 overs) (G.M. Wood 91, S.B. Smith 117). New Zealand 153 (39.5 overs) (B.L. Cairns 52, including 6 sixes off 10 balls).

AUSTRALIA won the WSC Finals by two matches to nil, the third Final being unnecessary. Player of the Series: D.I. Gower. Player of the Finals: K.J. Hughes.

Leading Averages

Batting	M	I	NO	HS	R	Avge	100	50
D.I. Gower (England	10	10	1	158	563	62.55	3	1
D.W. Hookes (Australia)	12	11	2	76	391	43.44	-	4
J. Dyson (Australia)	9	9	1	78*	317	39.62	-	2
D.W. Randall (England)	10	9	1	57	294	36.75	-	2
A.J. Lamb (England)	10	10	1	108*	326	36.22	1	1
K.C. Wessels (Australia)	8	8	1	79	249	35.57	-	3
B.A. Edgar (New Zealand)	8	8	0	74	276	34.50	-	1
G.M. Turner (New Zealand)	11	11	0	84	332	30.18	-	2
J.G. Wright (New Zealand)	12	12	0	84	362	30.16	-	3
J.V. Coney (New Zealand)	11	11	4	47*	200	28.57	-	-

Bowling	O	M	R	W	Avge	Best	r/o
G.F. Lawson (Australia)	93.3	19	254	16	15.87	3-11	2.7
C.G. Rackemann (Australia)	54.4	3	247	15	16.46	4-39	4.5
D.K. Lillee (Australia)	53	8	222	11	20.18	3-34	4.2
R.G.D. Willis (England)	81	10	296	14	21.14	4-23	3.7
I.T. Botham (England)	68.2	5	364	17	21.41	3-29	5.3
R.J. Hadlee (New Zealand)	85.1	16	267	12	22.25	3-15	3.1
R.M. Hogg (Australia)	111	10	377	16	23.56	3-44	3.4
J.R. Thomson (Australia)	89	5	357	14	25.50	3-27	4.0
V.J. Marks (England)	72	5	277	10	27.70	3-30	3.8
E.J. Chatfield (New Zealand)	113	18	425	14	30.35	3-27	3.8

*not out. r/o = runs per over.

England in New Zealand

England, unable to disguise their staleness after their struggles in Australia, performed mostly with mediocrity in their three one-day games for the Rothman's Cup and were comfortably beaten in each. The series ended on an unsavoury note when David Gower grappled with a spectator who had been allowed to walk unchecked to the middle when the England vice-captain was batting in Christchurch.

In the opening match, at Auckland, a capacity crowd of 41,000 saw England's batsmen – after a two-week lay-off – struggle to come to terms with a slow, low and slightly variable pitch. Even Gower needed some moments of luck in his top score of 84. With Glenn Turner making an imperious 88, which won him the Man of the Match award, New Zealand triumphed by 6 wickets with 21 balls to spare. They moved on to Wellington, where, after being put in on what proved to be the best pitch of the three, Turner inspired them to a total of 295 for 6, again being named Man of the Match. Predictably, such a daunting total proved beyond England, who lost by 103 runs.

And their problems continued in Christchurch, where, on a poor pitch, New Zealand were allowed to make 211 for 8. Gower, coping well with the pitch's eccentricities, seemed capable of steering his side close to victory, but lost concentration after the pitch invasion, precipitating a collapse in which the last seven wickets fell for 24 runs. Man of the Match was Snedden, whose 2 for 14 in 7 overs complemented his 31 in a vital unbroken partnership of 55 with Morrison for New Zealand's ninth wicket.

One-Day Internationals (The Rothman's Cup)

19 February at Eden Park, Auckland. NEW ZEALAND won by 6 wickets. Toss: England. Match award: G.M. Turner (88). England 184-9 (50 overs) (D.I. Gower 84). New Zealand 187-4 (46.3 overs) (G.M. Turner 88).

23 February at Basin Reserve, Wellington. NEW ZEALAND won by 103 runs. Toss: England. Match award: G.M. Turner (94). New Zealand 295-6 (50 overs) (G.M. Turner 94, B.A. Edgar 60). England 192 (44.5 overs).

26 February at Lancaster Park, Christchurch. NEW ZEALAND won by 84 runs. Toss: New Zealand. Match award: M.C. Snedden (31* and 7-3-14-2). New Zealand 211-8 (50 overs). England 127 (40.1 overs) (D.I. Gower 53).

NEW ZEALAND won the Rothman's Cup by three matches to nil.

Overseas cricket 1982-83

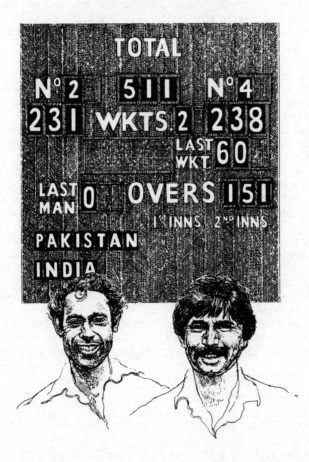

India v Sri Lanka

The inaugural Test match between India and Sri Lanka almost resulted in a famous initial victory for the visitors. It also produced an exceptional scoring rate by modern standards and, despite the loss of 165 minutes to rain on the third day, a record aggregate of 1,441 runs for any Test in India.

Although they were surprisingly outplayed in the one-day internationals – the type of cricket upon which they have been reared – Warnapura's team rattled up a handsome total of 311-8 in 330 minutes off 84 overs on the first day. After Gavaskar had established a bizarre Test record by losing his ninth successive toss, Dias and Mendis raced to 126-2 at lunch. Mendis reached his first Test hundred with a six, and also hit 17 fours in an innings lasting 179 minutes, before becoming the second of Doshi's five prizes. The left-arm spinner bowled unchanged on a placid pitch throughout an afternoon of overpowering heat, which caused Kirmani to retire with giddiness. Doshi's third wicket was the hundredth of a 28-match Test career that began on the same ground almost exactly three years earlier.

India's mammoth response was founded upon Gavaskar's 25th Test hundred in his first important innings since Botham's square-drive had dented his left fibula ten weeks previously at The Oval.

Although trailing by 220 runs and again losing both openers cheaply, Mendis and Dias (97 off 108 balls) again scored at a tremendous rate to reach 150 in 105 minutes off 22.4 overs. Mendis, an obvious Man of the Match, joined Bradman and Weekes by making a hundred in each innings of a Test against India, and, incidentally, became the first to achieve an identical three-figure score in both innings of any Test.

India started well in pursuit of 175 runs in 53 minutes and 20 overs. But they lost their way dramatically after Patil and Kapil Dev found each other in the same crease. Fortunately, Gavaskar, batting at No. 9 because of a strained neck, was on hand to prevent De Mel (5-68) from making further inroads.

A month later, Warnapura and three of his colleagues in this match were effectively banned from all Sri Lankan cricket for life for engaging upon a clandestine tour of South Africa.

One-Day Internationals

12 September at Amritsar. INDIA won by 78 runs. Toss: Sri Lanka. India 269-7 (46 overs) (K. Srikkanth 57, Kapil Dev 49 off 31 balls). Sri Lanka 191-8 (46 overs) (D.R. Doshi 10-0-44-4).

15 September at Delhi. INDIA won by 6 wickets. Sri Lanka 277-8 (50 overs) (S. Wettimuny 74, R.L. Dias 102). India 281-4 (40.5 overs) (K. Srikkanth 95, D.B. Vengsarkar 53, S.M. Patil 64).

26 September at Bangalore. INDIA won by 6 wickets. Toss: Sri Lanka. Sri Lanka 233-8 (50 overs) (R.L. Dias 121). India 234-4 (39.2 overs) (K. Srikkanth 92).

India v Sri Lanka 1982-83 (only Test)
Match Drawn
Played at Chidambaram Stadium, Chepauk, Madras, September 17, 18, 19, 21, 22
Toss: Sri Lanka. Umpires: M.V. Gothoskar and Swaroop Kishen
Debuts: India, Arun Lal, R. Shukla

Sri Lanka

B. Warnapura*	c Yashpal b Madan Lal	4		c Yashpal b Kapil Dev	6
H.M. Goonatillake†	c Patil b Kapil Dev	7	(10)	c sub (K. Srikkanth) b Kapil Dev	0
R.L. Dias	c Arun Lal b Doshi	60		c Gavaskar b Shukla	97
L.R.D. Mendis	lbw b Doshi	105		b Shukla	105
A. Ranatunga	c Vengsarkar b Doshi	25		c Kirmani b Doshi	15
R.S. Madugalle	c Madan Lal b Doshi	46		c Patil b Doshi	4
A.N. Ranasinghe	c Arun Lal b Doshi	0		b Kapil Dev	77
D.S. de Silva	c Gavaskar b Madan Lal	49		not out	46
J.R. Ratnayeke	lbw b Kapil Dev	23	(2)	c Yashpal b Kapil Dev	6
A.L.F. de Mel	not out	18	(9)	b Doshi	12
G.R.A. de Silva	c Viswanath b Kapil Dev	0		b Kapil Dev	14
Extras	(B 4, LB 5)	9		(B 4, LB 5, W 1, NB 2)	12
		346			**394**

India

S.M. Gavaskar*	c De Mel b D.S. de Silva	155	(9)	not out	4
Arun Lal	b De Mel	63	(1)	c Dias b De Mel	1
D.B. Vengsarkar	run out	90	(2)	c and b De Mel	5
G.R. Viswanath	c Warnapura b DS de Silva	9	(6)	lbw b De Mel	2
S.M. Patil	not out	114	(3)	run out	46
Yashpal Sharma	c Goonatillake b De Mel	17	(5)	not out	31
Kapil Dev	c Goonatillake b Ratnayeke	31	(4)	c Goonatillake b De Mel	30
Madan Lal	not out	37	(7)	c and b D.S. de Silva	9
S.M.H. Kirmani†	did not bat		(8)	b De Mel	5
R. Shukla	,,				
D.R. Doshi	,,				
Extras	(B 11, LB 8, W 2, NB 29)	50		(NB 2)	2
	(6 wickets declared)	**566**		(7 wickets)	**135**

India	O	M	R	W	O	M	R	W
Kapil Dev	22.5	2	97	3	24.3	3	110	5
Madan Lal	16	1	72	2	7	1	43	0
Patil	2	0	13	0				
Doshi	30	8	85	5	38	4	147	3
Shukla	22	4	70	0	27	5	82	2

Sri Lanka	O	M	R	W	O	M	R	W
De Mel	29	2	133	2	14	0	68	5
Ratnayeke	19	1	75	1	5	0	36	0
G.R.A. de Silva	18	2	78	0				
Warnapura	9	3	27	0				
D.S. de Silva	48	4	162	2	9	1	29	1
Ranasinghe	7	0	29	0				
Ranatunga	1	0	12	0				

Fall of Wickets

Wkt	SL 1st	I 1st	SL 2nd	I 2nd
1st	11	156	6	3
2nd	11	329	47	16
3rd	164	347	157	78
4th	203	363	198	90
5th	204	403	202	94
6th	204	488	291	125
7th	281		340	130
8th	304		361	
9th	346		362	
10th	346		394	

*Captain †Wicket-keeper

Pakistan v Australia

Fresh from their exploits in England, where they lost the series 2-1, Pakistan took on the Australians at home, inflicting a crushing defeat by winning the Wills Test Series by three matches to none. This sweeping victory against Australia was the first occasion in Pakistan's 30 years of Test cricket that a series was won by beating the opponents in every Test played. The margin of victory was extraordinary – two Tests were won by 9 wickets and one by an innings.

Coming from an Australian winter, the tourists were taken by surprise by Imran and his men. In the heat of Pakistan, where the temperature rarely dropped below 30°C, Kim Hughes' side crashed against some fine bowling, fielding, and batting.

The scourge of the Australian batsmen was Abdul Qadir. The wristy little leg-spinner totally mesmerized the visitors with his deceptive flight and well-disguised googlies. He took 22 wickets, winning the Wills Man of the Series award.

With Imran firing his thunderbolts from the other end, there was hardly any respite for the Australians. In the absence of their star batsman, Greg Chappell, who did not make the trip, there was lack of depth in the visitors' batting. Allan Border and Hughes failed on the tour, though John Dyson and Bruce Laird played a few innings of note, and the Australians found in young Greg Ritchie a promising batsman in the making. Playing in his first Test series, Ritchie batted with a lot of confidence and resilience. Though unable to spot Qadir's googlies, he was to make Australia's only hundred of the tour, a not-out 106 at Faisalabad in a vain attempt to make Pakistan bat again.

It was not only Australia's batsmen and bowlers who failed them, but also their overall fielding. This was the major reason for their dismal showing in Pakistan. They dropped catches at crucial stages, and their bowlers suffered because of it.

In the absence of Dennis Lillee, who also did not make the tour, their bowling lacked penetration. Thomson, Alderman, Bright, Sleep, and Yardley were reduced to mediocrity by the Pakistani batsmen, who plundered their attack to their hearts' content. Zaheer Abbas, Mohsin Khan, Javed Miandad, and Mansoor Akhtar scored hundreds, and helped Pakistan put on huge scores in every Test. The only exception among the Australian bowlers was Geoff Lawson. Though unlucky most of the time because of poor support in the field, Lawson finished with 9 wickets and was Australia's Wills Man of the Series.

With the series lost, Australia nevertheless tried to salvage some pride in the final Test, at Lahore. Put in to bat, they struggled to a respectable 316, thanks to a last-wicket stand of 52 dominated by Lawson, who made 57 not out. It was a vain effort, however, and Pakistan again ran out easy winners.

Pakistan also took the one-day series, winning two of the three matches. The third, at Karachi, was abandoned when the crowd rioted.

Pakistan v Australia 1982-83 1st Test
Pakistan won by 9 wickets
Played at National Stadium, Karachi, September 22, 23, 24, 26, 27
Toss: Australia. Umpires: Khizer Hayat and Mahboob Shah
Debuts: Australia, G.M. Ritchie

Australia

G.M. Wood	c Bari b Imran	0	(2) c sub (Salim Malik) b Qadir	17
B.M. Laird	run out	32	(1) c Mansoor b Imran	3
J. Dyson	b Qasim	87	b Qadir	6
K.J. Hughes*	c Bari b Qasim	54	(5) c Bari b Qadir	14
A.R. Border	not out	55	(4) c sub (Salim Malik) b Qadir	8
G.M. Ritchie	c Haroon b Qadir	4	b Qasim	17
R.W. Marsh†	b Tahir	19	lbw b Imran	32
B. Yardley	c Miandad b Tahir	0	lbw b Qadir	0
R.J. Bright	c Haroon b Tahir	2	not out	32
G.F. Lawson	c Bari b Tahir	0	run out	11
J.R. Thomson	st Bari b Qadir	14	c Bari b Qasim	18
Extras	(B 4, LB 10, W 1, NB 2)	17	(B 2, LB 19)	21
		284		**179**

Pakistan

Mohsin Khan	handled the ball	58	not out	14
Mansoor Akhtar	c Bright b Thomson	32	(3) not out	26
Haroon Rashid	c Laird b Yardley	82		
Javed Miandad	b Lawson	32		
Zaheer Abbas	c Marsh b Lawson	91		
Mudassar Nazar	not out	52	(2) c Border b Thomson	5
Imran Khan*	c Yardley b Bright	1		
Tahir Naqqash	st Marsh b Bright	15		
Wasim Bari†	b Bright	0		
Abdul Qadir	run out	29		
Iqbal Qasim	not out	2		
Extras	(B 4, LB 8, W 1, NB 12)	25	(NB 2)	2
	(9 wickets declared)	**419**	(1 wicket)	**47**

Pakistan	O	M	R	W	O	M	R	W
Imran	23	3	38	1	12	5	17	2
Tahir	16	3	61	4	7	3	17	0
Mudassar	13	0	33	0				
Qadir	21.4	1	80	2	26	7	76	5
Qasim	26	10	55	2	21.5	6	48	2

Australia	O	M	R	W	O	M	R	W
Thomson	29	5	103	1	3	1	16	1
Lawson	39	10	93	2				
Bright	36	8	96	3	5	0	14	0
Yardley	23	2	98	1	3	1	9	0
Border	1	0	4	0				
Hughes					0.1	0	6	0

Fall of Wickets

Wkt	A 1st	P 1st	A 2nd	P 2nd
1st	0	43	10	5
2nd	71	168	29	
3rd	169	188	32	
4th	202	277	45	
5th	212	328	72	
6th	249	329	72	
7th	249	351	73	
8th	255	353	137	
9th	255	404	160	
10th	284		179	

*Captain †Wicket-keeper

Pakistan v Australia 1982-83 2nd Test
Pakistan won by an innings and 3 runs
Played at Iqbal Stadium, Faisalabad, September 30, October 1, 2, 4, 5
Toss: Pakistan. Umpires: Khizer Hayat and Mahboob Shah
Debuts: Nil

Pakistan

Mohsin Khan	c Marsh b Lawson	76
Mudassar Nazar	c Hughes b Border	79
Mansoor Akhtar	c Marsh b Lawson	111
Javed Miandad	c Laird b Lawson	6
Zaheer Abbas	b Sleep	126
Haroon Rashid	c Laird b Lawson	51
Imran Khan*	not out	24
Tahir Naqqash	not out	15
Wasim Bari†	did not bat	
Abdul Qadir	,,	
Iqbal Qasim	,,	
Extras	(B 4, LB 1, NB 8)	13
	(6 wickets declared)	**501**

Australia

B.M. Laird	lbw b Qadir	8	c Mudassar b Qadir		60
G.M. Wood	c Bari b Mudassar	49	(7) c Bari b Qasim		22
J. Dyson	c Mudassar b Qasim	23	(2) c Qasim b Qadir		43
A.R. Border	c Miandad b Imran	9	(3) c Haroon b Qadir		31
K.J. Hughes*	c Imran b Qadir	11	(4) lbw b Qadir		7
G.M. Ritchie	run out	34	(5) not out		106
P.R. Sleep	lbw b Imran	0	(6) c Mohsin b Qadir		29
R.W. Marsh†	b Qadir	0	run out		8
R.J. Bright	c Haroon b Qadir	0	c sub (Salim Malik) b Qasim		0
G.F. Lawson	c Zaheer b Qasim	14	lbw b Qadir		0
J.R. Thomson	not out	1	st Bari b Qadir		11
Extras	(B 6, LB 8, W 2, NB 3)	19	(LB 7, W 1, NB 5)		13
		168			**330**

Australia	O	M	R	W				
Thomson	23	5	79	0				
Lawson	33	6	97	4				
Sleep	36	3	158	1				
Bright	41	5	107	0				
Border	11	3	47	1				

Pakistan	O	M	R	W	O	M	R	W
Imran	14	6	16	2	10	5	20	0
Tahir	15	4	21	0	9	1	25	0
Qadir	42	14	76	4	50.5	12	142	7
Qasim	24.5	11	28	2	46	18	97	2
Mudassar	7	2	8	1	9	3	26	0
Zaheer					3	0	5	0
Miandad					1	0	2	0

Fall of Wickets

Wkt	P 1st	A 1st	A 2nd
1st	123	20	73
2nd	181	82	125
3rd	201	96	133
4th	356	113	162
5th	428	123	218
6th	482	123	290
7th		124	309
8th		124	309
9th		167	310
10th		168	330

*Captain †Wicket-keeper

Pakistan v Australia 1982-83 3rd Test
Pakistan won by 9 wickets
Played at Gaddafi Stadium, Lahore, October 14, 15, 16, 18, 19
Toss: Pakistan. Umpires: Javed Ahtar and Shakoor Rana
Debuts: Pakistan, Jalal Uddin

Australia

G.M. Wood	c Miadad b Qadir	85	(2) c Mudassar b Jalal		30
B.M. Laird	lbw b Qadir	28	(1) lbw b Tahir		6
J. Dyson	b Jalal	10	lbw b Tahir		51
A.R. Border	lbw b Imran	9	st Bari b Qadir		6
K.J. Hughes*	b Tahir	29	st Bari b Qadir		39
G.M. Ritchie	lbw b Imran	26	lbw b Imran		18
R.W. Marsh†	c sub (Iqbal Sikander) b Imran	1	c Mudassar b Jalal		12
B. Yardley	c Haroon b Jalal	40	b Imran		21
G.F. Lawson	not out	57	c sub Iqbal Sikander) b Imran		9
J.R. Thomson	lbw b Jalal	0	not out		5
T.M. Alderman	b Imran	7	c Zaheer b Imran		0
Extras	(B 1, LB 13, W 5, NB 5)	24	(B 4, LB 5, NB 8)		17
		316			**214**

Pakistan

Mohsin Khan	b Border	135	lbw b Lawson		14
Mudassar Nazar	lbw b Lawson	23	not out		39
Abdul Qadir	c Laird b Yardley	1			
Mansoor Akhtar	lbw b Lawson	12	(3) not out		2
Javed Miandad	c Hughes b Alderman	138			
Zaheer Abbas	c Yardley b Alderman	52			
Haroon Rashid	c Ritchie b Thomson	15			
Imran Khan*	not out	39			
Tahir Naqqash	not out	7			
Wasim Bari†	did not bat				
Jalal Uddin	,,				
Extras	(B 3, LB 13, W 2, NB 27)	45	(B 4, LB 5)		9
	(7 wickets declared)	**467**	(1 wicket)		**64**

Pakistan	O	M	R	W	O	M	R	W
Imran	24.2	10	45	4	20	6	35	4
Tahir	18	4	65	1	16	3	39	2
Mudassar	6	1	17	0	2	0	5	0
Jalal	19	4	77	3	16	8	15	2
Qadir	37	7	86	2	35	7	102	2
Zaheer	2	0	2	0	1	0	1	0

Australia	O	M	R	W	O	M	R	W
Thomson	19	1	73	1	5	0	24	0
Lawson	35	4	91	2	7	1	21	1
Alderman	34	4	144	2	3	0	10	0
Yardley	27	6	102	1				
Border	4	1	12	1				

Fall of Wickets

Wkt	A 1st	P 1st	A 2nd	P 2nd
1st	85	92	21	55
2nd	120	93	58	
3rd	140	119	64	
4th	140	269	138	
5th	197	392	157	
6th	202	404	170	
7th	203	442	198	
8th	264		203	
9th	264		203	
10th	316		214	

*Captain †Wicket-keeper

Test Match Averages: Pakistan v Australia 1982-83

Pakistan

Batting/Fielding	M	I	NO	HS	R	Avge	100	50	Ct	St
Zaheer Abbas	3	3	0	126	269	89.66	1	2	2	-
Mohsin Khan	3	5	1	135	297	74.25	1	2	1	-
Mudassar Nazar	3	5	2	79	198	66.00	-	2	4	-
Imran Khan	3	3	2	39*	64	64.00	-	-	1	-
Mansoor Akhtar	3	5	2	111	183	61.00	1	-	1	-
Javed Miandad	3	3	0	138	176	58.66	1	-	3	-
Haroon Rashid	3	3	0	82	148	49.33	-	2	5	-
Tahir Naqqash	3	3	2	15*	37	37.00	-	-	-	-
Abdul Qadir	3	2	0	29	30	15.00	-	-	-	-

Also batted: Iqbal Qasim (2 matches) 2* (1 ct); Wasim Bari (3) 0 (7 ct, 4 st).
Jalal Uddin played in one Test without batting.

Bowling	O	M	R	W	Avge	Best	5w/I	10w/M
Imran Khan	103.2	35	171	13	13.15	4-35	-	-
Jalal Uddin	35	12	92	5	18.40	3-77	-	-
Abdul Qadir	212.3	48	562	22	25.54	7-142	2	1
Iqbal Qasim	118.4	45	228	8	28.50	2-28	-	-
Tahir Naqqash	81	18	228	7	32.57	4-61	-	-
Mudassar Nazar	37	6	89	1	89.00	1-8	-	-

Also bowled: Javed Miandad 1-0-2-0; Zaheer Abbas 6-0-8-0.

Australia

Batting/Fielding	M	I	NO	HS	R	Avge	100	50	Ct	St
G.M. Ritchie	3	6	1	106*	205	41.00	1	-	1	-
J. Dyson	3	6	0	87	220	36.66	-	2	-	-
G.M. Wood	3	6	0	85	203	33.83	-	1	-	-
K.J. Hughes	3	6	0	54	154	25.66	-	1	2	-
A.R. Border	3	6	1	55*	118	23.60	-	1	1	-
B.M. Laird	3	6	0	60	137	22.83	-	1	4	-
G.F. Lawson	3	6	1	57*	91	18.20	-	1	-	-
B. Yardley	2	4	0	40	61	15.25	-	-	2	-
P.R. Sleep	1	2	0	29	29	14.50	-	-	-	-
J.R. Thomson	3	6	2	18	49	12.25	-	-	-	-
R.W. Marsh	3	6	0	32	72	12.00	-	-	3	1
R.J. Bright	2	4	1	32*	34	11.33	-	-	1	-
T.M. Alderman	1	2	0	7	7	3.50	-	-	-	-

Bowling	O	M	R	W	Avge	Best	5w/I	10w/M
A.R. Border	16	4	63	2	31.50	1-12	-	-
G.F. Lawson	114	21	302	9	33.55	4-96	-	-
R.J. Bright	82	13	217	3	72.33	3-96	-	-
T.M. Alderman	37	4	154	2	77.00	2-144	-	-
J.R. Thomson	79	12	295	3	98.33	1-16	-	-
B. Yardley	53	9	209	2	104.50	1-98	-	-
P.R. Sleep	36	3	158	1	158.00	1-158	-	-

Also bowled: K.J. Hughes 0.1-0-6-0.

*not out

Statistical Highlights of Tests

1st Test, Karachi. Tahir Naqqash claimed 4 first-innings wickets (Marsh, Yardley, Bright, and Lawson) for 2 runs in 8 balls, twice being on a hat-trick. Mohsin Khan played defensively to a delivery from Lawson and handled the ball as it bounced towards his stumps. He became the third batsman to be given out 'handled the ball', following W.R. Endean for South Africa v England at Cape Town in 1956-57 and A.M.J. Hilditch for Australia v Pakistan at Perth in 1978-79. Crowd disturbances caused the Australians to leave the field twice on the third day.

2nd Test, Faisalabad. The partnership of 155 between Mansoor Akhtar and Zaheer Abbas was a record for Pakistan's 4th wicket against Australia, beating 128 by Javed Miandad and Zaheer at Melbourne in 1981-82. With his score on 23 in the first innings, Ritchie exercised his right to hit a stationary ball which had slipped from the grasp of the bowler (Qadir), and struck it for four. Abdul Qadir's second-innings and match figures of 7-142 and 11-218, respectively, were both career bests and records for all Tests at Faisalabad.

3rd Test, Lahore. Australia lost every Test of a series for only the second time this century, the first occasion being their 4-0 defeat in South Africa in 1969-70. Not once did they succeed in bowling out Pakistan, who won three Tests in a series for the first time. The partnership of 52 between Lawson and Alderman equalled Australia's 10th-wicket record against Pakistan set by D.K. Lillee and M.H.N. Walker at Sydney in 1976-77.

General. Zaheer Abbas took his aggregate of runs against Australia to 1,088 (avg 45.33) in 15 Tests, and passed the previous record of 915 runs by Majid Khan, which had also been scored in 15 matches. Imran Khan extended his own Pakistan record aggregate of wickets against Australia to 60 (avg 23.85) from 13 matches. Abdul Qadir's total of 22 wickets in the series set a new record for either side in Tests between Pakistan and Australia. Wasim Bari's 11 dismissals established a new record for a Pakistan wicket-keeper in a home series against Australia – one more than Imtiaz Ahmed achieved in 1959-60. Zaheer Abbas and K.J. Hughes made their 50th Test appearance, at Karachi and Faisalabad, respectively.

Australia Tour of Pakistan 1982-83
First-Class Match Statistics
Results: Played 6; Won 0, Lost 3, Drawn 3

Batting/Fielding	M	I	NO	HS	R	Avge	100	50	Ct	St
G.M. Ritchie	5	9	2	106*	293	41.85	1	1	2	-
J. Dyson	6	10	1	87	361	40.11	-	3	-	-
K.J. Hughes	6	11	1	101*	396	39.60	1	2	2	-
W.B. Phillips	2	3	0	92	118	39.33	-	1	1	1
G.M. Wood	6	10	1	85	343	38.11	-	3	2	-
A.R. Border	6	11	1	59	259	25.90	-	2	6	-
B.M. Laird	5	10	0	60	258	25.80	-	1	6	-
G.F. Lawson	4	7	1	57*	107	17.83	-	1	-	-
B. Yardley	5	7	0	40	111	15.85	-	-	2	-
J.R. Thomson	4	8	3	18	67	13.40	-	-	1	-
R.W. Marsh	4	7	0	32	83	11.85	-	-	5	2
R.J. Bright	5	7	2	32*	55	11.00	-	-	1	-
P.R. Sleep	3	5	1	29	38	9.50	-	-	-	-

Also batted: T.M. Alderman (3 matches) 7, 0 (1 ct); I.W. Callen (2) 1*.

Bowling	O	M	R	W	Avge	Best	5w/I	10w/M
I.W. Callen	20	3	60	4	15.00	2-15	-	-
A.R. Border	28	9	77	4	19.25	2-14	-	-
G.F. Lawson	134.3	23	365	15	24.33	5-32	1	-
R.J. Bright	146	36	375	12	31.25	5-40	1	-
T.M. Alderman	68	12	260	4	65.00	2-144	-	-
B. Yardley	110	23	431	5	86.20	2-136	-	-
J.R. Thomson	89	13	352	3	117.33	1-16	-	-
P.R. Sleep	56.2	7	246	1	246.00	1-158	-	-

Also bowled: K.J. Hughes 0.1-0-6-0.

*not out

One-Day Internationals

20 September at Niaz Stadium, Hyderabad. PAKISTAN won by 59 runs. Toss: Australia. Match award: Mohsin Khan (104 & 1-0-2-1). Pakistan 229-6 (40 overs) (Mohsin Khan 104). Australia 170-9 (40 overs) (G.M. Wood 52; Jalal Uddin 8-1-32-4, including the first hat-trick in limited-overs internationals).

8 October at Gaddafi Stadium, Lahore. PAKISTAN won by 27 runs. Toss: Australia. Match award: Zaheer Abbas (109 & 2-0-12-0). Pakistan 233-3 (40 overs) (Zaheer Abbas 109, Javed Miandad 60*). Australia 206-4 (40 overs) (B.M. Laird 93*, K.J. Hughes 64).

22 October at National Stadium, Karachi. MATCH ABANDONED because of crowd disturbances. Toss: Australia. Pakistan 44-1 (12 overs).

Pakistan v India

Pakistan swept to victory against India, beating them 3-0 in a six-match Test series. The only consolation for India was a win in the one-day international at Lahore on a better run-rate. Pakistan, however, won the one-day series by a 3-1 margin.

By the time the Indians landed in Pakistan, Imran and his men were in top gear, bubbling with confidence after their resounding success against Australia. Imran especially was in devastating form with bat and ball. Bowling with venomous pace, he accounted for 40 Indian batsmen at an average of 13.95. In the Faisalabad Test, he not only took 11 wickets, but also scored an exhilarating century.

While Imran was creating havoc with his pace, the Pakistani batsmen were thrashing the Indian bowlers to the tune of 12 Test centuries. Zaheer Abbas, Javed Miandad, and Mudassar Nazar each scored a double century. Zaheer and Mudassar were in prolific form, both notching up three successive hundreds in Test matches, besides taking toll of the weak Indian attack in the one-day games.

Mudassar and Javed established a record stand in the fourth Test, at Hyderabad, beating the third-wicket partnership of 370 made by Bill Edrich and Denis Compton, and going on to equal that for any wicket in Test cricket, the 451 of Australia's Bill Ponsford and Don Bradman.

After losing three Tests in a row, the Indians resigned themselves to their fate and few offered any resistance. The failure of most of their star batsmen against Imran's pace did not do much to help their bowlers, who were already being let down by poor fielding. The outstanding exception was Mohinder Amarnath, who scored three hundreds and aggregated at least 100 runs in five of the six Tests. Time and time again, he attempted to give respectability to the Indian innings, but mostly ran out of partners. Sunil Gavaskar, the captain, was in low-key form, but compiled some respectable scores. With his century at Faisalabad, he not only equalled Sir Garfield Sobers's 26 Test hundreds, but also became the first Indian to carry his bat through a completed innings.

The biggest disappointment of the tour was Viswanath, who in eight innings scored only 134 runs. Kapil Dev also failed to impress with the bat, but he took 24 Test wickets.

Apart from an umpiring controversy at the beginning of the tour, the series was played in a most cordial atmosphere.

Pakistan v India 1982-83 1st Test
Match Drawn
Played at Lahore (Gadaffi) Stadium, December 10, 11, 12, 14, 15
Toss: India. Umpires: Amanullah Khan and Mahboob Shah
Debuts: Nil

Pakistan

Mohsin Khan	c Amarnath b Madan Lal	94	not out		101
Mudassar Nazar	c Gavaskar b Kapil Dev	50	c Arun Lal b Doshi		17
Mansoor Akhtar	c Gavaskar b Kapil Dev	3	not out		14
Javed Miandad	c Gavaskar b Madan Lal	17			
Zaheer Abbas	b Doshi	215			
Salim Malik	b Madan Lal	6			
Imran Khan*	c Madan Lal b Doshi	45			
Wasim Bari†	c Arun Lal b Doshi	12			
Tahir Naqqash	st Kirmani b Doshi	20			
Sarfraz Nawaz	c Amarnath b Doshi	18			
Jalal Uddin	not out	1			
Extras	(LB 3, NB 1)	4	(LB 3)		3
		485	(1 wicket)		**135**

India

S.M. Gavaskar*	c Bari b Sarfraz	83
Arun Lal	c Mudassar b Imran	51
D.B. Vengsarkar	c Mudassar b Imran	3
G.R. Viswanath	c Bari b Imran	1
M. Amarnath	not out	109
S.M. Patil	run out	68
Kapil Dev	c Bari b Sarfraz	9
R.J. Shastri	lbw b Jalal	7
S.M.H. Kirmani†	c Bari b Jalal	10
Madan Lal	c Malik b Sarfraz	7
D.R. Doshi	b Sarfraz	0
Extras	(B 2, LB 11, NB 18)	31
		379

India	O	M	R	W	O	M	R	W
Kapil Dev	39	3	149	2	8	2	27	0
Madan Lal	27	2	101	3	5	1	10	0
Amarnath	23	5	60	0	3	1	5	0
Doshi	32.5	6	90	5	15	2	57	1
Shastri	22	3	81	0	14	1	33	0
Gavaskar					1	1	0	0

Pakistan	O	M	R	W
Imran	27	8	68	3
Sarfraz	31.5	11	63	4
Jalal	34	10	93	2
Tahir	29	6	114	0
Mudassar	3	1	10	0

Fall of Wickets

Wkt	P 1st	I 1st	P 2nd
1st	85	105	55
2nd	100	111	
3rd	126	123	
4th	238	188	
5th	250	294	
6th	367	305	
7th	438	322	
8th	447	348	
9th	478	375	
10th	485	379	

*Captain †Wicket-keeper

Pakistan v India 1982-83 2nd Test
Pakistan won by an innings and 86 runs
Played at National Stadium, Karachi, December 23, 24, 25, 27
Toss: Pakistan. Umpires: Khizar Hayat and Shakoor Rana
Debuts: India, Maninder Singh

India

S.M. Gavaskar*	run out	8
Arun Lal	lbw b Sarfraz	35
D.B. Vengsarkar	c Mohsin b Imran	0
G.R. Viswanath	c Bari b Qadir	24
M. Amarnath	lbw b Imran	5
S.M. Patil	c Miandad b Qadir	4
Kapil Dev	c and b Sarfraz	73
S.M.H. Kirmani†	c Mohsin b Qadir	11
Madan Lal	not out	3
Maninder Singh	lbw b Qadir	0
D.R. Doshi	b Imran	0
Extras	(LB 4, NB 2)	6
		169

	b Imran	42
	lbw b Qadir	11
	c Bari b Imran	79
	b Imran	0
	lbw b Imran	3
	b Imran	0
(8)	b Imran	1
(7)	c Malik b Qadir	1
	not out	52
	lbw b Imran	0
	b Imran	0
	(B 1, LB 3, W 1, NB 3)	8
		197

Pakistan

Mohsin Khan	c Amarnath b Madan Lal	12
Mansoor Akhtar	c Kirmani b Madan Lal	0
Salim Malik	c Kirmani b Madan Lal	3
Javed Miandad	b Amarnath	39
Zaheer Abbas	lbw b Kapil Dev	186
Mudassar Nazar	c Kirmani b Kapil Dev	119
Imran Khan*	c Amarnath b Kapil Dev	33
Wasim Bari†	c Arun Lal b Doshi	30
Abdul Qadir	b Kapil Dev	0
Sarfraz Nawaz	lbw b Kapil Dev	13
Jalal Uddin	not out	0
Extras	(B 2, LB 6, W 2, NB 7)	17
		452

Pakistan	O	M	R	W	O	M	R	W
Imran	12.1	6	19	3	20.1	4	60	8
Jalal	10	2	28	0	7	2	31	0
Sarfraz	16	2	49	2	10	2	23	0
Qadir	15	3	67	4	23	3	75	2

India	O	M	R	W
Kapil Dev	28.5	3	102	5
Madan Lal	23	1	129	3
Maninder	23	2	67	0
Amarnath	17	1	69	1
Doshi	18	1	68	1

*Captain †Wicket-keeper

Fall of Wickets

Wkt	I 1st	P 1st	I 2nd
1st	10	6	28
2nd	10	15	102
3rd	48	18	108
4th	55	128	112
5th	70	341	112
6th	130	397	113
7th	165	427	114
8th	168	427	197
9th	168	452	197
10th	169	452	197

OVERSEAS CRICKET 1982-83/PAKISTAN v INDIA

Pakistan v India 1982-83 3rd Test
Pakistan won by 10 wickets
Played at Iqbal Stadium, Faisalabad, January 3, 4, 5, 7, 8
Toss: Pakistan. Umpires: Mahboob Shah and Shakil Khan
Debuts: Nil

India

S.M. Gavaskar*	c Malik b Imran	12	not out		127
Arun Lal	b Sarfraz	0	c Zaheer b Sarfraz		3
D.B. Vengsarkar	lbw b Imran	6	lbw b Imran		1
G.R. Viswanath	b Mudassar	53	c Miandad b Sarfraz		9
M. Amarnath	b Mudassar	22	lbw b Imran		78
S.M. Patil	c Bari b Imran	84	b Imran		6
Kapil Dev	lbw b Imran	41	c Sikander b Sarfraz		16
S.M.H. Kirmani†	lbw b Imran	66	c Bari b Sikander		6
Madan Lal	c Malik b Imran	54	lbw b Sarfraz		10
Maninder Singh	c Mohsin b Qadir	6	lbw b Imran		2
D.R. Doshi	not out	2	b Imran		4
Extras	(B 6, LB 8 W 4, NB 8)	26	(B 1, LB 9, NB 14)		24
		372			**286**

Pakistan

Mohsin Khan	c Kirmani b Kapil Dev	4	not out	8
Mudassar Nazar	c Kirmani b Kapil Dev	38	not out	2
Mansoor Akhtar	c Kirmani b Kapil Dev	23		
Javed Miandad	c Gavaskar b Madan Lal	126		
Zaheer Abbas	c Kirmani b Madan Lal	168		
Salim Malik	b Kapil Dev	107		
Imran Khan*	c Madan Lal b Maninder	117		
Wasim Bari†	c Kirmani b Kapil Dev	6		
Sarfraz Nawaz	c Gavaskar b Kapil Dev	4		
Abdul Qadir	not out	38		
Sikander Bakht	b Kapil Dev	9		
Extras	(LB 10, NB 2)	12		
		652	(0 wickets)	**10**

Pakistan	O	M	R	W	O	M	R	W
Imran	25	3	98	6	30.5	12	82	5
Sarfraz	23	4	95	1	33	11	79	4
Sikander	13	1	66	0	9	3	41	1
Mudassar	12	2	39	2	11	3	27	0
Qadir	12.3	1	48	1	11	1	33	0

India	O	M	R	W	O	M	R	W
Kapil Dev	38.4	3	220	7				
Madan Lal	28	5	109	2				
Doshi	29	2	130	0				
Amarnath	16	1	68	0				
Maninder	29	3	103	1				
Gavaskar	2	0	10	0				
Arun Lal					1.1	0	6	0
Vengsarkar					1	0	4	0

Fall of Wickets

Wkt	I 1st	P 1st	I 2nd	P 2nd
1st	6	4	27	
2nd	17	66	28	
3rd	22	79	48	
4th	82	366	193	
5th	122	367	201	
6th	220	574	227	
7th	235	595	236	
8th	357	599	261	
9th	370	612	282	
10th	372	652	286	

*Captain †Wicket-keeper

Pakistan v India 1982-83 4th Test
Pakistan won by an innings and 119 runs
Played at Niaz Stadium, Hyderabad, January 14, 15, 16, 18, 19
Toss: Pakistan. Umpires: Javed Akhtar and Khizar Hayat
Debuts: India, B.S. Sandhu

Pakistan

Mohsin Khan	lbw b Sandhu	24
Mudassar Nazar	c Maninder b Doshi	231
Haroon Rashid	b Sandhu	0
Javed Miandad	not out	280
Zaheer Abbas	not out	25
Salim Malik	did not bat	
Imran Khan*	,,	
Wasim Bari†	,,	
Sarfraz Nawaz	,,	
Abdul Qadir	,,	
Iqbal Qasim	,,	
Extras	(B 9, LB 12)	21
	(3 wickets declared)	**581**

India

S.M. Gavaskar*	c Bari b Imran	17	c and b Qasim	60
K. Srikkanth	lbw b Sarfraz	2	c Malik b Imran	5
M. Amarnath	st Bari b Qasim	61	c Imran b Qasim	64
G.R. Viswanath	lbw b Imran	0	lbw b Sarfraz	37
D.B. Vengsarkar	c Bari b Imran	4	not out	58
Kapil Dev	b Imran	3	b Sarfraz	2
S.M.H. Kirmani†	b Imran	1	lbw b Sarfraz	0
S.M. Patil	c Imran b Sarfraz	2	c Imran b Qadir	9
B.S. Sandhu	b Sarfraz	71	c Imran b Qadir	12
Maninder Singh	not out	12	lbw b Sarfraz	4
D.R. Doshi	lbw b Imran	1	b Imran	14
Extras	(B 1, LB 7, NB 7)	15	(B 1, LB 1, NB 6)	8
		189		**273**

India	O	M	R	W				
Kapil Dev	27	2	111	0				
Sandhu	33	7	107	2				
Amarnath	15	0	64	0				
Maninder	50	10	135	0				
Doshi	41	9	143	1				

Pakistan	O	M	R	W	O	M	R	W
Imran	17.2	3	35	6	24.4	14	45	2
Sarfraz	19	4	56	3	30	4	85	4
Qadir	11	2	35	0	26	7	77	2
Qasim	9	3	48	1	31	9	58	2

Fall of Wickets

Wkt	P 1st	I 1st	I 2nd
1st	60	3	8
2nd	60	44	133
3rd	511	44	134
4th		52	201
5th		61	203
6th		65	203
7th		72	223
8th		131	249
9th		184	254
10th		189	273

*Captain †Wicket-keeper

Pakistan v India 1982-83 5th Test
Match Drawn
Played at Lahore (Gadaffi) Stadium, January 23, 24, 25, 27 (no play), 28 (no play)
Toss: India. Umpires: Javed Akhtar and Khizar Hayat
Debuts: India, T.A. Sekhar

Pakistan

Mohsin Khan	c Srikkanth b Kapil Dev	7
Mudassar Nazar	not out	152
Majid Khan	c Kirmani b Kapil Dev	0
Javed Miandad	c Viswanath b Maninder	85
Zaheer Abbas	c Kirmani b Kapil Dev	13
Salim Malik	b Maninder	6
Imran Khan*	c Kirmani b Kapil Dev	20
Wasim Bari†	c Amarnath b Kapil Dev	8
Sarfraz Nawaz	c Yashpal b Kapil Dev	26
Abdul Qadir	b Kapil Dev	0
Iqbal Qasim	lbw b Kapil Dev	0
Extras	(LB 6)	6
		323

India

S.M. Gavaskar*	lbw b Imran	13
K. Srikkanth	b Qadir	21
M. Amarnath	c Bari b Imran	120
Yashpal Sharma	not out	63
D.B. Vengsarkar	not out	1
G.R. Viswanath	did not bat	
Kapil Dev	,,	
S.M.H. Kirmani†	,,	
B.S. Sandhu	,,	
Maninder Singh	,,	
T.A. Sekhar	,,	
Extras	(B 6, LB 5, W 1, NB 5)	17
	(3 wickets)	**235**

India	O	M	R	W
Kapil Dev	30.5	7	85	8
Sandhu	21	2	56	0
Sekhar	20	2	86	0
Maninder	32	7	90	2

Pakistan	O	M	R	W
Imran	18	5	45	2
Sarfraz	23.2	9	46	0
Qadir	16	1	63	1
Majid	1	0	4	0
Mudassar	11	1	41	0
Qasim	12	3	19	0

Fall of Wickets

Wkt	P 1st	I 1st
1st	22	29
2nd	26	41
3rd	178	231
4th	191	
5th	202	
6th	244	
7th	276	
8th	323	
9th	323	
10th	323	

*Captain †Wicket-keeper

Pakistan v India 1982-83 6th Test
Match Drawn
Played at National Stadium, Karachi, January 30, 31, February 1, 3, 4
Toss: India. Umpires: Javed Akhtar and Khizar Hayat
Debuts: Nil

India

S.M. Gavaskar*	c Bari b Tahir	5	b Imran		67
R.J. Shastri	st Bari b Qadir	128	c Bari b Imran		17
M. Amarnath	c Bari b Imran	19	not out		103
Yashpal Sharma	c Bari b Imran	9	not out		19
D.B. Vengsarkar	c and b Tahir	89			
G.R. Viswanath	b Mudassar	10			
S.M.H. Kirmani†	c Zaheer b Sarfraz	18			
Kapil Dev	lbw b Imran	33			
B.S. Sandhu	not out	32			
T.A. Sekhar	not out	0			
Maninder Singh	did not bat				
Extras	(B 13, LB 9, NB 28)	50	(B 10, W 3, NB 5)		18
	(8 wickets declared)	393	(2 wickets)		224

Pakistan

Mohsin Khan	lbw b Kapil Dev	91
Mudassar Nazar	lbw b Kapil Dev	152
Javed Miandad	c Kirmani b Sandhu	47
Zaheer Abbas	c Amarnath b Shastri	43
Wasim Raja	run out	10
Imran Khan*	not out	32
Wasim Bari†	c Kirmani b Sandhu	12
Sarfraz Nawaz	not out	6
Salim Malik	did not bat	
Abdul Qadir	,,	
Tahir Naqqash	,,	
Extras	(B 5, LB 12, W 1, NB 9)	27
	(6 wickets declared)	420

Pakistan	O	M	R	W	O	M	R	W
Imran	32	11	65	3	16	3	41	2
Sarfraz	41	10	92	1	14	4	45	0
Tahir	24	7	69	2	8	1	28	0
Qadir	23	3	86	1	14	2	42	0
Mudassar	15	4	30	1				
Raja	1	0	1	0	5	2	12	0
Zaheer					8	0	24	0
Mohsin					1	0	3	0
Miandad					2	0	11	0

India	O	M	R	W
Kapil Dev	33	2	137	2
Sandhu	28.2	4	87	2
Sekhar	14	1	43	0
Maninder	16	3	49	0
Shastri	22	1	62	1
Amarnath	4	1	15	0

Fall of Wickets

	I	P	I
Wkt	1st	1st	2nd
1st	47	157	43
2nd	86	269	150
3rd	109	342	
4th	178	363	
5th	218	371	
6th	267	411	
7th	316		
8th	393		
9th			
10th			

*Captain †Wicket-keeper
Vengsarkar retired hurt when 17, at 140-3, and resumed at 218-5.

Test Match Averages: Pakistan v India 1982-83

Pakistan

Batting/Fielding	M	I	NO	HS	R	Avge	100	50	Ct	St
Zaheer Abbas	6	6	1	215	650	130.00	3	-	2	-
Mudassar Nazar	6	8	2	231	761	126.83	4	1	2	-
Javed Miandad	6	6	1	280*	594	118.80	2	1	2	-
Imran Khan	6	5	1	117	247	61.75	1	-	4	-
Mohsin Khan	6	8	2	101*	341	56.83	1	2	3	-
Salim Malik	6	4	0	107	122	30.50	1	-	5	2
Abdul Qadir	5	3	1	38	38	19.00	-	-	-	-
Sarfraz Nawaz	6	5	1	26	67	16.75	-	-	1	-
Wasim Bari	6	5	0	30	68	13.60	-	-	15	-
Mansoor Akhtar	3	4	1	23	40	13.33	-	-	-	-

Also bowled: Haroon Rashid (1 match) 0; Iqbal Qasim (2) 0 (1 ct); Jalal Uddin (2) 1*, 0*; Majid Khan (1) 0; Sikander Bakht (1) 9 (1 ct); Tahir Naqqash (2) 20 (1 ct); Wasim Raja (1) 10.

Bowling	O	M	R	W	Avge	Best	5w/I	10w/M
Imran Khan	223.1	69	558	40	13.95	8-60	4	2
Sarfraz Nawaz	241.1	62	633	19	33.31	4-63	-	-
Abdul Qadir	151.3	23	526	11	47.81	4-67	-	-

Also bowled: Iqbal Qasim 52-15-125-3; Jalal Uddin 51-14-152-2; Javed Miandad 2-0-11-0; Majid Khan 1-0-4-0; Mohsin Khan 1-0-3-0; Mudassar Nazar 52-11-147-3; Sikander Bakht 22-4-107-1; Tahir Naqqash 61-14-211-2; Wasim Raja 6-2-13-0; Zaheer Abbas 8-0-24-0.

India

Batting/Fielding	M	I	NO	HS	R	Avge	100	50	Ct	St
Yashpal Sharma	2	3	2	63*	91	91.00	-	1	1	-
M. Amarnath	6	10	2	120	584	73.00	3	3	6	-
B.S. Sandhu	3	3	1	71	115	57.50	-	1	-	-
R.J. Shastri	2	3	0	128	152	50.66	1	-	-	-
S.M. Gavaskar	6	10	1	127*	434	48.22	1	3	5	-
Madan Lal	3	5	2	54	126	42.00	-	2	2	-
D.B. Vengsarkar	6	9	2	89	241	34.42	-	3	-	-
S.M. Patil	4	7	0	85	173	24.71	-	2	-	-
Kapil Dev	6	8	0	73	178	22.25	-	1	-	-
Arun Lal	3	5	0	51	100	20.00	-	1	3	-
G.R. Viswanath	6	8	0	53	134	16.75	-	1	1	-
S.M.H. Kirmani	6	8	0	66	113	14.12	-	1	13	1
K. Srikkanth	2	3	0	21	28	9.33	-	-	1	-
Maninder Singh	5	6	1	12*	24	4.80	-	-	1	-
D.R. Doshi	4	7	1	14	21	3.50	-	-	-	-

Also batted: T.A. Sekhar (2 matches) 0*.

Bowling	O	M	R	W	Avge	Best	5w/I	10w/M
Kapil Dev	205.2	22	831	24	34.62	8-85	3	-
Madan Lal	83	9	349	8	43.62	3-101	-	-
D.R. Doshi	135.5	20	488	8	61.00	5-91	1	-
B.S. Sandhu	82.2	13	250	4	62.50	2-87	-	-

Also bowled: M. Amarnath 78-9-281-1; Arun Lal 1.1-0-6-0; S.M. Gavaskar 3-1-10-0; Maninder Singh 150-25-444-3; T.A. Sekhar 34-3-129-0; R.J. Shastri 58-5-176-1; D.B. Vengsarkar 1-0-4-0.

*not out

India Tour of Pakistan 1982-83
First-Class Match Statistics
Results: Played 10; Won 1, Lost 3, Drawn 6

Batting/Fielding	M	I	NO	HS	R	Avge	100	50	Ct	St
M. Amarnath	9	14	4	120	738	73.80	3	4	6	-
D.B. Vengsarkar	9	14	6	100*	499	62.37	2	3	1	-
R.J. Shastri	4	4	0	128	245	61.25	1	1	1	-
S.M. Gavaskar	8	13	2	127*	579	52.63	1	5	8	-
S.M. Patil	6	10	0	137	413	41.30	1	3	-	-
K. Srikkanth	6	10	0	135	357	35.70	1	2	1	-
Madan Lal	4	6	2	54	129	32.25	-	2	2	-
B.S. Sandhu	6	6	1	71	133	26.60	-	1	-	-
Yashpal Sharma	5	7	2	63*	131	26.20	-	1	2	-
Arun Lal	7	12	0	84	299	24.91	-	3	5	-
Kapil Dev	7	8	0	73	178	22.25	-	1	2	-
L. Sivaramakrishnan	4	2	1	21*	22	22.00	-	-	1	-
G.R. Viswanath	10	14	3	53	238	21.63	-	2	3	-
S.M.H. Kirmani	8	9	0	66	140	15.55	-	1	15	2
Maninder Singh	9	6	1	12*	24	4.80	-	-	3	-
D.R. Doshi	6	8	2	14	26	4.33	-	-	1	-

Also batted: T.A. Sekhar (2 matches) 0*.

Bowling	O	M	R	W	Avge	Best	5w/I	10w/M
Kapil Dev	216.2	23	879	25	35.16	8-85	3	-
Madan Lal	102	16	393	11	35.72	3-37	-	-
Maninder Singh	316	64	861	16	53.81	6-35	1	1
D.R. Doshi	190	26	651	12	54.25	5-91	1	-
R.J. Shastri	142	26	335	6	55.83	4-80	-	-
B.S. Sandhu	150.2	29	466	8	58.25	2-87	-	-

Also bowled: M. Amarnath 108-19-389-2; Arun Lal 6.1-0-29-0; S.M. Gavaskar 3-1-10-0; T.A. Sekhar 34-3-129-0; L. Sivaramakrishnan 94.2-12-348-14; K. Srikkanth 13-1-61-0; D.B. Vengsarkar 6-0-25-0; G.R. Viswanath 2-0-12-0.

*not out

One-Day Internationals

3 December at Gujranwala. PAKISTAN won by 14 runs. Toss: India. Pakistan 224-4 (40 overs) (Javed Miandad 106*). India 210-6 (40 overs) (M. Amarnath 51, Yashpal Sharma 56*).

17 December at Multan. PAKISTAN won by 37 runs. Pakistan 263-2 (40 overs) (Mohsin Khan 117* and Zaheer Abbas 118 added 205 for the 2nd wicket). India 226-7 (40 overs) (S.M. Patil 84).

31 December at Lahore. INDIA won by a faster scoring rate in a match curtailed by rain and bad light. Pakistan 252-3 (33 overs) (Zaheer Abbas 105, Javed Miandad 119*). India 193-4 (27 overs) (S.M. Gavaskar 69, S.M. Patil 51).

21 January at Karachi. PAKISTAN won by 8 wickets. Toss: India. India 197-6 (40 overs). Pakistan 198-2 (34 overs) (Mudassar Nazar 61*, Zaheer Abbas 113).

New Zealand v Sri Lanka

Sri Lanka made their inaugural tour of New Zealand in February-March seeking their first test win, but it was their hosts who passed the landmarks. The Kiwis' wins at Christchurch and Wellington in the Tests meant that for the first time they took a series by a margin of more than one match. More remarkable, New Zealand had never before won successive Tests. When Geoff Howarth's side made a clean sweep of the three one-day matches as well, they completed a sequence of nine consecutive international victories – two Tests and seven one-day matches – over England, Australia, and Sri Lanka. The New Zealanders' busiest international season, of 21 games for 15 wins, was also easily their most successful.

The Sri Lankans were outplayed for most of their visit, and joined the 1980 West Indians in leaving New Zealand without a first-class win. Their only victory was in a one-day fixture against the Minor Associations, and the Minors took revenge for that in the return match.

New Zealand has long known about the fortunes of war favouring the bigger battalions. The novel feature was that this time theirs was the bigger battalion in question. The Sri Lankans started with the handicap of not being able to use the banned players who had been to South Africa earlier in the season. Those who did make it to New Zealand then suffered some wretched luck.

Dayle Hadlee, making a comeback first as Canterbury's 'cricket adviser' (coach), then as a player, not only scored his maiden first-class century 16 years after he entered the top level, he also broke Duleep Mendis's right index finger from the first delivery the Sri Lankan skipper faced in New Zealand. Later, Roy Dias, Mendis's deputy and the next most experienced batsman, broke a thumb, and the best regarded pace bowler, Asantha de Mel, tore muscles in his left side.

The only time the tourists had New Zealand in serious difficulties was during the home team's first innings in the second Test. Then, as Lance Cairns, in characteristically vigorous style, led a tail-end recovery, the television replays twice cast doubts on the umpires' negative responses to Sri Lankan appeals. Their lead was limited to 39, and New Zealand went on to win in comfort.

New Zealand's victory at Christchurch had been easier, accomplished for the first time ever within three days. The injuries following the bannings meant that Sri Lanka needed to field seven new caps there. In a series without centuries, Warren Lees (89) and Jeremy Coney (84) played the highest Test knocks of the season in the same innings. New Zealand successfully fielded an attack entirely composed of right-arm pace bowlers.

For the tourists, acting-captain D.S. de Silva batted courageously and could have given himself more overs of leg-spin. Ranjan Madugalle was an attractive if rather unsafe middle-order batsman, and Rumesh Ratnayake a promising teenage pace bowler.

New Zealand v Sri Lanka 1982-83 1st Test

New Zealand won by an innings and 25 runs
Played at Lancaster Park, Christchurch, March 4, 5, 6.
Toss: Sri Lanka. Umpires: F.R. Goodall and D.A. Kinsella
Debuts: New Zealand, J.J. Crowe; Sri Lanka, R.G. de Alwis, E.R.N.S. Fernando,
Y. Goonasekera, S. Jeganathan, V.B. John, R.J. Ratnayake, M. de S. Wettimuny.

New Zealand

G.M. Turner	c De Alwis b John	32
B.A. Edgar	c M. de S. Wettimuny b J.R. Ratnayeke	39
J.G. Wright	b R.J. Ratnayake	13
G.P. Howarth*	c Goonasekera b J.R. Ratnayeke	0
J.J. Crowe	run out	12
J.V. Coney	run out	84
R.J. Hadlee	b John	12
B.L. Cairns	c M. de S. Wettimuny b R.J. Ratnayake	3
W.K. Lees†	b De Silva	89
M.C. Snedden	c sub (S.A.R. Silva) b J.R. Ratnayeke	22
E.J. Chatfield	not out	10
Extras	(LB 14, W 2, NB 12)	28
		344

Sri Lanka

S. Wettimuny	not out	63	lbw b Cairns	7
M. de S. Wettimuny	c Lees b Cairns	17	c Lees b Snedden	5
E.R.N.S. Fernando	b Cairns	0	b Cairns	46
Y. Goonasekera	c Lees b Cairns	4	c Turner b Cairns	8
R.S. Madugalle	run out	34	c Lees b Snedden	23
D.S. de Silva*	c Lees b Hadlee	7	b Chatfield	52
J.R. Ratnayeke	run out	0	lbw b Cairns	7
R.G. de Alwis†	c Turner b Hadlee	0	c Hadlee b Snedden	3
S. Jeganathan	lbw b Cairns	6	b Chatfield	8
R.J. Ratnayake	c Coney b Hadlee	1	c Howarth b Chatfield	0
V.B. John	lbw b Hadlee	0	not out	3
Extras	(B 2, LB 7, NB 3)	12	(B 1, LB 6, W 5, NB 1)	13
		144		**175**

Bowling

Sri Lanka	O	M	R	W	O	M	R	W
R.J. Ratnayake	31	8	125	2				
John	12	2	45	2				
J.R. Ratnayeke	31	9	93	3				
De Silva	22.5	10	41	1				
Jeganathan	5	2	12	0				

New Zealand	O	M	R	W	O	M	R	W
Hadlee	13.3	1	33	4	22	12	27	0
Snedden	10	1	30	0	23	6	48	3
Cairns	15	6	49	4	20	7	47	4
Chatfield	15	4	20	0	16.5	3	40	3

Fall of Wickets

Wkt	NZ 1st	SL 1st	SL 2nd
1st	59	49	14
2nd	93	49	26
3rd	93	56	46
4th	93	104	95
5th	137	121	108
6th	159	129	124
7th	171	133	133
8th	250	141	168
9th	292	144	170
10th	344	144	175

*Captain †Wicket-keeper

New Zealand v Sri Lanka 1982-83 2nd Test
New Zealand won by 6 wickets
Played at Basin Reserve, Wellington, March 11, 12, 13, 14, 15
Toss: New Zealand. Umpires: I.C. Higginson and S.J. Woodward
Debuts: Sri Lanka, S.A.R. Silva

Sri Lanka

S. Wettimuny	c Cairns b Hadlee	8	c Coney b Hadlee	9
M. de S. Wettimuny	c Coney b Snedden	6	c Cairns b Snedden	0
E.R.N.S. Fernando	c Wright b Hadlee	12	c Lees b Snedden	12
Y. Goonasekera	c Lees b Cairns	13	(5) c Lees b Chatfield	23
R.S. Madugalle	run out	79	(6) c Lees b Hadlee	13
D.S. de Silva*	lbw b Chatfield	61	(7) c Lees b Snedden	0
S.A.R. Silva†	c Lees b Chatfield	8	(4) c Crowe b Hadlee	0
J.R. Ratnayeke	not out	29	b Hadlee	12
S. Jeganathan	c Lees b Chatfield	5	c Lees b Chatfield	0
R.J. Ratnayake	b Snedden	12	c sub (M.D. Crowe) b Chatfield	1
V.B. John	c Wright b Chatfield	0	not out	8
Extras	(B 1, LB 5, NB 1)	7	(B 5, LB 10)	15
		240		**93**

New Zealand

G.M. Turner	c Goonasekera b John	10	b J.R. Ratnayeke	29
B.A. Edgar	c John b R.J. Ratnayake	10	not out	47
J.G. Wright	c De Silva b R.J. Ratnayake	14		
G.P. Howarth*	c S. Wettimuny b De Silva	36	(3) c Silva b John	1
J.J. Crowe	c Silva b R.J. Ratnayake	36	(4) b R.J. Ratnayake	11
J.V. Coney	c Goonasekera b John	2	(5) c Goonasekera b De Silva	17
R.J. Hadlee	c Goonasekera b John	30	(6) not out	17
W.K. Lees†	c Goonasekera b John	0		
B.L. Cairns	c De Silva b John	45		
M.C. Snedden	lbw b R.J. Ratnayake	5		
E.J. Chatfield	not out	2		
Extras	(B 4, LB 3, W 3, NB 1)	11	(LB 11, NB 1)	12
		201	(4 wickets)	**134**

New Zealand	O	M	R	W	O	M	R	W
Hadlee	25	9	47	2	17	5	34	4
Snedden	24	5	56	2	17	7	21	3
Chatfield	27	7	66	4	12	5	15	3
Cairns	20	5	53	1	7	2	8	0
Coney	5	2	11	0				

Sri Lanka	O	M	R	W	O	M	R	W
R.J. Ratnayake	24	5	81	4	15	0	46	1
John	25.2	9	60	5	8	2	38	1
J.R. Ratnayeke	14	3	36	0	8.1	4	20	1
De Silva	9	5	13	1	6	1	18	1

*Captain †Wicket-keeper

Fall of Wickets

Wkt	SL 1st	NZ 1st	SL 2nd	NZ 2nd
1st	14	12	0	59
2nd	14	33	12	62
3rd	34	104	12	81
4th	48	107	57	116
5th	178	141	61	
6th	191	141	61	
7th	194	145	78	
8th	220	163	81	
9th	239	169	83	
10th	240	201	93	

Test Match Averages: New Zealand v Sri Lanka 1982-83

New Zealand

Batting/Fielding	M	I	NO	HS	R	Avge	100	50	Ct	St
B.A. Edgar	2	3	1	47*	96	48.00	-	-	-	-
W.K. Lees	2	2	0	89	89	44.50	-	1	13	-
J.V. Coney	2	3	0	84	103	34.33	-	1	3	-
R.J. Hadlee	2	3	1	30	59	29.50	-	-	1	-
B.L. Cairns	2	2	0	45	48	24.00	-	-	2	-
G.M. Turner	2	3	0	32	71	23.66	-	-	2	-
J.J. Crowe	2	3	0	36	59	19.66	-	-	1	-
M.C. Snedden	2	2	0	22	27	13.50	-	-	-	-
J.G. Wright	2	2	0	14	27	13.50	-	-	2	-
G.P. Howarth	2	3	0	36	37	12.33	-	-	1	-
E.J. Chatfield	2	2	2	10*	12	-	-	-	-	-

Bowling	O	M	R	W	Avge	Best	5w/I	10w/M
E.J. Chatfield	70.5	19	141	10	14.10	4-66	-	-
R.J. Hadlee	77.3	27	141	10	14.10	4-33	-	-
B.L. Cairns	62	20	157	9	17.44	4-47	-	-
M.C. Snedden	74	19	155	8	19.37	3-21	-	-

Also bowled: J.V. Coney 5-2-11-0.

Sri Lanka

Batting/Fielding	M	I	NO	HS	R	Avge	100	50	Ct	St
R.S. Madugalle	2	4	0	79	149	37.25	-	1	-	-
D.S. de Silva	2	4	0	61	120	30.00	-	2	2	-
S. Wettimuny	2	4	1	63*	87	29.00	-	1	1	-
E.R.N.S. Fernando	2	4	0	46	70	17.50	-	-	-	-
J.R. Ratnayeke	2	4	1	29*	48	16.00	-	-	-	-
Y. Goonasekera	2	4	0	23	48	12.00	-	-	6	-
M. de S. Wettimuny	2	4	0	17	28	7.00	-	-	2	-
V.B. John	2	4	2	8*	11	5.50	-	-	1	-
S. Jeganathan	2	4	0	8	19	4.75	-	-	-	-
S.A.R. Silva	1	2	0	8	8	4.00	-	-	2	-
R.J. Ratnayake	2	4	0	12	14	3.50	-	-	-	-
R.G. de Alwis	1	2	0	3	3	1.50	-	-	1	-

Bowling	O	M	R	W	Avge	Best	5w/I	10w/M
V.B. John	45.2	13	143	8	17.87	5-60	1	-
D.S. de Silva	37.5	16	72	3	24.00	1-13	-	-
R.J. Ratnayake	70	13	252	7	36.00	4-81	-	-
J.R. Ratnayeke	53.1	16	149	4	37.25	3-93	-	-

Also bowled: S. Jeganathan 5-2-12-0.

*not out

Sri Lanka Tour of Australia and New Zealand 1982-83
First-Class Match Statistics
Results: Played 6; Won 0, Lost 3, Drawn 3

Batting/Fielding	M	I	NO	HS	R	Avge	100	50	Ct	St
R.S. Madugalle	6	10	0	81	392	39.20	-	3	2	-
D.S. de Silva	5	8	1	65	243	34.71	-	3	3	-
S. Wettimuny	5	8	1	105	231	33.00	1	1	1	-
J.R. Ratnayeke	5	9	3	64*	174	29.00	-	1	3	-
E.R.N.S. Fernando	4	7	0	72	188	26.85	-	1	1	-
R.L. Dias	3	5	0	40	112	22.40	-	-	-	-
S. Jeganathan	6	10	1	74	170	18.88	-	1	3	-
Y. Goonasekera	4	7	0	27	89	12.71	-	-	8	-
M. de S. Wettimuny	6	10	0	31	126	12.60	-	-	2	-
R.G. de Alwis	3	5	0	42	53	10.60	-	-	6	-
S.A.R. Silva	3	5	0	43	51	10.20	-	-	7	-
V.B. John	6	7	3	8*	20	5.00	-	-	1	-
R.J. Ratnayake	5	7	0	12	14	2.00	-	-	-	-

Also batted: A.L.F. de Mel (2 matches) 0*, 12 (2 ct); L.R.D. Mendis (2) 15, 0*; R.G.C.E. Wijesuriya (1) 1 (1 ct).

Bowling	O	M	R	W	Avge	Best	5w/I	10w/M
R.J. Ratnayake	163	42	524	22	23.81	5-50	1	-
J.R. Ratnayeke	92.1	22	255	10	25.50	4-34	-	-
V.B. John	135.3	31	421	16	26.31	5-60	1	-
D.S. de Silva	128.5	41	311	8	38.87	2-44	-	-

Also bowled: A.L.F. de Mel 40-10-122-3; Y. Goonasekera 16-3-33-1; S. Jeganathan 99-26-243-3; R.G.C.E. Wijesuriya 5-1-20-0; M. de S. Wettimuny 11-5-24-0.
*not out

One-Day Internationals

2 March at Carisbrook, Dunedin. NEW ZEALAND won by 65 runs. Toss: Sri Lanka. Match award: J.G. Wright (45 and 1-1-0-0). New Zealand 183-8 (50 overs). Sri Lanka 118-9 (50 overs) (R.J. Hadlee 8-3-9-3).

19 March at McLean Park, Napier. NEW ZEALAND won by 7 wickets. Toss: New Zealand. Sri Lanka 167-8 (50 overs). New Zealand 168-3 (36.4 overs). The Crowe brothers appeared together at international level for the first time, Jeff scoring 46* and Martin 43*.

20 March at Eden Park, Auckland. NEW ZEALAND won by 116 runs. Toss: New Zealand. Match award: G.M. Turner (140, 1-1-0-0, and 1 ct). New Zealand 304-5 (50 overs) (G.M. Turner 140, B.A. Edgar 52). Sri Lanka 188-6 (50 overs) (B.L. Cairns 10-2-23-4).

West Indies v India

For the first time in five consecutive rubbers between them, West Indies beat India without losing a single Test. The margin was 2-0, with a clear possibility of a third West Indies win had the second Test, in Trinidad, been free of rain. At the same time, India might have given a better account of themselves in the first Test – also badly affected by the weather and eventually decided in a thrilling, last-over finish – had they had more than just one match to acclimatize before the start of the Test series. The short preparation was a particular disadvantage in view of a new captain in Kapil Dev having taken command.

Despite their pronounced superiority in the Test matches, West Indies looked a declining side. It was, in the circumstances, paradoxical that their batting and bowling averages were headed by the senior members of each department, Clive Lloyd and Andy Roberts, who used their experience to the fullest.

Lloyd made centuries in the second and fifth Tests, each of them having roots in a dreadful crisis. All the first seven batsmen in their batting order made a century during the series, and four of them averaged above 50. A fifth, Viv Richards, fell just below the mark. By his standards, Richards had a moderate series. Only in the first Test, when he was in the thick of a furious run chase, was Richards seen at his best.

Although the need to infuse new blood seemed pressing, West Indies capped only two new players during the series. Augustine Logie, an ebullient, pint-sized batsman of 23, was given the full series to prove his worth. In the bowling department, Joel Garner never looked the bowler of old, but it was not until the 'dead' fifth Test that Winston Davis won his spurs. Jeffrey Dujon, wicket-keeper batsman, was still a comparative newcomer to the side. Lithe and agile, he caught almost everything the Indian batsmen snicked. But it was as a batsman, stylish, technically accomplished and effective, that Dujon, from Jamaica, was most impressive.

Roberts's place at the top of the bowling aggregates was tribute to his durability and his guile. But for speed and consistent aggression, Malcolm Marshall (21 wickets) was the pick of the West Indies bowlers. Principally, it was he who undermined Gavaskar's confidence.

Gavaskar had a disastrous series, which largely explains the disparity between the sides. The Indian batting was erratic, and the forceful Sandeep Patil, unavailable for private reasons, was badly missed.

But Mohinder Amarnath, defending and hooking fearlessly, so enhanced his reputation that one of the West Indies fast bowlers said that he was the best batsman West Indies had encountered since the formation of their lethal four-pronged fast attack in the late 1970s.

India's three seam bowlers, Kapil Dev, Sandhu, and Madan Lal, performed beyond expectations. But the spinners did not come up to the mark, and India's outcricket suffered from indifferent fielding and wicket-keeper Kirmani's wretched form.

West Indies v India 1982-83 1st Test

West Indies won by 4 wickets
Played at Sabina Park, Kingston, Jamaica, February 23, 24, 26, 27 (no play), 28
Toss: West Indies. Umpires: D.M. Archer and W. Malcolm
Debuts: West Indies, A.L. Logie

India

S.M. Gavaskar	c Dujon b Marshall	20	b Holding	0
A.D. Gaekwad	c Dujon b Holding	1	c Greenidge b Marshall	23
M. Amarnath	c Dujon b Garner	29	c Garner b Marshall	40
D.B. Vengsarkar	c Richards b Roberts	30	c Garner b Marshall	20
Yashpal Sharma	c Haynes b Garner	63	c Gomes b Holding	24
R.J. Shastri	c Dujon b Holding	1	not out	25
Kapil Dev*	c Marshall b Roberts	5	c Dujon b Roberts	12
S.M.H. Kirmani†	c Dujon b Marshall	5	c Haynes b Roberts	10
B.S. Sandhu	c Garner b Roberts	68	c Garner b Roberts	0
S. Venkataraghavan	hit wkt b Roberts	0	c Greenidge b Roberts	0
Maninder Singh	not out	3	c Holding b Roberts	2
Extras	(B 1, LB 15, NB 10)	26	(B 1, LB 5, W 1, NB 11)	18
		251		**174**

West Indies

C.G. Greenidge	c Venkataraghavan b Shastri	70	b Kapil Dev	42
D.L. Haynes	c Amarnath b Kapil Dev	25	b Kapil Dev	34
I.V.A. Richards	c Venkataraghavan b Shastri	29	(4) c Kapil Dev b Amarnath	61
H.A. Gomes	c Yashpal b Shastri	4		
A.L. Logie	run out	13	(7) lbw b Kapil Dev	10
C.H. Lloyd*	b Venkataraghavan	24	(3) c Amarnath b Kapil Dev	3
P.J. Dujon†	lbw b Kapil Dev	29	(6) not out	17
M.D. Marshall	c Yashpal b Kapil Dev	23	not out	0
A.M.E. Roberts	c Sandhu b Shastri	17	(5) c Kirmani b Amarnath	1
M.A. Holding	c Kirmani b Kapil Dev	1		
J. Garner	not out	0		
Extras	(B 1, LB 8, NB 10)	19	(LB 5)	5
		254	(6 wickets)	**173**

West Indies

	O	M	R	W	O	M	R	W
Holding	24	5	57	2	17	4	36	2
Roberts	22	4	61	4	24.3	9	39	5
Garner	15.4	4	41	2	13	6	16	0
Marshall	16	4	35	2	24	6	56	3
Gomes	9	0	31	0	7	2	9	0
Richards	1	1	0	0				

India

	O	M	R	W	O	M	R	W
Kapil Dev	25.3	6	45	4	13	0	73	4
Sandhu	11	4	30	0	3	0	22	0
Venkataraghavan	25	3	66	1	7	0	39	0
Maninder	31	6	51	0				
Shastri	24	8	43	4				
Amarnath					2.2	0	34	2

Fall of Wickets

Wkt	I 1st	WI 1st	I 2nd	WI 2nd
1st	10	36	0	47
2nd	58	83	68	65
3rd	66	91	69	131
4th	98	114	112	132
5th	99	157	118	156
6th	104	186	136	167
7th	127	228	168	
8th	234	244	168	
9th	238	254	168	
10th	251	254	174	

*Captain †Wicket-keeper

West Indies v India 1982-83 2nd Test
Match Drawn
Played at Queen's Park Oval, Port-of-Spain, Trinidad, March 11, 12, 13, 15, 16
Toss: West Indies. Umpires: S.E. Parris and Sadiq Mohammad
Debuts: Nil

India

S.M. Gavaskar	c Dujon b Holding	1	c Dujon b Garner		32
A.D. Gaekwad	run out	0	c sub (S.F.A.F. Bacchus) b Gomes		35
M. Amarnath	c Lloyd b Roberts	58	lbw b Richards		117
D.B. Vengsarkar	c Holding b Marshall	7	c Dujon b Roberts		45
Yashpal Sharma	not out	11	b Roberts		50
R.J. Shastri	c Gomes b Marshall	42	lbw b Holding		9
Kapil Dev*	c Haynes b Marshall	13	not out		100
S.M.H. Kirmani†	b Roberts	7	run out		30
B.S. Sandhu	c Richards b Marshall	11	not out		0
S. Venkataraghavan	c Richards b Roberts	1			
Maninder Singh	c Dujon b Marshall	1			
Extras	(B 5, LB 1, W 3, NB 14)	23	(B 10, LB 20, NB 21)		51
		175	(7 wickets)		**469**

West Indies

C.G. Greenidge	b Sandhu	0
D.L. Haynes	c Kirmani b Sandhu	0
I.V.A. Richards	c Kirmani b Kapil Dev	1
H.A. Gomes	c Gavaskar b Venkataraghavan	123
C.H. Lloyd*	st Kirmani b Shastri	143
A.L. Logie	c Kapil Dev b Venkataraghavan	13
P.J. Dujon†	lbw b Kapil Dev	31
M.D. Marshall	lbw b Shastri	14
A.M.E. Roberts	b Kapil Dev	9
M.A. Holding	c Vengsarkar b Maninder	24
J. Garner	not out	21
Extras	(B 4, LB 7, W 1, NB 3)	15
		394

West Indies	O	M	R	W	O	M	R	W
Holding	13	2	24	1	31	2	106	1
Roberts	22	5	72	3	25	3	100	2
Marshall	19.1	6	37	5	27.1	8	72	0
Garner	10	5	17	0	30	8	81	1
Gomes	2	1	2	0	19	7	45	1
Richards					7	4	14	1

India	O	M	R	W
Kapil Dev	31	6	91	3
Sandhu	19	2	69	2
Venkataraghavan	41	13	97	2
Shastri	21	2	71	2
Maninder	26.3	7	51	1

Fall of Wickets

Wkt	I 1st	WI 1st	I 2nd
1st	1	0	63
2nd	5	1	132
3rd	28	1	206
4th	131	238	312
5th	146	255	325
6th	147	316	329
7th	164	324	463
8th	166	340	
9th	171	346	
10th	175	394	

*Captain †Wicket-keeper
In the first innings, Yashpal Sharma retired hurt at 44-3 and resumed at 166-8.

64 OVERSEAS CRICKET 1982-83/WEST INDIES v INDIA

West Indies v India 1982-83 3rd Test
Match Drawn
Played at Bourda, Georgetown, Guyana, March 31, April 2 (no play), 3, 4 (no play), 5
Toss: West Indies. Umpires: D.M. Archer and D. Narine
Debuts: Nil

West Indies

C.G. Greenidge	c Kirmani b Maninder	70
D.L. Haynes	c Yashpal b Venkataraghavan	46
I.V.A. Richards	c Venkataraghavan b Sandhu	109
H.A. Gomes	c Gaekwad b Kapil Dev	36
M.A. Holding	run out	0
A.L. Logie	c Kirmani b Sandhu	0
C.H. Lloyd*	c Kirmani b Shastri	81
P.J. Dujon†	c and b Venkataraghavan	47
M.D. Marshall	lbw b Kapil Dev	27
A.M.E. Roberts	c Gavaskar b Sandhu	36
J. Garner	not out	1
Extras	(B 1, LB 14, W 1, NB 1)	17
		470

India

S.M. Gavaskar	not out	147
A.D. Gaekwad	c Dujon b Holding	8
M. Amarnath	c Richards b Marshall	13
D.B. Vengsarkar	c Richards b Garner	62
Yashpal Sharma	not out	35
R.J. Shastri	did not bat	
Kapil Dev*	,,	
S.M.H. Kirmani†	,,	
B.S. Sandhu	,,	
Maninder Singh	,,	
S. Venkataraghavan	,,	
Extras	(B 1, LB 3, NB 15)	19
	(3 wickets)	**284**

India	O	M	R	W
Kapil Dev	30	7	68	2
Sandhu	25.4	5	87	3
Shastri	22	3	84	1
Maninder	27	3	90	1
Venkataraghavan	38	4	124	2

West Indies	O	M	R	W
Roberts	15	2	38	0
Holding	16	1	72	1
Garner	17	4	57	1
Marshall	13	2	39	1
Gomes	14	5	35	0
Richards	4	0	24	0

Fall of Wickets

Wkt	WI 1st	I 1st
1st	89	24
2nd	157	68
3rd	251	180
4th	253	
5th	256	
6th	299	
7th	387	
8th	417	
9th	460	
10th	470	

*Captain †Wicket-keeper

West Indies v India 1982-83 4th Test

West Indies won by 10 wickets
Played at Kensington Oval, Bridgetown, Barbados, April 15, 16 17, 19, 20
Toss: West Indies. Umpires: D.M. Archer and S.E. Parris

India

S.M. Gavaskar	c Dujon b Holding	2	c Roberts b Garner	19
A.D. Gaekwad	c Marshall b Roberts	3	b Holding	55
M. Amarnath	c Dujon b Marshall	91	c Dujon b Roberts	80
D.B. Vengsarkar	c Marshall b Holding	15	lbw b Holding	6
Yashpal Sharma	c Richards b Roberts	24	c Greenidge b Roberts	12
R.J. Shastri	c Richards b Roberts	29	c Lloyd b Marshall	19
Kapil Dev*	c Lloyd b Marshall	0	(8) c Lloyd b Marshall	26
S.M.H. Kirmani†	c Haynes b Roberts	11	(9) run out	33
Madan Lal	c Holding b Garner	6	(10) lbw b Roberts	0
B.S. Sandhu	not out	8	(7) lbw b Roberts	4
S. Venkataraghavan	c Dujon b Garner	5	(11) not out	0
Extras	(LB 1, NB 14)	15	(B 5, LB 2, NB 16)	23
		209		**277**

West Indies

C.G. Greenidge	c Gavaskar b Madan Lal	57
D.L. Haynes	c Kapil Dev b Shastri	92
I.V.A. Richards	c Gavaskar b Venkataraghavan	80
H.A. Gomes	c sub‡ b Venkataraghavan	6
A.L. Logie	c Amarnath b Shastri	130
C.H. Lloyd*	c sub‡ b Venkataraghavan	50
P.J. Dujon†	c Vengsarkar b Kapil Dev	25
M.D. Marshall	c Venkataraghavan b Kapil Dev	8
A.M.E. Roberts	c Kapil Dev b Madan Lal	20
M.A. Holding	c Kirmani b Kapil Dev	2
J. Garner	not out	2
Extras	(B 1, LB 11, NB 2)	14
		486

	not out	0
	not out	0
	(NB 1)	1
	(0 wickets)	**1**

West Indies	O	M	R	W	O	M	R	W
Holding	14	4	46	2	21	2	75	2
Roberts	16	4	48	4	19.2	5	31	4
Marshall	13	1	56	2	16	1	80	2
Garner	12.2	5	41	2	15	4	48	1
Gomes	2	1	3	0	8	3	20	0

India	O	M	R	W	O	M	R	W
Kapil Dev	32.2	7	76	3				
Sandhu	5	1	21	0				
Madan Lal	27	2	96	2				
Shastri	50	13	133	2				
Venkataraghavan	43	6	146	3				
Gaekwad	1	1	0	0				
Kirmani					0.1	0	0	0

Fall of Wickets

Wkt	I 1st	WI 1st	I 2nd	WI 2nd
1st	2	98	61	
2nd	10	220	108	
3rd	39	230	109	
4th	91	262	132	
5th	172	395	139	
6th	172	454	155	
7th	180	458	214	
8th	196	481	276	
9th	200	483	276	
10th	209	486	277	

*Captain †Wicket-keeper ‡L. Sivaramakrishnan
Amarnath (2nd innings) retired hurt at 96-1 and resumed at 139-5.

West Indies v India 1982-83 5th Test
Match Drawn
Played at Recreation Ground, St John's, Antigua, April 28, 29, 30, May 1, 3
Toss: West Indies. Umpires: D.M. Archer and A. Weekes
Debuts: West Indies, W.W. Davis; India, L. Sivaramakrishnan

India

S.M. Gavaskar	c Dujon b Marshall	18	c Dujon b Davis	1
A.D. Gaekwad	c Richards b Roberts	3	lbw b Marshall	72
M. Amarnath	c Lloyd b Davis	54	c Logie b Davis	116
D.B. Vengsarkar	c Davis b Marshall	94	c Dujon b Marshall	0
Yashpal Sharma	c Gomes b Roberts	3	c sub (S.F.A.F. Bacchus) b Gomes	20
R.J. Shastri	st Dujon b Gomes	102	not out	9
Kapil Dev*	lbw b Holding	98	not out	0
S.M.H. Kirmani†	c Greenidge b Davis	2		
Madan Lal	not out	35		
L. Sivaramakrishnan	c sub (S.F.A.F. Bacchus) b Marshall	17		
S. Venkataraghavan	b Marshall	0		
Extras	(B 14, LB 7, W 1, NB 9)	31	(B 11, LB 8, NB 10)	29
		457	(5 wickets declared)	247

West Indies

C.G. Greenidge	retired, not out	154
D.L. Haynes	c Shastri b Yashpal	136
W.W. Davis	b Madan Lal	14
I.V.A. Richards	c Gaekwad b Madan Lal	2
H.A. Gomes	lbw b Madan Lal	9
A.L. Logie	hit wkt b Kapil Dev	1
P.J. Dujon†	c Gaekwad b Venkataraghavan	110
C.H. Lloyd*	c Yashpal b Shastri	106
M.D. Marshall	b Venkataraghavan	2
A.M.E. Roberts	not out	1
M.A. Holding	run out	0
Extras	(B 6, LB 5, NB 4)	15
		550

Fall of Wickets

Wkt	I 1st	WI 1st	I 2nd
1st	5	296	1
2nd	51	303	201
3rd	128	323	201
4th	181	324	235
5th	337	334	245
6th	372	541	
7th	376	546	
8th	419	549	
9th	457	550	
10th	457		

West Indies	O	M	R	W	O	M	R	W
Roberts	29	3	110	2	15	3	46	0
Holding	26	3	86	1				
Marshall	27.5	5	87	4	18	7	33	2
Davis	29	1	121	2	23	4	54	2
Richards	11	3	13	0	13	1	36	0
Gomes	4	1	9	1	19	0	49	1

India	O	M	R	W
Kapil Dev	22	6	71	1
Madan Lal	35	7	105	3
Sivaramakrishnan	25	1	95	0
Shastri	46.4	5	141	1
Venkataraghavan	36	1	114	2
Gaekwad	1	0	3	0
Yashpal	1	0	6	1

*Captain †Wicket-keeper
Greenidge retired at 301-1 to visit his baby daughter seriously ill in Barbados. Amarnath (1st innings) retired hurt at 98-2 and resumed at 337-5.

Test Match Averages: West Indies v India 1982-83

West Indies

Batting/Fielding	M	I	NO	HS	R	Avge	100	50	Ct	St
C.G. Greenidge	5	7	2	154*	393	78.60	1	3	4	-
C.H. Lloyd	5	6	0	143	407	67.83	2	2	5	-
D.L. Haynes	5	7	1	136	333	55.50	1	1	4	-
P.J. Dujon	5	6	1	110	259	51.80	1	-	18	1
I.V.A. Richards	5	6	0	109	282	47.00	1	2	8	-
H.A. Gomes	5	5	0	123	178	35.60	1	-	3	-
A.L. Logie	5	6	0	130	167	27.83	1	-	1	-
J. Garner	4	4	4	21*	24	-	-	-	4	-
A.M.E. Roberts	5	6	1	36	84	16.80	-	-	1	-
M.D. Marshall	5	6	1	27	74	14.80	-	-	3	-
M.A. Holding	5	5	0	24	27	5.40	-	-	3	-

Played in one Test: W.W. Davis 14 (1 ct).

Bowling	O	M	R	W	Avge	Best	5w/I	10w/M
A.M.E. Roberts	187.5	38	545	24	22.70	5-39	1	-
M.D. Marshall	174.1	40	495	21	23.57	5-37	1	-
M.A. Holding	162	23	502	12	41.83	2-36	-	-
J. Garner	113	36	301	7	43.00	2-41	-	-

Also bowled: W.W. Davis 52-5-175-4; H.A. Gomes 84-20-203-3; I.V.A. Richards 36-9-87-1.

India

Batting/Fielding	M	I	NO	HS	R	Avge	100	50	Ct	St
M. Amarnath	5	9	0	117	598	66.44	2	4	3	-
Kapil Dev	5	8	2	100*	254	42.33	1	1	4	-
R.J. Shastri	5	8	2	102	236	39.33	1	-	1	-
Yashpal Sharma	5	9	2	63	242	34.57	-	2	4	-
D.B. Vengsarkar	5	9	0	94	279	31.00	-	2	2	-
S.M. Gavaskar	5	9	1	147*	240	30.00	1	-	4	-
B.S. Sandhu	4	6	2	68	91	22.75	-	1	1	-
A.D. Gaekwad	5	9	0	72	200	22.22	-	2	3	-
Madan Lal	2	3	1	35*	41	20.50	-	-	-	-
S.M.H. Kirmani	5	7	0	33	98	14.00	-	-	8	1
Maninder Singh	3	3	1	3*	6	3.00	-	-	-	-
S. Venkataraghavan	5	6	1	5	6	1.20	-	-	5	-

Played in one Test: L. Sivaramakrishnan 17.

Bowling	O	M	R	W	Avge	Best	5w/I	10w/M
Kapil Dev	153.5	32	424	17	24.94	4-45	-	-
Madan Lal	62	9	201	5	40.20	3-105	-	-
B.S. Sandhu	63.4	12	229	5	45.80	3-87	-	-
R.J. Shastri	163.4	31	472	10	47.20	4-43	-	-
S. Venkataraghavan	190	27	586	10	58.60	3-146	-	-

Also bowled: M. Amarnath 2.2-0-34-2; A.D. Gaekwad 2-1-3-0; S.M.H. Kirmani 0.1-0-0-0; Maninder Singh 84.3-16-192-2; L. Sivaramakrishnan 25-1-95-0; Yashpal Sharma 1-0-6-1.

*not out

India Tour of West Indies 1982-83
First-Class Match Statistics
Results: Played 10; Won 3, Lost 2, Drawn 5

Batting/Fielding	M	I	NO	HS	R	Avge	100	50	Ct	St
M. Amarnath	8	14	1	117	959	73.76	4	6	4	-
Madan Lal	6	9	2	97	290	41.42	-	2	3	-
R.J. Shastri	9	14	3	102	422	38.36	1	2	2	-
D.B. Vengsarkar	8	14	0	94	502	35.85	-	5	3	-
Kapil Dev	7	11	2	100*	315	35.00	1	2	5	-
Yashpal Sharma	9	16	2	63	478	34.14	-	4	6	-
K. More	3	4	2	31	66	33.00	-	-	5	5
S.M. Gavaskar	6	10	1	147*	245	27.22	1	-	4	-
A. Malhotra	4	7	1	59	157	26.16	-	2	-	-
A.D. Gaekwad	9	16	0	89	414	25.87	-	4	4	-
Arun Lal	5	9	1	77	170	21.25	-	1	5	-
Gursharan Singh	4	6	0	89	123	20.50	-	1	7	-
B.S. Sandhu	5	8	2	68	110	18.33	-	1	1	-
L. Sivaramakrishnan	5	7	1	32	109	18.16	-	-	1	-
S.M.H. Kirmani	8	12	1	74	199	18.09	-	-	10	2
Maninder Singh	6	7	4	14	40	13.33	-	-	3	-
S. Venkataraghavan	8	10	1	14	32	3.55	-	-	9	-

Bowling	O	M	R	W	Avge	Best	5w/I	10w/M
Kapil Dev	196.5	40	539	25	21.56	4-45	-	-
Madan Lal	145.2	14	504	20	25.20	5-68	1	-
Maninder Singh	188.4	39	464	18	25.77	7-47	2	1
S. Venkataraghavan	291.2	60	768	21	36.57	4-5	-	-
R.J. Shastri	272.1	50	734	17	43.17	5-22	1	-

Also bowled: M. Amarnath 35.2-8-142-7; A.D. Gaekwad 63-10-188-6; S.M.H. Kirmani 0.1-0-0-0; B.S. Sandhu 87.4-19-293-7; L. Sivaramakrishnan 118-15-400-9; Yashpal Sharma 22-4-68-2.

*not out.

One-Day Internationals

9 March at Queen's Park Oval, Port-of-Spain. WEST INDIES won by 52 runs. Toss: India. Match award: D.L. Haynes (97 and 1 ct). West Indies 215-4 dec (38.5 overs) (C.G. Greenidge 66, D.L. Haynes 97). India 163-7 (39 overs).

29 March at Albion, Berbice. INDIA won by 27 runs. Toss: West Indies. Match award: Kapil Dev (72, 10-1-33-2, and 2 ct). India 282-5 (47 overs) (S.M. Gavaskar 91, Kapil Dev 72). West Indies 255-9 (47 overs) (I.V.A. Richards 64, S.F.A.F. Bacchus 52, P.J. Dujon 53*).

7 April at St George's, Grenada. WEST INDIES won by 7 wickets. Toss: India. Match award: H.A. Gomes (10-0-38-4). India 166 (44.4 overs) (D.B. Vengsarkar 54; Gomes 10-0-38-4). West Indies 167-3 (40.2 overs) (C.G. Greenidge 64).

Sri Lanka v Australia

Shortly after 2 pm on the fourth day, Australia concluded a resounding innings victory in their first official encounter with Sri Lanka. It avenged two recent defeats on successive days in the limited-overs series, and extended the painful initiation of Test cricket's most recent recruit to six defeats and no victories after eight matches.

Australia were in control from the moment that Chappell won a vital toss in his 48th and final Test as captain. The relaid pitch at the newly relandscaped Asgiriya Stadium took appreciable turn from the first afternoon. Sri Lanka's selectors had made the task easier for Australia's galaxy of left-handers by not including an off-spinner.

A sound start was essential for the visitors, whose attack was extremely suspect. Hogg began the match with severe food poisoning, Lillee had still to test his damaged knee in a five-day game, and Hogan was playing in his first Test. After a slow first session, Wessels and Yallop paved the way for a final onslaught by Hookes. Wessels reached his second hundred in five Tests, while Yallop fell two runs short – a commanding innings that celebrated his recall after breaking Ponsford's record aggregate for a season of Sheffield Shield cricket. Chappell, the only right-hander to bat in the innings, took his Test aggregate to 6,746 – exactly 250 runs short of Bradman's Australian record. It was Hookes who delighted the spectators, though, with a maiden hundred in his 24th Test innings. His undefeated 143 was made off only 152 balls, and included 2 sixes and 17 fours, with the last 100 scored between lunch and tea.

Sri Lanka, needing to survive three days and one session, were soon struggling at 9 for 3. Although some fine batting by Mendis – in his first Test as captain – and the 19-year-old left-handed Ranatunga enabled Sri Lanka to reach a respectable total, they were unable to avoid being asked to follow on. Their one-day background produced a series of reckless heaves against Yardley's off-breaks.

Their second attempt was even less successful, and only Wettimuny demonstrated the necessary technique in a three-hour vigil sadly ended just 4 runs short of his second Test century.

One-Day Internationals

13 April at Saravanamuttu Stadium, Colombo. SRI LANKA won by 2 wickets. Toss: Australia. Match award: R.G. de Alwis (6 and 5 ct). Australia 168-9 (45 overs) (G.M. Wood 50). Sri Lanka 169-8 (44.1 overs).

16 April at Saravanamuttu Stadium, Colombo. SRI LANKA won by 4 wickets. Toss: Sri Lanka. Australia 207-5 (45 overs) (G.N. Yallop 59, G.S. Chappell 54*). Sri Lanka 213-6 (43.2 overs) (S. Wettimuny 56, A. Ranatunga 55* off 36 balls).

29 April at Sinhalese Sports Club Ground, Colombo. MATCH ABANDONED – rain. Toss: Sri Lanka. Australia 194-5 (39.2 overs) (G.N. Yallop 51).

30 April at SSC Ground, Colombo. MATCH ABANDONED – rain. Australia 124-3 (19.2 overs) (G.N. Yallop 60*).

Sri Lanka v Australia 1982-83 only Test

Australia won by an innings and 38 runs
Played at Asgiriya Stadium, Kandy, April 22, 23, 24, 26
Toss: Australia. Umpires: C.E.B. Anthony and H.C. Felsinger
Debuts: Sri Lanka, R.P.W. Guneratne; Australia, T.G. Hogan, R.D. Woolley

Australia

K.C. Wessels	c Dias b De Silva	141
G.M. Wood	c Ratnayake b Ranatunga	4
G.N. Yallop	lbw b De Mel	98
G.S. Chappell*	lbw b De Mel	66
D.W. Hookes	not out	143
A.R. Border	not out	47
R.D. Woolley†	did not bat	
T.G. Hogan	,,	
B. Yardley	,,	
D.K. Lillee	,,	
R.M. Hogg	,,	
Extras	(LB 11, W 1, NB 3)	15
	(4 wickets declared)	**514**

Sri Lanka

S. Wettimuny	c Woolley b Lillee	0	b Hogan	96
E.R.N.S. Fernando	c Woolley b Hogg	0	c Woolley b Lillee	3
R.L. Dias	c Border b Lillee	4	b Hogan	10
L.R.D. Mendis*	c Hookes b Yardley	74	(5) c Border b Yardley	6
R.S. Madugalle	c and b Yardley	9	(6) b Yardley	0
A. Ranatunga	c Lillee b Yardley	90	(7) b Hogan	32
D.S. de Silva	c Hogan b Yardley	26	(8) c Woolley b Hogan	5
A.L.F. de Mel	c Hookes b Hogan	29	(9) c Yallop b Hogan	0
R.G. de Alwis†	c Border b Yardley	3	(10) run out	9
R.J. Ratnayake	c Woolley b Border	14	(4) run out	30
R.P.W. Guneratne	not out	0	not out	0
Extras	(B 4, LB 5, W 1, NB 12)	22	(B 6, LB 7, NB 1)	14
		271		**205**

Sri Lanka	O	M	R	W
De Mel	23	3	113	2
Ratnayake	28	4	108	0
Ranatunga	19	2	72	1
De Silva	44	7	122	1
Guneratne	17	1	84	0

Australia	O	M	R	W	O	M	R	W
Lillee	19	3	67	2	11	3	40	1
Hogg	12	4	31	1	3	2	7	0
Chappell	1	0	2	0				
Yardley	25	7	88	5	26	6	78	2
Hogan	11	1	50	1	25.2	6	66	5
Border	4.5	0	11	1				

Fall of Wickets

Wkt	A 1st	SL 1st	SL 2nd
1st	43	1	17
2nd	213	5	59
3rd	290	9	120
4th	359	46	151
5th		142	155
6th		220	155
7th		224	162
8th		247	164
9th		270	191
10th		271	205

*Captain †Wicket-keeper

Cricket in Australia

New South Wales proved worthy winners of their first Sheffield Shield for 17 years, beating Western Australia by 54 runs on the fifth day of a tense, inaugural final at Perth's WACA Ground. New South Wales had finished a close second to Western Australia in 1980-81 and to South Australia in 1981-82, and they would have been an honorable second to Western Australia again in 1982-83 but for the introduction of a final, which provided the showcase for Rick McCosker's men to reveal their depth and versatility.

McCosker, 36, rated New South Wales' triumph as the 'second greatest moment' of his career, after his Test debut in 1974 against England. Later, he relinquished the captaincy. Dirk Wellham is his successor. Western Australian captain Kim Hughes said the final was 'harder than any of the Tests we played against England this summer'. New South Wales scored 271 and 280, Western Australia managed 259 and 238.

New South Wales made a slow start to the season, gaining only 8 points from their first 3 matches and 20 from 5. Two outright wins against Queensland helped lift them to 60 points from 10 matches. South Australia also had 60 points, but New South Wales had one more first innings win. Under the old system, Western Australia (64 points) would have won the Shield.

McCosker and Wellham were two of only three batsmen (Victorian captain Graham Yallop was the other) to amass 1,000 Shield runs for the season. Steve Smith's 709 included the season's highest score – a marvellous 263 against Victoria in Melbourne, an innings that clinched his selection in the Australian team late in the World Series Cup one-day competition. Trevor Chappell and Peter Toohey topped 500 and 400, respectively, and New South Wales found two capable all-rounders, left-arm orthodox spinner Murray Bennett and off-spinner Greg Matthews.

Left-arm opener Michael Whitney was New South Wales' most successful bowler, with 38 wickets at 29.89, including 5 in the final when medium-pacer Chappell and Test speedster Geoff Lawson claimed 7 wickets each. Lawson took 30 wickets in only 5 Shield games. His Test team-mate John Dyson also was restricted to 5 games, in which he passed 50 four times, including an important 57 in the first innings of the final.

Western Australia again provided the most players (eight) to Australia's Test and World Series Cup teams, and their only four losses until the final coincided with the absence of the Test men. Injury prevented Western Australia's best two pace bowlers, Dennis Lillee and Terry Alderman, from playing in the final. The batting revolved around Greg Shipperd, Hughes, Bruce Laird, and Graeme Wood. Hughes hit three centuries and completed a fine double of 66 and 55 in the final. Former Test opener Wayne Clark proved a competent replacement for Alderman, with 31 wickets at 25.84, including 6 in the final. Medium-pacer Ken MacLeay underlined his developing all-round talent with 25 wickets, and Bruce Yardley and Tom Hogan formed the competition's most successful spinning combination.

Defending champions South Australia crumpled in the second half of the season, mostly because their batting and bowling lacked the depth and consistency of the previous season. Captain David Hookes missed 3 of their 10 Shield matches because of Test duty, yet still accumulated 967 runs at 74.38. He just failed to join Sir Donald Bradman and South African Barry Richards as the only batsmen to score 1,000 for South Australia in a Shield season. The first of Hookes' four centuries was a sensational effort against Victoria, with his hundred coming off only 34 balls in 43 minutes, the fastest first-class century in Australian cricket and the equal fifth-fastest in the world. Three other South Australian batsmen passed 600 – outstanding youngster Michael Haysman, veteran John Inverarity, and left-hand opener Wayne Phillips. West Indian Test giant Joel Garner and Australian Test fast bowler Rodney Hogg shared 93 wickets, Garner's 53 (at 17.74) coming in the first eight matches before he had to return to the Caribbean.

In their first full season in the Shield competition, Tasmania beat New South Wales outright, had first-innings wins against Queensland, Victoria, South Australia, and New South Wales, and lost only one match outright – to Western Australia. Tasmania rightly gained recognition from the Australian selectors when captain and wicket-keeper-batsman Roger Woolley deputized for Western Australia's Rod Marsh (unavailable) on Australia's tour of Sri Lanka. Three other players – batsman David Boon, left-arm medium-pacer Phil Blizzard, and leg-spinning all-rounder Stuart Saunders – went to Zimbabwe with the Australian Under-25 side. Tasmania also celebrated their first hat-trick in first-class cricket – opener Peter Clough's dismissal of Dyson, Smith, and Trevor Chappell off three balls in successive overs against New South Wales in Hobart. Clough, West Indian Test import Michael Holding, and Blizzard (24 at 31.38) dominated Tasmania's bowling, while Boon, David Smith, Woolley, Saunders, and Middlesex's Roland Butcher scored most of the runs.

Queensland supplied seven players to Australia's Test and one-day squads, but had their services often enough to have finished higher than fifth. Kepler Wessels, Robbie Kerr, and Allan Border carried the batting, while John Maguire, Carl Rackemann, and Harry Frei were the only bowlers to speak of.

Victoria finished bottom for the second successive season, and had to seek consolation in captain Yallop's breaking of fellow-Victorian Bill Ponsford's 55-year-old record for the most runs scored in a Shield season. Yallop made 1,254 at 69.67, with four centuries, including 246 against Queensland – his highest first-class score. He had 18 innings. In 1927-28, Ponsford's eight Shield innings produced 1,217 at 152.12 – 133, 437, 202, 38, 336, 6, 2, 63.

Western Australia v New South Wales 1982-83 Sheffield Shield Final
NSW won by 54 runs
Played at W.A.C.A. Ground, Perth, March 4, 5, 6, 7, 8
Toss: NSW. Umpires: R.A. French and P.J. McConnell

New South Wales

R.B. McCosker*	c Boyd b Yardley	71		lbw b Macleay	44
J. Dyson	c Shipperd b Yardley	57		c R.W. Marsh b Yardley	10
S.B. Smith	c Hughes b Yardley	3	(6)	c R.W. Marsh b Boyd	37
D.M. Wellham	c Laird b Macleay	6		c R.W. Marsh b Macleay	70
P.M. Toohey	lbw b Clark	40		c Macleay b Clark	26
T.M. Chappell	c Laird b Hogan	10	(3)	run out	33
G. Matthews	lbw b Hogan	34		c Macleay b Boyd	24
M.J. Bennett	c Wood b Yardley	10		c R.W. Marsh b Clark	9
S.J. Rixon†	c R.W. Marsh b Clark	20		not out	10
G.F. Lawson	not out	7		b Clark	2
M.R. Whitney	c R.W. Marsh b Clark	0		run out	0
Extras	(B 3, LB 8, NB 2)	13		(B 8, LB 5, NB 2)	15
		271			280

Western Australia

G.M. Wood	c Toohey b Whitney	45		c Chappell b Lawson	0
B.M. Laird	run out	24		lbw b Whitney	15
G. Shipperd	lbw b Lawson	10		c Toohey b Lawson	48
K.J. Hughes*	b Lawson	66		c Toohey b Lawson	55
G.R. Marsh	c Rixon b Chappell	32		c Dyson b Chappell	18
R.W. Marsh†	c Smith b Whitney	36		c Dyson b Lawson	58
D. Boyd	lbw b Whitney	16	(10)	not out	9
K.H. Macleay	st Rixon b Chappell	1	(7)	c Matthews b Chappell	24
B. Yardley	not out	14	(8)	c Rixon b Chappell	4
T.G. Hogan	lbw b Chappell	2	(9)	lbw b Lawson	0
W.M. Clark	b Whitney	3		c Whitney b Chappell	0
Extras	(B 2, LB 5, W 3)	10		(B 5, LB 1, NB 1)	7
		259			238

WA	O	M	R	W	O	M	R	W
Boyd	12	3	51	0	13.3	2	39	2
Clark	24	4	42	3	25	8	48	3
Macleay	22	7	45	1	21	3	64	2
Yardley	29	8	92	4	28	5	81	1
Hogan	16	7	28	2	12	2	33	0

NSW	O	M	R	W	O	M	R	W
Lawson	22	6	58	2	28	10	52	5
Whitney	25.2	4	67	4	18	4	45	1
Chappell	16	5	32	3	20.5	6	45	4
Bennett	29	12	50	0	22	9	39	0
Matthews	20	9	42	0	18	4	50	0

Fall of Wickets

Wkt	N 1st	W 1st	N 2nd	W 2nd
1st	110	70	32	3
2nd	123	76	84	40
3rd	142	105	101	67
4th	149	183	155	125
5th	188	200	218	186
6th	216	234	252	206
7th	237	235	265	222
8th	243	247	273	229
9th	271	256	275	229
10th	271	259	280	238

*Captain †Wicket-keeper

McDonald's Cup
Semi-Finals
12 March at Perth. WESTERN AUSTRALIA beat VICTORIA by 3 wickets. Victoria 112 (D. Boyd 5-15). Western Australia 115-7 (S.F. Graf 4-15).
13 March at Brisbane. NEW SOUTH WALES beat QUEENSLAND by 2 wickets. Queensland 205-9 (G.S. Chappell 71, G.M. Ritchie 69). NSW 206-8 (S.B. Smith 59*; G.S. Chappell 4-35).
Final
20 March at Sydney; match abandoned without a ball being bowled and replayed 8 October at Perth. WESTERN AUSTRALIA beat NEW SOUTH WALES by 4 wickets. NSW 195-6 (50 overs) (D.M. Wellham 65*). W. Australia 198-6 (49.1 overs) (K.J. Hughes 61, G. Shipperd 54).

Sheffield Shield 1982-83

Final Table	P	W	L	D	1st Inngs points	Total points
Western Australia	10	3	1	6	28	64
New South Wales	10	3	2	5	24	60†
South Australia	10	3	1	6	24	60
Tasmania	10	1	1	8	20	32
Queensland	10	1	4	5	16	28
Victoria	10	0	2	8	8	8

†New South Wales, who had to win the final outright to claim the championship, qualified ahead of South Australia by having won more drawn matches on first innings (4-3).

Leading First-Class Averages

Batting	State(s)	M	I	NO	HS	R	Avge	100	50
A.R. Border	Q/A	11	20	5	165	1081	72.06	2	7
G.N. Yallop	V	12	22	1	246	1418	67.52	4	6
D.M. Wellham	NSW	13	23	5	136*	1205	66.94	2	10
D.W. Hookes	SA/A	13	23	1	193	1424	64.72	4	9
K.J. Hughes	WA/A	13	21	1	137	1280	64.00	4	7
K.C. Wessels	Q/A	12	23	0	249	1325	57.60	5	3
M.D. Haysman	SA	7	14	2	153	684	57.00	2	4
R.B. McCosker	NSW	13	25	4	124	1153	54.90	3	9
D.M. Jones	V	7	11	0	199	603	54.81	2	2
G.R.J. Matthews	NSW	7	11	4	81*	343	49.00	-	1
M.D. Taylor	V	11	19	3	144	771	48.18	1	6
G. Shipperd	WA	12	19	1	166	816	45.33	2	3

Qualification: 8 innings.

Bowling	State(s)	O	M	R	W	Avge	Best	5w/I
C.G. Rackemann	Q/A	238.5	65	553	35	15.80	7-49	3
J. Garner	SA	403.1	131	976	55	17.74	7-78	4
T.M. Chappell	NSW	192.5	52	482	27	17.85	4-23	-
G.F. Lawson	NSW/A	493.4	110	1368	65	21.04	6-47	5
J.R. Thomson	Q/A	254.4	50	766	34	22.52	5-50	2
R.M. Hogg	SA/A	401.5	85	1120	49	22.85	7-53	3
W.M. Clark	WA	337.2	90	801	31	25.83	5-125	1
M.A. Holding	T	371.4	93	946	36	26.27	7-59	2
P.M. Clough	T	414.1	91	1089	41	26.56	6-53	2
T.G. Hogan	WA	415.2	134	939	35	26.82	6-91	2
M.J. Bennett	NSW	507.5	203	1102	39	28.25	5-39	2
D.K. Lillee	WA/A	343	103	907	32	28.34	4-29	-

Qualification: 20 wickets.

Cricket in South Africa

There can seldom have been a season in the history of South African cricket that was so completely dominated by one team as the past one. Transvaal, under the captaincy of Springbok all-rounder Clive Rice, won every trophy that was available to them: the SAB Currie Cup, the Datsun Shield (limited-overs), the Benson and Hedges night series, the Computer Sciences triangular (contested between the top three provinces from the previous season), and the Protea Challenge (Western Province v Transvaal).

They provided the top five batsmen in the final Currie Cup averages – Henry Fotheringham, Jimmy Cook, Alvin Kallicharran, Kevin McKenzie, and Clive Rice, with Graeme Pollock a notable absentee down in 25th position – the leading bowler in Vintcent van der Bijl, the leading wicket-taker in Alan Kourie, and the number one wicket-keeper in Ray Jennings, who broke the Currie Cup record.

Kallicharran, a man well placed to pass opinion, equated the Transvaal batting strength with that of the West Indies Test line-up. Certainly, the strength of their batting turned the limited-overs competitions into virtual non-contests.

In both the major competitions – the Datsun Shield and the Benson and Hedges – their opponents were Western Province in the final. In the former they scored 303 for 5 in 55 overs, with Cook and Fotheringham putting on a record-equalling 135 runs in only 31 overs. And then in the night competition these same two batsmen put on 73 for the first wicket in the final, as Transvaal made light work of matching Western Province's total of 275 (in 45 overs), losing only 4 wickets in the process.

In the Currie Cup, the story was fairly similar. This competition was also a two-horse race between Western Province and Transvaal. Third-placed Natal represented little more than nuisance value. They held Transvaal to a draw at the Wanderers Stadium, but achieved a similar result against Western Province at Kingsmead.

In the latter match, the defending champions managed only three bonus points, and this, coupled with their home defeat against Transvaal at the New Year, left them with too much ground to make up.

Both Western Province and Transvaal won all their matches coming up the home straight, against Eastern Province, Natal, and Northern Transvaal, which meant that Peter Kirsten's men had to down Transvaal at the Wanderers to top the log.

This proved beyond them in a match that was dominated by injuries to key players on both sides. The Springbok left-arm opening bowler, Stephen Jefferies, had to carry the visiting attack single-handed, which he did magnificently, while Transvaal were without both Van der Bijl and Rupert Hanley for a substantial part of the game.

The highlight of the match was the century on A-section debut by a young university student, Paul Rayner, for Western Province. But Transvaal took the bonus-points honours 9-7 in a drawn encounter to top the final table by 22 points.

This position gave them the all-important home ground advantage in the inaugural four-day Currie Cup final against Western Province. There had been much criticism of the need for a final, particularly after Transvaal's convincing victory in the round-robin league. But in any event, the final produced much excellent cricket, even if the public support was poor – some 10,000 spectators spread over the four days.

Cook and Fotheringham gave Transvaal another splendid start with 106 for the first wicket, after Rice had won the toss in perfect batting conditions. Cook, who had scored a maiden double century against Eastern Province shortly before, needed 218 to match Barry Richards' South African record for a first-class season of 1,285. But his dismissal for 49 in the first innings ruled this out of the question.

The innings belonged to the brilliant little Guyanan left-hander, Kallicharran. His knock of 151 won him the Man of the Match award, as it ruled victory for Western Province out of the question. It was his highest innings in South Africa, but it was the first fifty that really grabbed the imagination of those who saw it.

He blocked the first two overs he received from the left-arm spinner Omar Henry, and then cut loose to hit 11 boundaries in racing to his first half-century off only 41 balls. In sheer contrast, his second half-century contained only two boundaries, but he had still faced a meagre 138 balls by this stage of his innings.

In the end, Transvaal made the huge total of 475 and then bowled Western Province out for 228. The outgoing champions salvaged their honour with a follow-on total of 490 for 7 before making a token declaration. It was their highest ever at this venue, thanks to fine centuries by Peter Kirsten and Ken McEwan.

The season ended with two events of major importance concerning the two outstanding batsmen in South Africa for the past decade. Following a very congested season, which clearly took its toll on him physically, Graeme Pollock announced that he was considering standing down from Springbok selection, although he would probably play for Transvaal for a couple of seasons more.

And Barry Richards announced that, in future, he would play only for Natal in the event of injury disrupting the team, which means that he, too, has probably played his last game at this level.

Next season will be an important one to find younger players of quality, as Richards and Pollock are by no means the only Springboks getting a bit long in the tooth. A few young players have already started to emerge, such as the two Western Province batsmen, Rayner and Roy Pienaar, and the Natal opening batsman, Brian Whitfield.

These players are, of course, very short on experience, and for the second West Indian visit, the national selectors are likely to call up Fotheringham and McEwan, both of whom have surprisingly still to win their Springbok colours.

Transvaal v Western Province 1982-83 Currie Cup Challenge Match
Match drawn
Played at Johannesburg, April 2, 3, 4, 5

Transvaal

S.J. Cook	c and b Henry	49	lbw b Emburey		26
H.R. Fotheringham	c Pienaar b Jefferies	89	not out		44
A.I. Kallicharran	c Ryall b Jefferies	151	not out		23
R.G. Pollock	c Ryall b Gooch	17			
C.E.B. Rice*	c Henry b Emburey	15			
K.A. McKenzie	c Seeff b Henry	92			
A.J. Kourie	b Jefferies	11			
R.V. Jennings†	not out	28			
N.V. Radford	c Emburey b Henry	7			
V.A.P. Van der Bijl	b Henry	5			
R.W. Hanley	b Emburey	3			
Extras	(LB 5, W 1, NB 2)	8	(B 4)		4
		475	(1 wicket)		97

Western Province

G.A. Gooch	b Van der Bijl	11	lbw b Kourie		36
L. Seeff	c Jennings b Van der Bijl	7	lbw b Van der Bijl		71
P.N. Kirsten*	b Hanley	19	b Van der Bijl		168
K.S. McEwan	c Rice b Radford	9	not out		130
R.F. Pienaar	b Radford	51	c Jennings b Radford		19
P.H. Rayner	c and b Kourie	13	c Jennings b Van der Bijl		8
A.P. Kuiper	b Radford	4	not out		23
S.T. Jefferies	c Fotheringham b Kourie	38	c Jennings b Van der Bijl		10
O. Henry	c Kourie b Hanley	50	c Jennings b Radford		1
J.E. Emburey	lbw b Van der Bijl	0			
R.J. Ryall†	not out	12			
Extras	(B 3, LB 7, NB 4)	14	(B 1, LB 16, NB 7)		24
		228	(7 wickets declared)		490

W. Province	O	M	R	W	O	M	R	W
Jefferies	32	2	161	3	10	0	31	0
Kuiper	5	2	16	0				
Gooch	27	5	63	1				
Emburey	40.5	6	137	2	16	5	33	1
Henry	16	2	48	4	7	4	24	0
Pienaar	11	2	42	0				
Kirsten					1	0	5	0

Transvaal	O	M	R	W	O	M	R	W
Hanley	18.1	3	55	2	21	2	107	0
Van der Bijl	21	13	23	3	35	5	109	4
Kourie	28	14	63	2	24	2	84	1
Radford	11	0	68	3	30	3	143	2
Kallicharran	2	0	5	0	3	0	23	0

Fall of Wickets

Wkt	T 1st	WP 1st	WP 2nd	T 2nd
1st	106	18	53	47
2nd	214	21	190	
3rd	248	35	371	
4th	299	75	407	
5th	362	112	428	
6th	380	124	440	
7th	440	124	441	
8th	450	204		
9th	470	207		
10th	475	228		

*Captain †Wicket-keeper

OVERSEAS CRICKET 1982-83/SOUTH AFRICA

Currie Cup

Final Table	P	W	L	D	Bonus points Batting	Bonus points Bowling	Total Points
TRANSVAAL	8	6	0	3	54	45	137†
Western Province	8	5	1	2	30	35	115
Natal	8	1	2	5	28	31	69
Northern Transvaal	8	0	5	3	14	34	48
Eastern Province	8	0	4	4	15	24	39

†Competition record

Currie Cup Wins
20 Transvaal, 18 Natal, 12 Western Province, 1 Kimberley (now Griqualand West)
Shared Titles: 4 Transvaal, 3 Natal, 2 Western Province

Leading Currie Cup Averages

Batting	Prov	M	I	NO	HS	R	Avge	100	50
H.R. Fotheringham	T	7	12	2	116	615	61.50	1	4
S.J. Cook	T	9	15	2	201*	755	58.07	2	4
A.I. Kallicharran	T	8	12	1	151	627	57.00	2	2
K.A. McKenzie	T	9	12	1	164*	618	56.18	1	5
C.E.B. Rice	T	9	13	3	104	516	51.60	1	2
P.N. Kirsten	WP	9	16	3	168	659	50.69	1	5

Qualification: 8 innings.

Bowling	Prov	O	M	R	W	Avge	Best	5w/I
V.A.P. van der Bijl	T	351.2	116	715	41	17.43	7-42	1
G.S. le Roux	WP	178	42	442	21	21.04	5-34	2
J.E. Emburey	WP	355.4	92	785	36	21.80	6-33	3
S.T. Jefferies	WP	341.4	63	980	40	24.50	6-91	3
A.J. Kourie	T	423.1	130	1121	45	24.91	7-79	3
W.K. Watson	EP	226.3	42	675	26	25.96	7-50	2

Qualification: 20 wickets.

Note: R.V. Jennings (Transvaal) established a Currie Cup record by making 38 dismissals (34 ct, 4 st).

Datsun Shield Final
19 February at Johannesburg. TRANSVAAL beat WESTERN PROVINCE by 109 runs. Match award: R.G. Pollock (55). Transvaal 303-5 (S.J. Cook 70, H.R. Fotheringham 67, A.I. Kallicharran 74, R.G. Pollock 55). Western Province 194 (K.S. McEwan 57; R.V. Jennings 5 dismissals).

SAB Bowl

Final Table	P	W	L	D	Bonus points Batting	Bonus points Bowling	Total points
WESTERN PROVINCE B	6	5	0	1	19	23	92
Transvaal B	6	3	2	1	16	27	73
Natal B	6	3	3	0	14	26	70
Orange Free State	6	2	3	1	13	24	57
Border	6	2	0	4	10	26	56
Boland	6	1	2	3	13	24	47
Eastern Province B	6	0	1	5	23	22	45
Northern Transvaal B	6	1	4	1	9	24	43
Griqualand West	6	1	3	2	12	18	40

Cricket in West Indies

In a remarkable transformation of fortunes and form, Guyana completely dominated inter-territorial cricket in the West Indies in the 1983 season, becoming the first team to win both the Shell Shield and the limited-overs Geddes Grant/Harrison Line Trophy in the same year.

Guyana had last won the Shield in 1975. In the seven intervening seasons, they had been last four times and had managed only one victory. Now they were unbeaten, winning four of their five Shield matches and drawing the other, against defending champions Barbados. Their margin over Jamaica in the final of the limited-overs competition was a decisive 128 runs. The main reason for the revival was not difficult to identify. Clive Lloyd returned as captain, and his influence, on and off the field, was enormous. So, too, was that of former Test opening batsman Roy Fredericks, now junior minister of sport in the Guyana government, who was manager/player.

Lloyd brought self-confidence to his talented but youthful team, and scored important centuries against Barbados and Trinidad & Tobago. Fredericks, still trim and fit despite his 40 years, played for the first time since 1980. He came into the side for the final two matches, and proceeded to score 103 against Trinidad & Tobago and 217 against Jamaica, the season's only double-century.

Yet Guyana did not owe its triumph to the two veterans alone. Andrew Lyght, an opening batsman with a positive approach, averaged over 60, while Leslaine Lambert, a well-built fast bowler with genuine speed, and three off-spinners, Clyde Butts, Roger Harper, and Derek Kallicharran (younger brother of Alvin), comprised a penetrative attack.

The Windward Islands proved their previous season's performance was no fluke by again finishing runners-up in the Shield. Barbados, who lost eight of their players from the previous season, and Jamaica, stripped of their four leading batsmen, were particularly hard hit by the controversial tour of South Africa. The 'rebel' team of West Indians were automatically banned by the West Indies Cricket Board of Control.

Ironically, one of the positions thus left open in the Barbados team went to Thelston Payne, a neat left-hander, who took his chance with three centuries, 517 runs, and the season's best average (73.85). The diminutive Trinidadian Augustine Logie was the only other batsman to pass 500, and his consistent performance earned him a place in the Test team against India.

The lively Windward Islands fast bowler Winston Davis topped his previous Shield record of 32 wickets by one, while the ageless Andy Roberts had 28 wickets for the Leewards, including a hat-trick against Barbados and match figures of 13 for 114 against the Windwards.

Two Leeward Islanders impressed as players with a future. Richie Richardson, a well-organized 21-year-old opening batsman, took centuries off Barbados and Jamaica, while Eldine Baptiste (also of Kent) took 26 wickets with lively fast-medium bowling, and scored useful runs in the low order.

Shell Shield

Final Table	P	W	L	D	Points
GUYANA	5	4	0	1	68
Windward Islands	5	3	1	1	61
Barbados	5	3	1	1	56
Leeward Islands	5	1	3	1	29
Trinidad and Tobago	5	0	3	2	13
Jamaica	5	0	3	2	12

Shell Shield Winners
9 Barbados
3 Guyana
2 Trinidad
1 Combined Islands, Jamaica
Shared Titles: 1 Barbados, Trinidad

Leading Shell Shield Averages

Batting	Team	M	I	NO	HS	R	Avge	100	50
T.R.O. Payne	B	5	9	2	123	517	73.85	3	2
A.A. Lyght	G	5	9	1	112	493	61.62	2	3
A.L. Logie	T	5	10	1	138	540	60.00	2	2
C.H. Lloyd	G	5	8	1	136	412	58.85	2	1
V.A. Eddy	LI	4	7	1	124	337	56.16	1	2
L.C. Sebastien	WI	5	10	1	122	470	52.22	1	3
S.I. Williams	LI	3	5	0	120	255	51.00	1	1
Bowling	Team	O	M	R	W	Avge	Best	5w/I	
H.L. Alleyne	B	80.2	20	245	15	16.33	6-63	1	
L.A. Lambert	G	112.2	21	358	20	17.90	7-59	1	
C. Butts	G	209.3	59	458	25	18.32	5-23	3	
A.M.E. Roberts	LI	162.1	29	514	28	18.35	8-62	3	
W.W. Daniel	B	109.3	11	409	22	18.59	7-55	2	
W.W. Davis	WI	226.1	49	620	33†	18.78	6-54	3	
E.A.E. Baptiste	LI	154.4	31	508	26	19.53	4-46	-	

†Shell Shield record.

Geddes Grant/Harrison Line Trophy
Final: 19 March at Bourda, Georgetown. GUYANA beat JAMAICA by 128 runs. Toss: Guyana. Match award: D.I. Kallicharran (67*). Guyana 211-8 (41 overs) (D.I. Kallicharran 67*). Jamaica 83 (25 overs) (G.E. Charles 8-1-18-5).

Cricket in New Zealand

While the amount of New Zealand domestic first-class cricket expanded in 1982-83, interest in it diminished as the Kiwis concentrated their attention chiefly on events across the Tasman. For the second time in three summers, New Zealand cricket administrators decided to send the national team to Australia with the Shell Series hardly begun. Even during the Shell Cup final – a major occasion in the domestic season – that minority of the cricket public who had pulled themselves away from the television relay of the World Series Cup were more interested in the radio commentary from Perth.

The Shell Series encompasses two separate competitions among the six major associations. The Shell Trophy is a three-day contest for the equivalent of England's County Championship. Englishmen worried about the effects of reducing the number of championship fixtures in recent years to 22 or 24 will be interested that Shell Trophy series were increased in 1982-83 – from 7 to 8. Wellington retained the Trophy, the first province to do so since Shell entered provincial cricket in 1975-76.

The Shell Cup is awarded for limited-overs cricket. It originated as a knock-out. For the last two summers, a round-robin contest has been played, and then the two leading sides meet in a final. Auckland won one final place easily. Northern Districts gained the other from Wellington, both having three wins, because their 'differential' was better. This method of separating teams involves comparing the runs per wicket each scores with those it concedes. It thus puts importance on bowling and fielding as well as batting, and seems preferable to the method used in the World Cup, which takes into account only batting.

The finalists had enjoyed an extraordinary match at Gisborne during the round-robin section of the competition, with 615 runs off 99.2 overs. Northern Districts' 306 for 2 was exceeded by Auckland's 309 for 8. They contained rather better in the final, at Auckland, but their opponents again won in the last over.

Ian Smith (Central Districts) has always been called a wicket-keeper-batsman, but had never scored a first-class century till he hit three in four innings during the Shell Trophy. Young Aucklanders Martin Crowe and Trevor Franklin also made three hundreds, and the trio all made their way into the touring side for England. Wellington's left-handed Test opener Bruce Edgar contributed a fine 146 against Northern Districts before he left for Australia, and he topped the averages at 65.75. Tony Pigott of Sussex, unlike most of the English professionals wintering in New Zealand, was chosen for the Shell Series, and his 33 wickets for Wellington was the leading haul. And Roger Broughton became the first Maori to make a Shell Series century when he hit 122 for Northern Districts against Central Districts at Palmerston North.

Hawkes Bay celebrated their centenary by staging a one-day international at Napier against Sri Lanka, and by winning the minor associations' challenge trophy, the Hawke Cup.

Shell Trophy

Final Table	P	W	L	D	1st inngs points	Penalty points	Total points
WELLINGTON	8	4	1	3	24	1	71
Central Districts	8	3	2	3	24	1	59
Otago	8	2	4	2	20	0	44
Northern Districts	8	2	1	5	12	1	35
Auckland	8	2	2	4	8	1	31
Canterbury	8	2	5	1	8	1	31

Leading First-Class Averages

Batting	Team(s)	M	I	NO	HS	R	Avge	100	50
B.A. Edgar	W/NZ	4	7	3	146	263	65.75	1	–
I.D.S. Smith	CD	7	8	0	145	446	55.75	3	–
M.D. Crowe	A	9	16	2	119	736	52.57	3	3
E.B. McSweeney	W	8	9	3	130	314	52.33	1	1
B.R. Blair	O	8	13	0	143	680	52.30	2	4
T.J. Franklin	A	8	15	2	136	664	51.07	3	3

Qualification: 8 innings.

Bowling	Team(s)	O	M	R	W	Avge	Best	5w/I
R.J. Hadlee	C/NZ	152.5	52	277	23	12.04	6-43	1
V.R. Brown	C	202.2	64	452	30	15.06	7-28	2
M.C. Snedden	A/NZ	149.2	38	372	24	15.50	7-49	2
E.J. Chatfield	W/NZ	189.5	66	389	25	15.56	6-76	2
A.C.S. Pigott	W	196.4	56	581	33	17.60	5-47	2
R.J. Webb	O	165.4	50	394	22	17.90	4-33	–

Qualification: 20 wickets.

Shell Cup
Final: 6 February at Auckland. AUCKLAND beat NORTHERN DISTRICTS by 5 wickets with 5 balls to spare. Northern Districts 210 (R.D. Broughton 52, J.M. Parker 77; J.A.J. Cushen 4-38). Auckland 212-5 (T.J. Franklin 76, M.D. Crowe 54).

Cricket in India

Where Karnataka failed in 1981-82 in the Ranji Trophy final against Delhi, being unable to win despite a first innings tally of 705, the 1982-83 season saw them chase and achieve the imposing 534 made by Bombay in the first innings, to win the Championship. Bombay, until recently regarded as invincible in the Championship, were without Test stars Gavaskar, Vengsarkar, Shastri, and Sandhu, while Karnataka missed stumper Kirmani, all away in the West Indies.

In a five-day encounter on a flawless pitch, dropped catches by both sides contributed in the main to the huge scores, but there was plenty of excitement. Nobody quite gave Karnataka a chance of overhauling Bombay's total, which was due to a massive 157 by Chandrakant Pandit, a wicket-keeper and batsman regarded quite highly in western India. However, Karnataka's wicket-keeper and batsman S. Viswanath, with scores of 92 and 71, and Roger Binny, with an assured 115, provided a fitting reply. Determined contributions from the rank and file enabled Karnataka to gain a lead, decisive in the ultimate analysis, of 17.

Karnataka's triumph was the work of bowlers right until the final. With the batsmen not making runs in the qualifying knock-out matches, spinners Bhatt and Vijayakrishna (left-arm) and the fast-medium Binny took the team to Bombay. Bombay in their turn can look to Pandit as a future international player. And there could be a lot heard about the Delhi swing bowler Manoj Prabakhar and the Tamil Nadu opening batsman C.S. Suresh Kumar (three centuries), whose technique and ability to concentrate have the Gavaskar touch.

With India engaged in two Test series in quick succession, all 11 Test matches away, in Pakistan and the West Indies, the Cricket Board used the Duleep Trophy and the Irani Trophy as selection matches. North Zone, the strongest combination in the country, won the Duleep Trophy without much difficulty, inspired by all-rounder Kapil Dev. In the final against West Zone, with Kapil prising out Gavaskar cheaply in the first innings and Madan Lal finishing with a match haul of 11 for 122 (seaming and cutting the ball with a vengeance), North had the match by 8 wickets. North earlier had proved too good for both Central and East Zones. Mohinder Amarnath's 207 against East Zone was the best score in the tournament.

The Irani Trophy was unexpectedly won by the Rest of India, led by Gavaskar, against Delhi. Delhi must have believed that everything was safe when they set the Rest 421 to get in 4 hours and 20 mandatory overs. But with Krishnamachari Srikkanth (110) leading the way with an innings of unbelievable aggression, and with support from Arun Lal (82) and Ashok Malhotra (116 not out), victory was achieved. There has never quite been a match like this in Indian cricket history.

Bombay won the Wills Trophy thanks to the tactical brilliance of skipper Ashok Mankad, while West Zone prevailed quite surprisingly over a strong North Zone in the Deodhar Trophy. Both are limited-overs tournaments conducted by the Cricket Board.

Karnataka v Bombay 1982-83 Ranji Trophy Final
Match drawn; Karnataka won Ranji Trophy by leading on 1st innings
Played at Wankhede Stadium, Bombay, March 11, 12, 13, 14, 15

Bombay

S. Hattangadi	c Sudhakar b Binny	13	c Binny b Abhiram	3
J. Singhani	c Jayaprakash b Binny	78	c Sudhakar b Khanwilkar	0
R.V. Mankad	c Prasad b Abhiram	14	c Viswanath b Khanwilkar	23
S.M. Patil	b Vijayakrishna	48	not out	121
G.A. Parkar	c S. Viswanath b Bhatt	60	c S. Viswanath b Abhiram	7
C. Pandit	c S. Viswanath b Khanwilkar	157	not out	33
A.V. Mankad*	c Prasad b Binny	13		
S.V. Nayak	c Prasad b Bhatt	67		
R. Kulkarni	c G.R. Viswanath b Bhatt	40		
S. Shetty	not out	22		
R. Thakkar	c G.R. Viswanath b Bhatt	0		
Extras	(B 3, LB 7, W 2, NB 10)	22	(LB 4, NB 2)	6
Penalty runs		–		20
		534	(4 wickets declared)	**213**

Karnataka

M. Srinivasa Prasad	lbw b Kulkarni	29	c Pandit b Kulkarni	2
S. Viswanath†	c Pandit b Shetty	92	b Shetty	77
A.V. Jayaprakash	c and b Thakkar	89	lbw b Shetty	10
R.M.H. Binny	c Hattangadi b Thakkar	115	c Singhani b Thakkar	45
G.R. Viswanath*	lbw b Shetty	3	c Pandit b Shetty	20
B.G. Patel	c Pandit b Kulkarni	18	not out	4
Sudhakar Rao	c Parkar b Kulkarni	9		
J. Abhiram	c A.V. Mankad b Nayak	69	(7) not out	11
R. Khanwilkar	b Kulkarni	32		
B. Vijayakrishna	lbw b Kulkarni	42		
R. Bhatt	not out	0		
Extras	(B 10, LB 19, W 1, NB 7)	37	(LB 6, NB 4)	10
		551	(5 wickets)	**179**

Karnataka	O	M	R	W	O	M	R	W
Binny	43	12	119	3				
Khanwilkar	34	4	116	1	11	3	51	2
Jayaprakash	5	2	8	0				
Abhiram	11	1	43	1	8	0	48	2
Vijayakrishna	37	5	86	1	4	1	39	0
Bhatt	52.4	15	121	4	4	0	49	0
Sudhakar Rao	10	2	19	0				
Bombay	O	M	R	W	O	M	R	W
Kulkarni	40.4	3	157	5	19	6	57	1
Nayak	27	8	58	1	7	3	24	0
Shetty	26	4	75	2	19	7	34	3
Patil	3	0	16	0				
Thakkar	49	6	167	2	25	9	54	1
A.V. Mankad	9	1	25	0				

Fall of Wickets

Wkt	B 1st	K 1st	B 2nd	K 2nd
1st	27	51	4	6
2nd	57	225	24	39
3rd	138	227	36	124
4th	186	237	57	149
5th	298	273		161
6th	329	293		
7th	462	447		
8th	493	470		
9th	534	526		
10th	534	551		

*Captain †Wicket-keeper

Duleep Trophy
Final
14, 15, 16, 17 October at Wankhede Stadium, Bombay. NORTH ZONE beat WEST ZONE by 8 wickets. West Zone 168 (Madan Lal 6-59) and 330 (A.D. Gaekwad 104, D.B. Vengsarkar 50; Madan Lal 5-63). North Zone 329 (A. Malhotra 76, M. Amarnath 80, Yashpal Sharma 83; R.J. Shastri 7-105) and 170-2 (C.P.S. Chauhan 63*, M. Amarnath 67*).

Leading First-Class Averages†

Batting	I	NO	HS	R	Avge	100
M. Amarnath (Delhi)	6	1	207	537	107.40	2
A. Malhotra (Haryana)	9	1	228	859	107.37	4
A.D. Gaekwad (Baroda)	10	1	225	859	95.44	4
A.V. Mankad (Bombay)	10	3	150*	526	75.14	2
S.S. Hattangadi (Bombay)	11	2	141	554	61.55	1
K.B.J. Azad (Delhi)	14	3	186	668	60.72	2
R.M.H. Binny (Karnataka)	15	3	115	635	52.91	1
R.C. Shukla (Delhi)	13	1	163*	506	42.16	1

Qualification: 500 runs.

Bowling	O	M	R	W	Avge
D.V. Pardeshi (Baroda)	201.2	117	403	31	13.00
S. Talwar (Haryana)	247.5	55	535	37	14.45
B. Vijayakrishna (Karnataka)	216.3	84	530	30	17.66
R.V. Kulkarni (Bombay)	193.4	43	540	30	18.00
A. Raghuram Bhat (Karnataka)	338.5	107	798	43	18.55
S.S. Hazare (Baroda)	165.1	32	501	27	18.55
R.M.H. Binny (Karnataka)	185.5	40	518	25	20.72
R. Thakkar (Bombay)	327.1	100	724	34	21.29
R. Goel (Harayana)	314.4	110	558	26	21.46
R.S. Hans (Uttar Pradesh)	247.5	64	577	26	22.19
Chetan Sharma (Haryana)	158.1	27	618	27	22.88
Maninder Singh (Delhi)	215.2	58	612	26	23.53
K.B.J. Azad (Delhi)	300.4	55	731	30	24.36
T.A. Sekhar (Tamil Nadu)	199	28	667	27	24.70
R.C. Shukla (Delhi)	300.5	59	774	30	25.80

Qualification: 25 wickets.

*not out. †For Ranji, Irani, and Duleep trophy matches and Test against Sri Lanka.

Ranji Trophy Winners
28 Bombay
 4 Baroda, Holkar
 3 Delhi, Karnataka (formerly Mysore)
 2 Maharashtra
 1 Bengal, Hyderabad, Madras (now Tamil Nadu), Nawanagar, Western India States

Cricket in Pakistan

The 1982-83 domestic season in Pakistan was one of satisfaction and jubilation. Not only was a record number of first-class matches played, but the two visiting teams, the Australians and the neighbouring Indians, were well beaten in successive Test series.

As in previous years, the banks teams dominated the first-class scene by winning the major tournaments. Pakistan's premier domestic championship, the Quaid-e-Azam Trophy, which for the first time in its 25-year history was sponsored (by Fujicolor), was won by United Bank. And Habib Bank, under Javed Miandad, took the PACO pentangular Cup. The Railways finished third in both competitions. The season saw more than seventy matches played. There were 45 in the Quaid-e-Azam Trophy and 10 in the PACO Cup, while the Australians played 6 including 3 Tests, and the Indians 10 including 6 Tests. One of the PACO Cup matches was abandoned owing to crowd rioting, which has sadly become a regular feature of Pakistan cricket.

It was a season in which the batsmen flourished. Records were shattered. No fewer than 11 batsmen scored more than a thousand runs, as opposed to only 4 in 1981-82.

Zaheer Abbas, captain of PIA, topped the batting averages, scoring 1,371 runs. His team-mate Rizwan-uz-Zaman was not far behind. Nairobi-born Qasim Umar of Muslim Commercial Bank stood second in the averages with 91.07 from his 1,275 runs. He scored more than a thousand runs in only seven games. His six hundreds included two double centuries in the Quaid-e-Azam Trophy, besides centuries in each innings twice. Prolific run-getter Zaheer Abbas hit seven centuries, while Qasim Umar and Saleem Malik made six each.

Pakistan's captain, Imran Khan, topped the bowling averages with 53 wickets (all in Test matches), at an average of 13.75. Abdul Qadir, the tiny leg-spinner, finished with 103 wickets, the only bowler to reach a hundred wickets. Twice he took nine wickets in an innings. Iqbal Qasim of National Bank was the only bowler to perform a hat-trick.

The country's leading wicket-keeper was PIA's Anil Dalpat, with 41 victims, closely followed by Zulqarnain and Ashraf Ali with 40 each. Karachi's Kamal Najamuddin had the distinction of dismissing 10 batsmen in a match.

In the only one-day competition played in Pakistan, PIA won the Wills Cup for the third time in a row, beating Habib Bank in the final.

From next season, however, the BCCP will be reshaping the domestic competitions. The Quaid-e-Azam Trophy will now be played on a league-cum-knock-out basis, and the relegation and promotion system will be abolished.

Leading First-Class Averages

Batting/Fielding	Team	M	I	NO	HS	R	Avge	100	50
Zaheer Abbas	PIA/P	13	15	1	215	1371	97.92	7	4
Qasim Omer	MCB	9	18	4	210*	1275	91.07	6	3
Mudassar Nazar	UB/P	11	17	4	231	1110	85.38	4	5
Javed Miandad	HB/P	14	16	2	280*	1124	80.28	4	3
Zafar Ahmed	K	10	18	7	140	800	72.72	2	5
Imran Khan	P	9	8	3	117	311	62.20	1	–
Agha Zahid	HB	14	23	2	175	1220	58.09	3	8
Majid Khan	L/P	8	13	2	128*	629	57.18	3	3
Mohsin Khan	HB/P	12	18	4	135	797	56.92	3	4
Ashraf Ali	UB	14	20	7	111*	719	55.30	1	5
Shafiq Ahmed	NB	13	23	3	118	1104	55.20	3	8

Bowling	Team	O	M	R	W	Avge	Best	5w/I
Imran Khan	P	326.3	104	729	53	13.75	8-60	4
Khatib Rizwan	R	181.1	28	568	31	18.32	6-19	3
Shahid Mahboob	AB	293	50	800	43	18.60	7-65	5
Jalal Uddin	AB/P	284	77	784	41	19.12	6-45	3
Tausif Ahmed	UB	365.4	77	956	48	19.91	6-49	2
Mohammad Nazir	Rwy	841.1	269	1451	70	20.72	7-74	4
Abdul Wahab	R	232	40	652	31	21.03	7-74	2
Iqbal Qasim	NB/P	578.5	161	1477	65	22.72	7-78	6
Khurshid Akhtar	UB	393.1	91	1011	44	22.97	7-101	3
Abdul Qadir	HB/P	827.2	184	2367	103	22.98	9-49	9

Teams: Allied Bank (AB), Habib Bank (HB), Karachi (K), Lahore (L), Muslim Commercial Bank (MCB), National Bank (NB), Pakistan (P), Pakistan International Airlines (PIA), Railways (Rwy), Rawalpindi (R), United Bank (UB).

Quaid-e-Azam Trophy

Final Table	P	W	L	D	Bonus points Batting	Bonus points Bowling	Total points
1 UNITED BANK (2)	9	5	0	4	31	25	106
2 National Bank (1)	9	4	1	4	25	26	91
3 Railways (6)	9	3	3	3	27	29	86
4 Habib Bank (3)	9	2	0	7	31	31	82
PIA (4)	9	2	2	5	30	32	82
6 Muslim Commercial Bank (5)	9	2	2	5	27	28	75
7 Allied Bank	9	2	3	4	22	28	70
8 Karachi (10)	9	1	4	4	30	22	62
9 Rawalpindi (7)	9	2	5	2	16	24	60
10 Lahore (9)	9	0	3	6	20	31	51

1981-82 positions are shown in brackets.

Cricket in Sri Lanka

Sri Lanka's major domestic competition was sponsored for the first time, by Sri Lanka Milk Foods (CWE) Ltd, who also replaced the 52-year-old P. Saravanamuttu Trophy with the Lakspray Trophy. The tournament, consisting of three-day matches, was won by Bloomfield. Against Colombo, they produced the highest total of the competition, 602 for 9 declared, and the highest individual score, Sunil Jayasinghe's 283. Colombo's Charith Senanayake, however, led the batting averages, with 68.77 (619 runs), and the two most successful bowlers were Tamil Union's S. Munaweera and A.J. Samarasekera, with 36 wickets apiece. In the field, Arjuna Ranatunga took 13 catches.

Division I(B), for the Rahaman Hathy Trophy, was won by Burgher Recreation Club, Division II (Donovan Andree Trophy) by Sinhalese SC, and Division III (Daily News Trophy) by Kurunegala Youth SC. In local limited-over cricket, Tamil Union's Lakshman Aloysius took all 10 wickets (9.5-1-36-10) against Catamarans. And in under-19 schools cricket, Jude de Silva (St Johns College, Panadura), with 17 sixes and 24 fours in his 240 against Piliyandala Central College, hit the most number of sixes in an innings by a schoolboy, breaking a record that had stood since 1917.

At international level, Sri Lanka's performances were disappointing, apart from success in the one-day series against Australia. The inaugural Test with Australia was the first at the Asgiriya International Stadium, the world's 54th Test venue. In addition to this new Test venue, Sri Lanka's Board of Control has paved the way for several improvements, including better pay for players, sponsorship of domestic tournaments, and the appointment of Sir Garfield Sobers as coach. Next season will almost certainly see a third Test venue, at Galle, and four-day matches in the major domestic tournament at district level.

After the painful but valuable Test experiences of their first two seasons (six defeats and no wins in eight matches), Sri Lanka have more international cricket scheduled for next season. A visit from Zimbabwe in December is followed by five Tests in the first half of 1984 (two against India and three against New Zealand). And their first Test in England will take place in August.

Prudential World Cup 1983

World Cup

From first ball to last, the third Prudential World Cup was a triumph. With help from the English climate and the new, extended format, in which teams met twice in Group matches, it was watched by more spectators then before, and, after a series of surprises, was fittingly won by India, who overcame the favourites, West Indies, at Lord's.

The decision to take matches to cricketing outposts such as Tunbridge Wells, Taunton, Worcester, Leicester, Chelmsford, and Derby gave more of the public a sense of involvement. And with matches broadcast live to overseas countries by radio and television, the sponsors ended their association with the competition on a high note.

Most of the cricket, too, was of a rewarding nature, with surprises galore and no reputations respected. Apart from India, who, dangerously underestimated by all beforehand, beat the West Indies, Australia, and England on their way to Lord's, Zimbabwe began with an unexpected victory over Australia, while Sri Lanka upset New Zealand and deprived them of a place in the semi-finals.

For the purist, too, there was the sight of spin bowlers proving their point. Pakistan's leg-spinner Qadir twice won Man-of-the-Match awards, while at various times his Sri Lankan counterpart De Silva and off-spinners Marks (England) and Traicos (Zimbabwe) were also successful.

India's success, ironically, owed not so much to spin as to accurate medium-paced bowling and measured stroke-play by a deep batting line-up. Nevertheless, slow-left-armer Shastri played a crucial role in the initial win over the holders, which must have done wonders for India's all-round self-confidence.

England, meanwhile, began by erasing memories of the previous winter by amassing a match-winning 322 for 6 against New Zealand, built around Allan Lamb's splendid 102. And Zimbabwe sent echoes round the world by defeating Australia by 13 runs, thanks to a sterling all-round display by their captain Duncan Fletcher (69 not out and 4 for 42).

Australia, short on team spirit and lacking discipline with both bat and ball, were to be a disappointment. Pakistan, their attack diminished in power by Imran Khan's inability to bowl because of injury, lost to New Zealand, having been reduced to 0 for 3 by Richard Hadlee and Lance Cairns, and were then outplayed by England at Lord's.

West Indies, having had problems with their own fast bowlers for a change, discovered a new one in Winston Davis, aged 24, of St Vincent and Glamorgan. He destroyed Australia at Headingley on a pitch too variable to be satisfactory for a one-day game, and his figures of 7 for 51 were a record for the competition.

The holders continued their return to form by beating Zimbabwe, who made them work hard. And after Australia had deceptively overwhelmed the future champions – with a brilliant century by Trevor Chappell, but without the services of Lillee – England lapsed in their second game against New Zealand, who won by 2 wickets with one ball left. They had recovered from the loss of Turner and Edgar with only 3 runs on the board. Victory owed much to Coney's all-round work – and also, arguably, to England's decision to tinker with their batting order after Fowler and Tavaré had given them an excellent start.

India then found themselves reduced to 17 for 5 by Zimbabwe and facing elimination, before Kapil Dev's sterling, unbeaten 175, the highest score so far in the competition, led to victory. They then reached the semi-finals by outplaying Australia.

In the other group, with England already through, Pakistan needed to beat New Zealand at Trent Bridge to qualify on a better run rate. This they did, thanks largely to an unbeaten stand of 147 in 27 overs between Zaheer (103) and Imran (79). After they bowled New Zealand out in the last over, 11 short of their total, umpire David Evans was flattened as the excited crowd invaded the pitch.

In the semi-finals, India overcame England, who lacked the discipline required on a slow Old Trafford pitch and were hard put to reach 213 runs – all out on the last ball of the innings. India, not without some alarms, knocked off the required runs with 6 wickets and more than 5 overs to spare.

In the other semi-final, at the Oval, Pakistan were no match for the West Indies, who had little trouble in exceeding a target of 185, making their subsequent failure to reach a similar target against India in the final even more surprising.

Group A

9 June at Kennington Oval, London, ENGLAND beat NEW ZEALAND by 106 runs. Toss: England. Match award: A.J. Lamb (102 & 2 ct). England 322-6 (60 overs) (A.J. Lamb 102). New Zealand 216 (59 overs) (M.D. Crowe 97).

9 June at St Helen's, Swansea. PAKISTAN beat SRI LANKA by 50 runs. Toss: Sri Lanka. Match award: Mohsin Khan (82). Pakistan 338-5 (60 overs) (Mohsin Khan 82, Zaheer Abbas 82, Javed Miandad 72, Imran Khan 56*). Sri Lanka 288-9 (60 overs) (B. Kuruppu 72, R.G. de Alwis 59*).

11, 12 June at Edgbaston, Birmingham. NEW ZEALAND beat PAKISTAN by 52 runs. Toss: Pakistan. Match award: Abdul Qadir (41* & 4-21). New Zealand 238-9 (60 overs) (Abdul Qadir 12-4-21-4). Pakistan 186 (55.2 overs).

11 June at Taunton. ENGLAND beat SRI LANKA by 47 runs. Toss: England. Match award: D.I. Gower (130). England 333-9 (60 overs) (D.I. Gower 130, A.J. Lamb 53). Sri Lanka 286 (58 overs) (L.R.D. Mendis 56, R.G. de Alwis 58*; V.J. Marks 12-3-39-5; G.R. Dilley 11-0-45-4).

13 June at Lord's, London. ENGLAND beat PAKISTAN by 8 wickets. Toss: Pakistan. Match award: Zaheer Abbas (83*). Pakistan 193-8 (60 overs) (Zaheer Abbas 83*). England 199-2 (50.4 overs) (G. Fowler 78*).

13 June at Phoenix County Ground, Bristol. NEW ZEALAND beat SRI LANKA by 5 wickets. Toss: New Zealand. Match award: R.J. Hadlee (5-25 & 2 ct). Sri Lanka 206 (56.1 overs) (R.S. Madugalle 60; R.J. Hadlee 10.1-4-25-5). New Zealand 209-5 (39.2 overs) (G.M. Turner 50, G.P. Howarth 76).

15 June at Edgbaston, Birmingham. NEW ZEALAND beat ENGLAND by 2 wickets. Toss: England. Match award: J.V. Coney (66* & 12-2-27-1). England 234 (55.2 overs) (G. Fowler 69, D.I. Gower 92*). New Zealand 238-8 (59.5 overs) (G.P. Howarth 60, J.V. Coney 66*; R.G.D. Willis 12-1-42-4).

16 June at Headingley, Leeds. PAKISTAN beat SRI LANKA by 11 runs. Toss: Sri Lanka. Match award: Abdul Qadir (5*, 5-44, & 1 ct). Pakistan 235-7 (60 overs) (Imran Khan 102*, Shahid Mahboob 77; A.L.F. de Mel 12-1-39-5). Sri Lanka 224 (58.3 overs) (S. Wettimuny 50; Abdul Qadir 12-1-44-5).

18 June at Old Trafford, Manchester. ENGLAND beat PAKISTAN by 7 wickets. Toss: Pakistan. Match award: G. Fowler (69). Pakistan 232-8 (60 overs) (Javed Miandad 67). England 233-3 (57.2 overs) (G. Fowler 69, C.J. Tavaré 58).

18 June at Racecourse Ground, Derby. SRI LANKA beat NEW ZEALAND by 3 wickets. Toss: Sri Lanka. Match award: A.L.F. de Mel (5-32). New Zealand 181 (58.2 overs) (A.L.F. de Mel 12-4-32-5). Sri Lanka 184-7 (52.5 overs) (B. Kuruppu 62, R.L. Dias 64*).

20 June at Headingley, Leeds. ENGLAND beat SRI LANKA by 9 wickets. Toss: England. Match award: R.G.D. Willis (9-4-9-1). Sri Lanka 136 (50.4 overs). England 137-1 (24.1 overs) (G. Fowler 81*).

20 June at Trent Bridge, Nottingham. PAKISTAN beat NEW ZEALAND by 11 runs. Toss: Pakistan. Match award: Imran Khan (79* & 2 ct). Pakistan 261-3 (60 overs) (Zaheer Abbas 103*, Imran Khan 79*). New Zealand 250 (59.1 overs) (J.V. Coney 51).

Final Group A Table	P	W	L	Points	Runs	Overs	Run-rate
ENGLAND	6	5	1	20	1458	312.1	4.67
PAKISTAN	6	3	3	12	1445	360	4.01
New Zealand	6	3	3	12	1332	339.1	3.93
Sri Lanka	6	1	5	4	1324	353.5	3.75

Pakistan qualified for the semi-finals by faster run-rate (0.08 per over faster than New Zealand).

Group B

9, 10 June at Old Trafford, Manchester. INDIA beat WEST INDIES by 34 runs. Toss: West Indies. Match award: Yashpal Sharma (89). India 262-8 (60 overs) (Yashpal Sharma 89). West Indies 228 (54.1 overs).

9 June at Trent Bridge, Nottingham. ZIMBABWE beat AUSTRALIA by 13 runs. Toss: Australia. Match award: D.A.G. Fletcher (69* & 4-42). Zimbabwe 239-6 (60 overs) (D.A.G. Fletcher 69*). Australia 226-7 (60 overs) (K.C. Wessels 76, R.W. Marsh 50*; D.A.G. Fletcher 11-1-42-4).

11, 12 June at Headingley, Leeds. WEST INDIES beat AUSTRALIA by 101 runs. Toss: Australia. Match award: W.W. Davis (7-51). West Indies 252-9 (60 overs) (H.A. Gomes 78). Australia 151 (30.3 overs) (W.W. Davis 10.3-0-51-7).

11 June at Grace Road, Leicester. INDIA beat ZIMBABWE by 5 wickets. Toss: India. Match award: Madan Lal (10.4-0-27-3). Zimbabwe 155 (51.4 overs) (S.M.H. Kirmani 5 ct). India 157-5 (37.3 overs) (S.M. Patil 50).

13 June at Trent Bridge, Nottingham. AUSTRALIA beat INDIA by 162 runs. Toss: Australia. Match award: T.M. Chappell (110). Australia 320-9 (60 overs) (T.M. Chappell 110, K.J. Hughes 52, G.N. Yallop 66*; Kapil Dev 12-2-43-5). India 158 (37.5 overs) (K.H. MacLeay 11.5-3-39-6).

13 June at New Road, Worcester. WEST INDIES beat ZIMBABWE by 8 wickets. Toss: West Indies. Match award: C.G. Greenidge (105*). Zimbabwe 217-7 (60 overs) (D.L. Houghton 54, D.A.G. Fletcher 71*). West Indies 218-2 (48.3 overs) (C.G. Greenidge 105*, H.A. Gomes 75*).

15 June at Kennington Oval, London. WEST INDIES beat INDIA by 66 runs. Toss: West Indies. Match award: I.V.A. Richards (119). West Indies 282-9 (60 overs) (I.V.A. Richards 119). India 216 (53.1 overs) (M. Amarnath 80).

16 June at Southampton. AUSTRALIA beat ZIMBABWE by 32 runs. Toss: Australia. Match award: D.L. Houghton (84 & 1 ct). Australia 272-7 (60 overs) (G.M. Wood 73). Zimbabwe 240 (59.5 overs) (D.L. Houghton 84).

18 June at Lord's, London. WEST INDIES beat AUSTRALIA by 7 wickets. Toss: Australia. Match award: I.V.A. Richards (95*). Australia 273-6 (60 overs) (K.J. Hughes 69, D.W. Hookes 56, G.N. Yallop 52*). West Indies 276-3 (57.5 overs) (C.G. Greenidge 90, I.V.A. Richards 95*).

18 June at Nevill Ground, Tunbridge Wells. INDIA beat ZIMBABWE by 31 runs. Toss: India. Match award: Kapil Dev (175*, 11-1-32-1, & 2 ct). India 266-8 (60 overs) (Kapil Dev 175*). Zimbabwe 235 (57 overs) (K.M. Curran 73).

20 June at Chelmsford. INDIA beat AUSTRALIA by 118 runs. Toss: India. Match award: R.M.H. Binny (21, 4-29, & 1 ct). India 247 (55.5 overs). Australia 129 (38.2 overs) (Madan Lal 8.2-3-20-4; R.M.H. Binny 8-2-29-4).

20 June at Edgbaston, Birmingham. WEST INDIES beat ZIMBABWE by 10 wickets. Toss: Zimbabwe. Match award: S.F.A.F. Bacchus (80*). Zimbabwe 171 (60 overs) (K.M. Curran 62). West Indies 172-0 (45.1 overs) (D.L. Haynes 88*, S.F.A.F. Bacchus 80*).

Final Group B Table	P	W	L	Points	Runs	Overs	Run-rate
WEST INDIES	6	5	1	20	1428	331.3	4.31
INDIA	6	4	2	16	1306	337.3	3.87
Australia	6	2	4	8	1371	360	3.81
Zimbabwe	6	1	5	4	1257	360	4.19

England v India 1983 Prudential Cup Semi-Final
India won by 6 wickets
Played at Old Trafford, Manchester, 22 June
Toss: England. Umpires: D.G.L. Evans and D.O. Oslear
Man of the Match: M. Amarnath (Adjudicator: J.B. Statham)

England		Runs	Mins	Balls	6s	4s
G. Fowler	b Binny	33	93	59	-	3
C.J. Tavaré	c Kirmani b Binny	32	70	51	-	4
D.I. Gower	c Kirmani b Amarnath	17	51	30	-	1
A.J. Lamb	run out (Yashpal)	29	64	58	-	1
M.W. Gatting	b Amarnath	18	45	46	-	1
I.T. Botham	b Azad	6	28	26	-	-
I.J. Gould†	run out (Kirmani)	13	43	36	-	-
V.J. Marks	b Kapil Dev	8	31	18	-	-
G.R. Dilley	not out	20	34	26	-	2
P.J.W. Allott	c Patil b Kapil Dev	8	22	14	-	-
R.G.D. Willis*	b Kapil Dev	0	3	2	-	-
Extras	(B 1, LB 17, W 7, NB 4)	29				
	(60 overs; 251 minutes)	**213**				

India		Runs	Mins	Balls	6s	4s
S.M. Gavaskar	c Gould b Allott	25	58	41	-	3
K. Srikkanth	c Willis b Botham	19	66	44	-	3
M. Amarnath	run out (Allott/Botham)	46	110	92	-	4
Yashpal Sharma	c Allott b Willis	61	143	115	2	3
S.M. Patil	not out	51	49	32	-	8
Kapil Dev*	not out	1	10	6	-	-
K. Azad	did not bat					
R.M.H. Binny	,,					
Madan Lal	,,					
S.M.H. Kirmani†	,,					
B.S. Sandhu	,,					
Extras	(B 5, LB 6, W 1, NB 2)	14				
	(54.4 overs; 223 minutes)	**217-4**				

India	O	M	R	W	Fall of Wickets		
Kapil Dev	11	1	35	3	Wkt	E	I
Sandhu	8	1	36	0	1st	69	46
Binny	12	1	43	2	2nd	84	50
Madan Lal	5	0	15	0	3rd	107	142
Azad	12	1	28	1	4th	141	205
Amarnath	12	1	27	2	5th	150	
England	O	M	R	W	6th	160	
Willis	10.4	2	42	1	7th	175	
Dilley	11	0	43	0	8th	177	
Allott	10	3	40	1	9th	202	
Botham	11	4	40	1	10th	213	
Marks	12	1	38	0			

*Captain †Wicket-keeper

West Indies v Pakistan 1983 Prudential Cup Semi-Final
West Indies won by 8 wickets
Played at Kennington Oval, London, 22 June
Toss: West Indies. Umpires: D.J. Constant and A.G.T. Whitehead
Man of the Match: I.V.A. Richards (Adjudicator: F.S. Trueman)

Pakistan

Mohsin Khan	b Roberts	70
Mudassar Nazar	c and b Garner	11
Ijaz Fakih	c Dujon b Holding	5
Zaheer Abbas	b Gomes	30
Imran Khan*	c Dujon b Marshall	17
Wasim Raja	lbw b Marshall	0
Shahid Mahboob	c Richards b Marshall	6
Sarfraz Nawaz	c Holding b Roberts	3
Abdul Qadir	not out	10
Wasim Bari†	not out	4
Rashid Khan	did not bat	
Extras	(B 6, LB 13, W 4, NB 5)	28
	(60 overs)	**184-8**

West Indies

C.G. Greenidge	lbw b Rashid Khan	17
D.L. Haynes	b Qadir	29
I.V.A. Richards	not out	80
H.A. Gomes	not out	50
C.H. Lloyd*	did not bat	
S.F.A.F. Bacchus	,,	
P.J. Dujon†	,,	
A.M.E. Roberts	,,	
M.D. Marshall	,,	
J. Garner	,,	
M.A. Holding	,,	
Extras	(B 2, LB 6, W 4)	12
	(48.4 overs)	**188-2**

West Indies	O	M	R	W
Roberts	12	3	25	2
Garner	12	1	31	1
Marshall	12	2	28	3
Holding	12	1	25	1
Gomes	7	0	29	1
Richards	5	0	18	0
Pakistan	O	M	R	W
Rashid	12	2	32	1
Sarfraz	8	0	23	0
Qadir	11	1	42	1
Mahboob	11	1	43	0
Raja	1	0	9	0
Zaheer	4.4	1	24	0
Mohsin	1	0	3	0

Fall of Wickets

Wkt	P	WI
1st	23	34
2nd	34	56
3rd	88	
4th	139	
5th	139	
6th	159	
7th	164	
8th	171	
9th		
10th		

*Captain †Wicket-keeper

Against most expectations, India won the Prudential Cup for the first time, beating West Indies, the holders, by 43 runs at Lord's. With previous wins over them, plus Australia and England, it was clear that India were far removed from the side who had played with embarrassing inefficiency in the first competition. Yet their total of 183, after being put in, looked inadequate against West Indies' batting strength on a good pitch.

The way that Clive Lloyd's team approached the task certainly hinted at complacency after Richards, having struck eight fours in his 33, fell to an over-ambitious stroke. With Lloyd needing a runner because of injury, West Indies lost their last eight wickets for 83 runs against accurate medium-paced bowling backed by highly efficient out-cricket.

In a remarkable match, no batsman scored more than Srikkanth's 38, which was full of exotic strokes, yet no bowler took more than three wickets. A sound and sensible innings by Amarnath, at a time when batting was at its most difficult, plus three wickets, earned him the Man of the Match award from Mike Brearley, who could not resist the wistful comment: 'If only the West Indies had batted like this against us in 1979. . . .'

Amarnath's good work had been undone, however, by India's middle order, who, restrained by the pace and accuracy of Marshall, Holding, and company, lost crucial wickets – including Kapil Dev's – when trying to lift the tempo of the innings against Gomes. The innings subsided in a way that suggested there could be only one result.

Although Greenidge was quickly and surprisingly bowled, offering no stroke to Sandhu, Richards, with three fours in one over from Madan Lal, swaggered into action so imperiously that a disappointingly one-sided final seemed inevitable. When West Indies had reached 57 for 2 from only 14 overs, however, Kapil Dev held a well-judged catch at mid-wicket to dismiss Richards. And when Lloyd, in much discomfort with a strained groin, mistimed an attempted off-drive soon afterwards, West Indies were 66 for 5, having lost Gomes cheaply.

Even then, with their depth of batting, they were not necessarily finished against opponents who could scarcely believe what was happening. India's triumph was delayed by some calm batting from Marshall and Dujon, which suggested that had West Indies' target been around 250 their early batsmen would have paced themselves more and probably succeeded.

PRUDENTIAL WORLD CUP 1983

INDIA INNINGS v WEST INDIES 1983 PRUDENTIAL CUP FINAL at LORD'S on 25 JUNE. TOSS: WEST INDIES

IN	OUT	MINS	No.	BATSMAN	HOW OUT	BOWLER	RUNS	WKT	TOTAL	6s	4s	BALLS	NOTES ON DISMISSAL	OVER OUT
10.45	10.58	13	1	S.M. GAVASKAR	c Dujon	ROBERTS	2	1	2	-	-	12	Followed ball that left him – firm-footed stroke.	5
10.45	12.06	81	2	K. SRIKKANTH	LBW	MARSHALL	38	2	59	-	7	57	Hit across line – beaten by pace.	19
11.00	12.48	108	3	M. AMARNATH	BOWLED	HOLDING	26	3	90	-	3	80	Missed offside steer at ball which hit off stump.	30
12.08	12.53	45	4	YASHPAL SHARMA	c sub (A.L. Logie)	GOMES	11	4	92	-	1	32	Scooped easy catch to deep cover.	31
12.50	2.17	45	5	S.M. PATIL	c Gomes	GARNER	27	8	153	1	-	29	Mistimed hook – mis-judged bounce – simple mid-on catch	42
12.55	1.44	8	6	KAPIL DEV*	c Holding	GOMES	15	5	110	-	3	8	Drove skier to long-on.	33
1.46	1.47	1	7	K. AZAD	c Garner	ROBERTS	0	6	111	-	-	3	Hooked long-hop to backward square-leg	34
1.49	1.58	9	8	R.M.H. BINNY	c Garner	ROBERTS	2	7	130	-	-	8	Spooned simple catch to mid-wicket.	36
2.00	2.30	30	9	MADAN LAL	BOWLED	MARSHALL	17	9	161	-	1	27	off stump – late on steer stroke.	45
2.19	3.13	54	10	S.M.H. KIRMANI†	BOWLED	HOLDING	14	10	183	-	-	43	Played on via pads.	55
2.32	(3.13)	41	11	B.S. SANDHU	NOT OUT		11			-	1	30		
				EXTRAS	b 5 lb 5 w 9 nb 1		20						3' 15" 329 balls (inc 1 no ball)	
				TOTAL	(54.4 OVERS, 227 MIN.)		183						183 all out at 3.13pm	

*CAPTAIN †WICKET-KEEPER

14 OVERS 3 BALLS/HOUR
3·35 RUNS/OVER
55 RUNS/100 BALLS

WKT	PARTNERSHIP		RUNS	MINS
1st	Gavaskar	Srikkanth	2	13
2nd	Srikkanth	Amarnath	57	66
3rd	Amarnath	Yashpal	31	40
4th	Yashpal	Patil	2	3
5th	Patil	Kapil	18	8
6th	Patil	Azad	1	1
7th	Patil	Binny	19	9
8th	Patil	Madan	23	17
9th	Madan	Kirmani	8	11
10th	Kirmani	Sandhu	22	41
			183	

BOWLER	O	M	R	W		HRS	OVERS	RUNS		RUNS	MINS	OVERS	LAST 50 (in mins)
ROBERTS	10	3	32	3		1	15	43		50	73	17.3	73
GARNER	12	4	24	1		2	14	46		100	134	31.5	61
MARSHALL	11	1	24	2		3	14	66		150	167	40.4	33
HOLDING	9.4	2	26	2									
GOMES	11	1	49	2									
RICHARDS	1	0	8	0									
			20										
	54.4	11	183	10									

LUNCH: 100-4 (32 OVERS) RATE: 3·13 135 MIN.
PATIL 3* (10 min.); KAPIL 6* (5 min.)

WEST INDIES REQUIRE 184 @ 3·07/OVER

UMPIRES: H.D. BIRD and B.J. MEYER

© BILL FRINDALL 1983

WEST INDIES INNINGS

REQUIRING 184 TO WIN @ 3.07 PER OVER

IN	OUT	MINS	No.	BATSMAN	HOW OUT	BOWLER	RUNS	WKT	TOTAL	6s	4s	BALLS	NOTES ON DISMISSAL	OVER OUT
3.26	3.57	11	1	C.G. GREENIDGE	BOWLED	SANDHU	1	1	5	.	.	12	No stroke - bowled off pads.	4
3.26	4.10	44	2	D.L. HAYNES	c' BINNY	MADAN LAL	13	2	50	.	2	33	Mistimed drive - cover.	12
3.39	4.20	41	3	I.V.A. RICHARDS	c' KAPIL DEV	MADAN LAL	33	3	57	.	7	28	Hooked skier to mid-wicket (backward running catch).	14
4.12	4.44	32	4	C.H. LLOYD*	c' KAPIL DEV	BINNY	8	5	66	.	1	17	Batsman's grip wrong first ball - Hayne as runner when 1 run only. Mistimed off-drive - mid-off catch.	19
4.22	4.40	18	5	H.A. GOMES	c' GAVASKAR	MADAN LAL	5	4	66	.	.	16	Top-edged cut at short ball to slip.	18
4.42	5.36	34	6	S.F.A.F. BACCHUS	c' KIRMANI	SANDHU	8	6	76	.	.	25	Edged outswinger (which ran) low in front of slip.	26
4.46	6.39	93	7	P.J. DUJON†	BOWLED	AMARNATH	25	7	119	.	.	73	Changed mind in removing bat - played on.	42
5.38	6.51	73	8	M.D. MARSHALL	c' GAVASKAR	AMARNATH	18	8	124	.	.	51	Flashed at which ball - edged to slip.	44
6.41	6.56	15	9	A.M.E. ROBERTS	LBW	KAPIL DEV	4	9	126	.	.	14	Played across line.	45
6.52	(7.24)	32	10	J. GARNER	NOT OUT		5			.	.	19		
6.58	7.24	26	11	M.A. HOLDING	LBW	AMARNATH	6	10	140	.	.	24	Ball kept low, played back.	52

*CAPTAIN †WICKET-KEEPER

EXTRAS b - 1 b 4 : 1 b 10* 312 balls ('no' no balls')

TOTAL (52 OVERS, 218 MIN) 140 all out at 7.24 pm

(WEST INDIES LOWEST PRUDENTIAL CUP TOTAL)

BOWLER	O	M	R	W	HRS	OVERS	RUNS	RUNS	MINS	OVERS	LAST 50 (in mins)
KAPIL DEV	11	4	21	1	1	14	61	50	44	11.2	44
SANDHU	9	1	32	2	2	13	19	100	144	33.3	100
MADAN LAL	12	2	31	3	3	16	43				
BINNY	10	1	23	1							
AMARNATH	7	0	12	3							
AZAD	3	0	7	0							
		8	14	10							
	52		140								

TEA: 76-5 (25 OVERS) RATE: 3.04
108 MIN.
BACCHUS 8* (32 MIN), DUJON (28 MIN)
REQUIRING A FURTHER 108 RUNS @ 3.09/OVER

INDIA beat WEST INDIES by 43 runs
to win 3RD PRUDENTIAL CUP FINAL

MAN OF THE MATCH: M. AMARNATH
(Adjudicator: J.M. Brearley)

14 OVERS 2 BALLS/HOUR
2.69 RUNS/OVER
45 RUNS/100 BALLS

WKT	PARTNERSHIP		RUNS	MINS
1st	Greenidge	Haynes	5	11
2nd	Haynes	Richards	45	31
3rd	Richards	Lloyd	7	8
4th	Lloyd	Gomes	9	18
5th	Lloyd	Bacchus	0	2
6th	Bacchus	Dujon	10	30
7th	Dujon	Marshall	43	61
8th	Marshall	Roberts	5	10
9th	Roberts	Garner	2	4
10th	Garner	Holding	14	26
				140

© BILL FRINDALL 1983

Prudential Cup Records

Highest total 338-5: Pakistan v Sri Lanka (Swansea, 1983)
Highest total batting second 288-9: Sri Lanka v Pakistan (Swansea, 1983)
Lowest total 45: Canada v England (Manchester, 1979)
Highest match aggregate 626: Pakistan v Sri Lanka (Swansea, 1983)
Lowest match aggregate 91: Canada v England (Manchester, 1979)
Biggest victories 10 wkts: India beat East Africa (Leeds, 1975)
   10 wkts: West Indies beat Zimbabwe (Birmingham, 1983)
   202 runs: England beat India (Lord's, 1975)
Narrowest victories 1 wkt: West Indies beat Pakistan (with 2 balls to spare) (Birmingham, 1975)
   9 runs: England beat New Zealand (Manchester, 1979)
Highest individual score 175*: Kapil Dev (I v Z, Tunbridge Wells, 1983)
Hundred before lunch 101: A. Turner (A v SL, Oval, 1975)
Best bowling 7 for 51: W.W. Davis (WI v A, Leeds, 1983)
Most economical bowling 12-8-6-1: B.S. Bedi (I v EA, Leeds, 1975)
Most expensive bowling 12-1-105-2: M.C. Snedden (NZ v E, Oval, 1983)
Wicket-keeping: Most dismissals 5: S.M.H. Kirmani (I v Z, Leicester, 1983)
Fielding: Most catches 3: C.H. Lloyd (WI v SL, Manchester, 1975)

Highest partnerships

Wkt	Runs	Partners
1st	182	R.B. McCosker & A. Turner (A v SL, Oval, 1975)
2nd	176	D.L. Amiss & K.W.R. Fletcher (E v I, Lord's, 1975)
3rd	195*	C.G. Greenidge & H.A. Gomes (WI v Z, Worcester, 1983)
4th	149	R.B. Kanhai & C.H. Lloyd (WI v A, Lord's, 1975)
5th	139	I.V.A. Richards & C.L. King (WI v E, Lord's, 1979)
6th	144	Imran Khan & Shahid Mahboob (P v SL, Leeds, 1983)
7th	75*	D.A.G. Fletcher & I.P. Butchart (Z v A, Nottingham, 1983)
8th	62	Kapil Dev & Madan Lal (I v Z, Tunbridge Wells, 1983)
9th	126*	Kapil Dev & S.M.H. Kirmani (I v Z, Tunbridge Wells, 1983)
10th	71	A.M.E. Roberts & J. Garner (WI v I, Manchester, 1983)

*denotes 'not out' innings or unbroken partnership.

Prudential Cup National Records

Australia				Opponents
Highest total	328-5			Sri Lanka (Oval, 1975)
Lowest total	129			India (Chelmsford, 1983)
Highest score	110		T.M. Chappell	India (Nottingham, 1983)
Best bowling	6-14		G.J. Gilmour	England (Leeds, 1975)

England				Opponents
Highest total	334-4			India (Lord's, 1975)
Lowest total	93			Australia (Leeds, 1975)
Highest score	137		D.L. Amiss	India (Lord's, 1975)
Best bowling	5-39		V.J. Marks	Sri Lanka (Taunton, 1983)

India				Opponents
Highest total	262-8			West Indies (Manchester, 1983)
Lowest total	132-3			England (Lord's 1975)
Highest score	175*		Kapil Dev	Zimbabwe (Tunbridge Wells, 1983)
Best bowling	5-43		Kapil Dev	Australia (Nottingham, 1983)

New Zealand				Opponents
Highest total	309-5			East Africa (Birmingham, 1975)
Lowest total	158			West Indies (Oval, 1975)
Highest score	171*		G.M. Turner	East Africa (Birmingham, 1975)
Best bowling	5-25		R.J. Hadlee	Sri Lanka (Bristol, 1983)

Pakistan				Opponents
Highest total	338-5			Sri Lanka (Swansea, 1983)
Lowest total	151			England (Leeds, 1979)
Highest score	103*		Zaheer Abbas	New Zealand (Nottingham, 1983)
Best bowling	5-44		Abdul Qadir	Sri Lanka (Leeds, 1983)

Sri Lanka				Opponents
Highest total	288-9			Pakistan (Swansea, 1983)
Lowest total	86			West Indies (Manchester, 1975)
Highest score	72		B. Kuruppu	Pakistan (Swansea, 1983)
Best bowling	5-32		A.L.F. de Mel	New Zealand (Derby, 1983)

West Indies				Opponents
Highest total	293-6			Pakistan (Oval, 1979)
Lowest total	140			India (Lord's, 1983)
Highest score	138*		I.V.A. Richards	England (Lord's 1979)
Best bowling	7-51		W.W. Davis	Australia (Leeds, 1983)

Zimbabwe				Opponents
Highest total	240			Australia (Southampton, 1983)
Lowest total	155			India (Leicester, 1983)
Highest score	84		D.L. Houghton	Australia (Southampton, 1983)
Best bowling	4-42		D.A.G. Fletcher	Australia (Nottingham, 1983)

*denotes 'not out' innings

New Zealand in England 1983

New Zealand in England

The 1983 Cornhill Test series was not only a triumph for England, who won the four-match rubber by 3-1, but also for the game of cricket itself, since it constituted something of a return to old-fashioned values of sportsmanship, dignity, and good humour, which have not been too much in evidence at international level in recent years.

Strong leadership in this respect from the two captains, Bob Willis and Geoff Howarth, ensured that behaviour on the field was of the highest order. Decisions or rejected appeals were accepted with good grace, and it was a pleasant rarity in a modern series to hear umpires praised rather than condemned at the end of it.

Inevitably, there would have been errors from time to time in this department, but the attitude of both sides went a long way to proving that, if these are not dwelt upon or magnified by complaining captains, the pressure on umpires is eased and a Test series results in which attention is focused primarily on the quality of the cricket.

This, like some of the pitches provided, tended to be variable, which was probably an accurate reflection of the strengths and weaknesses of two sides who would not claim to be of the highest class. But it meant that most days were eventful, and every Test produced a result.

Under the leadership of Willis - whose reappointment after defeat the previous winter did not meet with approval in all quarters - England showed a detectable improvement, though the balance of their side still left something to be desired. Willis himself bowled superbly for most of the series. He is still, by some way, England's leading fast bowler, and he finished within sight of F.S. Trueman's total of 307 Test wickets, a figure which he seemed likely to overhaul during the winter's series against New Zealand and Pakistan.

Of those who supported him, Cowans was the most successful, while clearly still serving his fast-bowling apprenticeship. It is worth noting, however, that such has been the scarcity of opening bowlers in recent years that some 25 per cent of all Cowans's limited first-class appearances have been made at Test level.

As it happened, in a summer that eventually produced prolonged, hot weather, England found themselves on turning pitches in the last two Tests, at Lord's and Trent Bridge, and Nick Cook, who was summoned from Leicestershire's game against Essex when Phil Edmonds developed back trouble on the eve of the game at Lord's, enjoyed a remarkably successful first appearance, with eight wickets.

He then confounded those who felt he was unlikely to repeat the feat by taking nine more on his second appearance, at Trent Bridge. Overall, the somewhat unexpected introduction of an intelligent slow-left-arm spin bowler, who was not afraid to flight the ball, was a stroke of good fortune for England, since Cook's county form had not been as impressive as in the previous year, when he and Edmonds were passed over for the tour of Australia.

By contrast, New Zealand depended largely on John Bracewell, who although often looking extremely promising, sometimes lacked the accuracy required at Test level and was often betrayed by his lack of experience of English conditions.

New Zealand also suffered through the lack of a penetrative new-ball partner for Richard Hadlee, who, although now content to cut down his pace, still produced many moments of high quality. With 21 wickets and 301 runs, he was indisputably named Man of the Series. At other times, New Zealand discovered that bowlers such as Jeremy Coney, Lance Cairns, and Ewan Chatfield, at around medium pace, could impose great restraint on slowish pitches.

Cairns, in fact, produced the best figures ever achieved by a New Zealand bowler in Tests between the countries when he took 7 for 74 at Headingley, a performance that enabled his side to win their first Test in England after 52 years and 28 earlier attempts.

This, following England's emphatic win on what was to prove the best pitch of the series at the Oval, put them level and ensured public interest would be sustained. Disappointingly for New Zealand, however, the expected continued improvement did not materialize, and England mostly outplayed them in the two remaining games.

Another gulf between the sides was in the quality of the batting. Although the admirable and well-organized Bruce Edgar achieved the distinction of occupying the crease longer than anyone – even Chris Tavaré – New Zealand had only two three-figure partnerships and no individual hundred.

For England, Tavaré, Graeme Fowler, Allan Lamb (two) and David Gower (two) all hit centuries, as did Ian Botham, whose variable all-round form at the start of the series was a problem for the selectors. Eventually, at Trent Bridge, he made his first Test hundred for a year, an innings that finished violently after a highly disciplined start and enabled his side to make a remarkable 362 for 7 on the first day.

While Botham did not succeed in completely erasing doubts about the current effectiveness of his bowling at Test level, that innings at least was gratifying. So too was the continuing flawless wicket-keeping of Bob Taylor at the age of 42, which emphasized New Zealand's problems in this department, especially when Ian Smith broke a finger late in the series. It is also worth noting the refreshingly positive attitude with which Howarth's team approached games against the counties, most of which were won, albeit sometimes against opponents who not only turned out below-strength sides – which unfortunately seems to be the fashion nowadays – but often entered the games with a questionable attitude.

This prompted strong and justified comment from Howarth, who felt the public were being 'cheated', and questioned the value of continuing with such fixtures if this attitude persisted. Certainly, it is a matter that demands the attention of the Test and County Cricket Board.

First Test: The Oval, July 14, 15, 16, 17, 18.
England won by 189 runs.

Despite being bowled out in their first innings for a modest 209 on a good pitch offering pace and bounce for the faster bowlers, England went one up in the series by a comprehensive margin. New Zealand, disappointingly for them, lost the last seven wickets of their second innings for only 73 runs in 23 overs, after suggesting that they might defy England by batting for some ten hours to save the match.

England were without Dilley (sore shins), and Foster, of Essex, who had been called in to replace him, did not play, though the decision to choose both spin bowlers was by no means unanimous. After winning the toss on a sultry, cloudless day, England batted unevenly, regularly finding ways of getting out to Hadlee, whose control and subtle changes of pace earned him 6 for 53.

With Tavaré run out when becoming established, and both Gower and Botham playing on to Hadlee, Randall – after much playing and missing – was the only England batsman to make the most of the conditions. He was left unbeaten with 75 after some 2½ hours, but Willis, bowling very fast, and Cowans left New Zealand at 17 for 3 at the end of the first day.

Willis continued to penetrate the next day, and at one stage had taken 4 for 10 in 12 overs. A vigorous innings of 84 from 79 balls by Hadlee, sensibly partnered by Coney, produced 84 runs for the sixth wicket in only 15 overs. It was ended only by Willis's brilliant running out of Coney, and, with Botham holding a low return catch from Hadlee, England managed a slender first innings lead.

The rest of the day was dominated by Tavaré and Fowler, who put on 146 together and next morning took their partnership to 223, the highest for England against New Zealand. Fowler completed his maiden Test century and Tavaré his second, the first time since 1960 that both openers had reached three figures. Curiously, on that occasion, they were also a left-hander from Lancashire and a right-hander from Kent – Pullar and Cowdrey.

Their dismissal in quick succession, however, led to a pawky batting performance in which England made only 194 runs from 98 overs during the day, admittedly against bowling that was shrewdly handled and gave little away. On the fourth morning, Lamb, surviving an escape at 53, gradually found his touch to make an unbeaten 102, the first time since 1974 that an England innings had contained three century-makers.

Willis's declaration left New Zealand to make 460. More hostile bowling by Willis plunged them into immediate trouble, but a partnership of 120 for the third wicket by Wright and Howarth suggested that Marks and Edmonds, who were now England's main attacking weapon, would have to work hard.

Wright, however, became the fourth run-out victim of the match early on the last morning and after Howarth had fallen to Edmonds. The spinners then worked their way with surprising ease through the remaining batting, leaving New Zealand with only the consolation of the Man of the Match award, deservedly won by Hadlee.

NEW ZEALAND IN ENGLAND 1983

ENGLAND 1st INNINGS v NEW ZEALAND (1st TEST) at KENNINGTON OVAL on 14, 15, 16, 17, 18 JULY 1983. TOSS: ENGLAND

IN	OUT	MINS	No.	BATSMAN	HOW OUT	BOWLER	RUNS	WKT	TOTAL	6s	4s	BALLS	NOTES ON DISMISSAL
11.00	11.21	21	1	G. FOWLER	LBW	HADLEE	1	1	2	.	.	19	Moved across stumps and played across late inswing.
11.00	12.42	145	2	C.J. TAVARÉ	RUN OUT [WRIGHT/LEES]		45	(3)	73	.	5	106	Retired hurt (22) at 73-3 — hit in mouth by Hadlee bouncer. 62 minutes
2.14	2.57						6		154				Randall refused run to extra cover.
11.24	11.39	15	3	D.I. GOWER	BOWLED	HADLEE	11	2	18	.	2	18	Played on to off stump — inside edge to late inswing.
11.41	12.33	52	4	A.J. LAMB	BOWLED	CAIRNS	24	3	67	.	4	44	Bowled off stump by inswinger — between bat and pad.
11.41	2.01	47	5	I.T. BOTHAM	BOWLED	HADLEE	15	4	104	.	2	32	Edged cover drive at off side ball into stumps.
12.45 (4.35)		172	6	D.W. RANDALL	NOT OUT		75	.	.	.	7	129	His highest score in 1983 first-class matches. So is 112 minutes.
2.03	2.12	9	7	V.J. MARKS	C† LEES	HADLEE	4	5	116	.	.	9	Fended lifting ball to keeper.
2.58	3.33	35	8	P.H. EDMONDS	C and BOWLED	BRACEWELL	12	7	184	.	1	39	Firm straight drive caught above bowler's head.
3.35	4.09	14	9	R.W. TAYLOR †	LBW	HADLEE	0	8	191	.	.	13	Pushed forward — hit on back leg.
4.11	4.23	12	10	R.G.D. WILLIS *	C† J.J. CROWE	BRACEWELL	4	9	202	.	.	10	Edged forward push at off break to forward short-leg.
4.24	4.35	11	11	N.G. COWANS	BOWLED	HADLEE	3	10	209	.	.	10	Late outswinger hit middle and off stumps.
				EXTRAS	b 6 lb 6 w – nb 3		15					21	429 balls (including 5 no balls)
				TOTAL	(70.4 OVERS, 277 MINUTES)		209						all out at 4.35pm on first day.

* CAPTAIN   † WICKET-KEEPER

15 OVERS   2 BALLS/HOUR
2.96 RUNS/OVER
49 RUNS/100 BALLS

WKT	PARTNERSHIP		RUNS	MINS
1st	Fowler	Tavaré	2	21
2nd	Tavaré	Gower	16	15
3rd	Tavaré	Lamb	49	52
4th	Tavaré	Botham	6	6
	Randall	Botham	31	38
5th	Randall	Marks	12	9
6th	Randall	Tavaré	38	43
7th	Randall	Edmonds	30	35
8th	Randall	Taylor	7	14
9th	Randall	Willis	11	12
10th	Randall	Cowans	7	11
			209	

LUNCH: 85-3   BOTHAM 11* (26 min)   RANDALL 5* (7 min)
31 OVERS   122 MINUTES

TEA: 184-7   RANDALL 59* (128 min)   TAYLOR 0* (6 min)
62 OVERS   243 MINUTES

ENGLAND'S THIRD-LOWEST TOTAL AGAINST NEW ZEALAND IN ENGLAND AND LOWEST AGAINST THEM AT THE OVAL.

HADLEE'S ANALYSIS, HIS 14th FIVE-WICKET INSTANCE IN 41 TESTS, SET A NEW RECORD FOR NEW ZEALAND IN ENGLAND — BEATING JACK COWIE'S 6-67 AT OLD TRAFFORD IN 1937.

BOWLER	O	M	R	W	nb	HRS	OVERS	RUNS		RUNS	MINS	OVERS	LAST 50 (in mins)
HADLEE	23.4	6	53	6	3	1	15	38		50	73	18.2	73
CHATFIELD	17	3	48	0	-	2	16	47		100	139	35.3	66
CAIRNS	17	3	63	1	1	3	15	48		150	194	48.3	55
BRACEWELL	8	4	16	2	0	4	15	51		200	262	66.5	68
M.D. CROWE	5	0	14	0	1								
			15	1									
	70.4	16	209	10									

© BILL FRINDALL

UMPIRES: H.D. BIRD and D.G.L. EVANS

106 NEW ZEALAND IN ENGLAND 1983

NEW ZEALAND 1ST INNINGS — In reply to ENGLAND'S 209 all out

IN	OUT	MINS	No.	BATSMAN	HOW OUT	BOWLER	RUNS	WKT	TOTAL	6s	4s	BALLS	NOTES ON DISMISSAL
4.46	4.48	2	1	J.G. WRIGHT	C GOWER	WILLIS	0	1	0	.	.	3	Fended lifting ball low to 3rd slip – superb left-handed catch
4.46	11.34	120	2	B.A. EDGAR	C TAYLOR	WILLIS	12	5	41	.	1	58	Top-edged square cut at ball slanted in from round wicket
4.50	4.58	8	3	J.J. CROWE	C RANDALL	WILLIS	0	2	1	.	.	4	Edged short off-side ball to 4th slip
5.00	5.32	32	4	G.P. HOWARTH*	BOWLED	COWANS	4	3	10	.	.	29	Beaten by sheer speed – pushed half-forward
5.34	11.04	42	5	M.D. CROWE	BOWLED	WILLIS	0	4	17	.	.	29	Late on ball of full length which removed off stump
11.06	12.53	97	6	J.V. CONEY	RUN OUT [WILLIS]		44	6	125	.	4	65	Beaten by direct return from mid-on to bowler's stumps
11.37	2.34	139	7	R.J. HADLEE	C AND BOWLED	BOTHAM	84	8	182	1	11	79	Mistimed back foot force. So off 46 balls in 71 min. Low catch.
12.55	1.59	26	8	J.G. BRACEWELL	C AND BOWLED	BOTHAM	7	7	149	.	1	26	Changed mind playing short ball – cocked up off-side catch
2.00	2.56	56	9	W.K. LEES †	NOT OUT		31	.	.	.	4	46	
2.36	2.46	10	10	B.L. CAIRNS	C LAMB	BOTHAM	2	9	188	.	.	6	Edged via pad to forward short leg – fending off short ball
2.48	2.56	8	11	E.J. CHATFIELD	C WILLIS	BOTHAM	0	10	196	.	.	5	Fended short ball to gully
				EXTRAS	b - 1 b 6	w - nb 6	12			1 5	21 4	350 balls (including 8 no balls)	

*CAPTAIN † WICKET-KEEPER

TOTAL (57 OVERS; 284 MINUTES) 196 all out at 2.56 (13 RUNS BEHIND)

© BILL FRINDALL

12 OVERS 0 BALLS/HOUR
3.44 RUNS/OVER
56 RUNS/100 BALLS

BOWLER	O	M	R	W	nb	w	HRS	OVERS	RUNS	RUNS	MINS	OVERS	LAST 50 (in mins)
WILLIS	20	8	43	4	2		1	12	11	50	135	26.3	135
COWANS	19	3	60	1	4		2	12	30	100	175	34.1	40
BOTHAM	16	2	62	4	.		3	11	73	150	229	45.2	54
EDMONDS	2	0	19	0	2		4	13	45				
			12	1									
	57	13	196	10									

STUMPS: 17-3 EDGAR 10* (86 min)
1ST DAY MD CROWE 0* (38 min)
BLSP at 6.12pm (34 min) 17.2 OVERS; 86 MINUTES

LUNCH: 136-6 HADLEE 64* (96 min)
BRACEWELL 1* (8 min)
41 OVERS; 209 MINUTES

WKT	PARTNERSHIP		RUNS	MINS
1st	Wright	Edgar	0	2
2nd	Edgar	JJ Crowe	1	8
3rd	Edgar	Howarth	9	32
4th	Edgar	MD Crowe	7	42
5th	Edgar	Coney	24	28
6th	Coney	Hadlee	84	76
7th	Hadlee	Bracewell	24	26
8th	Hadlee	Lees	33	34
9th	Lees	Cairns	6	10
10th	Lees	Chatfield	8	8
			196	

NEW ZEALAND IN ENGLAND 1983

ENGLAND 2ND INNINGS — 13 RUNS AHEAD ON FIRST INNINGS

IN	OUT	MINS	No.	BATSMAN	HOW OUT	BOWLER	RUNS	WKT	TOTAL	6s	4s	BALLS	NOTES ON DISMISSAL
3-08	1-59	324	1	G. FOWLER	RUN OUT [EDGAR/LEES]		105	2	225	–	11	8	303	1st in TESTS: 288; 2nd ball: Point returned to 'Keeper – Gower's stroke.
3-08	1-47	312	2	C. J. TAVARÉ	c HOWARTH	BRACEWELL	109	1	223		11		255	2nd in TEST: 277; 217 balls. Leading edge – simple extra-cover catch.
1-49	3-28	99	3	D. I. GOWER	c HOWARTH	HADLEE	25	3	269		3		76	Edged off-side steer low to 1st slip – 2nd ball with second new ball
2-02 (3-00)		356	4	A. J. LAMB	NOT OUT		102				10		293	2nd in TESTS
3-30	4-55	63	5	I. T. BOTHAM	RUN OUT [M. CROWE/LEES]		26	4	322		3		44	Attempted second run off mid-wicket's misfield – sent back.
4-58	5-20	22	6	D. W. RANDALL	c CONEY	HADLEE	3	5	329				22	Gloved throat ball to 2nd slip
5-22	5-53	31	7	V. J. MARKS	c M. D. CROWE	BRACEWELL	2	6	336				18	Jabbed off-break low to diving short square-leg.
5-55 (3-00)		145	8	P. H. EDMONDS	NOT OUT		43					5	125	
			9	R. W. TAYLOR †										
			10	R. G. D. WILLIS *	DID NOT BAT									
			11	N. G. COWANS										
				EXTRAS	b 8 lb 23 w – nb –		31							
				TOTAL	(189.2 OVERS; 684 MINUTES)		446-6		–'6s 40⁴ 1136 BALLS (0 no balls) DECLARED at 3.00pm 4TH DAY

* CAPTAIN † WICKET-KEEPER

© BILL FRINDALL

BOWLER	O	M	R	W	HRS	OVERS	RUNS		RUNS	MINS	OVERS	LAST 50 (in mins)
HADLEE	37.2	7	99	2	1	16	40		50	73	20	73
CAIRNS	30	7	67	0	2	18	51		100	140	40	67
CHATFIELD	35	9	85	0	3	18	47		150	198	57.2	58
M. D. CROWE	3	0	9	0	4	17	43		200	268	77.1	70
BRACEWELL	54	13	115	2	5	17	40		250	382	110.2	114
CONEY	27	11	39	0	6	19	15		300	448	128	66
HOWARTH	3	2	31	2	7	16	38		350	560	156.1	112
	189.2	49	444	6	8	15	46		400	640	177.3	80
					9	14	16					
					10	18	38					
					11	14	39					

2nd NEW BALL TAKEN at 3-27pm on 3rd day – ENGLAND 269-2 after 119.1 OVERS

16 OVERS 4 BALLS/HOUR
2·36 RUNS/OVER
39 RUNS/100 BALLS

WKT	PARTNERSHIP		RUNS	MINS
1st	Fowler	Tavaré	223	312
2nd	Fowler	Gower	2	10
3rd	Gower	Lamb	44	86
4th	Lamb	Botham	53	63
5th	Lamb	Randall	7	22
6th	Lamb	Marks	7	31
7th	Lamb	Edmonds	110*	145
			446	

TEA: 46-0 (19 OVERS) { FOWLER 22², TAVARÉ 23², } 69 min

STUMPS: 146-0   FOWLER 60* 54 OVERS
2nd DAY   TAVARÉ 78* 186 MIN.   LEAD: 159

LUNCH: 222-0   FOWLER 102*   89 OVERS
               TAVARÉ 105*   306 MIN

TEA: 280-3   LAMB 20* { 98 min } 122 OVERS
             BOTHAM 7* { 10 min } 425 MIN

STUMPS: 340-6   LAMB 48* (217 min) 152 OVERS
3rd DAY   EDMONDS 4* (6 min) 544 MIN   LEAD: 353 (ENGLAND ADDED 194 OFF 98 OVERS)

LUNCH: 420-6   LAMB 84* (393 min) 184 OVERS
               EDMONDS 36* (127 min) 665 MIN

NEW ZEALAND REQUIRE 460 TO WIN

108 NEW ZEALAND IN ENGLAND 1983

NEW ZEALAND 2ND INNINGS

REQUIRING 460 RUNS TO WIN

IN	OUT	MINS	No.	BATSMAN	HOW OUT	BOWLER	RUNS	WKT	TOTAL	6s	4s	BALLS	NOTES ON DISMISSAL
3·11	3·31	20	1	B.A.EDGAR	C' TAYLOR	WILLIS	3	1	10	·	·	14	Edged short ball that 'left' him.
3·11	11·19	234	2	J.G. WRIGHT	RUN OUT [AWARE TAYLOR]		88	3	146	·	11	188	Attempted suicidal run to cover - sent back by Howarth.
3·33	3·57	24	3	J.J. CROWE	C' LAMB	WILLIS	9	2	26	·	·	20	Fended inslanted ball off hip to square short-leg.
3·59	12·37	264	4	G.P. HOWARTH*	C' TAYLOR	EDMONDS	67	4	197	·	6	225	Edged off drive at widish leg-break.
11·22	1·47	105	5	M.D. CROWE	C' TAYLOR	EDMONDS	33	6	210	·	3	107	Leg-break 'kicked', hit glove & rebounded off his chest.
12·40	12·49	9	6	J.V. CONEY	LBW	MARKS	2	5	202	·	·	9	Played no stroke - padded up to 'arm' ball.
12·51	2·14	43	7	R.J. HADLEE	C' TAYLOR	MARKS	11	7	228	1	·	36	Edged forward push at leg-break (left-handed batsman).
1·49	2·25	36	8	W.K. LEES †	RUN OUT (COWANS)		8	9	228	·	2	33	Cairns attempted quick run to cover - direct hit on run.
2·16	2·22	6	9	J.G. BRACEWELL	C' GOWER	MARKS	0	8	228	·	·	6	Edged off break via pad to silly point (waist high).
2·24	2·42	18	10	B.L. CAIRNS	C' WILLIS	EDMONDS	32	10	270	4	1	20	Drove skier to long-off.
2·27	(2·42)	15	11	E.J. CHATFIELD	NOT OUT		10	·	·	·	2	8	
				EXTRAS	b 3 lb 1	w - nb 3	7		5b 25 666 balls (5 no balls)
				TOTAL	(110·1 OVERS; 397 MINUTES)		270 all out at 2·42 pm on FIFTH DAY

*CAPTAIN †WICKET-KEEPER

BOWLER	O	M	R	W	nb	HRS	OVERS	RUNS	RUNS	MINS	OVERS	LAST (6-mins)
WILLIS	12	3	26	2	3	1	12	32	50	93	21·2	93
COWANS	11	2	41	0	·	2	16	49	100	157	38	64
BOTHAM	4	0	17	0	·	3	18	37	150	252	68	95
MARKS	43	20	78	3	·	4	18	28	200	316	87·2	64
EDMONDS	40·1	16	101	3	2	5	18	41	250	391	108·2	75
			7	2		6	18	33				
	110·1	41	270	10								

© BILL FRINDALL

16 OVERS 4 BALLS/HOUR
2·45 RUNS/OVER
41 RUNS/100 BALLS

TEA: 48-2 21 OVERS 93 MINUTES

STUMPS: 130-2 56 OVERS 215 MIN WRIGHT 26* (93 min) HOWARTH 10* (45 min)
4TH DAY REQUIRING 330 RUNS OFF MINIMUM OF 96 OVERS WRIGHT 75* (215 min) HOWARTH 32* (67 min)

LUNCH: 203·5 92 OVERS 335 MIN CROWE 27* (98 min) HADLEE 0* (9 min)

ENGLAND won by 189 runs
at 2·42 pm on fifth day

MAN OF THE MATCH: R.J. HADLEE

ATTENDANCE: 34,043. RECEIPTS: £168,240.

WKT	PARTNERSHIP		RUNS	MINS
1st	Edgar	Wright	10	20
2nd	Wright	J.J. Crowe	16	24
3rd	Wright	Howarth	120	186
4th	Howarth	M.D. Crowe	51	75
5th	M.D. Crowe	Coney	5	9
6th	M.D. Crowe	Hadlee	8	16
7th	Hadlee	Lees	18	25
8th	Lees	Bracewell	0	6
9th	Lees	Cairns	0	1
10th	Cairns	Chatfield	42	15
			270	

Second Test: Headingley, July 28, 29, 30, Aug 1
New Zealand won by five wickets.
Taking advantage of England's deficiencies, especially in attack, New Zealand achieved their historic first Test win in England after an impressive all-round performance, although some fine fast bowling by Bob Willis played on their nerves before they got home with more than a day to spare.

Needing only 101, they lost five wickets for 83, all to Willis, which took him to the 300 mark, the fourth most successful bowler in Test history. Gower's unbeaten 112 was the highest score of the match and his first century in England since 1979.

The irony of England's defeat was that they had started the match strong favourites because of Headingley's tradition of helping seam and swing bowling. A pitch that started damp, however, allied itself to bowling of around medium pace, and New Zealand's attack exploited the conditions well.

After Howarth had won a crucial toss and put England in to bat, Cairns, with an intelligent mixture of inswingers and leg-cutters, swept through England's middle order to take 7 for 74.

Tavaré played the role of anchorman well, batting some five hours for 69. But both Lamb and Botham were unable to build on fluent starts, and by the end of the second day New Zealand led by 27 runs with five wickets standing, despite two disastrous run-out episodes.

First, Howarth was beaten by Lamb's direct hit, and later Jeff Crowe could not beat Cowans's powerful and accurate return from the boundary. In each case, Wright was the culpable partner, and, visibly upset, he was out soon after the second incident during a hostile spell of bowling by Cowans.

England, however, had lost their way earlier in the day. Their bowling lacked direction, Willis's captaincy lacked imagination, and, although Edgar had been forced to retire with an injured hip, he returned later to join Hadlee in a partnership that continued to embarrass England until the third morning, when Dilley did not bowl because of a sore heel. They added 86 together before falling in quick succession. When England went in again, with a deficit of 152, Hadlee had both openers dropped in an inspired spell. That New Zealand should triumph without Hadlee taking a wicket was another remarkable aspect of the match.

By this stage the bounce was more unpredictable and, Gower apart, England found various ways of falling to the accurate Coney and Chatfield. The latter went on to take five wickets in a Test for the first time.

England were only two runs ahead with four wickets standing on the fourth morning. Although Gower continued to play well, he was still eight short of his hundred when Cowans appeared, and he was obliged to refuse more than one single on 99 in the interests of protecting his partner.

Eventually, Gower was left unbeaten, and although Howarth had expressed fears of making much more than 100 in the fourth innings, the pitch was probably less awkward at this stage and Willis's great effort was not enough. Cairns, whose bowling in the first innings had given his side their first glimpse of a goal they had sought for 52 years, was the Man of the Match.

110 NEW ZEALAND IN ENGLAND 1983

ENGLAND 1ˢᵀ INNINGS v. NEW ZEALAND 2ⁿᵈ TEST at HEADINGLEY, LEEDS on 28, 29, 30 JULY, 1 AUGUST, 1983. TOSS: NEW ZEALAND

IN	OUT	MINS	No.	BATSMAN	HOW OUT	BOWLER	RUNS	WKT	TOTAL	6's	4's	BALLS	NOTES ON DISMISSAL
11.00	12.07	67	1	G. FOWLER	C⁺ SMITH	CHATFIELD	9	1	18	.	.	55	Edged offside push at ball which left him slightly.
11.00	4.54	296	2	C.J. TAVARÉ	C⁺ SMITH	CONEY	69	8	209	.	8	228	Edged push at away-swinger. Smith standing up.
12.09	12.31	22	3	D.I. GOWER	C⁺ CONEY	CAIRNS	9	2	35	.	1	18	Edged outswinger waist-high to 2nd slip.
12.33	2.52	99	4	A.J. LAMB	C⁺ M.D. CROWE	CAIRNS	58	3	135	1	9	83	Superb diving two-handed short square-leg catch.
2.54	3.30	36	5	I.T. BOTHAM	C⁺ HOWARTH	CAIRNS	38	4	175	1	6	33	Edged push at away-seamer to slip.
3.52	4.04	14	6	D.W. RANDALL	C⁺ CONEY	CAIRNS	4	5	185	.	.	10	Lifting ball hit but shoulder - high left-handed 2ⁿᵈ slip catch.
4.06	4.40	34	7	P.H. EDMONDS	C⁺ SMITH	CAIRNS	8	6	205	.	.	35	Edged leg-cutter to keeper's right - ran across slips.
4.41	4.43	2	8	G.R. DILLEY	BOWLED	CAIRNS	0	7	205	.	.	3	Beaten by leg-break - middle stump - slower ball.
4.44	(5.35)	51	9	R.W. TAYLOR†	NOT OUT		10	.	.	.	1	43	.
4.56	5.31	35	10	R.G.D. WILLIS*	C⁺ J.J. CROWE	CONEY	9	9	225	.	1	26	Edged attempted drive - diving catch at bat point
5.33	5.35	2	11	N.G. COWANS	C⁺ BRACEWELL	CAIRNS	0	10	225	.	.	2	Hoisted vast skier to long-leg.
				EXTRAS	b 4 lb 7 w - nb -		11					2ᵇ 2ᵇ 536 balls (0 no-balls)	
				TOTAL	(89.2 OVERS. 337 MINUTES)		225 all out at 5.35 pm on 1ˢᵗ day.						

* CAPTAIN † WICKET-KEEPER

15 OVERS   5 BALLS/HOUR
2.52   RUNS/OVER
42   RUNS/100 BALLS

BOWLER	O	M	R	W	HRS	OVERS	RUNS	RUNS	MINS	OVERS	LAST 50 (in overs)
HADLEE	21	9	44	0	1	17	13	50	111	30.2	111
CHATFIELD	22	8	67	1	2	16	37	100	163	44.5	52
CAIRNS	33.2	14	74	7	3	16	78	150	211	56.1	48
BRACEWELL	1	0	8	0	4	15	55	200	265	70.3	54
CONEY	12	3	21	2	5	15	26				
	89.2	34	225	10			11				

LUNCH: 50-2 [120 MIN. 33 OVERS] TAVARÉ 20* (20b) LAMB 11* (27)
TEA: 183-4 [242 MIN. 64 OVERS] TAVARÉ 55* (341) RANDALL 4* (10)

LANCE CAIRNS RECORDED HIS BEST
ANALYSIS IN 30 TESTS AND BECAME
THE FIRST NZ BOWLER TO TAKE SEVEN
WICKETS AGAINST ENGLAND.
ONLY 2 OTHER NEW ZEALANDERS HAVE
TAKEN 7 WICKETS IN A TEST INNINGS:
B.R. TAYLOR 7-74 v WI (Bridgetown) 1971-72
R.J. HADLEE 7-23 v IND (Wellington) 1975-76

WKT	PARTNERSHIP		RUNS	MINS
1ˢᵗ	Fowler	Tavaré	18	67
2ⁿᵈ	Tavaré	Gower	17	22
3ʳᵈ	Tavaré	Lamb	100	99
4ᵗʰ	Tavaré	Botham	40	36
5ᵗʰ	Tavaré	Randall	10	14
6ᵗʰ	Tavaré	Edmonds	20	34
7ᵗʰ	Tavaré	Dilley	0	2
8ᵗʰ	Tavaré	Taylor	4	10
9ᵗʰ	Taylor	Willis	16	35
10ᵗʰ	Taylor	Cowans	0	2
			225	

© BILL FRINDALL

UMPIRES: D.J. CONSTANT and B.J. MEYER

NEW ZEALAND 1st INNINGS
In reply to England's 225 all out

IN	OUT	MINS	No.	BATSMAN	HOW OUT	BOWLER	RUNS	WKT	TOTAL	6s	4s	BALLS	NOTES ON DISMISSAL
5.46	4.27	288	1	J.G. WRIGHT	c WILLIS	COWANS	93	4	169	.	13	223	Mistimed backfoot off-drive - simple catch to wide mid-off
5.46	11.52	279	2	B.A. EDGAR	BOWLED	WILLIS	84	(2)	26	.	11	211	Retired hurt when 19* four balls after being hit on hip looking at Botham. Resumed (with J.J. Crowe as runner) at 218.5. Middle stump, nasty lifted line.
5.36	2.14							9	377				
11.54	12.21	27	3	G.P. HOWARTH*	RUN OUT (LAMB)		13	1	52	.	3	13	Backed up for run (Wright) to cover - sent back - beaten by throw
12.22	4.16	176	4	M.D. CROWE	LBW	COWANS	37	2	168	.	5	135	Front foot - half-forward push - beaten by June leg.
4.18	4.21	3	5	J.J. CROWE	RUN OUT (COWANS/TAYLOR)		0	3	169	.	.	4	Wright unchanged mind over second run to deep fine leg.
4.23	5.34	71	6	J.V. CONEY	c GOWER	WILLIS	19	5	218	.	4	58	Edged to 3rd slip - playing short ball off back foot.
4.29	12.05	185	7	R.J. HADLEE	BOWLED	COWANS	75	6	304	.	9	135	Mistimed hook at short ball - played on.
12.07	1.41	55	8	J.G. BRACEWELL	c DILLEY	EDMONDS	16	7	348	.	3	40	Edged pull to deep backward point - gentle skier.
1.42	1.47	5	9	I.D.S. SMITH †	c TAVARÉ	WILLIS	2	8	351	.	.	6	Top-edged cut at long-hop to 1st slip.
1.49	(2.17)	28	10	B.L. CAIRNS	NOT OUT		24			2	1	21	
2.16	2.17	1	11	E.J. CHATFIELD	LBW	WILLIS	0	10	377	.	.	1	Missed turn to leg - out first ball.
				EXTRAS			b1 lb4 w1 nb8					2s 4½	847 balls (including 10 no balls)
				TOTAL	(139.3 overs; 568 minutes)		377						all out at 2.17 pm on 3rd day.

*CAPTAIN †WICKET-KEEPER

BOWLER	O	M	R	W	nb	w	HRS	OVERS	RUNS		RUNS	MINS	OVERS	LAST 50 (in mins)
WILLIS	23.3	6	57	4			1st	1	13	18	50	94	20	94
DILLEY	17	4	36	0	-		2nd	2	12	40	100	176	40.5	82
BOTHAM	26	9	81	0	7		3rd	3	16	42	150	254	62.1	78
COWANS	28	8	88	3	7/1		4th	4	18	41	200	323	80.3	69
EDMONDS	45	14	101	1	-		5th	5	15	34	250	406	98.5	83
					2		6th	6	14	43	300	471	116	65
	139.3	41	377	10			7th	7	14	34	350	534	132.3	63
							8th	8	15	52				
							9th	9	16	46				

2nd NEW BALL TAKEN AT 5.21 pm 2nd DAY
- NEW ZEALAND 212-4 AFTER 85.1 OVERS

© BILL FRINDALL

STUMPS (1st DAY): 11-0 [4 OVERS / 19 MIN WRIGHT 2* / EDGAR 9*]

LUNCH: 77-1 [31 OVERS / 141 MIN WRIGHT 39*(94) / MD CROWE 3*(16)]

TEA: 164-1 [65 OVERS / 266 MIN WRIGHT 88*(246) / MD CROWE 37 (65)]

STUMPS (2nd DAY): 252-5 [132 OVERS / 531 MIN EDGAR 28*(84) / HADLEE 52*(120)] OFF 100 OVERS IN 410 MINUTES

LUNCH: 346-6 [132 OVERS / 531 MIN EDGAR 83*(245) / BRACEWELL 14*(54)]

NEW ZEALAND LED BY 152 RUNS

- ONLY THEIR FOURTH FIRST INNINGS LEAD IN ENGLAND.

14 OVERS 4 BALLS/HOUR
2.70 RUNS/OVER
45 RUNS/100 BALLS

WKT	PARTNERSHIP		RUNS	MINS
1st	Wright	Edgar	26*	71
		Howarth	26	27
2nd	Wright	MD Crowe	116	176
3rd	Wright	J.J. Crowe	1	3
4th	Wright	Coney	0	4
5th	Coney	Hadlee	49	65
6th	Hadlee	Edgar	86	118
7th	Edgar	Bracewell	44	55
8th	Edgar	Smith	3	5
9th	Edgar	Cairns	26	25
10th	Cairns	Chatfield	0	1
			377	

112 NEW ZEALAND IN ENGLAND 1983

ENGLAND 2ND INNINGS — 152 RUNS BEHIND ON FIRST INNINGS

IN	OUT	MINS	No.	BATSMAN	HOW OUT	BOWLER	RUNS	WKT	TOTAL	6s	4s	BALLS	NOTES ON DISMISSAL
2:28	3:23	55	1	G. FOWLER	c Smith	CHATFIELD	19	1	39	.	1	41	Pushed forward - not at pitch of ball 'leaving him'.
2:28	3:30	62	2	C.J. TAVARÉ	BOWLED	CHATFIELD	23	2	44	.	4	64	off stump - played half-back to length ball - kept low
3:25	1:48	270	3	D.I. GOWER	NOT OUT		112	.	.	.	14	196	(6th in TESTS: (22nd in FIRST-CLASS MATCHES: (15th in TEST in England: 1983)
3:32	5:10	78	4	A.J. LAMB	BOWLED	CONEY	28	3	116	.	3	71	off stump - misread in-swinger - aimed back-foot drive
5:12	5:18	6	5	I.T. BOTHAM	c Howarth	CONEY	4	4	126	.	1	3	Top-edged sweep at midwish leg-side ball - clear behind 'keeper
5:20	5:34	14	6	D.W. RANDALL	c Smith	CHATFIELD	16	5	142	.	3	16	Edged ball that lifted sharply.
5:36	5:38	2	7	P.H. EDMONDS	c Smith	CHATFIELD	0	6	142	.	.	4	Edged forward, push to 'keeper's right
5:39	11:40	68	8	G.R. DILLEY	c Smith	CHATFIELD	15	7	190	.	1	72	Top-edged cut.
11:42	12:24	42	9	R.W. TAYLOR†	BOWLED	CAIRNS	9	8	217	.	1	35	Pushed half-forward - beaten by in-swinger 'straightened'
12:25	12:26	1	10	R.G.D. WILLIS*	c Coney	CAIRNS	4	9	221	.	1	2	Edged to 2nd slip's left.
12:28	1:48	40	11	N.G. COWANS	c M.D. Crowe	CAIRNS	10	10	252	.	2	18	Edged in-swinger to forward short-leg.
				EXTRAS	b 8 lb 3 w 1 nb —		12						
				TOTAL	(87 OVERS; 327 MINUTES)		252					31	522 balls (0 no balls).

*CAPTAIN †WICKET-KEEPER

252 all out at 1:48 pm on 4th day.

BOWLER	O	M	R	W	HRS	OVERS	RUNS		RUNS	MINS	OVERS	LAST 50 (in mins)
HADLEE	26	9	45	0	1	17	43		50	67	18.2	67
CHATFIELD	29	5	95	5	2	16	51		100	127	35.3	60
CAIRNS	24	2	70	3	3	15	48		150	193	52	66
CONEY	8	1	30	2	4	17	47		200	262	71.1	69
			12		5	15	44		250	322	85.4	60
	87	17	252	10								

© BILL FRINDALL

2nd NEW BALL TAKEN AT 1:40 pm on 4th day
- ENGLAND 249-9 AFTER 85 OVERS

TEA: 55-2 [20 OVERS / 72 MIN]

STUMPS: 154-6 (3rd DAY) [54 OVERS / 199 MIN] GOWER 54*(141) DILLEY 1*(28)

LUNCH: 249-9 [85 OVERS / 319 MIN] GOWER 110*(262) COWANS 10*(32)
LEAD: 97 RUNS

GOWER 5s(15) LAMB 7*(8)

15 OVERS 5 BALLS/HOUR
2.90 RUNS/OVER
48 RUNS/100 BALLS

WKT	PARTNERSHIP		RUNS	MINS
1st	Fowler	Tavaré	39	55
2nd	Tavaré	Gower	5	5
3rd	Gower	Lamb	72	78
4th	Gower	Botham	10	6
5th	Gower	Randall	16	14
6th	Gower	Edmonds	0	2
7th	Gower	Dilley	48	68
8th	Gower	Taylor	27	42
9th	Gower	Willis	4	1
10th	Gower	Cowans	31	40
			252	

NEW ZEALAND IN ENGLAND 1983

NEW ZEALAND 2ND INNINGS — REQUIRING 101 RUNS OFF A MINIMUM OF 157 OVERS

IN	OUT	MINS	No.	BATSMAN	HOW OUT	BOWLER	RUNS	WKT TOTAL	6s	4s	BALLS	NOTES ON DISMISSAL
1·58	3·12	74	1	J.G. WRIGHT	C' RANDALL	WILLIS	26	3 60	·	3	45	Lofted drive to short extra cover.
1·58	2·20	22	2	B.A. EDGAR	C' EDMONDS	WILLIS	2	1 11	·	·	15	Cut short ball to gully.
2·22	2·44	22	3	G.P. HOWARTH*	C' RANDALL	WILLIS	20	2 42	·	4	20	Chest-high catch to mid-wicket.
2·46	3·16	30	4	M.D. CROWE	C' LAMB	WILLIS	1	4 61	·	·	13	Edged via pad to short square-leg.
3·14	3·50	36	5	J.J. CROWE	BOWLED	WILLIS	13	5 83	·	·	23	Middle stump out. WILLIS'S 300TH TEST WICKET
3·18	(4·46)	68	6	J.V. CONEY	NOT OUT		10		·	1	38	Made winning hit - boundary off Botham's first ball.
3·52	(4·46)	34	7	R.J. HADLEE	NOT OUT		6		·	·	22	
			8	J.G. BRACEWELL								
			9	I.D.S. SMITH †								
			10	B.L. CAIRNS								
			11	E.J. CHATFIELD								
				EXTRAS	b 8 lb 7	w - nb 10	25			$^4_8$	176 balls (including 13 no balls)	
				TOTAL (27·1 OVERS; 148 MINUTES)			103-5					

* CAPTAIN   † WICKET-KEEPER

© BILL FRINDALL

BOWLER	O	M	R	W	nb	HRS	OVERS	RUNS		RUNS	MINS	OVERS	LAST 50 (in mins)
WILLIS	14	5	35	5		1	11	48		50	67	12·5	67
COWANS	5	0	23	0	1	2	11	35		100	148	27·1	81
DILLEY	8	2	16	0	1								
BOTHAM	0·1	0	4	0	·								
			25										
	27·1	7	103	5									

11 OVERS   0 BALLS/HOUR
3·79 RUNS/OVER
59 RUNS/100 BALLS

WKT	PARTNERSHIP		RUNS	MINS
1st	Wright	Edgar	11	22
2nd	Wright	Howarth	31	22
3rd	Wright	MD Crowe	18	26
4th	MD Crowe	JJ Crowe	1	2
5th	JJ Crowe	Coney	22	32
6th	Coney	Hadlee	20*	34*
			103	

TEA: 97-5 [26 OVERS] CONEY 5* (62')
REQUIRING 4 RUNS [142 MIN] HADLEE 6* (28')

NEW ZEALAND WON BY 5 WICKETS
at 4.46 pm on the fourth day.
NEW ZEALAND'S FIRST VICTORY IN 29
TESTS IN ENGLAND, SECOND AGAINST
ENGLAND, AND FIRST WIN OUTSIDE
NEW ZEALAND SINCE NOVEMBER 1969

MAN OF THE MATCH: B.L. CAIRNS
(Adjudicator: T.W. Graveney)

ATTENDANCE: 36,050.   RECEIPTS: £150,000.

Third Test: Lord's, August 11, 12, 13, 15.
England won by 127 runs.
England, forced by injury to include three new caps (Smith, Foster, and Cook) for the first time since 1964, made the most of the luck that went their way on the first day of the third Test, and took a 2-1 lead in the series. They owed much to the Leicestershire pair, Gower, Man of the Match and the only century-maker on an awkward pitch, and Cook, who took 5 for 35 (8 for 125 in the match) after being withdrawn from his county's game at Chelmsford.

The issue was virtually decided on the first day, when England, put in on a pitch that was to help the faster bowlers throughout, with its variations in bounce, reached 279 for 5, Gower making an excellent century after being dropped off a very straightforward chance to Cairns at 21. Smith had gone to his first ball, sharing the fate experienced by the last Hampshire batsman to play for England, Johnny Arnold, also against New Zealand. Gower's efforts were followed by a remarkably assured attacking innings, considering the conditions, by Gatting, who reached his highest Test score before falling disappointingly on the second morning. England's last five wickets went down at that stage for 47.

New Zealand immediately had problems against Willis, but Edgar and Crowe played with sound judgement and no little courage to add 98 for the third wicket before Botham broke through, and then Cook, with a spell of 3 for 7, put England well in control.

Botham, maintaining his new-found aggression, polished off the New Zealand tail quickly on the third morning, the last four wickets going down for 15 runs. This gave England a lead of 135, important on a pitch that remained uneven in bounce, especially at the Nursery End, where the ball had several times gone through the top surface.

Smith followed his first innings failure with a gritty performance for 61 overs in which he showed a sound technique and admirable temperament. He held the innings together while his more experienced colleagues found various ways of getting out at the other end. Eventually it took an extremely awkward ball from Hadlee to remove him, but Botham followed his example and, playing with great discipline for some two hours, reached his first Test half-century since Adelaide the previous December. New Zealand were required to make 347, the highest score of the match.

The fourth morning started badly for them, with Howarth struck over the eye during net practice and needing seven stitches in the wound. He also had to rest, and it was surprising that he appeared first wicket down when Wright was adjudged caught behind off Botham, becoming Taylor's 150th victim in Test cricket. Almost immediately Howarth met a good ball from Willis, and once again Crowe and Edgar found themselves needing to play exceptionally well to keep their side afloat. As it happened, both fell during a hostile spell by Cowans, who exploited the variations in bounce at the Nursery End. This left New Zealand at 61 for 4.

Coney, however, batted with much expertise and no little courage, taking several blows on the body in an innings of 68 before becoming Foster's first victim in Test cricket. Willis, returning to remove Hadlee, ended the other main source of resistance and, appropriately, Cook's juggling catch to dismiss Chatfield completed England's victory.

NEW ZEALAND IN ENGLAND 1983

ENGLAND 1st INNINGS v. NEW ZEALAND (3RD TEST) at LORD'S, LONDON on 11, 12, 13, 15 AUGUST, 1983.
TOSS: NEW ZEALAND

IN	OUT	MINS	No.	BATSMAN	HOW OUT	BOWLER	RUNS	WKT	TOTAL	6s	4s	BALLS	NOTES ON DISMISSAL
11.00	3.05	205	1	C.J. TAVARÉ	BOWLED	CROWE	51	2	152	.	1	173	Yorked leg stump - Crowe's first Test wicket.
11.00	11.03	3	2	C.L. SMITH	LBW	HADLEE	0	1	3	.	.	1	Out 1st ball in Test cricket - breakback - back leg.
11.05	3.32	227	3	D.I. GOWER	LBW	CROWE	108	3	174	.	16	198	(7th in Tests) Ball 'straightened' and kept low.
3.07	4.14	49	4	A.J. LAMB	C SUB (J. CROWE)	CHATFIELD	17	4	191	.	2	44	Edged lifter high to 2nd slip - held above head.
3.34	11.12	141	5	M.W. GATTING	C WRIGHT	HADLEE	81	6	288	.	13	128	HS in TESTS. Pulled short offside ball - top edged skier to sq/leg.
4.16	4.54	38	6	I.T. BOTHAM	LBW	CAIRNS	8	5	218	.	1	29	Played back - ball kept low.
4.56	11.21	86	7	R.W. TAYLOR†	BOWLED	HADLEE	16	7	290	.	1	58	Off stump out - played across outswinger.
11.14	11.43	29	8	N.A. FOSTER	C SMITH	CAIRNS	10	8	303	.	1	25	Fast. Lifting ball flicked glove - 'walked'.
11.23	12.18	55	9	N.G.B. COOK	BOWLED	CHATFIELD	16	10	326	.	1	50	Played no stroke - off stump out.
11.45	12.05	20	10	R.G.D. WILLIS*	C SMITH	HADLEE	7	9	318	.	1	13	Edged 'unge' low to keeper's right - superb diving catch.
12.07	12.18	11	11	N.G. COWANS	NOT OUT		11					7	
				EXTRAS	b 3 lb 3	w 2 nb 3	⁺37						⁺726 balls (inc 3 no balls)
				TOTAL	(120.3 OVERS, 441 MIN)		326	ALL OUT at 12:18 pm 2ND DAY

* CAPTAIN † WICKET-KEEPER

16 OVERS 2 BALLS/HOUR
2.71 RUNS/OVER
45 RUNS/100 BALLS

BOWLER	O	M	R	W	NB/W	HRS	OVERS	RUNS	RUNS	MINS	OVERS	LAST 50 (in mins)
HADLEE	40	15	93	5	3/1	1	17	36	50	75	20.1	75
CAIRNS	23	8	65	1	.	2	17	44	100	145	41.1	70
CHATFIELD	36.3	8	116	2	.	3	17	49	150	204	57.3	59
CROWE	13	1	35	2	7/1	4	17	45	200	271	76	67
CONEY	8	7	6	0	.	5	15	46	250	324	89	53
						6	16	56	300	395	108.4	71
	120.3	39	326	10		7	16	36				

2ND NEW BALL TAKEN AT 5:21 pm 1st DAY -
ENGLAND 249-5 AFTER 88.2 OVERS

LUNCH: 80-1 TAVARÉ 21* (120')
GOWER 49* (115)
34 OVERS 120 MINUTES
TEA: 174-3 68 OVERS LAMB 8* (35 min.)
242 MIN GATTING 0* (8 min.)
STUMPS: 279-5 GATTING 74* (129 min.)
(1ST DAY) TAYLOR 12* (65 min.)
OFF 100 OVERS IN 363 MIN

UMPIRES: D.J. CONSTANT and D.G.L. EVANS

WKT	PARTNERSHIP		RUNS	MINS
1st	Tavaré	Smith	3	3
2nd	Tavaré	Gower	149	200
3rd	Gower	Lamb	22	25
4th	Lamb	Gatting	17	22
5th	Gatting	Botham	27	38
6th	Gatting	Taylor	70	77
7th	Taylor	Foster	2	7
8th	Foster	Cook	13	20
9th	Cook	Willis	15	20
10th	Cook	Cowans	8	11
			326	

© BILL FRINDALL

116 NEW ZEALAND IN ENGLAND 1983

NEW ZEALAND 1ST INNINGS IN REPLY TO ENGLAND'S 326 ALL OUT

IN	OUT	MINS	No.	BATSMAN	HOW OUT	BOWLER	RUNS	WKT TOTAL	6s	4s	BALLS	NOTES ON DISMISSAL
12:29	2:01	54	1	J.G.WRIGHT	C' LAMB	WILLIS	11	1	18	.	2	43	Viciously lifting ball lobbed off glove to gully.
12:29	5:25	238	2	B.A.EDGAR	C' WILLIS	COOK	70	4	159	.	8	189	Down pitch - mistimed lofted on-drive - comfortable mid on catch
2:03	2:54	51	3	G.P.HOWARTH*	BOWLED	COOK	25	2	49	.	1	39	Leg stump - missed cut - good length, middle stump ball
2:56	5:11	115	4	M.D.CROWE	BOWLED	BOTHAM	46	3	147	.	3	98	His 1st Test. Played back - beaten by ball that 'straightened'
5:13	6:01	48	5	J.V.CONEY	BOWLED	COOK	7	5	176	.	1	36	Played back - bowled between bat and pad.
5:27	11:28	73	6	E.J.GRAY	C' LAMB	BOTHAM	11	9	184	.	2	59	Fended lifting ball low to gully
6:03	6:04	1	7	J.G.BRACEWELL	C' GOWER	COOK	0	6	176	.	.	2	Edged via pad to silly mid-off.
6:06	11:02	8	8	R.J.HADLEE	C' BOTHAM	COOK	0	7	176	.	.	6	Edged off-drive waist-high to slip - pitched in rough.
11:04	11:18	14	9	B.L.CAIRNS	C' LAMB	BOTHAM	5	8	183	.	.	11	Drove long half-volley hard above cover's head.
11:20	11:42	22	10	I.D.S.SMITH†	C' LAMB	BOTHAM	3	10	191	.	.	18	Edged hook via his shoulder to gully.
11:30	(11:42)	12	11	E.J.CHATFIELD	NOT OUT		5	.	.	.	1	13	.
				EXTRAS	b - lb 5	w - nb 3	8					18* 514 balls (inc 6 no balls)

TOTAL (84.4 OVERS, 327 MIN.) 191 ALL OUT at 11:42 pm on 3RD DAY

(135 RUNS BEHIND)

*CAPTAIN †WICKET-KEEPER

BOWLER	O	M	R	W	nb	HRS	OVERS	RUNS
WILLIS	13	6	28	1		1	13	19
FOSTER	16	5	40	0		2	17	37
COWANS	9	1	30	0		3	17	52
BOTHAM	20.4	6	50	4		4	14	50
COOK	26	11	35	5		5	16	24
			8					
	84.4	29	191	10				

RUNS	MINS	OVERS	LAST 50 (in mins)
50	117	28.3	117
100	171	44.5	54
150	230	59.3	59

LUNCH: 12-0 WEIGHT 10*, EDGAR 1*
8 OVERS - 33 MINUTES

TEA: 78-2 [41 OVERS] EDGAR 24* (55')
[153 MIN] CROWE 14* (44')

STUMPS: 176-6 GRAY 10* (45 min.)
(2ND DAY) (150 BEHIND) HADLEE 0* (6 min)
73 OVERS 285 MIN

THIRD MORNING:
NEW ZEALAND lost their last 4 wickets
for 15 runs off 11.4 overs in 42 minutes

COOK - first England slow bowler to
take 5 wickets in an innings in a
HOME TEST since 1975 (Edmonds + Aus. at Leeds)

15 OVERS 3 BALLS/HOUR
2:26 RUNS/OVER
37 RUNS/100 BALLS

WKT	PARTNERSHIP		RUNS	MINS
1st	Wright	Edgar	18	54
2nd	Edgar	Howarth	31	51
3rd	Edgar	Crowe	98	115
4th	Edgar	Coney	12	12
5th	Coney	Gray	17	34
6th	Gray	Bracewell	0	1
7th	Gray	Hadlee	0	8
8th	Gray	Cairns	7	14
9th	Gray	Smith	1	8
10th	Smith	Chatfield	7	12
			191	

© BILL FRINDALL

NEW ZEALAND IN ENGLAND 1983

ENGLAND 2ND INNINGS — 135 RUNS AHEAD ON FIRST INNINGS

IN	OUT	MINS	No.	BATSMAN	HOW OUT	BOWLER	RUNS	WKT	TOTAL	6s	4s	BALLS	NOTES ON DISMISSAL
11·53	12:26	33	1	C.J. TAVARÉ	c CROWE	HADLEE	16	1	26	.	2	28	Pushed forward at shortish ball - bat/pad to silly point
11·53	4·17	204	2	C.L. SMITH	c CONEY	HADLEE	43	5	147	.	3	176	Viciously lifting ball lobbed off glove-shoulder to 2nd slip
12·28	2·11	64	3	D.I. GOWER	c CROWE	GRAY	34	2	79	.	5	67	Edged flick to mid-wicket via pad to forward short leg
2·13	2·26	13	4	A.J. LAMB	c HADLEE	GRAY	4	3	87	.	1	15	Edged backfoot defensive stroke to slip - lifting leg-break
2·27	3·17	50	5	M.W. GATTING	BOWLED	GRAY	15	4	119	.	2	50	Well down wicket - played across line
3·19	5·45	125	6	I.T. BOTHAM	c CONEY	CHATFIELD	61	7	199	.	7	101	Miscued big hit - skier to cover
4·19	5·27	68	7	R.W. TAYLOR†	c AND BOWLED	CONEY	7	6	195	.	1	41	Mistimed push to mid-wicker - leading edge - easy catch
5·29	11·12	42	8	N.A. FOSTER	c WRIGHT	HADLEE	3	9	210	.	.	35	Mistimed onside hit - gentle skier to mid-on
5·48	11·06	17	9	N.G.B. COOK	c BRACEWELL	CHATFIELD	5	8	208	.	1	15	Superb low catch at mid-on
11·08	(11·17)	9	10	R.G.D. WILLIS*	NOT OUT		2	.	.	.	.	5	HIS 50th 'NOT OUT' - WORLD TEST RECORD
11·14	11·17	3	11	N.G. COWANS	c SMITH	CHATFIELD	1	10	211	.	.	5	Offside edge to keeper - simple catch
				EXTRAS	b 5 lb 6	w 9 nb -	20				-6 22+	538	balls (inc. 1 no ball)
				TOTAL	(89·3 OVERS, 323 MIN.)		211	ALL OUT at 11·17 am on 4th day

*CAPTAIN †WICKET-KEEPER

16 OVERS 4 BALLS/HOUR
2.36 RUNS/OVER
39 RUNS/100 BALLS

BOWLER	O	M	R	W	nb	w	HRS	OVERS	RUNS		RUNS	MINS	OVERS	LAST 50 (in mins)
HADLEE	26	7	42	3	-	1/6	1	16	56		50	55	14.2	55
CHATFIELD	13·3	4	29	3	-	2	2	19	35		100	138	40.2	83
CAIRNS	3	0	9	0	-	3	3	18	41		150	215	63.2	77
BRACEWELL	11	4	29	0	-		4	17	42		200	300	83.5	85
GRAY	30	8	73	3	-	1/1	5	14	27					
CONEY	6	4	9	1					20					
	89·3	27	211	10										

LUNCH: 62-1 [19 OVERS / 68 MIN] SMITH 18* (68') / GOWER 23* (38')

TEA: 138-4 [56 OVERS / 188 MIN] SMITH 38* (188') / BOTHAM 15* (21')

STUMPS: 206-7 FOSTER 2* (31 min) / COOK 5* (12 min)
(3RD DAY) OFF 86 OVERS IN 307 MIN
ENGLAND LEAD BY 341 RUNS

4TH DAY :
ENGLAND LOST THEIR 3 WICKETS IN 16 MINUTES FOR 5 RUNS OFF 3.3 OVERS.
NEW ZEALAND REQUIRE 347 TO WIN

WKT	PARTNERSHIP		RUNS	MINS
1st	Tavaré	Smith	26	33
2nd	Smith	Gower	53	64
3rd	Smith	Lamb	8	13
4th	Smith	Gatting	32	50
5th	Smith	Botham	28	37
6th	Botham	Taylor	48	68
7th	Botham	Foster	4	16
8th	Foster	Cook	9	17
9th	Foster	Willis	2	4
10th	Willis	Cowans	1	3
			211	

© BILL FRINDALL

NEW ZEALAND 2ND INNINGS

REQUIRING 347 RUNS TO WIN IN A MINIMUM OF 186 OVERS

IN	OUT	MINS	No.	BATSMAN	HOW OUT	BOWLER	RUNS	WKT	TOTAL	6s	4s	BALLS	NOTES ON DISMISSAL
11-29	11-45	16	1	J.G. WRIGHT	C' TAYLOR	BOTHAM	12	1	15	·	3	15	Edged lifting outswinger – TAYLOR'S 150th CATCH
11-29	2-13	126	2	B.A. EDGAR	C' LAMB	COWANS	27	4	61	·	3	95	Fended viciously lifting ball to gully – little skier
11-47	12-00	13	3	G.P. HOWARTH*	C' TAYLOR	WILLIS	0	2	17	·	·	7	Ball reared from just short of a length – flicked gloves
12-02	2-02	82	4	M.D. CROWE	C' FOSTER	COWANS	12	3	57	·	1	55	Mistimed cut at short ball – skier to cover point (caught on run)
2-04	4-55	152	5	J.V. CONEY	C' GATTING	FOSTER	68	9	206	·	8	117	Top-edged hook at bouncer – gentle skier to square leg
2-15	2-55	40	6	E.J. GRAY	C' LAMB	COOK	17	5	108	·	1	33	Fended lifting leg break to silly point – gentle skier
2-57	3-34	37	7	R.J. HADLEE	BOWLED	WILLIS	30	6	154	·	5	36	Off stump out – misjudged line
3-36	3-43	7	8	J.G. BRACEWELL	LBW	WILLIS	4	7	158	·	1	6	Shuffled across stumps – late on stroke
3-45	4-35	30	9	B.L. CAIRNS	BOWLED	COOK	16	8	190	2	·	20	Hit across line of quicker 'arm' ball
4-37	5-12	35	10	I.D.S. SMITH †	NOT OUT		17			·	2	30	·
4-57	5-12	15	11	E.J. CHATFIELD	C' AND BOWLED	COOK	2	10	219	·	·	11	Held firmly struck cross-batted high catch at 2nd attempt
				EXTRAS	b 3 lb 4 w – nb 7		14					2⁶ 2⁴	425 balls (inc. 9 no balls)
				TOTAL	(69.2 OVERS; 286 MINUTES)		219		ALL OUT at 5:12 pm on 4th day				

*CAPTAIN †WICKET-KEEPER

14 OVERS 3 BALLS/HOUR
3.16 RUNS/OVER
52 RUNS/100 BALLS

	RUNS	MINS	OVERS	LAST 50 (in mins)
	50	108	24.2	108
	100	161	37.1	53
	150	202	49.2	41
	200	259	62	57

BOWLER	O	M	R	W	nb	HRS	OVERS	RUNS
WILLIS	12	5	24	3	9	1	11	34
BOTHAM	7	2	20	1	·	2	16	26
COWANS	11	1	36	2	·	3	16	53
COOK	27.2	9	90	3	·	4	14	68
FOSTER	12	0	35	1	·			
			14					
	69.2	17	219	10				

© BILL FRINDALL

LUNCH: 43-2 [20 OVERS] EDGAR 21* (93)
              [93 MIN] CROWE 3* (66)

TEA: 175-7 [55 OVERS] CONEY 51* (114)
            [231 MIN] CAIRNS 10* (13)

ENGLAND beat NEW ZEALAND
by 127 RUNS at 5:12 pm on 4th day

MAN OF THE MATCH: D.I. GOWER
(Adjudicator: A.R. LEWIS)

ATTENDANCE: 70,831. RECEIPTS: £344,050.

WKT	PARTNERSHIP		RUNS	MINS
1st	Wright	Edgar	15	16
2nd	Edgar	Howarth	2	13
3rd	Edgar	Crowe	40	82
4th	Edgar	Coney	4	9
5th	Coney	Gray	47	40
6th	Coney	Hadlee	46	37
7th	Coney	Bracewell	4	7
8th	Coney	Cairns	32	30
9th	Coney	Smith	16	18
10th	Smith	Chatfield	13	15
			219	

Fourth Test: Trent Bridge, August 25, 26, 27, 28, 29.
England won by 165 runs.
Despite opting to go into the match with only four recognized bowlers, England overcame an awkward start to triumph by the emphatic margin of 165 runs, thus winning the series by three matches to one. Nick Cook, with figures of 9 for 150, was the Man of the Match, but Ian Botham's first Test century for a year, made when his side were in trouble on the first day, was crucial to their success.

Botham and Randall took the New Zealand attack apart with a partnership of 186 in 32 overs, after the earlier batsmen had struggled on a slow but variable pitch. Gower's 72 was made in the face of considerable difficulties after he had ducked into a delivery from Hadlee, which struck his unprotected head. After a restrained start, Botham cut loose, making his second 50 from only 28 deliveries and facing only 103 in all. At one point, he and Randall scored at five an over, enabling England to total 362 for 7 on the first day.

Both sides had their problems on the second day, with Willis, twice warned for running on the pitch, facing a ban if he transgressed a third time. Cowans was alarmingly erratic, bearing in mind England's self-imposed shortage of bowling options. New Zealand reached three figures with only two men out, but five wickets fell in eleven overs, mostly to Cook, and with Martin Crowe nursing an injured wrist and batting lower down the order than usual, they were dismissed early on the third day, giving England a first innings lead of 213.

The follow-on was not enforced for a number of reasons, not least the fact that England's restricted attack could hardly have been expected to dismiss their opponents so cheaply a second time. By the close, the lead had been increased to 465 with two wickets still standing.

England's strong position led to a curiously undisciplined batting performance, with a number of players sacrificing the heaven-sent opportunity to play a lengthy innings under the minimum of pressure. But for Lamb's second century of the series, an unbeaten 137 made in 263 minutes, there was some danger, however slight, that they might have been dismissed extremely and unnecessarily cheaply.

On the fourth morning, England predictably batted on so that New Zealand were required to make an unattainable 511 for victory. Despite Edgar's steadfast innings of 76, they were facing defeat at the close with 167 for 5, and they went down boldly on the final day. Coney again played well for 68, and Hadlee, the Man of the Series, remained unbeaten eight short of becoming his side's first century-maker of the series.

ENGLAND 1st INNINGS v. NEW ZEALAND (4th TEST) at TRENT BRIDGE, NOTTINGHAM on 25,26,27,28,29 AUGUST, 1983. TOSS: ENGLAND

IN	OUT	MINS	No.	BATSMAN	HOW OUT	BOWLER	RUNS	WKT	TOTAL	6's	4's	BALLS	NOTES ON DISMISSAL
11.00	11.07	7	1	C.J. TAVARÉ	c' CAIRNS	SNEDDEN	4	1	5	.	.	7	Steered widish outswinger to 3rd slip - left-handed catch.
11.00	1.50	130	2	C.L. SMITH	c' HOWARTH	BRACEWELL	31	2	94	.	4	93	Edged. prod. at off break via pad to silly point.
11.09	2.27	158	3	D.I. GOWER	BOWLED	CAIRNS	72	3	136	.	9	141	Played across late outswinger - off stump out-yorked.
1.52	2.53	61	4	A.J. LAMB	c' HOWARTH	BRACEWELL	22	4	156	.	3	51	Edged push at off break via pad to silly point.
2.29	3.15	46	5	M.W. GATTING	LBW	BRACEWELL	14	5	169	.	1	44	Missed sweep at arm' ball.
2.55	5.51	156	6	I.T. BOTHAM	LBW	SNEDDEN	103	6	355	3	14	103	(12th Test). (23rd F.C.) (1st for 23 Test innings. Missed 'cow'shot.
3.17	6.03	146	7	D.W. RANDALL	c' EDGAR	HADLEE	83	7	356	.	11	115	Stepped back and flat-batted catch to cover.
5.53	12.30	113	8	R.W. TAYLOR†	BOWLED	BRACEWELL	21	9	407	.	1	93	Bowled through gate driving outside off break.
6.05	11.30	41	9	N.G.B. COOK	c' LEES	SNEDDEN	4	8	379	.	.	38	Edged grope at outswinger low to 'keeper.
11.33	(2.47)	74	10	R.G.D. WILLIS*	NOT OUT		25			.	2	52	His 51st 'not out' in Test cricket.
12.32	12.47	15	11	N.G. COWANS	c' BRACEWELL	CAIRNS	7	10	420	.	1	20	Drove to mid-on.
				EXTRAS	b 11 lb 14	w - nb 9	34				5b 44	757	balls (including 9 no balls)

* CAPTAIN † WICKET-KEEPER

TOTAL (off 124.4 overs in 483 min) 420 all out at 12.47 pm on 2nd day.

15 OVERS 3 BALLS/HOUR
3·37 RUNS/OVER
55 RUNS/100 BALLS

LUNCH: 88-1	30 OVERS 120 MIN	SMITH 31*(26') GOWER 41*(111')
TEA: 198-5	64 OVERS 240 MIN	BOTHAM 19*(45') RANDALL 14*(23')
STUMPS: 362-7 (1st DAY)	96 OVERS 376 MIN	TAYLOR 1*(23') COOK 4*(11')

ENGLAND added 58 runs off 28.4 overs in 107 minutes for their last 3 wickets on second day.

UMPIRES: H.D. BIRD and B.J. MEYER

WKT	PARTNERSHIP		RUNS	MINS
1st	Tavaré	Smith	5	7
2nd	Smith	Gower	89	121
3rd	Gower	Lamb	42	35
4th	Lamb	Gatting	20	24
5th	Gatting	Botham	13	20
6th	Botham	Randall	186	135
7th	Randall	Taylor	1	10
8th	Taylor	Cook	23	41
9th	Taylor	Willis	28	57
10th	Willis	Cowans	13	15
			420	

© BILL FRINDALL

BOWLER	O	M	R	W	nb	w	HRS	OVERS	RUNS	RUNS	MINS	OVERS	LAST 50 (in mins)
HADLEE	30	7	98	1			1	15	52	50	58	14.2	58
SNEDDEN	28	7	69	3	8		2	15	36	100	136	34.5	78
CAIRNS	33.4	9	77	2	-		3	18	59	150	187	49.2	51
BRACEWELL	28	5	108	4	-		4	16	51	200	246	65.2	59
CONEY	2	0	10	0	-		5	15	55	250	299	79	53
GRAY	3	0	24	0	1		6	12	102	300	325	83.5	26
			34				7	16	30	350	348	88.4	23
	124.4	28	420	10			8	16	28	400	455	115.4	107

2nd NEW BALL taken at 5.35 pm 1st day
- ENGLAND 312-5 after 86 overs.

NEW ZEALAND IN ENGLAND 1983

NEW ZEALAND 1st INNINGS

IN REPLY TO ENGLAND'S 420 ALL OUT

IN	OUT	MINS	No.	BATSMAN	HOW OUT	BOWLER	RUNS	WKT	TOTAL	6s	4s	BALLS	NOTES ON DISMISSAL
12.58	1.55	18	1	T.J. FRANKLIN	c SMITH	BOTHAM	2	1	4	·	·	18	Edged inswinger via pad to short square-leg - one-handed falling cat.
12.58	5.18	201	2	B.A. EDGAR	c GATTING	COOK	62	4	127	·	6	164	Turned off-break (LHB) to diving short mid-wicket.
1.57	3.33	96	3	G.P. HOWARTH*	c AND BOWLED	COOK	36	2	80	·	4	65	Mistimed on-drive - leg-break took outside edge.
3.35	5.09	74	4	J.V. CONEY	c GATTING	COOK	20	3	124	·	2	69	Drove to short mid-off.
5.11	5.25	14	5	E.J. GRAY	RUN OUT [BOTHAM / TAYLOR]		7	5	131	·	·	12	Called Hadlee for run to backward point.
5.20	5.39	19	6	R.J. HADLEE	c SMITH	COWANS	3	6	135	·	·	12	Fended lifting short ball to short square leg - easy catch.
5.27	5.51	24	7	W.K. LEES†	LBW	COOK	1	7	135	·	·	20	Padded up to 'arm ball'.
5.41	11.58	84	8	M.D. CROWE	c AND BOWLED	COOK	24	9	201	·	7	72	Mistimed on-drive - waist-high catch.
5.53	11.26	40	9	M.C. SNEDDEN	BOWLED	COWANS	9	8	157	·	·	34	Off stump out - late on stroke - full length, fast ball.
11.28	12.06	38	10	B.L. CAIRNS	c GOWER	COWANS	26	10	207	·	5	26	Mistimed on-drive - low mid-on catch taken falling forward.
12.02	(12.06)	4	11	J.G. BRACEWELL	NOT OUT		1			·	·	2	
				EXTRAS	b - 1 b 5	w - nb 1	6					-6 24	494 balls (including 2 no balls)
				TOTAL	(OFF 82 OVERS IN 316 MINUTES)		207		ALL OUT AT 12.06 pm on 3rd day.				

*CAPTAIN †WICKET-KEEPER

15 OVERS 3 BALLS/HOUR
2.52 RUNS/OVER
42 RUNS/100 BALLS

BOWLER	O	M	R	W	nb	w	HRS	OVERS	RUNS	RUNS	MINS	OVERS	LAST (in mins)
BOTHAM	14	4	33	1	-	-	1	14	38	50	74	17	74
WILLIS	10	2	23	0	1	-	2	15	42	100	143	37.2	69
COWANS	21	8	74	3	-	-	3	19	37	150	257	66.3	114
COOK	32	14	63	5	-	-	4	14	18	200	306	80.1	49
GATTING	5	2	8	0	-	-	5	16	52				
			6	1									
	82	30	207	10									

LUNCH: 1—0 (1 OVER, 3 MIN) FRANKLIN 1* FACING
TEA: 84-2 (31 OVERS / 124 MIN) EDGAR 44* (104) / CONEY 0* (61)
STUMPS: 135-7 (2nd DAY) (65 OVERS / 250 MIN) CROWE 0* (26) / SNEDDEN 0* (14)
285 BEHIND — 86 TO AVOID FOLLOW ON

WKT	PARTNERSHIP		RUNS	MINS
1st	Franklin	Edgar	4	18
2nd	Edgar	Howarth	76	96
3rd	Edgar	Coney	44	74
4th	Edgar	Gray	3	7
5th	Gray	Hadlee	4	5
6th	Hadlee	Lees	4	12
7th	Lees	Crowe	0	10
8th	Crowe	Snedden	22	40
9th	Crowe	Cairns	44	30
10th	Cairns	Bracewell	6	4
			207	

© BILL FRINDALL

ENGLAND 2ND INNINGS — 213 RUNS AHEAD ON FIRST INNINGS

IN	OUT	MINS	No.	BATSMAN	HOW OUT	BOWLER	RUNS	WKT	TOTAL	6s	4s	BALLS	NOTES ON DISMISSAL
12:18	1:55	57	1	C.J. TAVARÉ	C sub (J.J. Crowe)	BRACEWELL	13	2	58	.	.	59	Edged on-drive via pad to short square-leg.
12:18	12:23	5	2	C.L. SMITH	C' HOWARTH	SNEDDEN	4	1	5	.	1	3	Top-edged firm-footed cut at long-hop to 1st slip.
12:25	2:00	55	3	D.I. GOWER	C' CAIRNS	BRACEWELL	33	3	61	.	5	39	Edged leg-break (to LHB) via pad to silly-point-swing.
1:57	(12:40)	262	4	A.J. LAMB	NOT OUT		137			.	22	219	(5th in TEST) (33rd F.C.) 1000 RUNS in TEST. HS in TESTS
2:02	2:30	28	5	M.W. GATTING	C' LEES	CAIRNS	11	4	92	.	2	28	Edged firm-footed flat-bat drive at midwish long-hop.
2:32	3:37	65	6	I.T. BOTHAM	C' EDGAR	GRAY	27	5	149	.	4	70	Edged drive at midwish half-volley - low catch-th. 3rd man
3:39	4:47	48	7	D.W. RANDALL	BOWLED	HADLEE	13	6	188	.	1	37	Beaten by breakback - leg stump hit. (via pads)
4:49	4:51	2	8	R.W. TAYLOR†	BOWLED	HADLEE	0	7	188	.	.	2	off stump out - late on stroke - breakback. (via pads)
4:53	5:59	66	9	N.G.B. COOK	C' LEES	CAIRNS	26	8	252	.	3	61	HS in TESTS Bouncer hit glove as he ducked to avoid it.
12:00	12:36	36	10	R.G.D. WILLIS*	BOWLED	HADLEE	16	9	297	.	2	29	Hadlee's first delivery from round the wicket
12:37	12:40	3	11	N.G. COWANS	BOWLED	HADLEE	0	10	297	.	.	5	HADLEE'S 200th TEST WICKET 21 wkts in SERIES (RECORD)
				EXTRAS	b 6 lb 10 w 1 nb -		17				4	40	552 balls (0 no balls)
				TOTAL	(OFF 92 OVERS IN 321 MIN)		297		ALL OUT at 12:40pm on 4th day.				

*CAPTAIN †WICKET-KEEPER   © BILL FRINDALL

(510 AHEAD)

LUNCH: 45-1 [11 OVERS / 42 MIN.]   TAVARÉ 9* (42') GOWER 22* (35')

TEA: 151-5 [48 OVERS / 163 MIN.]   LAMB 43* (104') RANDALL 2* (21')

STUMPS: 252-8 80.1 OVERS LAMB 109* (221') 281 MIN (82 min, 17*)   LEAD: 465

BOWLER	O	M	R	W		HRS	OVERS	RUNS		RUNS	MINS	OVERS	LAST 50 (in mins)
HADLEE	28	5	85	4	1	16	58		50	51	13.4	51
SNEDDEN	8	1	40	1	.	2	18	57		100	104	30	53
BRACEWELL	21	2	88	2	.	3	18	54		150	163	47.5	59
CAIRNS	20	9	36	2	.	4	15	32		200	237	66.3	74
GRAY	15	4	31	1	.	5	19	76		250	278	79	41
	92	21	297	10									

2nd NEW BALL TAKEN at 12:15pm 4th day - ENGLAND 270-8 after 85 overs

17 OVERS 1 BALLS/HOUR
3.23 RUNS/OVER
54 RUNS/100 BALLS

WKT	PARTNERSHIP		RUNS	MINS
1st	Tavaré	Smith	5	5
2nd	Tavaré	Gower	53	55
3rd	Gower	Lamb	3	3
4th	Lamb	Gatting	31	28
5th	Lamb	Botham	57	65
6th	Lamb	Randall	39	48
7th	Lamb	Taylor	0	2
8th	Lamb	Cook	64	66
9th	Lamb	Willis	45	36
10th	Lamb	Cowans	0	3
			297	

NEW ZEALAND IN ENGLAND 1983   123

NEW ZEALAND 2ND INNINGS — REQUIRING 511 RUNS TO WIN FROM A MINIMUM OF 178 OVERS (2·87 PER OVER)

IN	OUT	MINS	No.	BATSMAN	HOW OUT	BOWLER	RUNS	6s	4s	BALLS	NOTES ON DISMISSAL
12:50	1:18	28	1	T.J. FRANKLIN	BOWLED	WILLIS	7	.	1	20	Played on — tried to evade ball angled in from edge of crease
12:50	6:18	268	2	B.A. EDGAR	c' GOWER	COOK	76	.	8	229	Edged via pad to silly point
1:20	3:29	89	3	G.P. HOWARTH*	c' TAVARÉ	COWANS	24	.	2	67	2000 RUNS (when 10") Top-edged square-slash to 1st slip
3:31	3:36	5	4	M.D. CROWE	c' TAYLOR	COWANS	0	.	3	3	Fast lifting ball hit glove — lifted from near a 'length'
3:37	12:34	277	5	J.V. CONEY	c' TAYLOR	COOK	68	.	7	218	Equalled HS v England. Under-edged cut
6:20	6:33	13	6	E.J. GRAY	c' GATTING	SMITH	3	.	.	14	Edged off break via pad to short square-leg
6:35	11:34	59	7	W.K. LEES †	c' LAMB	COWANS	7	.	.	53	Cut short ball low to gully's right — fine catch
11:36	(2:41)	144	8	R.J. HADLEE	NOT OUT	.	92	.	13	119	HS v ENGLAND
12:36	1:00	24	9	M.C. SNEDDEN	c' TAYLOR	COOK	12	.	2	24	Lifting off-break (LHB) hit gloves & pad — dropped behind stumps — sweeping Reid
1:41	2:02	21	10	B.L. CAIRNS	BOWLED	COOK	11	.	1	17	Missed vast heave — off stump
2:04	2:41	37	11	J.G. BRACEWELL	c' TAYLOR	SMITH	28	.	3	26	HS in Tests. Top-edged cut at off-break
				EXTRAS	b – lb 2 w 1 nb 14		17		1* 34	790 balls (inc 15 no balls)
				TOTAL	(OFF 129 OVERS IN 490 MIN)		345				all out at 2:41 pm on 5th day

*CAPTAIN   †WICKET-KEEPER

© BILL FRINDALL

BOWLER	O	M	R	W	HRS	OVERS	RUNS	MINS	OVERS	LAST 50 (in mins)
WILLIS	19	3	37	1	1	13	26	50	100	24·1	100
BOTHAM	25	4	73	0	2	15	38	100	181	44·3	81
COOK	50	22	87	4	3	16	32	150	262	70·5	81
COWANS	21	2	95	3	¾ 4	21	40	200	359	94·1	97
GATTING	2	1	5	0	5	16	30	250	422	111·1	63
SMITH	12	2	31	2	6	13	30	300	463	121	41
			17		7	17	53				
	129	34	345	10	8	14	84				

2ND NEW BALL TAKEN AT 11:03 ON 5TH DAY
– NEW ZEALAND 167-5 AFTER 85 OVERS

LUNCH: 27-1 [16 OVERS / 70 MIN]
TEA: 102-3 [48 OVERS / 190 MIN]
STUMPS: 167-5 [84 OVERS / 310 MIN] (4TH DAY)
LUNCH: 264-8 [114 OVERS / 430 MIN]

ENGLAND beat NEW ZEALAND by 165 RUNS at 2:41 pm on 5th day
ATTENDANCE 34,763   RECEIPTS: £161,300
MAN OF THE MATCH ($500): N.G.B. COOK
MAN OF THE SERIES (£1000): R.J. HADLEE
Adjudicator (both awards): J.C. LAKER

15 OVERS   4 BALLS/HOUR
            2·67 RUNS/OVER
            44   RUNS/100 BALLS

WKT	PARTNERSHIP		RUNS	MINS
1st	Franklin	Edgar	16	28
2nd	Edgar	Howarth	51	89
3rd	Edgar	Crowe	4	3
4th	Edgar	Coney	85	141
5th	Coney	Gray	5	13
6th	Coney	Lees	23	59
7th	Coney	Hadlee	44	58
8th	Hadlee	Snedden	36	24
9th	Hadlee	Cairns	26	21
10th	Hadlee	Bracewell	55	37
			345	

EDGAR 10* (70 min) / HOWARTH 3* (40 min)
EDGAR 46* (90 min) / CONEY 16* (63 min)
CONEY 46* (133 min) / LEES 2* (25 min)
HADLEE 52* (84 min) / NEEDING 247 16 MIN

Statistical Survey: England v New Zealand 1983 – England

England – Batting/Fielding

	M	I	NO	HS	Runs	Avge	100s	50s	6s	4s	Min	Balls	r/h	Ct	St
A.J. Lamb	4	8	2	137*	392	65.33	2	1	1	54	970	820	48	10	–
D.I. Gower	4	8	1	112*	404	57.71	2	1	–	55	910	753	54	6	–
C.J. Tavaré	4	8	0	109	330	41.25	1	2	–	31	1117	920	36	2	–
D.W. Randall	3	6	1	83	194	38.80	–	2	–	22	416	329	59	3	–
I.T. Botham	4	8	0	103	282	35.25	1	2	4	38	536	415	68	3	–
G. Fowler	2	4	0	105	134	33.50	1	–	–	9†	467	418	32	–	–
M.W. Gatting	2	4	1	81	121	30.25	–	1	1	17	265	250	48	4	–
P.H. Edmonds	2	4	0	43*	63	21.00	–	–	–	6	216	203	31	1	–
C.L. Smith	2	4	0	43	78	19.50	–	–	–	8	342	273	29	2	–
R.G.D. Willis	4	7	2	25*	67	13.40	–	–	–	7	187	137	49	4	–
N.G.B. Cook	2	4	0	26	51	12.75	–	–	–	5	179	164	31	3	–
R.W. Taylor	4	7	1	21	63	10.50	–	–	–	5	376	285	22	11	–
N.G. Cowans	4	7	1	10	22	3.66	–	–	1	2	85	67	33	–	–
Also batted:															
G.R. Dilley	1	2	0	15	15	7.50	–	–	–	1	70	75	20	1	–
N.A. Foster	1	2	0	10	13	6.50	–	–	–	1	71	60	22	1	–
V.J. Marks	1	2	0	4	6	3.00	–	–	–	–	40	27	22	–	–
Totals	44	85	9	(137*)	2235	29.40	7	8	7	261†	6247	5196	43	51	0

England – Bowling

	O	M	R	W	Avge	Best	5w/I	10w/M	b/w	r/h	NB	Wides
Willis	123.3	38	273	20	13.65	5-35	1	–	–	37	57	–
Cook	135.2	56	275	17	16.17	5-35	2	–	–	48	–	–
Botham	112.5	27	340	10	34.00	4-50	–	–	–	68	–	–
Cowans	125	25	447	12	37.25	3-74	–	–	–	63	6	2
Also bowled:												
Dilley	25	6	52	0	–	–	–	–	–	35	1	–
Edmonds	87.1	30	221	4	55.25	3-101	–	–	–	42	4	–
Foster	28	5	75	1	75.00	1-35	–	–	–	45	–	–
Gatting	7	3	13	0	–	–	–	–	–	31	–	–
Marks	43	20	78	3	26.00	3-78	–	–	–	30	–	–
Smith	12	2	31	2	15.50	2-31	–	–	–	43	–	–
Totals	698.5	212	1805	69	26.15	(5-35)	3	0	61	43	68	2

Statistical Survey: England v New Zealand 1983 – New Zealand

NZ – Batting/Fielding

	M	I	NO	HS	Runs	Avge	100s	50s	6s	4s	Min	Balls	r/h	Ct	St
R.J. Hadlee	4	8	2	92*	301	50.16	–	3	2	39+	609	445	73	1	–
B.A. Edgar	4	8	0	84	336	42.00	–	4	–	37	1274	975	34	2	–
J.G. Wright	3	6	0	93	230	38.33	–	2	–	32	668	517	44	2	–
J.V. Coney	4	8	1	68	238	34.00	–	2	–	24	796	610	39	7	–
G.P. Howarth	4	8	0	67	189	23.62	–	1	–	20	594	465	41	7	–
M.D. Crowe	4	8	0	46	163	20.37	–	–	–	19	639	512	32	5	–
B.L. Cairns	4	7	1	32	116	19.33	–	–	8	8	159	121	96	2	–
W.K. Lees	2	4	1	31*	47	15.66	–	–	–	6	175	152	31	4	–
I.D.S. Smith	2	3	1	17*	22	11.00	–	–	–	2	62	54	41	10	–
E.J. Gray	2	4	0	17	38	9.50	–	–	–	3	140	118	32	–	–
J.G. Bracewell	4	7	1	28	56	9.33	–	–	1	7	136	108	52	4	–
E.J. Chatfield	3	5	2	10*	17	5.66	–	–	–	3	51	38	45	–	–
J.J. Crowe	2	4	0	13	22	5.50	–	–	–	–	71	51	43	2	–
Also batted:															
T.J. Franklin	1	2	0	7	9	4.50	–	–	–	1	46	38	24	–	–
M.C. Snedden	1	2	0	12	21	10.50	–	–	–	2	64	58	36	–	–
Totals	44	84	9	(93)	1805	24.06	0	12	11	203†	5484	4262	43	46‡	0

NZ – Bowling

	O	M	R	W	Avge	Best	5w/I	10w/M	b/w	r/h	NB	Wides
Coney	63	26	115	5	23.00	2-21	–	–	76	30	1	1
Hadlee	232	65	559	21	26.61	6-53	2	–	66	40	7	11
Cairns	184	52	461	16	28.81	7-74	1	1	69	42	1	–
Bracewell	123	28	364	10	36.40	4-108	–	–	74	49	–	–
Chatfield	153	37	440	11	40.00	5-95	1	–	83	48	–	–
Also bowled:												
M.D. Crowe	21	1	58	2	29.00	2-35	–	–	63	46	1	1
Gray	48	12	128	4	32.00	3-73	–	–	72	44	–	–
Howarth	3	2	1	0	–	–	–	–	–	6	–	–
Snedden	36	8	109	4	27.25	3-69	–	–	54	50	8	–
Totals	863	231	2235	73	30.61	(7-74)	4	1	71	43	18	13

*not out. †plus one five. ‡plus 2 caught by substitute (J.J. Crowe). r/h = runs per 100 balls. 5w/I = 5 wickets in an innings. 10w/M = 10 wickets in a match. b/w = balls per wicket.

Statistical Highlights of Tests

1st Test, Kennington Oval. Willis became only the second specialist bowler after D.L. Underwood (86 caps) to play in 80 Tests. Gower became the first Leicestershire player to gain 50 England caps. R. Illingworth, 61 Tests, made 30 of his appearances during his first career with Yorkshire. Six of New Zealand's team (Bracewell, Chatfield, Coney, both Crowes, and Lees) made their first Test appearance in England after a collective 55 matches elsewhere. The first joint apperance of the Crowe brothers provided New Zealand's fourth such pairing after D.R. and R.J. Hadlee, G.P. and H.J. Howarth, and J.M. and N.M. Parker. Taylor, who celebrated his 42nd birthday on the fourth day, was England's oldest player since D.B. Close ended his international career at Old Trafford in 1976 at the age of 45 years 140 days. England's total of 209 was their lowest against New Zealand at The Oval and their third-lowest against them in England. Hadlee's analysis of 6-53 set a record for New Zealand in England, surpassing J. Cowie's 6-67 at Manchester in 1937. Wright's duck was only his second in 39 Test innings. The first was also inflicted by Willis, at Christchurch in February 1978. The partnership of 223 between Fowler and Tavaré was England's eleventh for the first wicket of 200 runs or more, their first since G. Boycott and D.L. Amiss put on 209 at Port-of-Spain in 1973-74, and their highest opening stand against New Zealand (beating 147 by L. Hutton and R.T. Simpson on the same ground in 1949). It was the ninth time that both of England's openers have scored hundreds in the same innings, the last instance being recorded by another left-handed Lancashire and right-handed Kent combination (G. Pullar and M.C. Cowdrey) against South Africa at The Oval in 1960. Fowler, Tavaré, and Lamb provided the first instance of three England batsmen scoring hundreds in the same innings since June 1974, when D.L. Amiss, M.H. Denness, and A.W. Greig achieved this feat against India at Lord's. All three batsmen were playing their first Test against New Zealand.

2nd Test, Headingley. New Zealand's first victory in 29 Tests and 52 years in England was their 16th against all countries, but only their fifth away from home, the last such success being against Pakistan at Lahore in November 1969. It was England's first defeat at Headingley since they lost to West Indies in 1976, and the first time in seven matches that Willis has captained a losing team in a home Test. However, during the match Willis became the fourth bowler after F.S. Trueman (307 wickets in 67 Tests), L.R. Gibbs (309 in 79) and D.K. Lillee (335 in 65) to claim 300 wickets in official Tests. His match figures of 9-92 were the best of his 81-match Test career. Cairns recorded his best analysis in 30 Tests, and became the first New Zealand bowler to take seven wickets against England. Only two other New Zealanders have taken seven wickets in a Test innings: B.R. Taylor, with 7-74 against West Indies at Bridgetown in 1971-72, and R.J. Hadlee, with 7-23 against India at Wellington in 1975-76. His match analysis of 10-144 was also Cairns's best in Test cricket. Chatfield took five wickets in a Test innings for the first time, but Hadlee failed to take a wicket for the first time in a Test in which he had bowled in both innings. Howarth won the toss for the seventh time in 15 Tests as New Zealand's captain, and for the seventh time opted to field first. New Zealand led England on first innings in England for only the fourth time in 29 Tests, the previous instances all occurring at Lord's – in 1949, 1973, and 1978.

3rd Test, Lord's. Lord's staged its 75th official Test match, equalling the record established in December 1982 by the Melbourne Cricket Ground. Taylor, who became the first Derbyshire player to appear in 50 Test matches, held his 150th catch. Willis became the first to be not out 50 times in Test cricket. Lamb equalled two England fielding records by holding four catches in an innings and six in the match. Coney took his Test aggregate past 1,000 runs during his first fifty against England. Botham became the first bowler from either country to take 50 wickets in Tests between England and New Zealand. The previous record of 48 was shared by D.L. Underwood and R.O. Collinge.

4th Test, Trent Bridge. Hadlee became the first bowler to take 200 Test wickets for New Zealand when he bowled Cowans in the second innings. He was not the first New Zealander to reach this landmark, as C.V. Grimmett, the first bowler to take 200 Test wickets (on 17 February 1936 for Australia), was born in Dunedin. Hadlee's total of 21 wickets set a New Zealand record for any series against England, beating 20 by A.R. MacGibbon in 1958.

Other Test career landmarks reached during this match involved **Randall** (2,000 runs), **Howarth** (2,000 runs), and **Lamb** (1,000 runs).

New Zealand in England 1983

Results: Played 13; Won 7, Lost 3, Drawn 3.

First-Class Averages

*not out

Batting and Fielding	M	I	NO	HS	R	Avge	100	50	Ct	St
M.D. Crowe	11	19	5	134*	819	58.50	3	3	13	–
R.J. Hadlee	8	11	2	92*	477	53.00	–	5	3	–
J.G. Wright	7	10	0	136	498	49.80	1	3	6	–
G.P. Howarth	11	18	1	144	697	41.00	1	5	12	–
B.A. Edgar	11	21	2	100	742	39.05	1	5	6	–
T.J. Franklin	9	18	3	98*	539	35.93	–	2	6	–
J.V. Coney	9	17	3	68	437	31.21	–	4	14	–
J.J. Crowe	11	19	2	79	470	27.64	–	3	13	–
W.K. Lees	6	9	4	42*	136	27.20	–	–	12	–
E.J. Gray	9	15	3	72	280	23.33	–	1	7	–
B.L. Cairns	11	14	2	60	254	21.16	–	1	6	–
M.C. Snedden	10	9	0	35	154	17.11	–	–	–	–
J.G. Bracewell	11	16	3	38	183	14.07	–	–	10	–
I.D.S. Smith	8	12	3	32*	104	11.55	–	–	19	2
E.J. Chatfield	9	8	4	13*	45	11.25	–	–	1	–

Also batted: S.R. Tracy (2 matches) 0, 4.

Hundreds (6)

3 M.D. Crowe: 134* v Middx (Lord's); 116* v Essex (Chelmsford); 110* v D.B. Close's XI (Scarborough).
1 B.A. Edgar: 100 v D.B. Close's XI (Scarborough).
  G.P. Howarth: 144 v Essex (Chelmsford).
  J.G. Wright: 136 v Glos (Bristol).

Bowling	O	M	R	W	Avge	Best	5w/I	10w/M
M.D. Crowe	76	12	284	12	23.66	3-21	–	–
R.J. Hadlee	345.1	95	855	36	23.75	6-53	2	–
J.V. Coney	124.5	40	339	14	24.21	3-19	–	–
E.J. Gray	143	40	398	16	24.87	4-24	–	–
J.G. Bracewell	325.5	73	1095	41	26.70	6-111	3	–
B.L. Cairns	341.1	101	877	32	27.40	7-46	2	1
M.C. Snedden	236.2	37	845	30	28.16	5-68	1	–
E.J. Chatfield	303.3	79	818	28	29.21	6-40	2	–

Also bowled: B.A. Edgar 5-0-17-1; G.P. Howarth 17-4-41-1; S.R. Tracy 33.1-5-115-8 (Best 5-29).

Bob Willis takes his 300th Test wicket by knocking out Jeff Crowe's middle stump in the second innings of the Headingley Test.

1

2

3

4

The Daily Telegraph Cricketers of the Year (see pages 15-16):

1 David Gower (England)
2 Imran Khan (Pakistan)
3 Geoff Lawson (Australia)
4 Jimmy Cook (South Africa)
5 Mohinder Amarnath (India)
6 Clive Lloyd (West Indies)
7 Richard Hadlee (New Zealand)
8 Duleep Mendis (Sri Lanka)

Winners of the Daily Telegraph 'Twin Hundreds' (see page 14): Steven O'Shaughnessy (left), who made his 100 in 35 minutes on the last day of the season; and John Emburey, first to 100 wickets and still an off-spinner of the highest class on all pitches and in all forms of cricket.

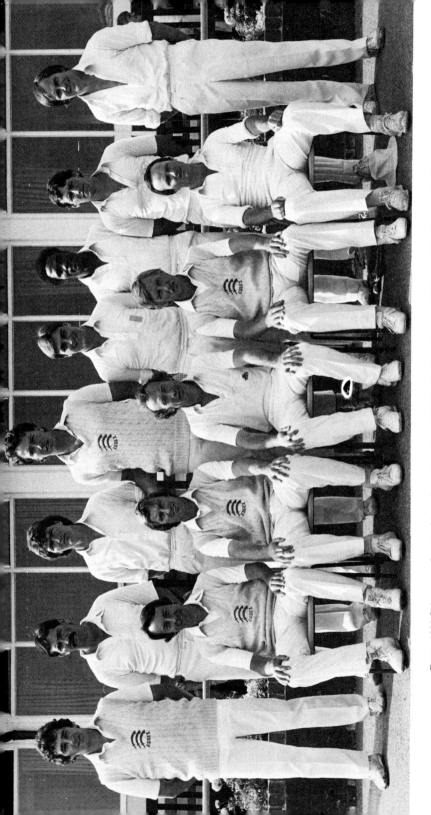

Essex, 1983 Schweppes County Champions. Standing: B.R. Hardie, G.A. Gooch, K.R. Pont, D.R. Pringle, C. Gladwin, N. Phillip, D.E. East, R.E. East. Seated: D.L. Acfield, J.K. Lever, K.W.R. Fletcher (captain), S. Turner, K.S. McEwan.

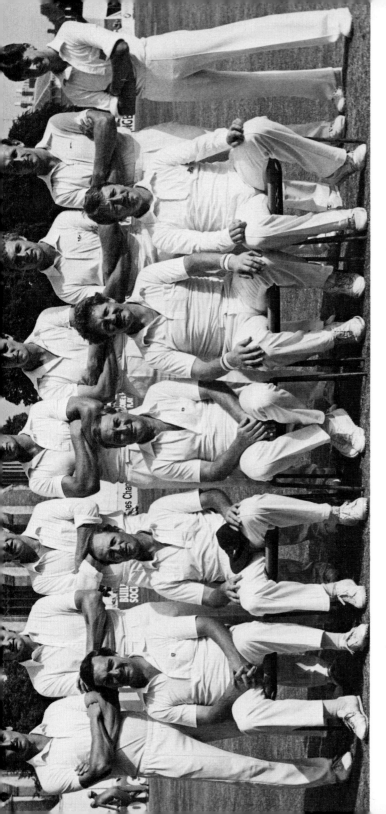

Yorkshire, 1983 John Player League winners. Standing: S.N. Hartley, M.D. Moxon, S.J. Dennis, N.S. Taylor, J.D. Love, K. Sharp, C.W.J. Athey, I.G. Swallow. Seated: P. Carrick, G. Boycott, R. Illingworth (captain), D.L. Bairstow, G.B. Stevenson.

The year's most disagreeable scene on a cricket field. Australia v England, First Test, Perth, November 1982. Terry Alderman lies on the ground with a shoulder injury suffered while he grappled with an intruder on the pitch. Allan Border and Dennis Lillee join in.

Tuesday 31st May

15p

MATCH BALLS: LAIDLAWS of BRENTWOOD.

WORLD CUP - AUSTRALIA v. INDIA - 20th JUNE, 1983
All reserved seats for the above Prudential World Cup match at Chelmsford are now sold, but there are unreserved seats available. These are priced at £1.80 (90p Juniors) for Members and £3.50 (£1.80 Juniors) for non-members.

BENSON & HEDGES CUP QUARTER FINAL - 1ST JUNE, 1983
In accordance with T.C.C.B. regulations members are required to pay the ground admission price of £3.50 (£1.80 for Pensioners and Juniors) and to avoid queueing on the day tickets may be purchased in advance.

PROMOTIONAL SHOPS
The Essex C.C.C. Yearbook (200 pages for £1.25), the Essex and the T.C.C.B. Prudential World Cup ties (each £4.50) and a wide variety of books and souvenirs are available from the shops on the ground.

MATCH DRAWN

B & H quarter final   TOSS WON BY: **SURREY**   (Essex to bat)   * Captain   + Wicketkeeper

SURREY	FIRST INNINGS		SECOND INNINGS	
1 A.R.BUTCHER	c EAST,D. b PHILLIP	2	c GOOCH b FOSTER	5
2 G.S.CLINTON	c EAST,D. b FOSTER	6	not out	61
3 A.NEEDHAM	b FOSTER	0	L.B.W. b PHILLIP	4
4 *R.D.V.KNIGHT	L.B.W. b PHILLIP	0	not out	101
5 M.A.LYNCH	L.B.W. b PHILLIP	0		
6 +C.J.RICHARDS	c TURNER b PHILLIP	0		
7 D.J.THOMAS	L.B.W. b FOSTER	0		
8 I.R.PAYNE	b PHILLIP	0		
9 S.T.CLARKE	b FOSTER	4		
10 G.MONKHOUSE	L.B.W. b PHILLIP	2		
11 P.I.POCOCK	not out	0		
Extras:	Byes.... Legbyes.... Wides.... No-Balls....		Byes 1 Legbyes 8 Wides 2 No-Balls 3	14
	TOTAL	**14**	**TOTAL**	**185**

FALL OF WICKETS

	FIRST INNINGS									SECOND INNINGS								
	1	2	3	4	5	6	7	8	9	1	2	3	4	5	6	7	8	9
	2	5	6	8	8	8	8	8	14	11	18							

FIRST INNINGS	O	M	R	W	SECOND INNINGS	O	M	R	W
PHILLIP	7.3	4	4	6	PHILLIP	13	2	39	1
FOSTER	7	3	10	4	FOSTER	13	2	33	1
					TURNER	7	3	16	0
					GOOCH	22	6	45	0
					ACFIELD	17	7	23	0
					EAST,R.	1	0	5	0
					PONT	5	1	10	0

Extract from the most remarkable score card of the year.

Kapil Dev, the Indian captain, during his brilliant innings of 175 not out against Zimbabwe at Tunbridge Wells. Having been 17 for 5, India recovered to win a vital Prudential Cup victory.

Almost there in the final! A delighted Yashpal Sharma dashes up to Kapil Dev who has just had Roberts lbw. West Indies are 126 for 9. Joel Garner turns sadly away.

Aftermath of victory. Syed Kirmani with the award made by Gordon's Gin to the best wicket-keeper in the 1983 Prudential Cup.

Left: Clive Radley, backbone of many a Middlesex innings in the last 20 years, batting during the Benson and Hedges final when his unbeaten 89 out of a total of 196 for 8 earned him the Gold Award.

Right: Robin Boyd-Moss of Cambridge, the first batsman to make a hundred in each innings of the University Match.

Below: Sir Donald Bradman, with last year's *Daily Telegraph Cricket Year Book* and two of its contributors, Bill Frindall (left) and Michael Carey.

England's newcomers: Neil Foster (left) in the third Test at Lord's. He retired for the season soon afterwards to have a metal plate removed from his back; Chris Smith (below), Hampshire's highly consistent opening batsman from South Africa, who qualified in 1983 to play for England and was first picked for the third Test at Lord's; Nick Cook (right), the young left-arm spinner who came in at Lord's, when Phil Edmonds injured himself in the car park, and took 17 wickets in the last two Tests.

A jubilant Ian Botham confirms his return to form. After his match-winning 98 not out for Somerset in the NatWest semi-final, he reaches a valuable and well played hundred in the final Test at Trent Bridge.

English season 1983

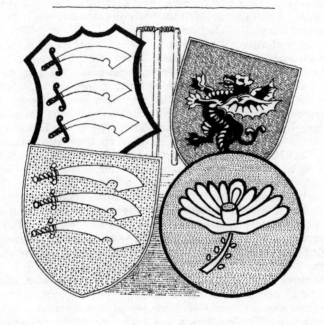

Schweppes County Championship

One of the closest fought county championships for some years ended in anticlimax and frustration in the rain of September, when Essex drew their last two matches to keep ahead of Middlesex by 16 points. Right up to the last day it was mathematically possible for Middlesex to win, but by then they were flagging and not making the same use of breaks in the rain as they might have done earlier.

At the end, there was no doubt that Essex were worthy winners, somewhat unexpectedly. At the start of the season, it was easy to dismiss them as a goodish side probably past their best, for they were still relying on nearly all the players who had won the championship for them in 1979. Graham Gooch and Ken McEwan were certainly still in their prime and, with Keith Fletcher, provided the basis of a side that was never likely to be bowled out easily. They now had a fine all-rounder in Derek Pringle available full time. With Stuart Turner, Norbert Phillip, and two seasoned spinners in Ray East and David Acfield, they had balance.

The difference between the seventh place of 1982 and the top was provided partly by the tremendous form of John Lever, who brushed aside the inconvenience of a nasty operation in mid-season and at 34 bowled better than ever, taking 106 wickets despite the lost matches. He was largely responsible for the regularity with which Essex bowled out opponents for 100 or less on the first morning. Even Middlesex mustered only 83 at Chelmsford, but they at least had the last laugh on a now benign pitch in the second innings when, starting 204 behind, they batted through the last 10 hours or so to make 634 for 7.

Another factor in Essex's success and a particularly encouraging one for the future was the introduction of highly promising young players in Neil Foster and Chris Gladwin and the continued progress of a very good young wicket-keeper, David East. Their amiable captain seemed fully entitled to say at the end of it all: 'We shall have an even stronger side next season.'

Yet until August, Essex were led by Middlesex, who, under their purposeful new captain, Mike Gatting, and his able deputy, John Emburey, nearly brought off what would have been an extraordinary performance. Whereas Essex lost only one player, Foster, for two matches while he was engaged in a Test match, Middlesex were at various times during the Prudential Cup and Test series without Gatting, Cowans, Edmonds, and Daniel, who missed between them a total of 31 championship matches. Every side has to find a few replacements during a season because of injuries, but when several more are absent it is hard to maintain form and confidence. To have won would have been a remarkable demonstration of reserve strength.

Middlesex played little cricket, if any, in their five home matches at Lord's in May, when Lord's was awash. And they won only one of their last nine, when bowling sides out became much harder. How, then, had they prospered to such an extent that in early August they still led Essex by 25 points with a match in hand?

They were lucky perhaps in June to find in different parts of the country pitches that took some spin – presumably pitches drying out on top after the inundations of May. Edmonds, only recently returned after a back problem, and Emburey swept through several sets of opponents, and four matches were won with a weakened side during the Prudential Cup.

The improvement of Neil Williams and the happy revival of Graham Barlow as an opening batsman played a big part, but as important as anything had been the speed with which Gatting and Butcher scored their runs, giving the bowlers extra time. Essex, of course, were succeeding in much the same admirable way, but in Middlesex's case it was not to last. Gatting went on attacking with marvellous consistency, but, after Butcher's awful blow in the face on July 18, had too much to do on his own. Nor was he always there.

Middlesex dug into their reserves, and in Andrew Miller, the third member of the 1983 Oxford side they had called on, they found a very useful opening batsman to deputize for Slack who, like Butcher, dropped out through injury. But the successful formula had been lost, and the lead was surrendered to Essex on August 23. Middlesex still had a match in hand, but that is a real asset only if rain spares it, which was not the case.

The pursuit of Essex and Middlesex was never very close. Hampshire finished third again, but were too badly hit by the absence of Greenidge, Marshall, and Jesty during the Prudential Cup to do better. It was in this period that they suffered their only two defeats, by Middlesex and Yorkshire. Leicestershire again looked nearly a championship-winning side. Warwickshire, bottom in 1982, were always just behind the leaders, profiting from the arrival of Gifford and Old to boost bowling that had seldom matched their batting. Northants, probably the strongest batting side, looked as if with one or two more bowlers they could beat anyone, and Kent's young side played as if they would soon be near the top.

And so, sadly, down to the bottom – and Yorkshire, heroes on Sundays, fairly friendless at other times. Never before had they finished lower than 14th.

They won just the one match, at Southampton, yet they lost only five, the same as champions Essex. They seldom seemed to be short of runs, but only Worcestershire earned fewer batting bonus points. They may have lacked the ability to bowl sides out twice, but so did other counties. The reasons for the indignity of 1983, which can scarcely include a dearth of talent, will doubtless be chewed over far into the winter.

Schweppes County Championship 1983 – Final Table

		P	W	L	D	1st Innings Points Batting	1st Innings Points Bowling	Total Points
1	ESSEX (7)	24	11	5	8	69	79	324
2	Middlesex (1)	23	11	4	8	60	72	308
3	Hampshire (3)	24	10	2	12	62	71	289
4	Leicestershire (2)	24	9	3	12	52	81	277
5	Warwickshire (17)	24	10	3	11	52	64	276
6	Northamptonshire (9)	24	7	4	13	63	77	252
7	Kent (13)	24	7	4	13	68	70	250
8	Surrey (5)	24	7	4	13	65	70	247
9	Derbyshire (11)	24	7	5	12	46	65	219
10	Somerset (6)	24	3	7	14	57	75	180
11	Sussex (8)	23	3	10	10	50	72	170
12	Gloucestershire (15)	23	3	8	12	56	61	165
	Lancashire (12)	24	3	4	17	56	61	165
14	Nottinghamshire (4)	24	3	10	11	39	62	149
15	Glamorgan (16)	24	2	10	12	45	64	141
16	Worcestershire (14)	24	2	11	11	43	54	129
17	Yorkshire (10)	23	1	5	17	45	64	125

1982 final positions are shown in brackets. The totals for Hampshire and Derbyshire include 12 points for winning a match reduced to one innings. The matches between Gloucestershire and Sussex at Gloucester and between Middlesex and Yorkshire at Lord's, both scheduled for 11, 12, 13 May, were abandoned without a ball being bowled and are excluded from the above table.

Points

For a win: 16 points, plus any first innings points. For winning a match reduced to a single innings because it started with less than eight hours of playing time remaining: 12 points. First innings points (awarded during the first 100 overs of each first innings and retained whatever the result of the match):

Batting		Bowling	
150 to 199 runs	1	3 or 4 wickets	1
200 to 249 runs	2	5 or 6 wickets	2
250 to 299 runs	3	7 or 8 wickets	3
300 runs and over	4	9 or 10 wickets	4

Final Positions 1890–1983

	D	E	Gm	Gs	H	K	La	Le	M	Nh	Nt	Sm	Sy	Sx	Wa	Wo	Y
1890	—	—	—	6	—	3	2	—	7	—	5	—	1	8	—	—	3
1891	—	—	—	9	—	5	2	—	3	—	4	5	1	7	—	—	8
1892	—	—	—	7	—	7	4	—	5	—	2	3	1	9	—	—	6
1893	—	—	—	9	—	4	2	—	3	—	6	8	5	7	—	—	1
1894	—	—	—	9	—	4	4	—	3	—	7	6	1	8	—	—	2
1895	5	9	—	4	10	14	2	12	6	—	12	8	1	11	6	—	3
1896	7	5	—	10	8	9	2	13	3	—	6	11	4	14	12	—	1
1897	14	3	—	5	9	12	1	13	8	—	10	11	2	6	7	—	4
1898	9	5	—	3	12	7	6	13	2	—	8	13	4	9	9	—	1
1899	15	6	—	9	10	8	4	13	2	—	10	13	1	5	7	12	3
1900	13	10	—	7	15	3	2	14	7	—	5	11	7	3	6	12	1
1901	15	10	—	14	7	7	3	12	2	—	9	12	6	4	5	11	1
1902	10	13	—	14	15	7	5	11	12	—	3	7	4	2	6	9	1
1903	12	8	—	13	14	8	4	14	1	—	5	10	11	2	7	6	3
1904	10	14	—	9	15	3	1	7	4	—	5	12	11	6	7	13	2
1905	14	12	—	8	16	6	2	5	11	13	10	15	4	3	7	8	1
1906	16	7	—	9	8	1	4	15	11	11	5	11	3	10	6	14	2
1907	16	7	—	10	12	8	6	11	5	15	1	14	4	13	9	2	2

ENGLISH SEASON 1983/COUNTY CHAMPIONSHIP

	D	E	Gm	Gs	H	K	La	Le	M	Nh	Nt	Sm	Sy	Sx	Wa	Wo	Y
1908	14	11	—	10	9	2	7	13	4	15	8	16	3	5	12	6	1
1909	15	14	—	16	8	1	2	13	6	7	10	11	5	4	12	8	3
1910	15	11	—	12	6	1	4	10	3	9	5	16	2	7	14	13	8
1911	14	6	—	12	11	2	4	15	3	10	8	16	5	13	1	9	7
1912	12	15	—	11	6	3	4	13	5	2	8	14	7	10	9	16	1
1913	13	15	—	9	10	1	8	14	6	4	5	16	3	7	11	12	2
1914	12	8	—	16	5	3	11	13	2	9	10	15	1	6	7	14	4
1919	9	14	—	8	7	2	5	9	13	12	3	5	4	11	15	—	1
1920	16	9	—	8	11	5	2	13	1	14	7	10	3	6	12	15	4
1921	12	15	17	7	6	4	5	11	1	13	8	10	2	9	16	14	3
1922	11	8	16	13	6	4	5	14	7	15	2	10	3	9	12	17	1
1923	10	13	16	11	7	5	3	14	8	17	2	9	4	6	12	15	1
1924	17	15	13	6	12	5	4	11	2	16	6	8	3	10	9	14	1
1925	14	7	17	10	9	5	3	12	6	11	4	15	2	13	8	16	1
1926	11	9	8	15	7	3	1	13	6	16	4	14	5	10	12	17	2
1927	5	8	15	12	13	4	1	7	9	16	2	14	6	10	11	17	3
1928	10	16	15	5	12	2	1	9	8	13	3	14	6	7	11	17	4
1929	7	12	17	4	11	8	2	9	6	13	1	15	10	4	14	16	2
1930	9	6	11	2	13	5	1	12	16	17	4	13	8	7	15	10	3
1931	7	10	15	2	12	3	6	16	11	17	5	13	8	4	9	14	1
1932	10	14	15	13	8	3	6	12	10	16	4	7	5	2	9	17	1
1933	6	4	16	10	14	3	5	17	12	13	8	11	9	2	7	15	1
1934	3	8	13	7	14	5	1	12	10	17	9	15	11	2	4	16	5
1935	2	9	13	15	16	10	4	6	3	17	5	14	11	7	8	12	1
1936	1	9	16	4	10	8	11	15	2	17	5	7	6	14	13	12	3
1937	3	6	7	4	14	12	9	16	2	17	10	13	8	5	11	15	1
1938	5	6	16	10	14	9	4	15	2	17	12	7	3	8	13	11	1
1939	9	4	13	3	15	5	6	17	2	16	12	14	8	10	11	7	1
1946	15	8	6	5	10	6	3	11	2	16	13	4	11	17	14	8	1
1947	5	11	9	2	16	4	3	14	1	17	11	11	6	9	15	7	7
1948	6	13	1	8	9	15	5	11	3	17	14	12	2	16	7	10	4
1949	15	9	8	7	16	13	11	17	1	6	11	9	5	13	4	3	1
1950	5	17	11	7	12	9	1	16	14	10	15	7	1	13	4	6	3
1951	11	8	5	12	9	16	3	15	7	13	17	14	6	10	1	4	2
1952	4	10	7	9	12	15	3	6	5	8	16	17	1	13	10	14	2
1953	6	12	10	6	14	16	3	3	5	11	8	17	1	2	9	15	12
1954	3	15	4	13	14	11	10	16	7	7	5	17	1	9	6	11	2
1955	8	14	16	12	3	13	9	6	5	7	11	17	1	4	9	15	2
1956	12	11	13	3	6	16	2	17	5	4	8	15	1	9	14	9	7
1957	4	5	9	12	13	14	6	17	7	2	15	8	1	9	11	16	3
1958	5	6	15	14	2	8	7	12	10	4	17	3	1	13	16	9	11
1959	7	9	6	2	8	13	5	16	10	11	17	12	3	15	4	14	1
1960	5	6	11	8	12	10	2	17	3	9	16	14	7	4	15	13	1
1961	7	6	14	5	1	11	13	9	3	16	17	10	15	8	12	4	2
1962	7	9	14	4	10	11	16	17	13	8	15	6	5	12	3	2	1
1963	17	12	2	8	10	13	15	16	6	7	9	3	11	4	4	14	1
1964	12	10	11	17	12	7	14	16	6	3	15	8	4	9	2	1	5
1965	9	15	3	10	12	5	13	14	6	2	17	7	8	16	11	1	4
1966	9	16	14	15	11	4	12	8	12	5	17	3	7	10	6	2	1
1967	6	15	14	17	12	2	11	3	7	9	16	8	4	13	10	5	1
1968	8	14	3	16	5	2	6	9	10	13	4	12	15	17	11	7	1
1969	16	6	1	2	5	10	15	14	11	9	8	17	3	7	4	12	13
1970	7	12	2	17	10	1	3	15	16	14	11	13	5	9	7	6	4
1971	17	10	16	8	9	4	3	5	6	14	12	7	1	11	2	15	13
1972	17	5	13	3	9	2	15	6	8	4	14	11	12	16	1	7	10
1973	16	8	11	5	1	4	12	9	13	3	17	10	2	15	7	6	14
1974	17	12	16	14	2	10	8	4	6	3	15	5	7	13	9	1	11
1975	15	7	9	16	3	5	4	1	11	8	13	12	6	17	14	10	2
1976	15	6	17	3	12	14	16	4	1	2	13	7	9	10	5	11	8
1977	7	6	14	3	11	1	16	5	1	9	17	4	14	8	10	13	12
1978	14	2	13	10	8	1	12	6	3	17	7	5	16	9	11	15	4
1979	16	1	17	10	12	5	13	6	14	11	9	8	3	4	15	2	7
1980	9	8	13	7	17	16	15	9	1	12	3	5	2	4	14	11	6
1981	12	5	14	13	7	9	16	8	4	15	1	3	6	2	17	11	10
1982	11	7	16	15	3	13	12	2	1	9	4	6	5	8	17	14	10
1983	9	1	15	12	3	7	12	4	2	6	14	10	8	11	5	16	17

Derbyshire

In any circumstances, Derbyshire's improvement by two places to ninth in the Championship and by six places to sixth in the John Player League is cause for some modest satisfaction. When these advances are considered against the backdrop of upheaval, controversy, and injury that afflicted the county during the 1983 season, they represent a very considerable achievement indeed for Kim Barnett, the youngest captain in their history, and a side frequently compelled to rely heavily on inexperienced players.

Derbyshire's decision to appoint Barnett to the captaincy at the age of 22 was a bold step. It was rewarded more prosperously than could have been anticipated, with seven Championship victories under his positive and resourceful leadership.

Only once in twenty seasons had they done better – eight wins in 1966 – and such a level of achievement could hardly have been suspected when Derbyshire lost three consecutive matches by heavy margins immediately after Barry Wood's peremptory and ill-timed resignation from the captaincy in May. With Wood and his employers involved in an unseemly display of mutual disaffection, there was a real danger of damage to morale within the club. But Barnett combined toughness with diplomacy, and found the ideal response in a string of successes during late June and early July, including a first Championship victory over Yorkshire since 1957.

With John Wright away on patriotic duties with New Zealand and Peter Kirsten remaining in South Africa to pursue business interests, most Derbyshire supporters were resigned to a season of modest attainment. The prolonged absence through injuries of John Hampshire, Geoff Miller, and Paul Newman exacerbated the difficulties, and Derbyshire must have felt the fates were conspiring unfairly when Michael Holding, whose registration had been delayed by the TCCB, was injured by fans who invaded the Lord's pitch at the end of the Prudential World Cup final.

Happily, the youngsters responded splendidly, and the advances made by Roger Finney, Bill Fowler, and John Morris were as much a cause for optimism as the success of Barnett, Iain Anderson, and Alan Hill, all of whom recorded career-best run aggregates.

The most outstanding success, however, was the least likely. The Dane, Ole Mortensen, registered as an 'honorary Englishman' thanks to Common Market regulations, was expected to be given a few senior appearances late in the season after 'learning his trade' in Second XI cricket. In the event, injuries accelerated his promotion, and he made an immediate impact with the ball – accurate, hostile, and unflagging despite suffering from sore shins much of the time. He took five wickets or more in an innings three times, and ended with 84 victims in all cricket, 66 of them in Championship matches at under 25 apiece.

Less encouraging was the contribution of the spin department, with Geoff Miller again inhibited by back problems and Dallas Moir, who took 75 first-class wickets the previous season, undergoing a crisis of form and confidence. Nonetheless, 1983 was a good season for Derbyshire and offered much to suggest better may lie ahead.

Schweppes County Championship: 9th; Won 7, Lost 5, Drawn 12
All First-Class Matches: Won 7, Lost 5, Drawn 12
NatWest Bank Trophy: Lost to Middlesex in 2nd round
Benson & Hedges Cup: Failed to qualify for Q-F (4th in Group B)
John Player League: 6th; Won 7, Lost 5, No result 4

Championship Averages   *not out

Batting and Fielding	M	I	NO	HS	R	Avge	100	50	Ct	St
K.J. Barnett	24	40	3	121	1423	38.45	3	9	13	-
A. Hill	24	40	5	137*	1311	37.45	4	6	3	-
I.S. Anderson	21	37	4	112	1233	37.36	1	9	23	-
G. Miller	21	30	7	84	699	30.39	-	4	13	-
J.H. Hampshire	14	19	2	84	485	28.52	-	3	5	-
W.P. Fowler	17	26	2	91	591	24.62	-	5	8	-
M.A. Holding	6	5	1	63	90	22.50	-	1	2	-
J.E. Morris	10	20	1	58	361	19.00	-	1	4	-
C.J. Tunnicliffe	17	25	0	91	461	18.44	-	2	3	-
R.W. Taylor	16	21	6	41*	267	17.80	-	-	37	2
R.J. Finney	20	35	2	71	578	17.51	-	3	4	-
B.J.M. Maher	8	12	2	52	150	15.00	-	1	13	3
S. Oldham	15	17	4	39	177	13.61	-	-	3	-
D.G. Moir	17	21	3	53	224	12.44	-	1	14	-
O.H. Mortensen	18	23	15	14*	76	9.50	-	-	5	-
P.G. Newman	7	5	0	12	14	2.80	-	-	3	-

Also batted: A. Watts (2 matches) 6, 33*; B. Wood (3) 18, 4; J.G. Wright (4) 60, 6, 41.

Hundreds (8)

4 A. Hill: 137* v Worcs, Derby; 121 v Warwicks, Birmingham; 106 v Lancs, Blackpool; 111 v Surrey, Oval.
3 K.J. Barnett: 103 v Northants, Derby; 106 v Kent, Chesterfield; 121 v Surrey, Oval.
1 I.S. Anderson: 112 v Kent, Chesterfield.

Bowling	O	M	R	W	Avge	Best	5w/I	10w/M
M.A. Holding	169	41	451	21	21.47	5-48	3	-
O.H. Mortensen	518.3	108	1605	66	24.31	6-27	3	1
R.J. Finney	281.5	43	970	30	32.33	5-58	1	-
G. Miller	492.5	132	1278	37	34.54	5-71	2	-
D.G. Moir	462.5	121	1385	40	34.62	5-44	2	-
C.J. Tunnicliffe	428.4	94	1372	39	35.17	4-30	-	-
S. Oldham	387.2	85	1120	31	36.12	4-56	-	-

Also bowled: I.S. Anderson 28-4-146-1; K.J. Barnett 3-0-13-0; W.P. Fowler 60-13-214-2; J.H. Hampshire 2-0-4-0; A. Hill 6.2-3-15-0; J.E. Morris 2-2-0-0; P.G. Newman 88.5-20-321-7; A. Watts 22-4-87-1; B. Wood 20-4-74-0.

Essex

Essex, champions after a three-years break, would be the first to admit that there was an element of ill-luck in the failure of Middlesex, their only realistic rivals, to retain the Schweppes Championship. But to stress this point would be to deny due credit to Essex for a worthy triumph. They and no other side in the Championship had the balance, flair, depth of talent, experience, and leadership to close the gap between themselves and Middlesex – a gap that, just before the competition reached its half-way mark, was 54 points.

At the end of May, Essex were among nine counties without a win. They were 10th in the table, but they had built up such a tidy balance of bonus points that their first win on June 7 sent them soaring to third place. Having broken the ice, Essex won five of their next six matches.

Essex's supporters, whose numbers swelled as their challenge gathered momentum, will remember 1983 not only for victory in the Championship but as the great season of Ken McEwan, the only batsman in the country to top the 2,000 runs mark. Gooch, by his own standards, had a moderate season, with the first of his two centuries delayed until mid-August. But McEwan's rich form compensated, and his panache was the main source of Essex's abundant crop of batting points, which proved so crucial at the end, with Essex and Middlesex equal on wins.

While McEwan's brilliance was the centrepiece of Essex's batting, Keith Fletcher too was a consistent scorer, his skill and footwork untarnished by his 39 years. An indication of Essex's batting strength was the fact that Keith Point got few opportunities.

There were, of course, occasions when the main batting broke down. Runs invariably came then from the lower order. David East, the wicket-keeper, usually had a major hand in these rescue operations. After only his second full season, East ranked high among the country's young wicket-keepers.

Essex's bowling matched the batting for depth. Despite a serious illness in mid-season, which called for an emergency operation, John Lever was (jointly with Derek Underwood) the season's highest wicket-taker (106). With Neil Foster coming into bloom, Norbert Phillip no longer commanded a regular place. Yet he finished the season with 69 wickets, playing a major role during the run-in. In a hot, dry summer, Acfield was also a principal wicket-taker.

Derek Pringle's all-round abilities were often to the fore, but Stewart Turner, 40, and Ray East performed below par. At the end of the season, East announced that he was retiring from first-class cricket, leaving the county scene the poorer for the loss of one of its few spinners, and depriving it of one of its richest characters. The great paradox of Essex's season was their dismissal of Surrey, at Chelmsford, for a mere 14 runs, the smallest total since 1907, and later being at the receiving end of Middlesex's gigantic total of 634 for 7.

ENGLISH SEASON 1983/ESSEX

Schweppes County Championship: 1st; Won 11, Lost 5, Drawn 8
All First-Class Matches: Won 11, Lost 6, Drawn 9
NatWest Bank Trophy: Lost to Kent in 2nd round
Benson & Hedges Cup: Lost to Middlesex in final
John Player League: 6th; Won 7, Lost 5, No result 4

Championship Averages

*not out

Batting and Fielding	M	I	NO	HS	R	Avge	100	50	Ct	St
K.S. McEwan	24	35	5	189*	2051	68.36	8	7	18	-
G.A. Gooch	24	35	1	111	1227	36.08	3	6	33	-
K.W.R. Fletcher	24	34	3	151*	1026	33.09	2	5	15	-
K.R. Pont	19	23	3	125*	658	32.90	2	3	3	-
D.R. Pringle	16	20	4	102*	503	31.43	1	1	2	-
C. Gladwin	8	12	0	61	375	31.25	-	1	3	-
B.R. Hardie	23	34	2	69	896	28.00	-	6	28	-
D.E. East	24	29	4	91	565	22.60	-	3	60	5
N.A. Foster	12	14	4	40*	219	21.90	-	-	5	-
R.E. East	19	24	4	80*	355	17.75	-	1	9	-
N. Phillip	18	24	0	80	406	16.91	-	1	7	-
J.K. Lever	17	16	3	44	207	15.92	-	-	7	-
S. Turner	14	18	2	30	161	10.06	-	-	5	-
D.L. Acfield	21	21	12	16	66	7.33	-	-	6	-

Also batted: A.W. Lilley (1 match) 2, 61 (1 ct).

Hundreds (16)

8 **K.S. McEwan:** 107 v Glam, Cardiff; 151 v Leics, Leicester; 142 v Kent, Tunbridge Wells; 178 v Derbys, Derby; 142 v Hants, Southend; 104 v Glam, Southend; 181 v Glos, Colchester; 189* v Worcs, Colchester.

3 **G.A. Gooch:** 110 v Leics, Chelmsford; 103 v Worcs, Chelmsford; 111 v Yorks, Chelmsford.

2 **K.W.R. Fletcher:** 151* v Glam, Cardiff; 110 v Surrey, Chelmsford.

K.R. Pont: 105 v Kent, Chelmsford; 125* v Glam, Southend.

1 **D.R. Pringle:** 102* v Hants, Southend.

Bowling	O	M	R	W	Avge	Best	5w/I	10w/M
J.K. Lever	541	127	1647	98	16.80	7-55	7	3
N. Phillip	454.2	84	1338	68	19.67	6-4	5	-
D.R. Pringle	267.4	47	872	40	21.80	7-32	2	-
N.A. Foster	389	73	1141	51	22.37	6-46	1	-
S. Turner	260	69	583	24	24.29	5-30	1	-
D.L. Acfield	482.1	132	1201	43	27.93	7-100	2	1
R.E. East	292.2	80	777	22	35.31	5-45	1	-

Also bowled: K.W.R. Fletcher 8.3-0-57-0; C. Gladwin 3-0-11-0; G.A. Gooch 187-37-514-8; K.S. McEwan 7-0-28-1; K.R. Pont 56-15-134-4.

Hat-trick: N. Phillip v Northants, Wellingborough.

Glamorgan

Glamorgan won one more Schweppes County Championship match than in 1982, finishing one place higher at 15th. Early on, for a couple of heady weeks, they led the John Player League. But for the most part they had a dismal season. Five successive defeats in Sunday League games in June and July ended their ambitions in that quarter, and they made swift exits from the Benson & Hedges and NatWest competitions. Their new captain, Mike Selvey, found himself struggling with batting that was frequently brittle and bowling that lacked penetration, and it is difficult to see how in the short term things can greatly alter.

Alan Jones completed his 1,000 runs for the 23rd consecutive time, but could not be expected to provide the solidity or the impetus of his prime years. Hopkins had an uneven season, at times batting with power and freedom but too often falling for low scores. A.L. Jones passed 1,000 runs for the first time, a feat long overdue, and batted capably in John Player League matches. Francis, though improving late in the season, was not helped by being moved up and down the order, and was a little disappointing after his improvement in 1982. The best of the batsmen was Ontong, who showed character and power of stroke and enjoyed his best season. Henderson, this year's Cambridge captain, played at least one significant innings and should benefit from the advice of Alan Jones, who will be coach in 1984, on ways of tightening up his technique.

The problems facing Glamorgan on the bowling front were highlighted by their need to play Winston Davis, as the only man who looked like bowling a side out, even though this meant leaving out Javed Miandad, a player of world class and far and away their best batsman. Though Davis was at times fast and hostile, his effectiveness was limited by his propensity for no-balls, of which he delivered over 250 in first-class games. Selvey, though he bowled as ever with intelligence and persistence, was rarely destructive, and Wilkins had a wretched season on returning to his native county from Gloucestershire.

Lack of penetration early in their opponents' innings put additional strain on the spin bowlers. Ontong, forsaking seam for off-spin during the season, showed potential, but he is learning a new trade and was not surprisingly a little expensive. Rowe also bowled a fair amount, but was rarely effective and paid a high price for his wickets. Lloyd, for some years Glamorgan's front-line spinner, rarely commanded a place in Championship matches, though he bowled with his usual economy in the Sunday League.

On a brighter note, Davies kept wicket efficiently and batted usefully. Selvey's positive attitude kept morale high, even in adversity. And if the self-belief that brought a Championship and John Player League double over the powerful Surrey side in August could be more regularly shown, the county's immediate future need not be bleak.

ENGLISH SEASON 1983/GLAMORGAN

Schweppes County Championship: 15th; Won 2, Lost 10, Drawn 12
All First-Class Matches: Won 2, Lost 10, Drawn 14
NatWest Bank Trophy: Lost to Hampshire in 2nd round
Benson & Hedges Cup: Failed to qualify for Q-F (3rd in Group D)
John Player League: 10th; Won 6, Lost 8, No result 2

Championship Averages   *not out

Batting and Fielding	M	I	NO	HS	R	Avge	100	50	Ct	St
R.C. Ontong	24	42	8	112	1259	37.02	3	6	12	-
A.L. Jones	22	39	7	99	1034	32.31	-	8	16	-
A. Jones	20	36	2	105	1020	30.00	1	5	6	-
S.P. Henderson	10	16	2	135*	411	29.35	1	1	6	-
G.C. Holmes	3	6	2	46	116	29.00	-	-	1	-
J.A. Hopkins	23	42	2	116	1087	27.17	2	3	16	-
D.A. Francis	22	39	5	89*	903	26.55	-	4	6	-
J. Derrick	4	4	2	24*	48	24.00	-	-	3	-
T. Davies	11	15	4	69*	260	23.63	-	2	18	2
C.J.C. Rowe	20	32	2	82	682	22.73	-	3	8	-
H. Morris	8	14	3	34	228	20.72	-	-	7	-
E.W. Jones	13	18	5	39	256	19.69	-	-	22	1
Javed Miandad	4	6	0	89	114	19.00	-	1	4	-
A.H. Wilkins	13	15	3	54	185	15.41	-	1	3	-
W.W. Davis	15	18	9	39*	135	15.00	-	-	4	-
B.J. Lloyd	12	12	2	38	135	13.50	-	-	3	-
J.G. Thomas	7	9	1	23	96	12.00	-	-	1	-
M.W.W. Selvey	22	24	3	63	250	11.90	-	1	5	-
S.R. Barwick	7	7	4	22*	31	10.33	-	-	1	-

Also batted: M.A. Nash (4 matches) 27*, 2 (2 ct).

Hundreds (7)

3 R.C. Ontong: 112 v Yorks, Middlesbrough; 109 v Surrey, Swansea; 105* v Kent, Cardiff.
2 J.A. Hopkins: 116 v Glos, Swansea; 109* v Derbys, Swansea.
1 S.P. Henderson: 135* v Warwicks, Birmingham.
  A. Jones: 105 v Sussex, Cardiff.

Bowling	O	M	R	W	Avge	Best	5w/I	10w/M
W.W. Davis	452.4	110	1389	52	26.71	7-70	3	-
J.G. Thomas	129.5	28	472	15	31.46	5-78	2	-
M.W.W. Selvey	597.4	126	1914	56	34.17	5-37	2	-
R.C. Ontong	611	122	1978	54	36.62	6-64	3	-
C.J.C. Rowe	455.4	85	1528	37	41.29	4-29	-	-
B.J. Lloyd	261.5	36	842	18	46.77	4-93	-	-
S.R. Barwick	129.3	21	532	11	48.36	8-42	1	-
A.H. Wilkins	197	24	795	10	79.50	2-82	-	-

Also bowled: J. Derrick 8-1-31-0; D.A. Francis 4-0-25-0; S.P. Henderson 8-0-65-2; J.A. Hopkins 4-0-23-0; Javed Miandad 2-0-11-0; A.L. Jones 3-0-25-0; H. Morris 3.5-0-23-0; M.A. Nash 75-22-226-3.

Gloucestershire

Gloucestershire will have drawn some comfort from their performances in 1983, particularly from an improvement in their batting which made them a more difficult side to beat. Their most notable efforts came in the Benson & Hedges Cup, where they won their group only to lose their washed-out quarter-final to Middlesex on the toss of a coin, and the NatWest, where, thanks principally to a marvellous 158 from Zaheer, they beat Leicestershire by 4 wickets, having been set 303 to win.

Yet they were as far away as ever from being a real force. A glance at their bowling figures shows where their problem lies. John Shepherd, who in his 40th year had an Indian summer with bat and ball, took most wickets. But they cost him 29 runs apiece and he had to bowl 11 overs for each success. Gary Sainsbury, recruited from Essex, bowled steadfastly but with less penetration than had been hoped for, and with Graveney under-bowling himself and Childs still unable to recapture his form of 1981, Gloucestershire did not have the fire-power to bowl sides out twice.

Their three Championship wins were against Glamorgan, twice, and Yorkshire, hardly top-class scalps. And even then, two of these victories came from fourth-innings chases after the opposition had declared, while the third was the direct result of winning the toss on a Cheltenham pitch that broke up on the second day. On three occasions, Gloucestershire failed to separate their opponent's last-wicket pair when in winning positions.

Gloucestershire's first priority is to find a strike bowler, and it is disappointing that 19-year-old David Lawrence, who has the potential to be genuinely fast, has made so little progress. His run-up is still far too long, his action needs smoothing out, and his 7 first-class wickets cost 86 apiece. However, in Sunday League matches, where his run was restricted, his 10 wickets cost only 16 each. It is to be hoped, for the sake of the player and the county, that their coaching staff appreciate the significance of these figures.

Despite their bowling difficulties, the side batted most attractively, even in the absence of Zaheer (due to the World Cup and later to the need to prepare for his country's tour of India). Stovold, in tremendous form at the start, recovered from a lean spell and had comfortably his best season. The cultured Romaines, who hit three centuries, fully earned his county cap. His ability to cope with the new ball will compensate for Broad's departure to seek fame and fortune with another county.

Hignell wound up his county career with some pugnacious displays, and though Bainbridge was inconsistent he passed 1,000 runs comfortably and remains a player of rich promise. Particularly encouraging was the progress made by the 19-year-old Russell, who kept wicket efficiently and whose gritty left-handed batting developed steadily during the season.

ENGLISH SEASON 1983/GLOUCESTERSHIRE

Schweppes County Championship: 12th; Won 3, Lost 8, Drawn 12 (Abandoned 1)
All First-Class Matches: Won 3, Lost 8, Drawn 13 (Abandoned 1)
NatWest Bank Trophy: Lost to Hampshire in quarter-final
Benson & Hedges Cup: Lost to Middlesex in quarter-final on toss
John Player League: 14th; Won 4, Lost 8, No result 4

Championship Averages

*not out

Batting and Fielding	M	I	NO	HS	R	Avge	100	50	Ct	St
Zaheer Abbas	12	19	0	116	867	45.63	3	4	3	-
A.W. Stovold	22	40	3	181	1592	43.02	4	7	16	-
B.C. Broad	16	27	2	145	1061	42.44	3	3	6	-
R.J. Doughty	6	9	6	32*	123	41.00	-	-	-	-
J.N. Shepherd	23	34	6	168	1025	36.60	2	6	16	-
A.J. Hignell	19	35	6	109*	1034	35.65	2	6	4	-
P.W. Romaines	22	39	4	135	1233	35.22	3	4	9	-
P. Bainbridge	23	41	2	99*	1068	27.38	-	6	14	-
A.J. Wright	9	15	2	56*	354	27.23	-	2	5	-
R.C. Russell	23	30	9	64*	469	22.33	-	3	45	17
D.A. Graveney	21	26	7	94	397	20.89	-	2	15	-
E.J. Cunningham	4	6	1	29*	83	16.60	-	-	4	-
J.H. Childs	19	16	1	19	79	5.26	-	-	5	-
D.V. Lawrence	8	9	4	9	22	4.40	-	-	1	-
G.E. Sainsbury	22	21	7	13	61	4.35	-	-	-	-

Also batted: B. Dudleston (2 matches) 35*, 11, 12; F.D. Stephenson (2) 21 (2 ct).

Hundreds (17)

4 **A.W. Stovold:** 181 v Derbys, Derby; 122 v Surrey, Bristol; 106 v Hants, Portsmouth; 164* v Warwks, Cheltenham.
3 **B.C. Broad:** 100 v Yorks, Cheltenham; 109 v Essex, Colchester; 145 v Notts, Bristol.
  P.W. Romaines: 135 v Kent, Bristol; 100* v Yorks, Cheltenham; 121 v Worcs, Bristol.
  Zaheer Abbas: 116 v Glam, Swansea; 112 v Lancs, Southport; 109 v Warwks, Cheltenham.
2 **A.J. Hignell:** 103 v Somerset, Bath; 109* v Hants, Bristol.
  J.N. Shepherd: 168 v Warwicks, Birmingham; 112 v Kent, Bristol.

Bowling	O	M	R	W	Avge	Best	5w/I	10w/M
F.D. Stephenson	52.4	13	140	11	12.72	5-56	1	-
J.N. Shepherd	776.1	209	2047	67	30.55	7-50	3	-
G.E. Sainsbury	602.4	142	1882	58	32.44	6-66	3	-
D.A. Graveney	498.1	153	1160	35	33.14	6-88	2	-
J.H. Childs	647.5	194	1691	48	35.22	6-81	2	-
P. Bainbridge	400.4	100	1160	29	40.00	4-67	-	-

Also bowled: E.J. Cunningham 49-10-181-4; R.J. Doughty 76.5-11-285-5; B. Dudleston 27.5-4-164-4; A.J. Hignell 7-1-46-0; D.V. Lawrence 157-21-613-7; A.J. Wright 1-0-3-0; Zaheer Abbas 26-7-79-0.

Hat-trick: D.A. Graveney v Leics, Leicester.

Hampshire

Scoring 10 wins, only one fewer than the champions and the runners-up, Hampshire finished third in the Championship for the second year running. This would seem a satisfactory state of affairs, but, considering the improvement in their final positions over the two previous seasons, Hampshire will have been disappointed not to have challenged more strongly for the title.

With Chris Smith having gained an English qualification and being able now to play alongside their two overseas stars, Gordon Greenidge and Malcolm Marshall, Hampshire had every reason to aspire to higher honours. Smith himself certainly lived up to expectations.

If just one reason had to be found for Hampshire's failing to contest the title more vigorously, it was because their great bowling find of 1982, Kevin Emery, failed by far to make the same impact again. Emery lost his rhythm so completely that, apart from his inability to reproduce the striking rate of his maiden season, he had intense trouble with no-balls and with keeping the ball on target. After four troublesome Championship games, Emery found himself out of the side. That was in early June. Having shown signs of a return to some semblance of form in the Second XI, Emery was reinstated at the end of July. But he had not bowled through a whole innings against Derbyshire, at Portsmouth, when his ankle broke down. So the bright young hope who had captured 78 championship wickets in 1982, coming close to an England cap, finished the 1983 season on July 28 with only 5 wickets.

Hampshire, then, did not have even one spinner of true class to exploit fully the pitches of a dry summer. Scoring their second win in consecutive matches, they went to the top of the table at the end of May, but headed the field only briefly. On June 24, they had slumped to ninth place, having played six matches in this span.

It is significant that this period of decline coincided with the dates of the Prudential Cup competition, which deprived them of Gordon Greenidge, Trevor Jesty, and Malcolm Marshall. For all his immense ability, Greenidge's absence was not a crushing hardship.

Robin Smith, 19, the younger brother of Chris, possessed the genius to fill the gap in terms of consistency as well as firepower (434 runs in 12 innings). But Marshall was irreplaceable, and while there was some amount of cover for Jesty the batsman, the unavailability of his medium-paced bowling put a limited attack under further stress. With the return of their stars, they soon recovered and were back in the upper reaches of the table by the end of July.

An event of note in Hampshire's season was Chris Smith's call-up for England. It had been many years since one of their ranks won an England cap. If Emery's eclipse was a major disappointment, there was encouragement in the progress as a batsman of Paul Terry, 24, and in Mark Nicholas's growing maturity. He was the first English-born batsman to complete 1,000 runs.

ENGLISH SEASON 1983/HAMPSHIRE

Schweppes County Championship: 3rd; Won 10, Lost 2, Drawn 12
All First-Class Matches: Won 11, Lost 3, Drawn 12
NatWest Bank Trophy: Lost to Kent in semi-final
Benson & Hedges Cup: Lost to Kent in quarter-final
John Player League: 5th; Won 9, Lost 6, No result 1

Championship Averages   *not out

Batting and Fielding	M	I	NO	HS	R	Avge	100	50	Ct	St
R.A. Smith	5	9	3	104*	401	66.83	3	-	1	-
C.G. Greenidge	15	27	5	154	1438	65.36	4	9	21	-
C.L. Smith	20	33	3	193	1831	61.03	6	8	16	-
M.D. Marshall	16	16	4	112	563	46.91	2	2	6	-
V.P. Terry	18	29	6	115	1039	45.17	3	4	15	-
T.E. Jesty	19	28	5	187	1019	44.30	1	5	11	-
M.C.J. Nicholas	24	39	5	110	1192	35.05	2	6	25	-
D.R. Turner	11	15	2	94*	425	32.69	-	2	3	-
N.E.J. Pocock	24	32	7	60*	681	27.24	-	6	27	-
T.M. Tremlett	22	17	5	59	229	19.08	-	1	16	-
N.G. Cowley	21	24	8	29	302	18.87	-	-	7	-
J.W. Southern	14	13	5	45*	146	18.25	-	-	8	-
R.J. Parks	24	15	2	52	180	13.84	-	1	48	9
K. Stevenson	6	7	3	25	51	12.75	-	-	1	-
S.J. Malone	20	13	4	12	37	4.11	-	-	4	-

Also batted: K. St J.D. Emery (5 matches) 8.

Hundreds (21)

6 **C.L. Smith:** 129* v Leics, Leicester; 193 v Derbys, Derby; 100 v Lancs, Bournemouth; 118 v Lancs, Liverpool; 163 v Essex, Southend; 125 v Glos, Portsmouth.
4 **C.G. Greenidge:** 116 v Worcs, Southampton; 104 and 100* v Lancs, Liverpool; 154 v Surrey, Southampton.
3 **R.A. Smith:** 100* v Lancs, Bournemouth; 104* v Sussex, Basingstoke; 100 v Glos, Bristol.
  V.P. Terry: 114 v Lancs, Bournemouth; 106* v Notts, Bournemouth; 115 v Sussex, Eastbourne.
2 **M.D. Marshall:** 100* v Surrey, Southampton; 112 v Kent, Bournemouth.
  M.C.J. Nicholas: 110 v Glos, Bristol; 100* v Derbys, Portsmouth.
1 **T.E. Jesty:** 187 v Derbys, Derby.

Bowling	O	M	R	W	Avge	Best	5w/I	10w/M
M.D. Marshall	532.5	144	1327	80	16.58	7-29	5	1
T.M. Tremlett	557.2	177	1285	58	22.15	6-82	1	-
N.G. Cowley	392.3	129	965	38	25.39	4-10	-	-
K. Stevenson	162.5	37	554	19	29.15	5-81	1	-
M.C.J. Nicholas	246.2	66	695	23	30.21	5-45	1	-
C.L. Smith	154	42	512	15	34.13	3-35	-	-
J.W. Southern	327.5	105	848	24	35.33	5-60	2	-
T.E. Jesty	256.5	70	804	21	38.28	3-48	-	-
S.J. Malone	481.1	104	1620	41	39.51	4-39	-	-

Also bowled: K. St J.D. Emery 75-22-204-5; N.E.J. Pocock 18-3-87-1.

Hat-trick and 4 wickets in 5 balls: M.D. Marshall v Somerset, Taunton.

Kent

If an admirable nursery system eventually played a significant role in elevating Kent from the lower to the upper half of the Championship, some of its elements were counter-productive. A healthy reserve of talented young batsmen certainly improved the performances of senior incumbents, but others became obsessed with their personal batting averages in the misguided belief that therein lay the guarantee of selection.

This occasionally resulted in the loss of maximum points – and the goodwill of adversaries and supporters alike – as Kent took far too long to reach the point of declaration. A notable example arose at Tunbridge Wells in mid-June, when Essex were offered a ludicrous target of 292 in 95 minutes. At Maidstone, a month later, Kent's declaration, 276 ahead of Lancashire, was not hastened by the performance of opener Neil Taylor who, at one point, had contributed only 39 to a total of 187 for 2.

Fortunately, Bob Woolmer – though somewhat injury-prone – was in superlative form, and when Mark Benson moved into a golden patch, with two centuries against Warwickshire at the end of July, the Kent batting assumed a lavish depth. Chris Tavaré, when available, was in excellent order, Derek Aslett soon joined Benson in achieving his thousand runs, and Chris Cowdrey, riding high on career-best centuries against Yorkshire and Essex (NatWest), enjoyed a magnificent season.

Kent's run-scoring capability was further enhanced by the burgeoning talents of Eldine Baptiste – exemplified by his maiden century against Yorkshire. Even so, it is curious that, despite the enforced absences of Woolmer and Tavaré, and the fluctuating form of Taylor, virtually no place could be found for Laurie Potter who, in 1982, scored 775 runs for the county at an average of 40.78.

Opportunities for the neglected Potter would appear to be a change of county or a transformation from batsman to strike or slow-left-arm bowler; for it is in these departments that Kent are in need of reinforcement. Graham Dilley's early form was sufficiently impressive to re-engage the interest of the England selectors, but recurring injuries resulted in a frustrating season. Neither was Kevin Jarvis a consistent force, and, though Baptiste and Richard Ellison seized their opportunities, no regular, incisive partnership was established.

Fortunately, Derek Underwood excelled as the man for all seasons. His 13 wickets against Notts at Trent Bridge and 14 against Worcestershire at Canterbury – taken for around 12 runs each – exemplified his long-serving skills. But where is his successor?

In reaching their lucrative, if unsuccessful, NatWest final, Kent were particularly well served by Ellison and Baptiste. In the second round, at Chelmsford, Essex appeared to be coasting to a comfortable victory when Ellison's spell of 4 for 12 polished them off. Similarly, Hampshire – needing only 174 to win the semi-final at Canterbury – were ripped apart by Baptiste's 5 for 20. The final, in many ways, reflected Kent's championship season: Woolmer unfit and the side's inexperience showing through when it mattered most. Ironically, too, Dilley chose this particular match to prove how good he can be when physically and psychologically in trim.

Schweppes County Championship: 7th; Won 7, Lost 4, Drawn 13
All First-Class Matches: Won 7, Lost 4, Drawn 14
NatWest Bank Trophy: Lost to Somerset in final
Benson & Hedges Cup: Lost to Essex in semi-final
John Player League: 3rd; Won 8, Lost 3, No result 5

Championship Averages   *not out

Batting and Fielding	M	I	NO	HS	R	Avge	100	50	Ct	St
C.S. Cowdrey	21	32	9	123	1256	54.60	4	5	27	–
R.A. Woolmer	13	20	1	129	969	51.00	4	5	6	–
C.J. Tavaré	10	14	0	94	633	45.21	–	7	8	–
D.G. Aslett	20	36	3	168	1437	43.54	3	8	19	–
M.R. Benson	22	36	3	152*	1410	42.72	3	10	15	–
A.P.E. Knott	22	29	8	92*	806	38.38	–	6	36	8
N.R. Taylor	22	38	6	155*	1161	36.28	4	3	18	–
E.A.E. Baptiste	17	26	5	136*	755	35.95	2	3	10	–
S.G. Hinks	6	10	0	87	253	25.30	–	1	2	–
R.M. Ellison	21	21	7	63	343	24.50	–	1	14	–
G.W. Johnson	24	28	11	79*	402	23.64	–	1	28	–
L. Potter	6	11	0	50	258	23.45	–	1	2	–
G.R. Dilley	10	7	1	29	99	16.50	–	–	8	–
D.L. Underwood	24	20	6	26*	142	10.14	–	–	5	–
K.B.S. Jarvis	20	13	5	9*	43	5.37	–	–	2	–
K.D. Masters	2	4	0	1	1	0.25	–	–	2	–

Also batted: S. Marsh (1 match) 5, 0; C. Penn (2) 24 (1 ct); S.N.V. Waterton (1) 8, 3 (3 ct).

Hundreds (20)

4 **C.S. Cowdrey:** 101* v Lancs, Maidstone; 113 v Yorks, Sheffield; 123 v Leics, Folkestone; 103* v Somerset, Taunton.
   N.R. Taylor: 116* v Essex, Tunbridge Wells; 155* v Glam, Cardiff; 111 v Leics, Leicester; 104 v Somerset, Taunton.
   R.A. Woolmer: 118 v Middx, Dartford; 129 v Lancs, Maidstone; 110 v Somerset, Maidstone; 120 v Surrey, Canterbury.
3 **D.G. Aslett:** 111 v Sussex, Hove; 168 and 119 v Derbys, Chesterfield.
   M.R. Benson: 102 and 152* v Warwicks, Birmingham; 111 v Glam, Cardiff.
2 **E.A.E. Baptiste:** 102* v Sussex, Hove; 136* v Yorks, Sheffield.

Bowling	O	M	R	W	Avge	Best	5w/I	10w/M
D.L. Underwood	919.3	349	2024	105	19.27	7-55	9	3
G.R. Dilley	232.3	60	601	28	21.46	5-70	1	–
E.A.E. Baptiste	376.3	88	1187	50	23.74	5-39	3	–
R.M. Ellison	580.4	161	1455	49	26.69	5-73	1	–
G.W. Johnson	616.1	160	1617	51	31.70	7-76	2	1
K.B.S. Jarvis	485.5	93	1545	29	53.27	3-32	–	–
C.S. Cowdrey	214.2	34	712	12	59.33	3-80	–	–

Also bowled: D.G. Aslett 37-5-218-3; M.R. Benson 5-1-16-0; K.D. Masters 33-4-121-2; C. Penn 35-8-116-2; L. Potter 6-2-14-0; C.J. Tavare 3-0-3-0; N.R. Taylor 35-9-108-1; R.A. Woolmer 76-26-148-7.

Lancashire

Whatever hilarity Yorkshire's embarrassments may provoke in Manchester, the fact is that Lancashire have not won the Championship outright for 50 years, and that record, for one of the traditional 'Big Six', is a disgrace. They do not even have the excuse of birthright, for Old Trafford has recruited overseas for longer than most counties.

Not that 1983 offered any real hope of distinction other than in limited overs. With Clive Lloyd required for the World Cup, the captaincy was inevitably split, Abrahams being the surprising but not unsuccessful choice. Popular and likeable, Abrahams responded with several vital innings and proved to be the bridge between the team of the 70s and the new generation, as represented by Fowler and O'Shaughnessy.

Paradoxically, Lancashire began well without their West Indian captain, for in his absence the qualification rules enabled the county to play Jefferies, the South African left-arm quick bowler who startled not a few with his Trueman-like gait. Had the rules and fitness permitted Jefferies a full summer in his spearhead role – as 1984 may provide – Lancashire might have had a very different season.

As the sun broke through in June, Lancashire's attack gradually faded. Speak and Folley, two seam bowlers who were expected to establish themselves, saw more of the junior dressing-room. Allott bowled well in the World Cup, McFarlane was mercurial, and with David Lloyd's departure in August, too much was expected of Watkinson and O'Shaughnessy, who are still learning.

The last six weeks were saved by a sparkling return to form by the 42-year-old Simmons, whose batting and off-spin once again rescued Lancashire from a dozen crises. On an Old Trafford square that might have been prepared for Tattersall and Hilton, Simmons, beaming and belligerent, gathered in a rich harvest.

The batting has to be restructured. The loss of Kennedy and now David Lloyd means that Fowler is left without a partner. O'Shaughnessy, despite his 101 in 35 minutes on the last day of the season, is not an opener. Hayes, unluckily injured again, may yet have an Indian summer, Clive Lloyd will be absent again in 1984, and Hughes could not sustain the advance of 1982. Maynard had a useful season with bat and gloves, but his wicket-keeping position will now be under challenge from Stanworth, who made a highly promising start in the closing weeks.

The one bright shining star of 1984 was Neil Harvey Fairbrother. Deprived, by a declaration, of a century on debut, the compact, well-balanced little left-hander from Warrington went on to hit 759 runs in his 26 innings, including seven more half-centuries, and looked, in technique and temperament, a prospect of the highest class.

It would be wrong to end without praising Lancashire for their persistence with Nasir Zaidi, a little leg-spinner who batted boldly, fielded bravely, sometimes brilliantly, and spiced the cricket wherever he played.

Schweppes County Championship: 12th; Won 3, Lost 4, Drawn 17
All First-Class Matches: Won 3, Lost 4, Drawn 18
NatWest Bank Trophy: Lost to Somerset in 2nd round
Benson & Hedges Cup: Lost to Middlesex in semi-final
John Player League: 8th; Won 5, Lost 5, Tied 1, No result 5

Championship Averages

*not out

Batting and Fielding	M	I	NO	HS	R	Avge	100	50	Ct	St
G. Fowler	15	25	2	156*	1253	54.47	4	6	4	-
D. Lloyd	9	14	2	123	485	40.41	1	4	6	-
J. Abrahams	23	39	7	178	1261	39.40	3	4	11	-
N.H. Fairbrother	16	26	5	94*	759	36.14	-	8	8	-
L.L. McFarlane	9	9	8	12*	35	35.00	-	-	-	-
S.T. Jefferies	9	12	4	75*	260	32.50	-	1	1	-
F.C. Hayes	19	28	1	149	866	32.07	3	4	13	-
C.H. Lloyd	11	16	11	86	447	29.80	-	3	11	-
S.J. O'Shaughnessy	17	28	3	105	685	27.40	2	1	5	-
J. Simmons	23	31	2	104	679	23.41	2	3	17	-
J. Stanworth	3	6	2	31*	90	22.50	-	-	2	-
Nasir Zaidi	12	16	6	51	215	21.50	-	1	9	-
I. Cockbain	8	15	1	52	291	20.78	-	1	4	-
D.P. Hughes	18	28	2	153	522	20.07	1	3	13	-
I. Folley	12	9	4	25	91	18.20	-	-	3	-
C. Maynard	21	27	3	61*	417	17.37	-	2	27	2
P.J.W. Allott	17	18	4	41	225	16.07	-	-	3	-
K.A. Hayes	5	8	0	32	103	12.87	-	-	1	-
M. Watkinson	15	20	4	29	168	10.50	-	-	2	-

Also batted: M.R. Chadwick (1 match) 1, 1 (1 ct); N.V. Radford (1) 24, 27.

Hundreds (16)

4 G. Fowler: 133 v Glam, Manchester; 156* v Yorks, Manchester; 107 v Northants, Northampton; 100 v Leics, Manchester.
3 J. Abrahams: 117* v Hants, Bournemouth; 105 v Kent, Maidstone; 178 v Worcs, Manchester.
  F.C. Hayes: 116 v Yorks, Manchester; 149 v Sussex, Horsham; 127* v Derbys, Blackpool.
2 S.J. O'Shaughnessy: 100* v Yorks, Leeds; 105 v Leics, Manchester.
  J. Simmons: 104 v Glam, Swansea; 101* v Derbys, Blackpool.
1 D.P. Hughes: 153 v Glam, Manchester.
  D. Lloyd: 123 v Northants, Northampton.

Bowling	O	M	R	W	Avge	Best	5w/I	10w/M
D. Lloyd	188	53	389	16	24.31	5-22	1	-
M. Watkinson	319.3	69	929	35	26.54	6-51	2	-
J. Simmons	744	214	1807	68	26.57	7-73	5	1
S.T. Jefferies	256.5	60	782	27	28.96	8-46	1	1
P.J.W. Allott	434.4	120	1154	38	30.36	5-45	1	-
Nasir Zaidi	170.3	51	491	15	32.73	3-27	-	-
S.J. O'Shaughnessy	227.2	40	816	22	37.09	4-73	-	-
L.L. McFarlane	204.4	32	726	15	48.40	3-53	-	-
J. Abrahams	216	41	658	13	50.61	3-83	-	-

Also bowled: N.H. Fairbrother 3-2-1-0; I. Folley 191-49-522-7; G. Fowler 2-0-7-0; D.P. Hughes 60.5-8-218-2; N.V. Radford 25-2-99-0.

Leicestershire

Leicestershire's confident hopes of going one better than the previous season's second place in the Championship were to a large degree based on the encouraging propect of having Andy Roberts, previously able to play only when free from League cricket duties, available on a fulltime basis to share the new ball with Les Taylor. In the event, Roberts was able to bowl only 101 overs for the county because of a recurring knee injury, which eventually required surgery, and Taylor had the misfortune to fracture an elbow during pre-season preparations, which kept him out of a dozen matches. This confined the pair to only one first-class match in harness together. But Leicestershire could hardly point to any shortfall in the seam-bowling department to account for their slip to fourth in the Championship and eleventh in the John Player League. Indeed, they gained more bowling bonus points than any other county, and had Taylor, Paddy Clift, and George Ferris high in the national averages with a combined aggregate of 205 victims.

The injuries to Roberts and Taylor were not the only ones to afflict Leicestershire during 1983. Clift, who had taken only 36 first-class wickets in the two previous seasons because of persistent ankle trouble, suffered from a strained tendon, which kept him out of ten matches. But recovered magnificently to claim 83 victims at under 20 each.

Test calls ruled David Gower out of a total of 16 three-day and one-day matches, and deprived the County of left-arm spinner Nick Cook for a further half dozen, making it something of a rarity for Leicestershire to field their strongest side. In these circumstances, their results must be regarded as very creditable indeed, the more so when considered alongside their achievement in winning both the Second XI and Under-25 competitions. Their prospects for the future became even brighter with the signing, after the season ended, of Peter Willey from Northants.

Only Norman Gifford, Derek Underwood, and John Emburey bowled more overs than Cook's 878 in first-class matches. He claimed 73 victims, while Ferris, a most important discovery, took 53 wickets from only 360 overs. With his uncomplicated action allied to unusual stamina for one of such youth, Ferris compensated impressively for the absence of Roberts, his mentor and Antiguan neighbour, and quickly learned that the bouncer is a more effective weapon if used sparingly.

Ian Butcher was another comparative newcomer to make a sustained impression, providing the typically productive Chris Balderstone with an enterprising partner and scoring three centuries, while Nigel Briers and Brian Davison both performed consistently to average better than 40.

Clift, whose batting seemed to decline or become neglected after his arrival in English cricket, had a marvellous season. A maiden century for the county and the ability to repair an innings or accelerate its momentum turned him back into a genuine all-rounder. Even more of a surprise was the batting form of Taylor, previously considered among the least adroit of tail-enders. A career-best 47 in the innings defeat of Derbyshire polished his confidence, and he ended with an average of above 20.

ENGLISH SEASON 1983/LEICESTERSHIRE

Schweppes County Championship: 4th; Won 9, Lost 3, Drawn 12
All First-Class Matches: Won 9, Lost 4, Drawn 13
NatWest Bank Trophy: Lost to Gloucestershire in 2nd round
Benson & Hedges Cup: Failed to qualify for Q-F (3rd in Group A)
John Player League: 11th; Won 4, Lost 7, No result 5

Championship Averages

*not out

Batting and Fielding	M	I	NO	HS	R	Avge	100	50	Ct	St
J.C. Balderstone	23	38	4	112	1443	42.44	3	9	16	-
N.E. Briers	23	35	6	201*	1206	41.58	1	7	14	-
D.I. Gower	13	21	4	140	702	41.29	2	4	12	-
B.F. Davison	24	38	5	106	1265	38.33	2	8	17	-
I.P. Butcher	17	30	1	139	973	33.55	3	3	17	-
P.B. Clift	21	30	6	100*	795	33.12	1	2	8	-
R.W. Tolchard	24	32	6	80*	671	25.80	-	3	41	8
J.J. Whitaker	10	16	4	56*	305	25.41	-	1	4	-
J.F. Steele	22	24	8	50	284	17.75	-	1	28	-
L.B. Taylor	18	17	5	47	213	17.75	-	-	8	-
G.J. Parsons	13	15	3	56	207	17.25	-	1	5	-
R.A. Cobb	7	9	0	28	98	10.88	-	-	4	-
N.G.B. Cook	21	19	5	32	150	10.71	-	-	7	-
J.P. Agnew	8	4	0	13	24	6.00	-	-	2	-
G.J.F. Ferris	13	12	4	11	38	4.75	-	-	1	-
T.J. Boon	4	7	0	5	18	2.57	-	-	-	-

Also batted: A.M.E. Roberts (4 matches) 15, 3, 4.

Hundreds (12)

3 J.C. Balderstone: 108 v Notts, Nottingham; 100* v Worcs, Hereford; 112 v Kent, Leicester.
  I.P. Butcher: 103 v Glos, Leicester; 139 v Notts, Leicester; 107 v Northants, Leicester.
2 B.F. Davison: 101 v Glam, Hinckley; 106 v Essex, Chelmsford.
  D.I. Gower: 108* v Glam, Hinckley; 140 v Sussex, Hove.
1 N.E. Briers: 201* v Warwicks, Birmingham.
  P.B. Clift: 100* v Sussex, Hove.

Bowling	O	M	R	W	Avge	Best	5w/I	10w/M
A.M.E. Roberts	101.2	19	294	16	18.37	5-26	1	-
L.B. Taylor	509.5	143	1338	69	19.39	7-73	3	1
P.B. Clift	573.3	152	1481	71	20.85	5-73	1	-
G.J.F. Ferris	360	74	1205	53	22.73	7-42	3	1
N.G.B. Cook	695.5	244	1489	54	27.57	4-53	-	-
J.F. Steele	476.1	148	1167	39	29.92	4-3	-	-
G.J. Parsons	241	65	732	26	28.15	5-51	1	-
J.P. Agnew	162	33	621	17	36.52	3-34	-	-

Also bowled: J.C. Balderstone 51-18-112-6; N.E. Briers 2-2-0-0; I.P. Butcher 2-0-2-1; B.F. Davison 4.4-0-18-0; D.I. Gower 9-0-102-0; J.J. Whitaker 10-2-88-0.

Hat-trick: G.J.F. Ferris v Northants, Leicester.

Middlesex

The wishful thoughts of rival counties that Mike Brearley's retirement could significantly weaken Middlesex were dispersed in two directions immediately the season emerged from its rain-swept start. Not only did Mike Gatting prove a shrewd, forceful, and popular successor to the former captain, but, in selecting Graham Barlow as a replacement opening bat, Middlesex made an inspired choice.

These speculative considerations resolved, there was never any doubt that the sheer breadth of the county's proven talents would carry them through another successful season. That they failed, in the end, to retain the Championship may be equally ascribed to injuries and Test calls, towards the latter part of the campaign, and the contemporary excellence of Essex.

The return to form of Barlow, who had played little in 1982, coincided with a similar resurgence of forceful certainty from Roland Butcher, whose highly productive exploits were cruelly curtailed by serious injury in mid-July.

With the incumbent opener Slack in fine fettle and Radley, Gatting, and Tomlins luxuriously enriching the middle order, such was the depth of batting that opponents then suffered not so much a flick from the tail but a hefty lumbar-punch from the likes of Emburey, Downton, Edmonds, and Williams. This pattern became splendidly familiar throughout June, as Middlesex swept to six successive Championship victories – against Kent, Derbyshire, Surrey, Hampshire, Worcestershire, and Derbyshire again.

Obviously, the bowling had to be of similar calibre and equally versatile. But, if Cowans, Williams, and Daniel provided a successful spearhead, the most arresting performances came from the spinners – notably Edmonds who, in the course of five consecutive matches, took 43 wickets at less than 11 runs each.

Ironically, it was Warwickshire spinner Norman Gifford who decisively ended Middlesex's imperious sequence of wins when, at Edgbaston on July 5, he took 6 for 22 as the Championship leaders were dismissed in the 70s (for the second time) and beaten by 167 runs.

Confidence was quickly restored, however, as successes against Gloucestershire and Leicestershire increased the total to eight wins in nine matches. Victory over Essex in the Benson & Hedges final boosted morale even further and, when August began, an eight-wicket win against Warwickshire gave Gatting's men a clear 25 points lead in the championship. There was reassurance, too, in saving the match against Essex, at Chelmsford, with a massive 634 for 7 in the second innings.

In the absence of Gatting, Cowans, and Edmonds, defeat at Northampton, on August 12, was to prove crucial, however, for as the fine weather ended, Middlesex's season ended with draws against Sussex and Yorkshire and defeat by Notts. Essex, meanwhile, had taken the lead and were not to be denied.

Even so, Gatting's disappointment must be tempered with the

satisfaction that Middlesex have maintained an awesome presence and are achieving evolution without revolution. If some of their senior players are possibly at the summit of their careers, there is plenty of youthful talent striding through the foothills. Among them, Andrew Miller, the left-hand bat and Oxford Blue, made a particularly good impression as the season drew to its close.

Schweppes County Championship: 2nd; Won 11, Lost 4, Drawn 8 (Abandoned 1)
All First-Class Matches: Won 12, Lost 4, Drawn 9 (Abandoned 1)
NatWest Bank Trophy: Lost to Somerset in semi-final
Benson & Hedges Cup: Winners
John Player League: 8th; Won 7, Lost 7, No result 2

Championship Averages   *not out

Batting and Fielding	M	I	NO	HS	R	Avge	100	50	Ct	St
M.W. Gatting	15	23	5	160	1157	64.27	5	4	15	-
G.D. Barlow	22	38	7	132	1519	49.00	4	9	22	-
R.O. Butcher	13	17	2	179	646	43.06	2	3	32	-
A.J.T. Miller	6	11	0	86	465	42.27	-	4	-	-
W.N. Slack	16	26	3	140	874	38.00	2	6	16	-
K.P. Tomlins	18	25	4	132*	606	28.85	1	2	21	-
J.E. Emburey	23	32	4	133	772	27.57	1	3	23	-
C.T. Radley	23	36	6	67	748	24.93	-	3	18	-
K.D. James	7	8	2	34	141	23.50	-	-	1	-
N.F. Williams	23	25	7	63	407	22.61	-	2	6	-
P.R. Downton	23	30	7	87	508	22.08	-	4	51	4
P.H. Edmonds	15	16	3	65	145	11.15	-	1	12	-
R.G.P. Ellis	6	11	0	34	107	9.72	-	-	2	-
W.W. Daniel	16	13	2	18	88	8.00	-	-	3	-
N.G. Cowans	10	8	3	9	34	6.80	-	-	2	-
S.P. Hughes	12	10	6	4*	13	3.25	-	-	2	-

Also batted: J.M. Brearley (1 match) 17; J.D. Carr (3) 9*, 12*, 1*; J.F. Sykes (1) 4.

Hundreds (15)

5 **M.W. Gatting:** 118 v Sussex, Lord's; 116 v Warwicks, Lord's; 160 v Essex, Chelmsford; 105 v Somerset, Lord's; 100* v Yorks, Leeds.
4 **G.D. Barlow:** 128 v Lancs, Lord's; 105 v Hants, Uxbridge; 132 v Essex, Chelmsford; 113 v Surrey, Lord's.
2 **R.O. Butcher:** 110 v Kent, Dartford; 179 v Derbys, Uxbridge.
 W.N. Slack: 140 v Glam, Lord's; 107 v Surrey, Oval.
1 **J.E. Emburey:** 133 v Essex, Chelmsford.
 K.P. Tomlins: 132* v Sussex, Hove.

Bowling	O	M	R	W	Avge	Best	5w/I	10w/M
J.E. Emburey	833	289	1677	96	17.46	6-13	4	-
P.H. Edmonds	615.5	169	1491	72	20.70	6-38	7	2
W.W. Daniel	307.2	48	1040	47	22.12	7-61	1	1
N.G. Cowans	155	33	455	18	25.27	5-43	1	-
S.P. Hughes	252.3	60	836	33	25.33	6-32	2	-
N.F. Williams	503.2	107	1571	62	25.33	5-77	1	-

Also bowled: G.D. Barlow 2-1-2-0; R.O. Butcher 1-1-0-0; J.D. Carr 15-4-31-0; M.W. Gatting 81.2-25-209-5; K.D. James 69-12-178-6; C.T. Radley 1-0-4-0; W.N. Slack 36-18-71-5; J.F. Sykes 21-6-54-1; K.P. Tomlins 6-2-19-0.

Northamptonshire

Northamptonshire relished the most consistent of batting orders last season, with Larkins, Willey, and Williams completing their 1,000 runs and averaging over 40 apiece, while the county averages were headed by Allan Lamb. It was not until the last match of the season that the captain, Geoff Cook, recorded his first hundred, but his soundness and example were revealed with an aggregate of over 1,500 runs. There was also much promising batting by the local Northampton boy Capel, 20, who hit his maiden hundred against Somerset at the end of July.

The success of the leading batsman, Larkins, came only in the second half of the season. He had had a poor start, with only one half-century by 1st June, and his next 50 not coming until the last week of that month. But Larkins hit 236 against Derbyshire in the middle of July and then compiled 816 runs in August. This aggregate included the highest score of his 11-year career, an innings of 252 against Glamorgan, at Cardiff. In that match, Lamb scored 119, and the county made 529 for 8 declared in 90 overs. This total was only 5 runs short of the record for the 100 overs of bonus points. It was also only 28 runs short of Northants' highest ever, 557 for 6 declared against Sussex, at Hove, in 1914.

Willey was Northants' next most prolific batsman to Larkins, but before the start of the season these two former England cricketers were involved in an Industrial Tribunal case, concerning the dismissal of the county's former groundsman, Les Bentley. Willey and Larkins both gave evidence for the groundsman against the club. They later had to assure the committee of their 'loyalty to the club'. But Willey - unlike other established players on a two-year signing - was offered, before the end of his fruitful season, a contract by the club of just one year's standing. This he refused, and left the county for Leicestershire.

Willey also confirmed his worth as an off-spin bowler, while Williams, who enjoyed his best batting season, took 47 wickets with well-flighted off-breaks. However, as in the previous year, it was the slow left-arm of Steele that gained most reward, with 68 wickets.

The fast-medium bowlers Griffiths and Mallender both did valuable work in the attack, but the South African Carse broke down at Oxford on 8th June and was then disappointing, until taking 5 wickets against Glamorgan towards the end of the season.

Another bowling disappointment for Northants was that Kapil Dev played only seven matches for the county. The Indian captain, of course, had World Cup commitments, followed by unexpected celebrations back in India, but he was again recalled to his country on 15th August - because of swollen knee worries and the prospect of further international cricket abroad.

There was certainly much good Northants cricket to admire, but the season ended somewhat restlessly, with the future of such leading players as Kapil Dev and Willey in deepening anxiety.

ENGLISH SEASON 1983/NORTHAMPTONSHIRE

Schweppes County Championship: 6th; Won 7, Lost 4, Drawn 13
All First-Class Matches: Won 8, Lost 4, Drawn 14
NatWest Bank Trophy: Lost to Middlesex in quarter-final
Benson & Hedges Cup: Lost to Lancashire in quarter-final
John Player League: 15th; Won 5, Lost 10, No result 1

Championship Averages

*not out

Batting and Fielding	M	I	NO	HS	R	Avge	100	50	Ct	St
J.A. Carse	10	10	8	36*	129	64.50	-	-	-	-
A.J. Lamb	13	21	5	119	840	52.50	3	2	9	-
P. Willey	22	38	7	175*	1483	47.83	4	8	5	-
Kapil Dev	7	10	2	120	349	43.62	1	1	10	-
W. Larkins	24	41	0	252	1739	42.41	5	4	12	-
G. Cook	23	40	3	128	1496	40.43	1	11	31	3
R.G. Williams	24	37	8	104*	1161	40.03	1	8	9	-
R.J. Boyd-Moss	15	24	2	101	704	32.00	1	5	4	-
G. Sharp	22	23	8	98	447	29.80	-	2	38	5
D.J. Capel	16	22	4	109*	470	26.11	1	2	10	-
D.S. Steele	24	29	6	60	506	22.00	-	2	27	-
M.J. Bamber	5	10	1	44	163	18.11	-	-	4	-
A. Walker	5	4	3	7*	18	18.00	-	-	3	-
N.A. Mallender	21	25	7	24*	238	13.22	-	-	7	-
D.J. Wild	3	5	0	29	64	12.80	-	-	1	-
T.M. Lamb	7	9	1	21	36	4.50	-	-	-	-
B.J. Griffiths	22	13	2	15	27	2.45	-	-	2	-

Also batted: R.J. Bailey (1 match) 4 (1 ct).

Hundreds (17)

5 **W. Larkins:** 236 v Derbys, Derby; 187 v Lancs, Northampton; 145 v Glam, Northampton; 252 v Glam, Cardiff; 100 v Middx, Lord's.
4 **P. Willey:** 175* v Hants, Northampton; 108 v Notts, Nottingham; 117* v Worcs, Northampton; 147* v Lancs, Northampton.
3 **A.J. Lamb:** 108 v Surrey, Oval; 107* v Yorks, Northampton; 119 v Glam, Cardiff.
1 **R.J. Boyd-Moss:** 101 v Leics, Leicester.
  D.J. Capel: 109* v Somerset, Northampton.
  G. Cook: 128 v Kent, Canterbury.
  Kapil Dev: 120 v Somerset, Weston-super-Mare.
  R.G. Williams: 104* v Yorks, Bradford.

Bowling	O	M	R	W	Avge	Best	5w/I	10w/M
D.S. Steele	643.2	235	1415	66	21.43	5-48	2	-
R.G. Williams	363.3	109	906	42	21.57	4-18	-	-
T.M. Lamb	122.1	36	261	11	23.72	4-49	-	-
Kapil Dev	161	47	385	16	24.06	4-24	-	-
A. Walker	123.4	22	438	17	25.76	4-61	-	-
B.J. Griffiths	536.2	130	1424	50	28.48	6-92	1	-
P. Willey	458.5	142	956	31	30.83	4-51	-	-
N.A. Mallender	465.1	95	1501	48	31.27	6-48	1	-
J.A. Carse	237	50	719	22	32.68	5-43	1	-

Also bowled: R.J. Boyd-Moss 11-5-15-1; D.J. Capel 57.5-12-194-3; G. Cook 11-3-43-0; A.J. Lamb 1-0-1-0; W. Larkins 25.4-3-67-5; D.J. Wild 23-7-72-2.

Nottinghamshire

Nottinghamshire, first and fourth in the County Championship in the two previous years, suffered a depressing decline in 1983 to finish fourth from the bottom of the table, winning only three matches and not one of them after early July. In the John Player League, Notts, who equalled their best-ever position in claiming fifth place the previous season, this time finished joint-bottom with Gloucestershire.

This sharp fall-off in standards could not be wholly excused by the loss of key players through international commitment or injury. Undoubtedly, however, the loss of Richard Hadlee to World Cup and Test duties with New Zealand did inhibit Notts, depriving them of their most penetrative bowler and of a batsman able to make runs at a gallop when necessary. Ironically, during an otherwise brilliant summer, four of the five Championship matches for which Hadlee was available were seriously affected by rain. Captain Clive Rice missed a month of the season with a fractured hand, off-spinner Eddie Hemmings was at times restricted by a shoulder injury, and Derek Randall had to cope not only with international commitments but also with the demands of an extremely packed testimonial programme. The fact that Randall scored fewer than 600 runs for Notts was certainly a factor in producing only 39 batting bonus points, fewer than any other county.

An unbeaten century carried Rice past 1,000 runs during the final game of the season, and Hemmings took 7 for 23 against Lancashire in June to set up one of the Championship victories. But most often Notts were heavily reliant for runs on opener Tim Robinson and for bowling penetration on Mike Hendrick.

Robinson, in his fifth season of first-class cricket, scored 1,545 runs for an average of over 40, and was awarded his county cap on completion of an impressive 207 against Warwickshire on September 1, only the fifth three-figure score of his career. Improved defensive technique and a greater capacity to concentrate and eschew the chancy strokes provided the basis of Robinson's emergence as an opener of England potential. John Birch was the other batsman to pass 1,000 runs, despite a marked decline while deputizing for Rice in the captaincy.

Hendrick, whose first season with Notts in 1982 yielded a disappointing 26 wickets, this time benefited from omission from Sunday cricket. He performed with consistent excellence to claim 66 wickets at 17 each and finish fourth in the national bowling averages. Kevin Cooper's 57 wickets equalled his highest total, and Kevin Saxelby, at a brisker pace with less movement, also made a useful contribution.

Bruce French did nothing to diminish his reputation as one of the best of the younger wicket-keepers, though a fall in productivity with the bat prevented him from advancing his international ambitions. Seamer Andy Pick, off-spinner Peter Such, and batsman Paul Johnson all confirmed their development, and their selection for the England under-19 team against the Australian tourists contributed to Notts' hopes of a more rewarding season in 1984.

Schweppes County Championship: 14th; Won 3, Lost 10, Drawn 11
All First-Class Matches: Won 4, Lost 10, Drawn 11
NatWest Bank Trophy: Lost to Sussex in 2nd round
Benson & Hedges Cup: Failed to qualify for Q-F (3rd in Group B)
John Player League: 15th; Won 4, Lost 9, Tied 1, No result 2

Championship Averages *not out

Batting and Fielding	M	I	NO	HS	R	Avge	100	50	Ct	St
R.T. Robinson	24	39	3	207	1464	40.66	2	10	6	-
C.E.B. Rice	19	30	2	101*	1026	36.64	2	3	14	-
R.J. Hadlee	5	4	0	103	119	29.75	1	-	3	-
J.D. Birch	23	36	2	95	1007	29.61	-	7	20	-
D.W. Randall	15	22	1	94	583	27.76	-	4	17	-
B. Hassan	21	34	1	112	890	26.96	1	5	17	-
P. Johnson	15	26	2	125	524	21.83	1	3	6	-
B.N. French	23	36	4	91	589	18.40	-	3	49	3
R.A. Pick	6	8	2	25*	84	14.00	-	-	-	-
K.E. Cooper	21	25	7	30*	245	13.61	-	-	5	-
E.E. Hemmings	23	32	3	38	377	13.00	-	-	11	-
M.K. Bore	12	15	4	24	131	11.90	-	-	7	-
K. Saxelby	20	26	3	35	259	11.26	-	-	1	-
M. Hendrick	21	26	13	15*	130	10.00	-	-	18	-
N.J.B. Illingworth	2	4	0	17	29	7.25	-	-	2	-
M.A. Fell	4	7	0	32	46	6.57	-	-	2	-
P.M. Such	9	14	4	5	13	1.30	-	-	7	-

C.W. Scott (1 st) played in one match without batting.

Hundreds (7)

2 C.E.B. Rice: 100* v Glos, Bristol; 101* v Middx, Nottingham.
  R.T. Robinson: 110 v Worcs, Worcester; 207 v Warwicks, Nottingham.
1 R.J. Hadlee: 103 v Sussex, Hove.
  B. Hassan: 112 v Essex, Chelmsford.
  P. Johnson: 125 v Glos, Bristol.

Bowling	O	M	R	W	Avge	Best	5w/I	10w/M
R.J. Hadlee	86.2	28	210	13	16.15	5-72	1	-
M. Hendrick	552.1	190	1122	66	17.00	6-17	4	-
K. Saxelby	387.2	93	1265	47	26.91	5-52	2	-
K.E. Cooper	545	149	1530	50	30.60	7-33	4	-
E.E. Hemmings	710.4	195	2000	59	33.89	7-23	2	1
P.M. Such	194	36	722	19	38.00	6-123	1	-
M.K. Bore	329.5	91	981	19	51.63	3-34	-	-

Also bowled: J.D. Birch 1-0-1-0; M.A. Fell 3-0-11-0; N.J.B. Illingworth 25-2-97-1; R.A. Pick 134.4-16-500-7; R.T. Robinson 1-0-1-0.

Somerset

Though Somerset had to be content with 10th place in the Schweppes County Championship, they were consoled by carrying off the NatWest Trophy for the first time. Despite the absence of Botham, Richards, and Garner during the World Cup and of Botham later on Test match duty, they came within a whisker of winning the John Player League as well. Only an uncharacteristically poor performance against Worcestershire on the Sunday after their NatWest triumph prevented them from achieving the double. As it was, they finished level on points with Yorkshire, who took the title by virtue of winning more away matches.

Generally, Somerset's successes came as a result of team-work rather than individual brilliance, although Richards, in towering form, topped the national averages and Botham, whose innings in the NatWest semifinal ranks with his finest, produced moments of magic. The figures of most of their colleagues were unremarkable, yet someone could normally be relied upon to deliver the goods when it mattered.

Somerset's batting was handicapped by their captain Brian Rose's back injury, which severely restricted his appearances. But the additional responsibility thrown on Roebuck brought some consistent batting from him, and he also captained the side capably when called upon. Lloyds and Popplewell made useful contributions from time to time without ever striking a rich vein of runs, and the same was true of Denning who reserved his best performances for the Sunday League. Late in the season, Felton confirmed the promise he had shown in 1982, and Wyatt, an opening batsman of phlegmatic temperament and solid technique, played some mature innings. Ollis, given an extended run, looked a player with possibilities, but Slocombe disappointed.

Somerset's real problem lay in their bowling. Garner, though he returned very respectable figures, was troubled throughout the season by a shoulder injury which limited his appearances and his effectiveness. This threw an additional burden on Dredge, who responded with characteristic energy and enthusiasm, but he is not the ideal spearhead. His task might have been easier but for injury to Wilson, who put in some whole-hearted performances when fit.

Marks, despite a fine record in one-day cricket, again obtained moderate results in the County Championship, where he was no more effective than Lloyds. Popplewell's medium-pacers were useful at times, and Booth, a young Yorkshire-born slow-left-arm bowler, did enough to suggest that he might eventually provide much-needed balance to the two off-spinners. Bearing in mind the limitations of their attack, it was not surprising that Somerset could win only three Championship matches.

A bright feature was the form of their wicket-keeper Gard, who had waited so long and so patiently in the shadow of Derek Taylor. Gard's excellent performance in the NatWest final set the seal on a splendid season's work. He earned high praise from a number of good judges, and though his career has started late, he could – if his batting continues to develop – become a candidate for international honours.

Schweppes County Championship: 10th; Won 3, Lost 7, Drawn 14
All First-Class Matches: Won 3, Lost 7, Drawn 15 (Abandoned 1)
NatWest Bank Trophy: Winners
Benson & Hedges Cup: Failed to qualify for Q-F (4th in Group C)
John Player League: 2nd; Won 10, Lost 3, No result 3

Championship Averages   *not out

Batting and Fielding	M	I	NO	HS	R	Avge	100	50	Ct	St
I.V.A. Richards	12	20	4	216	1204	75.25	5	3	6	-
I.T. Botham	10	13	0	152	570	43.84	2	1	7	-
J.G. Wyatt	5	10	2	82*	338	42.25	-	3	-	-
P.M. Roebuck	22	38	5	106*	1235	37.42	1	9	9	-
N.A. Felton	7	12	1	173*	376	34.18	1	1	2	-
J. Garner	9	14	6	44	223	27.87	-	-	9	-
J.W. Lloyds	20	33	2	100	803	25.90	1	3	12	-
N.F.M. Popplewell	23	37	3	143	879	25.85	1	4	21	-
R.L. Ollis	13	22	2	99*	517	25.85	-	3	3	-
V.J. Marks	15	23	2	44*	498	23.71	-	-	5	-
P.W. Denning	20	34	3	85	659	21.25	-	3	6	-
B.C. Rose	7	7	0	52	138	19.71	-	1	2	-
T. Gard	24	31	4	51	440	16.29	-	2	38	8
P.H.L. Wilson	10	9	6	25	45	15.00	-	-	3	-
C.H. Dredge	21	26	5	50	296	14.09	-	1	10	-
P.A. Slocombe	10	15	2	37	145	11.15	-	-	5	-
G.V. Palmer	10	13	2	78	119	10.81	-	1	8	-
M.R. Davis	13	15	4	20	105	9.54	-	-	3	-
S.C. Booth	10	12	5	9	24	3.42	-	-	6	-

Also batted: D. Breakwell (2 matches) 55*, 4, 13; N. Russom (1) 8.

Hundreds (11)

5 I.V.A. Richards: 216 v Leics, Leicester; 142* v Surrey, Taunton; 117* v Northants, Northampton; 128* v Northants, Weston-super-Mare; 103 v Kent, Taunton.
2 I.T. Botham: 107 v Worcs, Worcester; 152 v Leics, Leicester.
1 N.A. Felton: 173* v Kent, Taunton.
  J.W. Lloyds: 100 v Northants, Northampton.
  N.F.M. Popplewell: 143 v Glos, Bath.
  P.M. Roebuck: 106* v Hants, Taunton.

Bowling	O	M	R	W	Avge	Best	5w/I	10w/M
J. Garner	256	67	659	34	19.38	6-37	1	-
C.H. Dredge	492.3	127	1323	48	27.56	5-51	2	-
J.W. Lloyds	342.1	96	990	34	29.11	5-120	1	-
V.J. Marks	534.4	169	1488	49	30.36	6-79	3	-
G.V. Palmer	208.3	39	630	20	31.50	5-38	1	-
N.F.M. Popplewell	225	37	736	23	32.00	4-69	-	-
I.T. Botham	119.3	28	388	12	32.33	5-38	1	-
M.R. Davis	212.4	40	746	23	32.43	4-34	-	-
P.H.L. Wilson	213.3	37	717	21	34.14	4-77	-	-
I.V.A. Richards	188	61	462	12	38.50	3-56	-	-
S.C. Booth	296.2	85	849	21	40.42	4-26	-	-

Also bowled: D. Breakwell 49-17-121-4; T. Gard 0.2-0-8-0; R.L. Ollis 1-0-2-0; P.M. Roebuck 5-0-25-0; N. Russom 5-1-18-0; P.A. Slocombe 2-1-1-0.

Surrey

The throes of rebuilding were evident at The Oval long before contractors moved in on July 19 to demolish the Taverners stand. As the drills chattered and the dust flew, Surrey begged their supporters' forbearance – much as manager Micky Stewart had done before the season began.

As it transpired, the architect of Surrey's playing affairs proved accurate in predicting that the county would not readily overcome the retirement of strike bowler Robin Jackman and could not, therefore, anticipate significant success in the championship. Stewart was also near the mark in forecasting that Jackman's successor, David Thomas, would claim around 50-60 wickets, and that the batting would be generally strong and sometimes spectacular.

It was certainly spectacular at Chelmsford, on May 30, when, in the first innings against Essex, Surrey were dismissed for 14 in 14.3 overs. Remarkably, the match was subsequently saved by an unbroken third wicket partnership of 167 between Grahame Clinton and Roger Knight.

That was more typical of Surrey's style throughout a season in which, despite the absence of New Zealand's Geoff Howarth, the collective batsmanship was invariably solid, and high-scoring individual performances – such as Thomas's splendid century against Notts – were not the preserve of specialist batsmen. Of these, incidentally, Monte Lynch reeled off fifty after fifty in his irrepressible style, and the highly promising Duncan Pauline crowned increasing success with a fine maiden century against Sussex, at The Oval.

The bowling, however, lacked consistency. In the absence of Jackman, an opening attack of Clarke and Thomas tended to promote hostility at the expense of accuracy. Sometimes, on unhelpful wickets and in the bright light of a long, hot summer, Clarke bowled too short, Thomas too wide, and the new ball was wasted.

Often, on such occasions, the point was emphasized by the change bowlers, especially Monkhouse, whose admirable line and length rapidly brought him to the fore – notably in taking 7 for 51 against Notts. Payne, too, had his moments, not least at The Oval in July, when his career-best 5 for 13 hustled Gloucester to defeat by an innings and 84 runs.

Spinners Pocock and Needham coincidentally produced outstanding performances and provided Surrey with a notable double against Notts. At Trent Bridge, in June, Needham claimed 5 for 52 as Surrey won by 10 wickets, and, at The Oval in July, Pocock's contribution to a 9-wicket victory was 6 for 74 off 33 overs.

Another comprehensive result was achieved at Guildford, where the redoubtable Butcher and the up-and-coming Alec Stewart, with respective aggregates of 207 and 125, were prominent in Worcestershire's 227-run defeat.

But, set against such individual and corporate successes, were some equally salutary failures, not so much in defeat but in the frequency of drawn matches. This implies that, if the batting produced a rich spectrum of qualities, Stewart's reservations about the bowling were upheld. Furthermore, in Surrey's unexceptional fielding may lie a clue to their lack of success in the limited-over game.

Schweppes County Championship: 8th; Won 7, Lost 4, Drawn 13
All First-Class Matches: Won 8, Lost 4, Drawn 13
NatWest Bank Trophy: Lost to Warwickshire in 2nd round
Benson & Hedges Cup: Failed to qualify for Q-F (4th in Group D)
John Player League: 11th; Won 4, Lost 7, No result 5

Championship Averages

*not out

Batting and Fielding	M	I	NO	HS	R	Avge	100	50	Ct	St
M.A. Lynch	24	39	10	119	1558	53.72	3	11	15	-
D.M. Smith	13	20	4	131*	748	46.75	2	3	13	-
D.B. Pauline	11	20	1	115	758	39.89	1	7	3	-
R.D.V. Knight	24	38	6	101*	1235	38.59	1	9	28	-
D.J. Thomas	23	31	5	119	937	36.03	2	4	8	-
A.R. Butcher	24	43	3	128	1341	33.52	3	6	12	-
A.J. Stewart	9	16	3	82	407	31.30	-	2	4	1
G.P. Howarth	4	5	1	66	123	30.75	-	1	1	-
C.J. Richards	24	34	8	85*	718	27.61	-	2	46	7
I.R. Payne	9	10	4	43	139	23.16	-	-	11	-
G. Monkhouse	17	18	5	46	291	22.38	-	-	7	-
G.S. Clinton	12	21	3	105	371	20.61	1	2	-	-
S.T. Clarke	24	24	4	43	285	14.25	-	-	17	-
P.I. Pocock	23	19	7	23	110	9.16	-	-	8	-
A. Needham	8	13	1	18	88	7.33	-	-	1	-
I.J. Curtis	12	10	4	7	22	3.66	-	-	3	-

Also batted: K.S. Mackintosh (1 match) 18*, 5*; P.A. Waterman (2) 6*, 0.

Hundreds (13)

3 A.R. Butcher: 100 v Lancs, Oval; 128 v Glam, Swansea; 122 v Worcs, Guildford.
   M.A. Lynch: 112 v Worcs, Worcester; 119 v Hants, Southampton; 101* v Sussex, Hove.
2 D.M. Smith: 106* v Middx, Oval; 131* v Glam, Swansea.
   D.J. Thomas: 119 v Notts, Oval; 103* v Sussex, Hove.
1 G.S. Clinton: 105 v Glos, Bristol.
   R.D.V. Knight: 101* v Essex, Chelmsford.
   D.B. Pauline: 115 v Sussex, Oval.

Bowling	O	M	R	W	Avge	Best	5w/I	10w/M
G. Monkhouse	352.5	92	999	45	22.20	7-51	1	-
S.T. Clarke	693.1	183	1773	79	22.44	7-53	4	1
P.I. Pocock	681.2	200	1774	68	26.08	7-79	4	-
D.J. Thomas	547	113	1781	57	31.24	4-22	-	-
I.R. Payne	150.5	38	435	12	36.25	5-13	1	-
A. Needham	123	29	409	10	40.90	5-52	1	-
R.D.V. Knight	236	60	677	15	45.13	3-58	-	-
I.J. Curtis	239.5	65	647	11	58.81	4-14	-	-

Also bowled: A.R. Butcher 44.4-9-210-5; M.A. Lynch 7.3-0-47-0; K.S. Mackintosh 15-2-47-0; D.M. Smith 2.2-0-20-0; P.A. Waterman 39-7-151-1.

Sussex

Sussex, runners-up in the County Championship only two years ago, finished eleventh, their lowest position since they finished bottom in 1975. There must be some sympathy for them, because they had unending fitness problems, injuries being concentrated on their pace and seam bowlers.

In 1982, Sussex had slid to eighth place from having been second in 1981, and the main cause of their fall was the unavailability for half the season of Imran Khan, who was touring with Pakistan. In 1983, they should have missed him for only the three weeks of the World Cup. Instead, Sussex had to do without their great all-rounder until July. He had sustained stress fractures in the shins while fulfilling Pakistan's various international commitments during the winter, and had been advised total rest. In fact, it was very much against Sussex's counsel that Imran Khan played for Pakistan in the World Cup, even if purely as a batsman. He did not appear for Sussex at all before the World Cup, and when he at last began his season with the county, they were almost halfway through their fixtures, having won twice but lost five times, more often than any other county.

The cost to Sussex of Imran's absence can be measured by the fact that in their last 13 matches, in which he batted 25 times, Imran scored 1,260 runs at an average of 57.27. Able to concentrate on his batting, he had a run of high scores, all made with great authority. But as the season advanced and Sussex's injury list lengthened, Imran was compelled to lend a hand to their depleted attack. He did not feature as a front-line bowler, but operated from a short run. He still generated a great deal of pace, and in a mere 46.2 overs took 12 wickets for 86. This included 6 for 6 in 27 balls at Edgbaston, against Warwickshire, a hat-trick adding to the impact of his amazing feat.

Despite the added strength that Imran's success provided, Sussex scored only one more win, beating Surrey at the oval in a match of declarations at the tail end of the season.

Being without Imran was only one of Sussex's several misfortunes. One night in June, Sussex's other all-rounder, Ian Greig, found himself locked out of his Hove flat and attempted to get in the burglar's way. This hazardous operation ended with Greig acquiring a fracture in the foot, and he remained pavilion-bound until the week before the end of the season.

Garth le Roux, the other main prong in Sussex's attack, ruptured a groin muscle in mid-July and did not play again. Their season would have been a complete disaster had Tony Pigott not stayed fit right through the long hot summer, and had they not accidentally discovered a new pace bowler on the Lord's ground staff in Reeve, whom they registered in midseason. Although inexperienced, Reeve was accurate and strong enough to bowl for long periods.

It would not be accurate, however, to put all blame for Sussex's mediocrity in 1983 on their bowling limitations. Except for Gehan

ENGLISH SEASON 1983/SUSSEX

Mendis, who scored heavily, their batting was disappointingly erratic, and Paul Parker's form fell away so badly that a stage came when he had to step out of the side.

Schweppes County Championship: 11th; Won 3, Lost 10, Drawn 10 (Abandoned 1)
All First-Class Matches: Won 3, Lost 10, Drawn 11 (Abandoned 1)
NatWest Bank Trophy: Lost to Somerset in quarter-final
Benson & Hedges Cup: Failed to qualify for Q-F (3rd in Group C)
John Player League: 4th; Won 9, Lost 5, No result 2

Championship Averages   *not out

Batting and Fielding	M	I	NO	HS	R	Avge	100	50	Ct	St
Imran Khan	13	25	3	124*	1260	57.27	2	12	6	-
D.K. Standing	4	8	3	60	240	48.00	-	2	2	-
G.D. Mendis	23	45	6	133*	1608	41.23	4	8	8	-
I.J. Gould	17	22	6	59*	473	29.56	-	1	32	13
A.P. Wells	15	27	4	92	664	28.86	-	5	11	-
G.S. le Roux	12	16	1	80	379	25.26	-	1	2	-
C.M. Wells	23	40	6	71	857	25.20	-	5	8	-
J.R.T. Barclay	21	37	3	65	743	21.85	-	3	14	-
P.W.G. Parker	16	26	2	79	507	21.12	-	4	5	-
J.R.P. Heath	9	18	2	39	335	20.93	-	-	5	-
I.A. Greig	8	9	0	59	177	19.66	-	1	2	-
A.M. Green	15	29	2	53	519	19.22	-	1	10	-
A.C.S. Pigott	22	28	8	63	381	19.05	-	3	14	-
R.S. Cowan	5	10	0	50	154	15.40	-	1	2	-
D.A. Reeve	17	20	5	42*	192	12.80	-	-	7	-
C.E. Waller	21	22	11	21	98	8.90	-	-	6	-
D.J. Smith	5	7	2	13	22	4.40	-	-	9	-
A.N. Jones	5	7	3	4*	11	2.75	-	-	-	-

Also batted: C.P. Phillipson (1 match) 23, 28 (1 ct). A. Willows played in one match without batting.

Hundreds (6)

4 G.D. Mendis: 132 v Worcs, Hove; 121* v Northants, Hove; 105 v Middx, Hove; 133* v Worcs, Worcester.
2 Imran Khan: 101 v Hants, Eastbourne; 124* v Surrey, Oval.

Bowling	O	M	R	W	Avge	Best	5w/I	10w/M
Imran Khan	46.2	12	86	12	7.16	6-6	1	-
G.S. le Roux	358.3	90	944	37	25.51	5-17	2	-
A.C.S. Pigott	577.5	98	1879	72	26.09	6-22	4	-
D.A. Reeve	472.1	131	1233	42	29.35	4-15	-	-
C.E. Waller	752	223	1868	53	35.24	6-126	2	-
C.M. Wells	376.3	82	1135	32	35.46	4-69	-	-
I.A. Greig	185	26	681	17	40.05	4-42	-	-
J.R.T. Barclay	231.3	59	774	17	45.52	3-30	-	-

Also bowled: R.S. Cowan 8-2-27-0; I.J. Gould 2-0-9-0; A.M. Green 53.4-9-248-6; J.R.P. Heath 8-0-58-0; A.N. Jones 81.4-10-358-6; P.W.G. Parker 4.2-1-30-0; D.K. Standing 4.3-0-32-0; A. Willows 8-3-11-0.

Hat-trick: Imran Khan v Warwicks, Birmingham.

Warwickshire

A measure of Warwickshire's vast improvement is that they won more matches in the Schweppes Championship, albeit in a longer programme, than when the title pennant was last flying over Edgbaston in 1972. No-one could have envisaged the remarkable change in their cricket from the time they defeated Lancashire early in June. It was not only their first championship win at Edgbaston for four years, but the start of a sequence of seven consecutive victories. Lancashire (twice), Glamorgan, Northants, Yorkshire, Middlesex, and Essex were all swept aside in an almost violent upsurge which lifted them as high as third position, only 10 points behind the leaders, before Derbyshire ended the winning run only one short of the county record.

If such a transformation can be explained in individual terms, then the delighted, if somewhat stunned, Edgbaston membership had to look no further than the contributions by Gifford and Old. David Brown, the manager, and Bob Willis, the captain, set themselves before a storm of criticism by backing their judgement that the former England bowlers would improve an attack that had been sadly lacking in two years at the bottom of the Championship. The doubters saw them as ageing conscripts from other counties – and were proved hopelessly wrong.

Gifford became the first Warwickshire bowler to take 100 wickets in a season since Doshi in 1980, and his final total of 104 was the best by a Warwickshire spinner for a decade. It was also Gifford's highest return since 1970, proving that a new home brought an irresistible challenge, even at the age of 43. Old was the most successful seamer. He sacrificed pace for an economical run-up and re-discovered his away-swinger, thus enabling him to revert to long spells as a stock bowler after opening with the new ball.

Ferreira, the popular South African all-rounder, was equally consistent in Warwickshire's golden months of June and July. Sadly, his season terminated six weeks early because of a broken thumb, and with Willis away so often with England, the attack lost some of its penetration in the closing period. However, Hogg, despite problems with his run-up, was a steady and enthusiastic supporting seamer, and Ferreira's absence provided an opportunity for two teenage all-rounders, Paul Smith (brother of the opening batsman) and Thorne, to serve a brief apprenticeship at Championship level. Smith's whippy medium-pace became increasingly effective, while Thorne, who will be at Oxford University in 1984, hinted at possibilities as a batsman who can also bowl useful left-arm seamers.

Batting, of course, has rarely been a hardship for Warwickshire, and while the Edgbaston pitches were more tolerant than usual to bowlers (probably because the 'Brumbrella' cover was in permanent use during the rainy month of May), the five specialists automatically topped 1,000 runs. Lloyd, England's twelfth man at the Lord's Test, and the ever-consistent Amiss provided the foundation, while David Smith was a good opening partner for Lloyd, and Humpage was always a potential match-winner, as he proved by making a century when the last two wickets put on 122 to beat Yorkshire. Kallicharran started slowly but scored well over 1,000 runs, including five hundreds, in the last five weeks.

Schweppes County Championship: 5th; Won 10, Lost 3, Drawn 11
All First-Class Matches: Won 10, Lost 4, Drawn 13
NatWest Bank Trophy: Lost to Kent in quarter-final
Benson & Hedges Cup: Lost to Essex in quarter-final
John Player League: 15th; Won 4, Lost 9, Tied 1, No result 2

Championship Averages   *not out

Batting and Fielding	M	I	NO	HS	R	Avge	100	50	Ct	St
A.I. Kallicharran	22	34	4	243*	1637	54.56	6	4	16	-
T.A. Lloyd	22	39	4	208*	1659	47.40	5	5	12	-
D.L. Amiss	24	40	4	164	1571	43.63	3	10	22	-
G.W. Humpage	24	38	6	141*	1003	31.34	2	4	22	5
P.A. Smith	11	14	3	65	335	30.45	-	3	1	-
K.D. Smith	24	42	4	109	1133	29.81	2	7	7	-
C. Lethbridge	7	7	3	73*	110	27.50	-	1	-	-
Asif Din	12	18	2	65	361	22.56	-	2	10	-
A.M. Ferreira	16	22	4	66	399	22.16	-	1	8	-
D.A. Thorne	4	6	3	23*	62	20.66	-	-	3	-
C.M. Old	21	24	3	62	387	18.42	-	1	6	-
R.G.D. Willis	12	12	7	20*	79	15.80	-	-	2	-
R.I.H.B. Dyer	7	12	3	25	135	15.00	-	-	4	-
G.C. Small	5	7	3	31	59	14.75	-	-	2	-
N. Gifford	20	20	6	39	201	14.35	-	-	8	-
G.A. Tedstone	10	11	0	36	156	14.18	-	-	18	3
W. Hogg	20	16	6	27*	59	5.90	-	-	5	-

Also batted: G.J. Lord (3 matches) 61, 29, 1 (1 ct).

Hundreds (18)

6 A.I. Kallicharran: 209* v Lancs, Birmingham; 173* v Surrey, Oval; 111 v Kent, Folkestone; 152 and 118* v Sussex, Birmingham; 243* v Glam, Birmingham.
5 T.A. Lloyd: 208* v Glos, Birmingham; 126 v Lancs, Birmingham; 124* v Surrey, Oval; 123 v Glam, Birmingham; 112 v Somerset, Taunton.
3 D.L. Amiss: 142 v Glos, Birmingham; 111 v Essex, Nuneaton; 164 v Kent, Folkestone.
2 G.W. Humpage: 141* v Yorks, Birmingham; 105 v Kent, Birmingham.
  K.D. Smith: 103 v Middx, Lord's; 109 v Glos, Cheltenham.

Bowling	O	M	R	W	Avge	Best	5w/I	10w/M
N. Gifford	991.4	336	2220	99	22.42	6-22	7	2
C.M. Old	639.3	146	1786	61	29.27	5-50	2	-
G.C. Small	89.5	12	299	10	29.90	3-13	-	-
A.M. Ferreira	485.4	128	1237	39	31.71	5-19	1	-
W. Hogg	324.4	61	1073	31	34.61	5-63	1	-
R.G.D. Willis	247.2	58	772	21	36.76	3-8	-	-
P.A. Smith	169	21	628	16	39.25	3-56	-	-

Also bowled: Asif Din 39.1-5-149-1; G.W. Humpage 3-0-13-0; A.I. Kallicharran 135-18-476-8; C. Lethbridge 69.1-11-264-6; T.A. Lloyd 1-0-24-0; G.J. Lord 8-3-12-0; D.A. Thorne 21-0-115-2.

Worcestershire

It was not until the final weekend of the season that Worcestershire removed the ever-present probability that they would finish bottom in both the Schweppes Championship and the John Player League. Their escape from double indignity was seen as a substantial triumph for the county's decision, controversial at the time, to replace a number of senior players with the youngsters who had won the Second XI title in 1982.

Of the emerging batsmen, D'Oliveira, Weston, and Curtis were close to 1,000 runs. At times they were plagued by the inconsistency that comes with learning, but nothing in a season of adversity was more exciting than D'Oliveira's maiden century against the formidable Middlesex attack. Weston also scored his first Championship hundred, and Curtis, resolute and correct, played with maturity on coming down from Cambridge. Further encouragement was provided by McEvoy, the former Essex batsman, who scored his maiden century when elevated to open later in the season.

The batsmen carried an additional burden in that the pitches at New Road were far from satisfactory. Roy MacLaren, the new groundsman, inherited a square that had deteriorated in previous years, and he could not begin to seek a remedy until the autumn. Most of the batsmen were happier away from New Road. Neale, a caring captain who coaxed and cosseted his young team, recalled that, when he completed 1,000 runs he had scored only 250 at home. In the circumstances, it was a major achievement for Neale and Patel to pass 1,500 in a season for the first time. Patel was only one short of taking 50 wickets with his off-breaks for the second year in succession.

Patel's partnership with Illingworth, the Yorkshire-born left-arm spinner, will obviously become a cornerstone of Worcestershire's bowling for many years to come. Illingworth adapted particularly well to the different demands of one-day cricket, and finished his first full season with two career-best performances. His 5 for 24 against Somerset, a personal best in the John Player League, allowed Yorkshire to approach the final Sunday as League leaders, but his 5 for 26 against Gloucestershire, his best Championship return, consigned his native county to the wooden spoon in the Championship.

Pace bowling has not been Worcestershire's strongest department in recent years. Their hopes of resolving the problem by hiring the Australian fast-medium bowler Alderman were dashed by his serious shoulder injury. In the absence of a regular overseas player, Ellcock, still only 18, displayed obvious potential as a fast bowler in the true West Indian mould. Alternatively, Worcestershire called on the Barbadian all-rounder King, who played several explosive innings when he was available. Pridgeon eventually anchored the seam attack, taking more than 70 wickets in his most productive season, but injuries affected Inchmore and Warner, and Perryman was released after taking only 13 wickets in his limited appearances.

The county are hopeful of signing an overseas strike bowler for next season, and that would be a major step towards future prosperity.

Schweppes County Championship: 16th; Won 2, Lost 11, Drawn 11
All First-Class Matches: Won 4, Lost 12, Drawn 11
NatWest Bank Trophy: Lost to Nottinghamshire in 1st round
Benson & Hedges Cup: Failed to qualify for Q-F (4th in Group A)
John Player League: 11th; Won 4, Lost 7, Tied 3, No result 2

Championship Averages

*not out

Batting and Fielding	M	I	NO	HS	R	Avge	100	50	Ct	St
P.A. Neale	23	39	3	139	1500	41.66	2	11	8	-
D.N. Patel	23	39	2	112	1537	41.54	3	10	13	-
T.S. Curtis	8	16	2	84	363	25.92	-	2	6	-
M.J. Weston	19	33	1	115	823	25.71	1	2	7	-
D.B. D'Oliveira	19	34	2	102	775	24.21	1	2	11	-
P.J. Newport	4	4	1	41*	72	24.00	-	-	-	-
J.A. Ormrod	23	40	3	78	883	23.86	-	5	11	-
M.S. Scott	5	9	2	57*	155	22.14	-	1	-	-
D.A. Banks	5	9	1	44	174	21.75	-	-	1	-
D.J. Humphries	18	27	4	59	496	21.56	-	2	24	8
M.S.A. McEvoy	15	24	1	103	491	21.34	1	1	12	-
J.D. Inchmore	17	22	3	51	330	17.36	-	1	3	-
P. Moores	6	9	1	30	110	13.75	-	-	8	1
R.M. Ellcock	12	18	4	36	154	11.00	-	-	2	-
R.K. Illingworth	22	30	5	55	238	9.52	-	1	6	-
A.P. Pridgeon	24	30	8	23	186	8.45	-	-	5	-
A.E. Warner	7	12	2	20*	81	8.10	-	-	1	-
S.P. Perryman	10	13	6	22	54	7.71	-	-	3	-

Also batted: C.L. King (2 matches) 123, 8, 27 (1 ct); Younis Ahmed (2) 10*, 35*.

Hundreds (9)

3 **D.N. Patel:** 105 v Surrey, Guildford; 112 v Warwicks, Birmingham; 111 v Glos, Worcester.
2 **P.A. Neale:** 135 v Glam, Abergavenny; 139 v Lancs, Manchester.
1 **D.B. D'Oliveira:** 102 v Middx, Worcester.
  C.L. King: 123 v Somerset, Worcester.
  M.S.A. McEvoy: 103 v Warwicks, Birmingham.
  M.J. Weston: 115 v Sussex, Hove.

Bowling	O	M	R	W	Avge	Best	5w/I	10m/M
A.E. Warner	168.4	26	501	21	23.85	4-72	-	-
A.P. Pridgeon	581.2	130	1687	59	28.59	5-21	2	-
J.D. Inchmore	384.2	75	1107	32	34.59	5-45	1	-
R.M. Ellcock	244	39	931	25	37.24	4-70	-	-
D.N. Patel	638.4	185	1709	45	37.97	5-52	2	-
R.K. Illingworth	606.5	148	1680	41	40.97	5-26	1	-
S.P. Perryman	211.5	41	644	10	64.40	4-91	-	-

Also bowled: T.S. Curtis 3-1-6-0; D.B. D'Oliveira 65.1-13-250-3; C.L. King 15-2-39-1; P.J. Newport 41-3-118-3; M.J. Weston 14.2-3-69-2.

Yorkshire

It was a summer of contradictions for the White Rose. Bottom of the table in the Schweppes Championship for the first time, they were yet champions of the John Player League, a competition in which they had previously only been the shame-faced runners-up in 1973.

Boycott, who had hardly scored a run until July, just missed scoring 1,000 in August, almost reached 2,000 for the summer, and had his second-best season for the county. Moxon, languishing in the second team for a dreary two months, scored 153 against Lancashire and ended with K.W.R. Fletcher speaking of him as an England prospect.

Sharp finished in a storm of runs, Love was admirably consistent, and although Athey's form was patchy he did win, in one memorable and magnificent innings, a vital JPL match – with badly bruised ribs. Metcalfe, 19, became the youngest Yorkshire debutant to score a century, and a superb one it was, too. Sadly, Lumb, the beneficiary, and Hartley, the vice-captain, could retain neither fitness nor form for long.

Of the bowlers, Dennis won his cap and some acclaim. With his enthusiasm, his willingness and ability to learn, and the novelty of his left-arm fast-medium attack, he could go far. Stevenson remains an eternal contradiction in himself, an international one afternoon, a club cricketer the next morning. Ramage seemed to find the physical demands of three-day cricket beyond him, and sore shins inhibited Sidebottom later in the season. Under Illingworth's sympathetic eye, Carrick's left-arm spin blossomed again. He was encouraged to give the ball air and to dangle the carrot, while his deputy, Paul Booth, played successfully for Young England.

Bairstow's form, with bat and gloves, was a constant reproach to selectors. He became the first Yorkshire wicket-keeper who has twice passed 1,000 runs, while the reserve, Steven Rhodes, was outstanding in the Young England team.

To suggest that Yorkshire are inferior in ability to at least half the sides above them in the table is manifestly absurd. For various reasons, one of which, slow-scoring, caused another political storm, victory slipped away on at least five occasions. The instinct, and the ability, to finish off opponents quickly has gone. Illingworth, realizing this, succeeded in winning the one competition in which bowling the other side out is mostly irrelevant.

The fall to the very bottom of the Championship and the 'political' incident at Cheltenham, when Boycott's slow scoring contributed to the failure to beat Gloucestershire, led in October to the Yorkshire committee's decision not to renew his contract. Yorkshire supporters were split between those who immediately demanded Boycott's reinstatement and those who agreed with Ronnie Burnet, chairman of the cricket subcommittee, that 'it was time to end the rancour and controversy and to give the youngsters a chance'. Illingworth's proffered resignation was not accepted, and he remained as non-playing manager, with Bairstow the new captain.

ENGLISH SEASON 1983/YORKSHIRE

Schweppes County Championship: 17th; Won 1, Lost 5, Drawn 17 (Abandoned 1)
All First-Class Matches: Won 1, Lost 5, Drawn 17 (Abandoned 1)
NatWest Bank Trophy: Lost to Northamptonshire in 2nd round
Benson & Hedges Cup: Failed to qualify for Q-F (5th in Group B)
John Player League: 1st; Won 10, Lost 3, No result 3

Championship Averages

*not out

Batting and Fielding	M	I	NO	HS	R	Avge	100	50	Ct	St
G. Boycott	23	40	5	214*	1941	55.45	7	4	17	-
D.L. Bairstow	23	35	6	100*	1102	38.00	1	8	47	8
A. Sidebottom	16	21	7	78	490	35.00	-	2	2	-
M.D. Moxon	12	23	0	153	780	33.91	1	4	5	-
J.D. Love	23	38	7	76*	1020	32.90	-	7	8	-
K. Sharp	12	21	1	139	597	29.85	2	1	6	-
P. Carrick	23	32	8	83	697	29.04	-	4	9	-
C.W.J. Athey	20	32	1	90	758	24.45	-	5	15	-
R.G. Lumb	10	15	1	60	328	23.42	-	2	6	-
G.B. Stevenson	20	25	1	52	396	16.50	-	2	4	-
S.N. Hartley	14	19	1	69	261	14.50	-	1	5	-
S.D. Fletcher	3	4	2	12	14	7.00	-	-	-	-
R. Illingworth	21	16	4	16	71	5.91	-	-	11	-
S.J. Dennis	20	23	8	17	71	4.73	-	-	6	-
N.S. Taylor	4	5	0	4	10	2.00	-	-	1	-

Also batted: P.A. Booth (1 match) 0, 0; P.W. Jarvis (2) 5*, 1*, 11*; A.A. Metcalfe (1) 122, 7 (1 ct); A. Ramage (3) 0*, 14; I.G. Swallow (2) 4, 11*, 4* (1 ct).

Hundreds (12)

7 **G. Boycott:** 112* v Derbys, Sheffield; 101 v Kent, Sheffield; 214* v Notts, Worksop; 140* v Glos, Cheltenham; 163 and 141* v Notts, Bradford; 169* v Derbys, Chesterfield.
2 **K. Sharp:** 121 v Glos, Cheltenham; 139 v Surrey, Scarborough.
1 **D.L. Bairstow:** 100* v Middx, Leeds.
  A.A. Metcalfe: 122 v Notts, Bradford.
  M.D. Moxon: 153 v Lancs, Leeds.

Bowling	O	M	R	W	Avge	Best	5w/I	10w/M
G.B. Stevenson	460.1	103	1400	56	25.00	5-35	2	-
A. Sidebottom	361	81	1080	39	27.69	5-6	1	-
P. Carrick	848.1	303	1750	62	28.22	7-44	6	1
R. Illingworth	411.5	137	951	32	29.71	4-48	-	-
N.S. Taylor	111.1	23	427	14	30.50	5-49	1	-
S.J. Dennis	525.2	119	1600	52	30.76	4-32	-	-

Also bowled: C.W.J. Athey 38-8-110-3; D.L. Bairstow 10-4-27-1; P.A. Booth 17-3-50-0; G. Boycott 23-10-45-1; S.D. Fletcher 55.4-7-186-8; S.N. Hartley 15-4-40-1; P.W. Jarvis 44-8-155-3; J.D. Love 22-5-89-1; A.A. Metcalfe 2-0-6-0; M.D. Moxon 33-3-123-1; A. Ramage 39-4-145-2; I.G. Swallow 29.4-8-82-2.

University Cricket

The University Match has traditionally been a dour struggle with little quarter given or expected. However, judging by the evidence of the past two years, it is becoming a more decisive encounter between sides prepared to take a gamble for victory. In 1982 Oxford set a sporting target, which was duly accepted and reached, and last season Cambridge likewise offered their opponents a reasonable aspiration of 304 runs to win in 265 minutes.

Oxford's opening batsmen, Ellis and Miller, took up the challenge, with appropriately forceful batting, to score 123 for the first wicket. The straight driving of Ellis was the outstanding feature of this opening partnership, but when he was out, for 83 exciting runs, so Oxford's hopes and chances of any better result than a draw quickly vanished.

The batting prowess of Boyd-Moss, with a hundred in each innings, made him the first player in the 139 years' history of the University Match to have achieved such a feat. Following his hundred in 1982, Boyd-Moss's aggregate of 489 runs beat the overall record of 477 runs, previously held by M.J.K. Smith (1954-56).

Smith, admittedly, made hundreds in each of his three years at Lord's – including 201 not out as a freshman – but Boyd-Moss is the only other batsman to have completed three hundreds in this match.

The general achievements at Lord's this year accurately reflected the strengths and weaknesses of both teams: Cambridge were strong in batting, Oxford possessed a mature pair of opening batsmen, and neither team boasted bowling of much penetration. The latter aspect was somewhat unkindly confirmed at Lord's – with three declarations and not an innings completed.

Apart from Boyd-Moss's innings of 139, there was other batting to admire on the first day, from Curtis (75) and the left-handed Henderson, who for the second year completed a half-century. Earlier, at Fenners, Curtis (Worcestershire) played many an innings of sound judgement, and the Cambridge captain Henderson often set an attacking example himself.

Cambridge have a promising left-arm spinner in Cotterell, from Downside. He gave the ball plenty of air and on the last day at Lord's, when Ellis's hitting powers began arousing Dark Blue hopes, Cotterell's flight was rewarded by having the prime batsman caught on the midwicket boundary.

Ellis has been Oxford's most successful batsman since Imran Khan (1973-75), and he was given stalwart support for the first wicket from a fellow Haileyburian, Miller. It was, incidentally, the first time that the Oxford innings had been opened by two batsmen from the same school since the Wykehamists C.N. Bruce (later Lord Aberdare) and H. Teesdale in 1908. Further, on dates and records, Moulding, the 1981 Oxford captain, became the first cricketer ever to have played 6 years in the University Match.

ENGLISH SEASON 1983/UNIVERSITY CRICKET

Oxford University v Cambridge University
Match drawn
Played at Lord's, June 29, 30, July 1
Toss: Oxford. Umpires: D.G.L. Evans and B.J. Meyer

Cambridge

T.S. Curtis	b Petchey	75	b Hayes		0
D.W. Varey	c Cullinan b Hayes	6	b Carr		32
R.J. Boyd-Moss	c Carr b Petchey	139	c Heseltine b Petchey		124
S.P. Henderson*	not out	51	retired hurt		8
G. Pathmanathan	b Carr	5	c Carr b Rawlinson		64
S.J.G. Doggart	not out	31	b Carr		18
K.I. Hodgson	did not bat		not out		6
T.A. Cotterell	"		c Heseltine b Rawlinson		4
A.J. Pollock	"				
C.C. Ellison	"				
S.G.P. Hewitt†	"				
Extras	(B 4, LB 4, W 2, NB 5)	15	(LB 4, W 2, NB 2)		8
	(4 wickets declared)	322	(6 wickets declared)		264

Oxford

R.G.P. Ellis	lbw b Hodgson	18	c Curtis b Cotterell		83
A.J.T. Miller	c Ellison b Boyd-Moss	62	b Boyd-Moss		48
P.G. Heseltine	lbw b Doggart	13	c Pollock b Boyd-Moss		29
G.J. Toogood*	c Doggart b Boyd-Moss	14	lbw b Hodgson		5
K.A. Hayes	c Varey b Cotterell	45	b Hodgson		11
R.P. Moulding	lbw b Cotterell	66	c Ellison b Boyd-Moss		27
J.G. Varey	not out	40	c Doggart b Boyd-Moss		0
J.D. Carr	not out	16	lbw b Boyd-Moss		0
H.T. Rawlinson	did not bat		not out		2
M.R. Cullinan†	"		not out		18
M.D. Petchey	"				2
Extras	(B 1, LB 7, NB 1)	9	(LB 7, W 1, NB 5)		13
	(6 wickets declared)	283	(8 wickets)		236

Oxford	O	M	R	W	O	M	R	W
Petchey	26	3	127	2	25	3	129	1
Hayes	9.5	1	57	1	6	3	9	1
Varey	9	1	37	0				
Rawlinson	11	3	43	0	9	1	32	2
Carr	25	7	43	1	28	7	84	2
Moulding					1	0	2	0

Cambridge	O	M	R	W	O	M	R	W
Pollock	7.2	1	24	0	4	1	6	0
Hodgson	15	2	61	1	26	5	64	2
Ellison	3	2	6	0	6	0	26	0
Doggart	35	11	74	1	14	4	48	0
Cotterell	23	7	57	2	16	4	43	1
Boyd-Moss	20	9	41	2	12	4	27	5
Curtis	1	0	11	0	6	2	9	0

Fall of Wickets

Wkt	CU 1st	OU 1st	CU 2nd	OU 2nd
1st	12	34	10	123
2nd	227	78	83	143
3rd	240	100	195	152
4th	250	117	252	166
5th		182	254	194
6th		248	264	205
7th				205
8th				221
9th				
10th				

*Captain †Wicket-keeper

Cambridge University

Results: Played 10; Won 0, Lost 3, Drawn 7

First-Class Averages

Batting	M	I	NO	HS	R	Avge
R.J. Boyd-Moss†	10	19	0	139	733	38.57
T.S. Curtis†	10	20	3	92	506	29.76
K.I. Hodgson†	10	15	5	47	272	27.20
S.P. Henderson†	10	19	3	90	409	25.56
S.J.G. Doggart†	10	18	5	70	323	24.84
G. Pathmanathan	7	13	1	64	263	21.91
P.G.P. Roebuck	5	7	3	31*	82	20.50
D.W. Varey†	10	20	1	65	342	18.00
C.C. Ellison†	4	6	2	21	49	12.25
A. Odendaal	3	6	1	21*	56	11.20
T.A. Cotterell†	10	12	3	22	81	9.00
A.J. Pollock†	10	9	2	14*	38	5.42
S.G.P. Hewitt†	6	7	2	6	9	1.80

Also batted: A.G. Davies (4 matches) 0, 0; R.W.M. Palmer (1) 0.

Hundreds (2)

2 R.J. Boyd-Moss: 139 and 124 v Oxford Univ (Lord's).

Bowling	O	M	R	W	Avge
Ellison	56.4	17	153	7	21.85
Boyd-Moss	70	18	217	8	27.12
Pollock	230.2	49	750	21	35.71
Cotterell	273	67	758	17	44.58
Roebuck	75.5	17	269	6	44.83
Doggart	285.2	60	844	12	70.33
Hodgson	297	75	871	12	72.58

Also bowled: Curtis 40-6-144-3; Henderson 13-3-66-1; Palmer 12-0-75-1.

Fielding

9 Henderson; 7 Curtis, Hewitt (6 ct, 1 st); 4 Boyd-Moss, Doggart, Ellison, Pollock; 3 Varey; 2 Cotterell, Davies, Hodgson, Pathmanathan; 1 Palmer, Roebuck.

*not out †Blue 1983

Oxford University

Results: Played 9; Won 0, Lost 4, Drawn 5 (Abandoned 1)

First-Class Averages

Batting	M	I	NO	HS	R	Avge
R.P. Moulding†	8	13	3	80*	448	44.80
A.J.T. Miller†	9	15	3	127*	537	44.75
R.G.P. Ellis	9	15	2	103*	551	42.38
J.G. Varey†	6	10	3	69*	187	26.71
P.J. Heseltine†	6	10	1	40	176	19.55
K.A. Hayes†	3	4	0	45	62	15.50
J.G. Franks	5	7	0	29	98	14.00
H.T. Rawlinson†	8	9	2	24	91	13.00
M.R. Cullinan†	8	8	2	27	55	9.16
G.J. Toogood†	5	6	0	18	48	8.00
J.D. Carr†	6	7	1	18	45	7.50
A.H.K. Smail	6	6	1	13*	24	4.80
M.D. Petchey	6	6	0	18	21	3.50
J.R. Turnbull	7	7	4	5*	5	1.66

Also batted: D.S. Harrison (1 match) 1, 8; J.R. Chessher (1) 0, 11; R.M. Edbrooke (2) 0, 71; R.P. Gibaut (2) 7, 0. M.P. Lawrence played in one match without batting.

Hundreds (2)

1 R.G.P. Ellis: 103* v Glamorgan, Oxford.
A.J.T. Miller: 127* v Hants, Oxford.

Bowling	O	M	R	W	Avge
Hayes	33.5	10	124	8	15.50
Turnbull	130	34	424	12	35.33
Smail	70	18	222	5	44.40
Rawlinson	154.5	31	626	14	44.71
Carr	155	45	445	9	49.44
Petchey	206.2	36	804	12	67.00

Also bowled: Ellis 22-6-82-0; Lawrence 6-1-36-0; Moulding 9.4-0-22-0; Varey 77-10-316-3.

Fielding

14 Cullinan; 6 Turnbull; 5 Carr, Heseltine; 3 Ellis, Petchey; 2 Franks, Rawlinson; 1 Elbrooke, Harrison, Lawrence, Miller, Moulding, Smail, Varey.

*not out †Blue 1983

ENGLISH SEASON 1983/FIRST-CLASS AVERAGES

First-Class Averages

Batting (Qualifications: 8 innings, average 10.00)

	M	I	NO	HS	R	Avge	100	50
I.V.A. Richards	12	20	4	216	1204	75.25	5	3
C.G. Greenidge	15	27	5	154	1438	65.36	4	9
M.W. Gatting	18	28	5	216	1494	64.95	6	5
J.A. Carse	11	10	8	36*	129	64.50	-	-
K.S. McEwan	26	39	5	189*	2176	64.00	8	8
Imran Khan	13	25	3	124*	1260	57.27	2	12
C.S. Cowdrey	22	34	10	123	1364	56.83	5	5
A.J. Lamb	17	29	7	137*	1232	56.00	5	3
G. Boycott	23	40	5	214*	1941	55.45	7	4
A.I. Kallicharran	22	34	4	243*	1637	54.56	6	4
M.A. Lynch	24	39	10	119	1558	53.72	3	11
C.L. Smith	23	39	3	193	1923	53.41	6	8
G. Fowler	18	30	3	156*	1403	51.96	5	6
P. Willey	23	40	8	175*	1546	48.31	4	9
G.D. Barlow	23	39	7	132	1545	48.28	4	9
R.A. Smith	7	12	3	104*	434	48.22	3	-
D.K. Standing	4	8	3	60	240	48.00	-	2
R.A. Woolmer	14	22	1	129	994	47.33	4	5
M.D. Marshall	16	16	4	112	563	46.91	2	2
D.M. Smith (Sy)	13	20	4	131*	748	46.75	2	3
J.G. Wright	11	13	0	136	605	46.53	1	4
D.I. Gower	19	32	5	140	1253	46.40	5	5
R.J. Hadlee	13	15	2	103	596	45.84	1	5
Zaheer Abbas	12	19	0	116	867	45.63	3	4
T.A. Lloyd	23	41	4	208*	1673	45.21	5	5
R.P. Moulding	8	13	3	80*	448	44.80	-	4
M.R. Benson	23	37	3	152*	1515	44.55	4	10
D.L. Amiss	26	43	4	164	1721	44.12	3	12
Kapil Dev	7	10	2	120	349	43.62	1	1
A.J.T. Miller	15	26	3	127*	1002	43.56	1	7
D.G. Aslett	20	36	3	168	1437	43.54	3	8
R.G. Williams	26	40	10	104*	1305	43.50	1	10
W.N. Slack	18	28	4	140	1034	43.08	3	6
C.J. Tavaré	15	24	0	109	1030	42.91	1	9
T.E. Jesty	20	30	5	187	1072	42.88	1	5
A.W. Stovold	23	42	3	181	1671	42.84	4	8
D.R. Turner	12	17	3	122*	598	42.71	1	3
B.C. Broad	16	27	2	145	1061	42.44	3	3
D. Lloyd	10	15	3	123	507	42.25	1	4
W. Larkins	25	42	0	252	1774	42.23	5	4
D.B. Pauline	12	21	2	115	796	41.89	1	7
P.A. Neale	24	40	3	139	1521	41.10	2	11
R.O. Butcher	15	19	3	179	657	41.06	2	3
R.T. Robinson	25	41	3	207	1545	40.65	2	11
G.D. Mendis	24	46	6	133*	1624	40.60	4	8
V.P. Terry	20	33	6	115	1096	40.59	3	4
I.T. Botham	14	21	0	152	852	40.57	3	2
B.F. Davison	26	41	6	123*	1417	40.48	3	8
A.J. Stewart	10	17	4	118*	525	40.38	1	2
A.P.E. Knott	23	30	9	92*	848	40.38	-	6
N.E. Briers	25	38	6	201*	1289	40.28	1	8

ENGLISH SEASON 1983/FIRST-CLASS AVERAGES

Batting (contd)	M	I	NO	HS	R	Avge	100	50
G.A. Gooch	26	38	1	174	1481	40.02	4	7
J.C. Balderstone	25	41	4	112	1478	39.94	3	9
G. Cook	24	41	3	128	1510	39.73	1	11
J. Abrahams	24	39	7	178	1261	39.40	3	4
G.P. Howarth	15	23	2	144	820	39.04	1	6
N.R. Taylor	23	39	6	155*	1275	38.63	5	3
R.D.V. Knight	24	38	6	101*	1235	38.59	1	9
R.C. Ontong	26	43	9	112	1310	38.52	3	7
K.J. Barnett	24	40	3	121	1423	38.45	3	9
D.N. Patel	26	44	2	112	1615	38.45	3	10
D.L. Bairstow	23	35	6	100*	1102	38.00	1	8
A. Hill	24	40	5	137*	1311	37.45	4	6
P.M. Roebuck	22	38	5	106*	1235	37.42	1	9
I.S. Anderson	21	37	4	112	1233	37.36	1	9
M.C.J. Nicholas	26	43	5	158	1418	37.31	3	6
C.E.B. Rice	19	30	2	101*	1026	36.64	2	3
J.N. Shepherd	23	34	6	168	1025	36.60	2	6
N.H. Fairbrother	16	26	5	94*	759	36.14	-	8
D.J. Thomas	23	31	5	119	937	36.03	2	4
I.A. Greig	9	10	1	147*	324	36.00	1	1
E.A.E. Baptiste	17	26	5	136*	755	35.95	2	3
J.G. Wyatt	6	12	2	82*	352	35.20	-	3
R.J. Boyd-Moss	25	43	2	139	1437	35.04	3	7
A. Sidebottom	16	21	7	78	490	35.00	-	2
L.L. McFarlane	10	9	8	12*	35	35.00	-	-
K.R. Pont	21	27	4	125*	802	34.86	2	4
P.W. Romaines	23	41	4	135	1286	34.75	3	4
D.R. Pringle	17	21	4	102*	586	34.47	1	2
N.A. Felton	7	12	1	173*	376	34.18	1	1
M.D. Moxon	12	23	0	153	780	33.91	1	4
A.J. Hignell	20	37	6	109*	1044	33.67	2	6
C. Gladwin	9	14	0	89	470	33.57	-	2
I.P. Butcher	17	30	1	139	973	33.55	3	3
G. Sharp	23	24	8	98	536	33.50	-	3
J.D. Love	23	38	7	76*	1020	32.90	-	7
A.R. Butcher	25	44	3	128	1349	32.90	3	6
P.A. Smith	13	17	3	114	458	32.71	1	3
K.W.R. Fletcher	25	36	3	151*	1077	32.63	2	5
S.T. Jefferies	10	12	4	75*	260	32.50	-	1
P.B. Clift	23	33	7	100*	843	32.42	1	2
F.C. Hayes	20	28	1	149	866	32.07	3	4
J.H. Hampshire	15	21	2	85	601	31.63	-	4
A.L. Jones	23	40	7	99	1036	31.39	-	8
G.W. Humpage	26	42	6	141*	1116	31.00	2	5
K.P. Tomlins	20	27	5	132*	670	30.45	1	5
G. Miller	21	30	7	84	699	30.39	-	4
A. Jones	22	37	2	105	1059	30.25	1	5
D.A. Banks	7	13	1	100	363	30.25	1	1
J.D. Birch	24	38	2	95	1086	30.16	-	8
D.W. Randall	18	28	2	94	777	29.88	-	6
K. Sharp	12	21	1	139	597	29.85	2	1
C.H. Lloyd	11	16	1	86	447	29.80	-	3

Batting (contd)	M	I	NO	HS	R	Avge	100	50
B.R. Hardie	25	37	2	129	1042	29.77	1	6
M.S. Scott	7	12	2	76	297	29.70	-	3
P. Bainbridge	24	43	2	146	1217	29.68	1	6
K.D. Smith	27	47	4	109	1272	29.58	2	8
C.T. Radley	25	38	6	119	943	29.46	1	4
P. Carrick	23	32	8	83	697	29.04	-	4
D.J. Capel	17	24	5	109*	534	28.10	1	3
N.E.J. Pocock	26	35	8	60*	755	27.96	-	6
J.E. Emburey	25	33	5	133	782	27.92	1	3
I.J. Gould	18	23	6	59*	474	27.88	-	1
C.J. Richards	25	35	8	85*	751	27.81	-	2
A.P. Wells	16	28	4	92	665	27.70	-	5
M.J. Bamber	7	14	1	77	360	27.69	-	2
R.W. Tolchard	26	35	7	80*	775	27.67	-	4
T.S. Curtis	19	37	5	92	880	27.50	-	5
R.G.P. Ellis	15	26	2	103*	658	27.41	1	3
S.J. O'Shaughnessy	18	28	3	105	685	27.40	2	1
J.A. Hopkins	25	43	2	116	1123	27.39	2	3
S.P. Henderson	20	35	5	135*	820	27.33	1	4
J.W. Lloyds	21	35	2	100	901	27.30	1	4
K.I. Hodgson	10	15	5	47	272	27.20	-	-
R.J. Doughty	7	11	6	32*	135	27.00	-	-
B. Hassan	21	34	1	112	890	26.96	1	5
J.G. Varey	6	10	3	69*	187	26.71	-	1
D.A. Francis	23	39	5	89*	903	26.55	-	4
J. Garner	10	16	6	44	265	26.50	-	-
D.B. D'Oliveira	22	39	2	102	972	26.27	1	5
R.L. Ollis	13	22	2	99*	517	25.85	-	3
A.M. Ferreira	17	24	6	66	465	25.83	-	3
J.A. Ormrod	24	41	3	84	967	25.44	-	6
J.J. Whitaker	10	16	4	56*	305	25.41	-	1
A.J. Wright	10	17	2	56*	380	25.33	-	2
S.G. Hinks	6	10	0	87	253	25.30	-	1
C.M. Wells	24	40	6	71	857	25.20	-	5
G.S. le Roux	13	17	1	80	401	25.06	-	1
S.J.G. Doggart	10	18	5	70	323	24.84	-	2
W.P. Fowler	17	26	2	91	591	24.62	-	5
N.F.M. Popplewell	24	39	3	143	886	24.61	1	4
R.M. Ellison	22	21	7	63	343	24.50	-	1
C.W.J. Athey	20	32	1	90	758	24.45	-	5
G.W. Johnson	25	30	13	79*	413	24.29	-	1
I.R. Payne	10	11	4	43	167	23.85	-	-
T. Davies	11	15	4	69*	260	23.63	-	2
P. Johnson	16	28	2	125	612	23.53	1	4
K.D. James	8	8	2	34	141	23.50	-	-
L. Potter	6	11	0	50	258	23.45	-	1
R.G. Lumb	10	15	1	60	328	23.42	-	2
J. Simmons	23	31	2	104	679	23.41	2	3
M.J. Weston	22	38	1	115	862	23.29	1	2
C.J.C. Rowe	22	33	2	82	721	23.25	-	3
G.S. Clinton	13	22	3	105	439	23.10	1	3
P.W. Denning	21	36	3	99	758	22.96	-	4

Batting (contd)

	M	I	NO	HS	R	Avge	100	50
Asif Din	14	21	3	65	411	22.83	-	2
M.S.A. McEvoy	16	26	1	103	569	22.76	1	2
D.S. Steele	25	31	6	60	569	22.76	-	3
D.E. East	26	32	4	91	635	22.67	-	3
N.F. Williams	25	25	7	63	407	22.61	-	2
G. Monkhouse	18	18	5	46	291	22.38	-	-
P.R. Downton	25	30	7	87	508	22.08	-	4
V.J. Marks	17	27	3	44*	530	22.08	-	-
R.C. Russell	24	32	9	64*	507	22.04	-	3
G. Pathmanathan	7	13	1	64	263	21.91	-	2
J.R.T. Barclay	21	37	3	65	743	21.85	-	3
D.J. Humphries	20	30	4	59	560	21.53	-	2
Nasir Zaidi	13	16	6	51	215	21.50	-	1
D.A. Graveney	22	28	8	94	427	21.35	-	2
J.R.P. Heath	9	18	2	39	335	20.93	-	-
L.B. Taylor	19	18	6	47	250	20.83	-	-
I. Cockbain	8	15	1	52	291	20.78	-	1
H. Morris	8	14	3	34	228	20.72	-	-
P.W.G. Parker	17	27	2	79	512	20.48	-	4
B.C. Rose	8	9	0	52	184	20.44	-	1
R.I.H.B. Dyer	9	15	3	93	242	20.16	-	1
D.P. Hughes	19	28	2	153	522	20.07	1	3
A.M. Green	16	30	2	53	552	19.71	-	1
E.W. Jones	15	18	5	39	256	19.69	-	-
P.J. Heseltine	6	10	1	40	176	19.55	-	-
N.G. Cowley	23	27	9	29	351	19.50	-	-
A.C.S. Pigott	23	29	8	63	408	19.42	-	3
N.A. Foster	13	16	4	40*	232	19.33	-	-
J.F. Steele	24	26	9	50	327	19.23	-	1
R.E. East	21	27	5	80*	420	19.09	-	1
J.E. Morris	10	20	1	58	361	19.00	-	1
C.M. Old	22	25	4	62	396	18.85	-	1
T.M. Tremlett	24	19	5	59	263	18.78	-	1
G.A. Tedstone	13	16	3	67*	243	18.69	-	1
B.N. French	24	38	4	91	630	18.52	-	3
C.J. Tunnicliffe	17	25	0	91	461	18.44	-	2
J.W. Southern	15	13	5	45*	146	18.25	-	-
I. Folley	12	9	4	25	91	18.20	-	-
D.W. Varey	10	20	1	65	342	18.00	-	1
D.J. Wild	5	9	0	48	162	18.00	-	-
N.A. Mallender	23	27	9	71*	320	17.77	-	1
R.J. Finney	20	35	2	71	578	17.51	-	3
C. Maynard	22	27	3	61*	417	17.37	-	2
G.J. Parsons	14	15	3	56	207	17.25	-	-
J.D. Inchmore	20	26	4	51	377	17.13	-	1
R.G.D. Willis	17	20	9	37	183	16.63	-	-
G.B. Stevenson	20	25	1	52	396	16.50	-	2
P.J.W. Allott	18	18	4	41	225	16.07	-	-
R.W. Taylor	21	30	7	41*	366	15.91	-	-
N. Phillip	19	26	0	80	413	15.88	-	1
T. Gard	25	33	4	51	457	15.75	-	2
A.H. Wilkins	14	15	3	54	185	15.41	-	1

Batting (contd)	M	I	NO	HS	R	Avge	100	50
R.S. Cowan	5	10	0	50	154	15.40	-	1
P. Moores	7	11	1	30	154	15.40	-	-
J.K. Lever	18	17	3	44	211	15.07	-	-
W.W. Davis	15	18	9	39*	135	15.00	-	-
B.J.M. Maher	8	12	2	52	150	15.00	-	1
P.H.L. Wilson	11	11	7	25	60	15.00	-	-
P.A. Slocombe	11	17	2	66	224	14.93	-	1
S.N. Hartley	14	19	1	69	261	14.50	-	1
S.T. Clarke	24	24	4	43	285	14.25	-	-
G.R. Dilley	12	9	1	29	114	14.25	-	-
C.H. Dredge	21	26	5	50	296	14.09	-	1
R.A. Pick	6	8	2	25*	84	14.00	-	-
R.J. Parks	25	15	2	52	180	13.84	-	1
K.A. Hayes	8	12	0	45	165	13.75	-	-
S. Oldham	15	17	4	39	177	13.61	-	-
B.J. Lloyd	14	12	2	38	135	13.50	-	-
N. Gifford	22	21	6	39	201	13.40	-	-
A.E. Warner	9	15	5	26*	131	13.10	-	-
P.H. Edmonds	19	20	4	65	208	13.00	-	1
E.E. Hemmings	23	32	3	38	377	13.00	-	-
H.T. Rawlinson	8	9	2	24	91	13.00	-	-
K. Stevenson	7	9	3	25	77	12.83	-	-
D.A. Reeve	17	20	5	42*	192	12.80	-	-
K.E. Cooper	22	27	7	30*	254	12.70	-	-
D.G. Moir	17	21	3	53	224	12.44	-	1
G.C. Small	6	8	3	31	62	12.40	-	-
M.K. Bore	13	16	5	24	132	12.00	-	-
J.G. Thomas	9	9	1	23	96	12.00	-	-
M.W.W. Selvey	24	24	3	63	250	11.90	-	1
J.D. Carr	9	10	4	18	67	11.16	-	-
R.A. Cobb	8	10	0	28	110	11.00	-	-
R.M. Ellcock	12	18	4	36	154	11.00	-	-
K. Saxelby	21	28	3	35	274	10.96	-	-
G.V. Palmer	10	13	2	78	119	10.81	-	1
N.G.B. Cook	25	24	5	32	201	10.57	-	-
M. Watkinson	15	20	4	29	168	10.50	-	-
M.R. Davis	14	17	5	20*	125	10.41	-	-
S. Turner	15	19	2	30	177	10.41	-	-
M.A. Fell	5	9	0	41	93	10.33	-	-
D.L. Underwood	25	20	6	26*	142	10.14	-	-

Bowling (Qualification: 10 wickets in 10 innings)

	O	M	R	W	Avge	Best	5w/I
Imran Khan	46.2	12	86	12	7.16	6-6	1
J.K. Lever	569	137	1726	106	16.28	7-55	8
M.D. Marshall	532.5	144	1327	80	16.58	7-29	5
M. Hendrick	552.1	190	1122	66	17.00	6-17	4
R.A. Woolmer	86	29	170	10	17.00	3-13	-
J.E. Emburey	935	328	1842	103	17.88	6-13	4
P.B. Clift	619.4	167	1592	83	19.18	5-20	2

Bowling (contd)	O	M	R	W	Avge	Best	5w/I
D.L. Underwood	936.3	358	2044	106	19.28	7-55	9
K.D. James	89	20	217	11	19.72	5-28	1
T.M. Lamb	188.2	57	416	21	19.80	4-27	-
L.B. Taylor	529.5	151	1381	69	20.01	7-73	3
J. Garner	277	74	708	35	20.22	6-37	1
N. Phillip	477.2	87	1409	69	20.42	6-4	5
T.M. Tremlett	600.2	198	1346	63	21.36	6-82	1
P.H. Edmonds	820.3	230	1974	92	21.45	6-38	9
D.S. Steele	678	255	1460	68	21.47	5.48	2
M.A. Holding	169	41	451	21	21.47	5-48	3
R.J. Hadlee	431.3	123	1065	49	21.73	6.53	3
G.R. Dilley	275.3	73	681	31	21.96	5-70	1
R.G. Williams	434.1	148	1036	47	22.04	4-18	-
G. Monkhouse	373.3	97	1040	47	22.12	7-51	1
S.T. Clarke	693.1	183	1773	79	22.44	7-53	4
A.E. Warner	210.3	39	608	27	22.51	4-72	-
D.R. Pringle	288.4	53	928	41	22.63	7-32	2
G.J.F. Ferris	360	74	1205	53	22.73	7-42	3
N. Gifford	1043.4	346	2393	104	23.00	6-22	7
W.W. Daniel	324.3	51	1106	48	23.04	7-61	1
S. Turner	282.1	76	624	27	23.11	5-30	1
N.A. Foster	417	78	1216	52	23.38	6-46	1
D. Lloyd	199	60	400	17	23.52	5-22	1
E.A.E. Baptiste	376.3	88	1187	50	23.74	5-39	3
Kapil Dev	161	47	385	16	24.06	4-24	-
O.H. Mortensen	518.3	108	1605	66	24.31	6-27	3
A. Needham	164	50	470	19	24.73	6-30	2
S.T. Jefferies	278.1	74	797	32	24.90	8-46	2
G.B. Stevenson	460.1	103	1400	56	25.00	5-35	2
S.P. Hughes	268.3	61	910	36	25.27	6-32	2
N.G.B. Cook	878.1	321	1859	73	25.46	5-35	2
G.S. le Roux	362.3	92	950	37	25.67	5-17	2
N.G. Cowley	440.3	147	1053	41	25.68	4-10	-
R.G.D. Willis	376.5	98	1058	41	25.80	5-35	1
P.I. Pocock	681.2	200	1774	68	26.08	7-79	4
A.C.S. Pigott	582.5	98	1889	72	26.23	6-22	4
A. Walker	165.4	30	578	22	26.27	4-61	-
N.F. Williams	532.2	114	1659	63	26.33	5-77	1
M. Watkinson	319.3	69	929	35	26.54	6-51	2
J. Simmons	744	214	1807	68	26.57	7-73	5
W.W. Davis	452.4	110	1389	52	26.71	7-70	3
K. Saxelby	410.2	95	1337	50	26.74	5-52	2
A.P. Pridgeon	700	166	1978	72	27.47	5-21	2
C.H. Dredge	492.3	127	1323	48	27.56	5-51	2
A. Sidebottom	361	81	1080	39	27.69	5-6	1
J.G. Thomas	144.5	34	529	19	27.84	5-78	2
P. Carrick	848.1	303	1750	62	28.22	7-44	6
K.E. Cooper	579	164	1610	57	28.24	7-33	5
G.J. Parsons	269	73	823	29	28.37	5-51	1
D.L. Acfield	497.1	140	1222	43	28.41	7-100	2
B.J. Griffiths	536.2	130	1424	50	28.48	6-92	1
M.C.J. Nicholas	277.2	74	774	27	28.66	5-45	1

Bowling (contd)	O	M	R	W	Avge	Best	5w/I
J.D. Inchmore	488.3	104	1369	47	29.12	5-45	3
R.M. Ellison	598.4	167	1491	51	29.23	5-73	1
N.A. Mallender	525.2	112	1642	56	29.32	6-48	1
D.A. Reeve	472.1	131	1233	42	29.35	4-15	-
C.M. Old	656.3	152	1824	62	29.41	5-50	2
R. Illingworth	411.5	137	951	32	29.71	4-48	-
N.G. Cowans	286	60	912	30	30.40	5-43	1
J.N. Shepherd	776.1	209	2047	67	30.55	7-50	3
W. Hogg	384.4	74	1198	39	30.71	5.63	1
S.J. Dennis	525.2	119	1600	52	30.76	4-32	-
J.W. Lloyds	358.1	98	1079	35	30.82	5-120	1
P. Willey	483.5	159	991	32	30.96	4-51	-
P.J.W. Allott	457.4	131	1178	38	31.00	5-45	1
K. Stevenson	187.5	39	656	21	31.23	5-81	1
D.J. Thomas	547	113	1781	57	31.24	4-22	-
G.V. Palmer	208.3	39	630	20	31.50	5-38	1
A.M. Ferreira	502.4	131	1277	40	31.92	5-19	1
J.F. Steele	520.1	161	1280	40	32.00	4-3	-
V.J. Marks	615.3	199	1698	53	32.03	6-79	3
C.L. Smith	167	44	547	17	32.17	3-35	-
M.W.W. Selvey	629.4	138	2003	62	32.30	6-47	3
R.J. Finney	281.5	43	970	30	32.33	5-58	1
D.A. Graveney	512.1	156	1198	37	32.37	6-88	2
G.W. Johnson	631.1	166	1652	51	32.39	7-76	2
J.A. Carse	238.5	50	722	22	32.81	5-43	1
I.T. Botham	232.2	55	728	22	33.09	5-38	1
Nasir Zaidi	191.3	58	530	16	33.12	3-27	-
S.J. O'Shaughnessy	236.2	44	830	25	33.20	4.73	-
G.E. Sainsbury	625.4	150	1937	58	33.39	6-66	3
P.H.L. Wilson	248.3	45	837	25	33.48	4-77	-
E.E. Hemmings	710.4	195	2000	59	33.89	7-23	2
N.F.M. Popplewell	232	38	786	23	34.17	4-69	-
G. Miller	492.5	132	1278	37	34.54	5-71	2
D.G. Moir	462.5	121	1385	40	34.62	5-44	2
M.R. Davis	240.4	43	873	25	34.92	4-34	-
C.J. Tunnicliffe	428.4	94	1372	39	35.17	4-30	-
C.E. Waller	754	223	1873	53	35.33	6-126	2
C.M. Wells	376.3	82	1135	32	35.46	4-69	-
R.E. East	338	96	889	25	35.56	5-45	1
A.J. Pollock	230.2	49	750	21	35.71	5-107	1
J.W. Southern	369.5	115	966	27	35.77	5-60	2
S. Oldham	387.2	85	1120	31	36.12	4-56	-
R.C. Ontong	645	131	2053	56	36.66	6-64	3
J.H. Childs	664.5	200	1761	48	36.68	6-81	2
D.N. Patel	685.5	204	1799	49	36.71	5-52	2
R.M. Ellcock	244	39	931	25	37.24	4-70	-
S.J. Malone	547.1	123	1797	48	37.43	4.39	-
I.R. Payne	158.5	41	450	12	37.50	5-13	1
R.K. Illingworth	664.5	172	1830	48	38.12	5-26	1
T.E. Jesty	256.5	70	804	21	38.28	3-48	-
P.M. Such	214	44	767	20	38.35	6-123	1
I.V.A. Richards	188	61	462	12	38.50	3-56	-

Bowling (contd)	O	M	R	W	Avge	Best	5w/I
M.K. Bore	370.1	99	1040	27	38.51	4-29	-
P. Bainbridge	416.4	106	1199	30	39.96	4-67	-
I.A. Greig	185	26	681	17	40.05	4-42	-
P.A. Smith	218	29	844	21	40.19	3-56	-
S.C. Booth	296.2	85	849	21	40.42	4-26	-
J.P. Agnew	248	42	930	23	40.43	3-34	-
I.J. Curtis	269	82	690	17	40.58	6-28	1
C.J.C. Rowe	473.4	91	1572	38	41.36	4-29	-
B.J. Lloyd	288.5	47	876	21	41.71	4-93	-
T.A. Cotterell	273	67	758	17	44.58	5-89	1
H.T. Rawlinson	154.5	31	626	14	44.71	5-123	1
R.D.V. Knight	236	60	677	15	45.13	3-58	-
J.R.T. Barclay	231.3	59	774	17	45.52	3-30	-
S.R. Barwick	129.3	21	532	11	48.36	8-42	1
L.L. McFarlane	216.4	38	742	15	49.46	3-53	-
J. Abrahams	216	41	658	13	50.61	3-83	-
G.A. Gooch	212	46	572	11	52.00	3-40	-
K.B.S. Jarvis	500.5	95	1579	30	52.63	3-32	-
S.P. Perryman	253.5	54	750	14	53.57	4-91	-
C.S. Cowdrey	220.2	34	733	12	61.08	3-80	-
M.D. Petchey	206.2	36	804	12	67.00	2-70	-
A.H. Wilkins	205	24	820	12	68.33	2-25	-
S.J.G. Doggart	285.2	60	844	12	70.33	3-3	-
K.I. Hodgson	297	75	871	12	72.58	4-58	-

The following bowlers took 10 wickets but bowled in fewer than 10 innings:

	O	M	R	W	Avge	Best	5w/I
F.D. Stephenson	74.4	18	230	14	16.42	5-56	1
S.R. Tracy	54.1	10	170	10	17.00	5-29	-
A.M.E. Roberts	101.2	19	294	16	18.37	5-26	1
N.S. Taylor	111.1	23	427	14	30.50	5-49	1
G.C. Small	110.5	19	349	10	34.90	3-13	-
J.R. Turnbull	130	34	424	12	35.33	4-51	-

Fielding Statistics
Wicket-Keepers

68	D.E. East (63ct, 5st)	27	G.A. Tedstone (23ct, 4st)	23	I.S. Anderson
63	R.C. Russell (46ct, 17st)	25	E.W. Jones (24ct, 1st)	23	J.E. Emburey
60	R.J. Parks (51ct, 9st)	20	T. Davies (18ct, 2st)	22	D.L. Amiss
59	P.R. Downton (54ct, 5st)			22	G.D. Barlow
56	C.J. Richards (49ct, 7st)		**Fieldsmen**	22	C.T. Radley
	(Including 3ct in field)	37	R.O. Butcher	22	K.P. Tomlins
55	D.L. Bairstow (47ct, 8st)	35	G.A. Gooch	21	C.G. Greenidge
53	R.W. Tolchard (44ct, 9st)	30	B.R. Hardie	21	N.F.M. Popplewell
52	B.N. French (49ct, 3st)	30	N.E.J. Pocock		(Including 2ct as
51	R.W. Taylor (49ct, 2st)	30	J.F. Steele		wicket-keeper)
50	T. Gard (42ct, 8st)	29	D.S. Steele	20	J.D. Birch
47	A.P.E. Knott (39ct, 8st)	28	G.W. Johnson	20	D.W. Randall
45	I.J. Gould (32ct, 13st)	28	R.D.V. Knight		
45	G. Sharp (40ct, 5st)	27	G. Cook		
36	D.J. Humphries (27ct, 9st)		(Plus 5ct/3st as		
29	C. Maynard (27ct, 2st)		wicket-keeper)		
28	G.W. Humpage (23ct, 5st)	27	C.S. Cowdrey		
	(Including 7ct in field)	26	M.C.J. Nicholas		

Benson & Hedges Cup

Right at the end, the 1983 Benson and Hedges Cup competition overcame the ill luck that had haunted it – at the very end, when in the last hour of an apparently one-sided final lasting until nearly nine o'clock, Middlesex fought back to beat Essex by 4 runs. All the earlier disappointments, mostly attributable to the weather, were forgotten in that extraordinary finish.

In the zonal rounds amid the deluges of May, 11 matches out of 40 were lost. Essex were one of only four sides to play all their four matches. Middlesex would not have achieved their second win in only two matches had they not fitted in 20 overs (the exact number needed to make it a match) on a Saturday evening in case the ground should be unplayable on the Monday – which it was.

In the quarter-final round, one match took two days to complete, Kent beating Hampshire by 5 runs. Of the other winners, Essex and Lancashire each needed three days and Middlesex prevailed only by the toss of a coin against Gloucestershire at Bristol.

The weather improved in June during a five-week pause in which the Prudential Cup took place. But the semi-final day, July 6, proved not much more satisfactory, for in each case the side that won the toss and chose to bowl first won an overwhelming victory. Middlesex beat Lancashire at Lord's by 6 wickets, needing only 91, and Essex beat Kent by 9 wickets at Canterbury.

For most of a long day, it looked as if the final would be as one-sided as the semi-finals and both the 1982 Lord's finals. Play started 50 minutes late and was soon interrupted for 15 minutes by bad light on a cloudy humid morning after an early thunderstorm. There was surprise that Essex deliberated so long after winning the toss – they do in fact have a much better record batting first – but no surprise when their bowlers moved the ball about a lot and had Middlesex in serious trouble.

Two early wickets for the promising Neil Foster and his throw from the boundary that ran out Mike Gatting removed much of Middlesex's main batting strength. And though the dogged Radley, old master of improvisation, batted staunchly through to the end of the innings, the runs scrambled by the later batsmen to reach 196 merely emphasized that batting conditions were now easier.

They looked supremely easy as Graham Gooch, generously accommodated around his legs, made 16 off Cowans' first over and with Hardie took the score to 79, at 7 runs an over. Though Gooch was then out, the score passed 100 for 1 in the 21st over, and 150 with 18 overs left and 7 wickets standing.

But by then Middlesex had slowed the advance with the spin of Emburey and Edmonds, and were beginning to attack with a resilience that did their captain much credit. At 135, they had been rewarded by the wicket of Fletcher, caught off bat and pad at silly point, an unlikely position in this form of cricket. Now the initiative was with Gatting – and the luck. At 151, Pont hit his wicket when struck on the helmet. Pringle and Turner battled on from 156 for 5. But now, unbelievably for a side that had started so fast, Essex began to run short of overs. With 4 overs left, they still needed 12 runs, and though 5 wickets remained, panic was just around the corner. Middlesex were now inspired in the field, and Daniel and Cowans bowled an improved line and a fuller length. Pringle was lbw. Two marvellous catches by the young substitute, John Carr, and Gatting, a smart run-out by Radley, and finally a fast slanting ball between Foster's bat and pad from Cowans, the first ball of the final over, completed the astonishing transformation.

Zonal Results

Group A	P	W	L	NR	Pts	Group C	P	W	L	NR	Pts
GLOUCS	4	3	0	1	7	ESSEX	4	3	1	0	6
NORTHANTS	4	2	1	1	5	HAMPSHIRE	4	3	1	0	6
Leicestershire	4	1	1	2	4	Sussex	4	2	2	0	4
Worcestershire	4	1	2	1	3	Somerset	4	1	2	1	3
Scotland	4	0	3	1	1	Minor Counties	4	0	3	1	1

Group B	P	W	L	NR	Pts	Group D	P	W	L	NR	Pts
LANCASHIRE	4	2	0	2	6	KENT	4	3	1	0	6
WARWICKS	4	2	0	2	6	MIDDLESEX	4	2	0	2	6
Nottinghamshire	4	2	1	1	5	Glamorgan	4	1	1	2	4
Derbyshire	4	0	2	2	2	Surrey	4	1	2	1	3
Yorkshire	4	0	3	1	1	Combined Univ.	4	0	3	1	1

Final Rounds

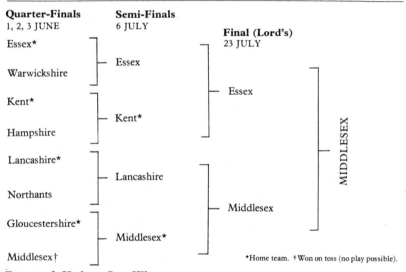

Quarter-Finals 1, 2, 3 JUNE
Semi-Finals 6 JULY
Final (Lord's) 23 JULY

Essex*
Warwickshire
Kent*
Hampshire
Lancashire*
Northants
Gloucestershire*
Middlesex†

Essex
Kent*
Lancashire
Middlesex*

Essex
Middlesex

MIDDLESEX

*Home team. †Won on toss (no play possible).

Benson & Hedges Cup Winners

1972	Leicestershire	1976	Kent	1980	Northamptonshire
1973	Kent	1977	Gloucestershire	1981	Somerset
1974	Surrey	1978	Kent	1982	Somerset
1975	Leicestershire	1979	Essex	1983	Middlesex

Essex v Middlesex 1983 Benson & Hedges Cup Final
Middlesex won by 4 runs
Played at Lord's, July 23
Toss: Essex. Umpires: H.D. Bird and B.J. Meyer
Man of the Match: C.T. Radley (Adjudicator: L.E.G. Ames)

Middlesex		Runs	Mins	Balls	6s	4s
G.D. Barlow	b Foster	14	43	31	–	3
W.N. Slack	c Gooch b Foster	1	13	8	–	–
C.T. Radley	not out	89	211	154	–	9
M.W. Gatting*	run out (Foster/D.E. East)	22	64	55	–	2
K.P. Tomlins	lbw b Gooch	0	1	1	–	–
J.E. Emburey	c D.E. East b Lever	17	57	44	–	1
P.R. Downton†	c Fletcher b Foster	10	15	14	–	1
P.H. Edmonds	b Pringle	9	21	18	–	–
N.F. Williams	c and b Pringle	13	11	9	–	1
W.W. Daniel	not out	2	2	3	–	–
N.G. Cowans	did not bat					
Extras	(B 3, LB 9, W 4, NB 3)	19				
	(55 overs; 225 minutes)	**196-8**				

Essex		Runs	Mins	Balls	6s	4s
G.A. Gooch	c Downton b Williams	46	53	51	–	6
B.R. Hardie	c Downton b Cowans	49	166	105	–	5
K.S. McEwan	c Cowans b Edmonds	34	57	64	–	3
K.W.R. Fletcher*	c Radley b Edmonds	3	8	9	–	–
K.R. Pont	hit wicket b Williams	7	27	24	–	–
D.R. Pringle	lbw b Daniel	16	56	38	–	2
S. Turner	c sub (J.D. Carr) b Cowans	9	49	30	–	1
D.E. East†	c Gatting b Cowans	5	9	10	–	1
R.E. East	run out (Radley)	0	5	5	–	–
N.A. Foster	b Cowans	0	6	1	–	–
J.K. Lever	not out	0	1	1	–	–
Extras	(LB 12, W 3, NB 8)	23				
	(54.1 overs, 227 minutes)	**192**				

Essex	O	M	R	W
Lever	11	1	52	1
Foster	11	2	26	3
Pringle	11	0	54	2
Turner	11	1	24	0
Gooch	11	2	21	1

Middlesex	O	M	R	W
Daniel	11	2	34	1
Cowans	10.1	0	39	4
Williams	11	0	45	2
Emburey	11	3	17	0
Edmonds	11	3	34	2

Fall of Wickets		
Wkt	M	E
1st	10	79
2nd	25	127
3rd	74	135
4th	74	151
5th	123	156
6th	141	185
7th	171	187
8th	191	191
9th		192
10th		192

*Captain †Wicket-keeper

NatWest Bank Trophy

Having claimed every other one-day title during the four previous years, Somerset completed the set in 1983 by taking the NatWest Trophy. No other county has so far won all the three existing competitions and the defunct Gillette Cup. Their opponents in the final were Kent, who, in the 1970s, were as powerful a force in limited-overs cricket as Somerset have become since 1979. It was ironic and unfortunate that in a season of record sunshine the final should have been marred by unkind weather.

Apart from two first-round matches spilling over, the competition had so far been unmolested by the elements. None of the Minor Counties or Ireland or Scotland reached the second round, although Oxfordshire, with schoolmaster Paul Fowler making a memorable century, stretched Warwickshire fully, and Norfolk gave a nasty fright to Glamorgan.

Surrey, the holders, bit the dust in the second round, decisively beaten on their home ground by Warwickshire, their victims in the 1982 final. Somerset, Hampshire, and Sussex brushed aside Lancashire, Glamorgan, and Nottinghamshire with equal ease.

However, the grounds at Chelmsford and Grace Road were thick with bitten-off fingernails. Essex were posed with a Kent total of 274 after Chris Cowdrey had made a rumbustious 122 not out. But Graham Gooch matched Cowdrey's innings blow for blow, and Essex were on target when Gooch was second out at 210. Though their grip was loosened, Essex were still favourites when the last over started with 6 runs wanted. But David East and Pringle fell in trying to overcome the accurate Ellison (4 for 12), and Kent won by 4 runs. With Zaheer Abbas at his vintage best in scoring 158, Gloucestershire overtook Leicestershire's 302 with 4 wickets in hand but only three balls to spare.

The quarter-finals were all won by substantial margins, but the one in which Somerset routed Sussex was unique in its one-sidedness. A record crowd was spilling out of the Hove ground at twenty past three – a record for an early finish – Somerset having been required to respond to a total no bigger than 65.

In the semi-finals, Somerset came back from an apparently hopeless position to beat Middlesex. A recovery of such proportions could be inspired only by one man – Ian Botham! The scores were level at 222 when Emburey started the last over. Rather than risk a calamity, Botham, needing only 4 for his century, played out a maiden, and remained content with Somerset winning on the basis of having lost fewer wickets in a tied match. Hampshire, the only county never to have figured in a Lord's final, missed out again, being comprehensively beaten by Kent.

The final was affected more by bad light than rain. It started late, and the limit of overs per side had to be reduced from 60 to an unsatisfactory 50. The bleak conditions made it inevitable that the contest would be dominated by the bowlers, as it indeed was. But the deciding factor was the art of the greatest batsman in the world, Viv Richards, who alone scored 50 in the match.

ENGLISH SEASON 1983/NATWEST BANK TROPHY

Gillette Cup Winners

1963	Sussex	1969	Yorkshire	1975	Lancashire
1964	Sussex	1970	Lancashire	1976	Northamptonshire
1965	Yorkshire	1971	Lancashire	1977	Middlesex
1966	Warwickshire	1972	Lancashire	1978	Sussex
1967	Kent	1973	Gloucestershire	1979	Somerset
1968	Warwickshire	1974	Kent	1980	Middlesex

NatWest Bank Trophy Winners

1981	Derbyshire	1982	Surrey	1983	Somerset

1983 Tournament

1st Round 29, 30 JUNE
2nd Round 20 JULY
Q-Finals 3 AUGUST
S-Finals 17 AUGUST
Final (Lord's) 3 SEPTEMBER

1st Round → 2nd Round → Q-Finals → S-Finals → Final:

- Cheshire / Kent* → Kent
- Dorset* / Essex → Essex* → Kent*
- Lincs* / Surrey → Surrey*
- Oxon / Warwicks* → Warwicks → Warwicks → Kent*
- Gloucs* / Scotland → Gloucs
- Devon / Leics* → Leics* → Gloucs*
- Glam / Norfolk* → Glam*
- Hants / Herts* → Hants → Hants → Hants → Somerset
- Northants / Wilts* → Northants
- Berks* / Yorks → Yorks* → Northants*
- Derbys / Suffolk* → Derbys*
- Cambs* / Middx → Middx → Middx → Middx* → SOMERSET
- Durham* / Lancs → Lancs*
- Shrops* / Somerset → Somerset → Somerset
- Notts / Worcs* → Notts
- Ireland* / Sussex → Sussex* → Sussex* → Somerset → Kent

Final: Somerset beat Kent — **SOMERSET**

*Home team.

Kent v Somerset 1983 NatWest Bank Trophy Final
Somerset won by 24 runs
Played at Lord's, September 3
Toss: Kent. Umpires: D.J. Constant and D.G.L. Evans
Man of the Match: V.J. Marks (Adjudicator: R.G.D. Willis)

Somerset		Runs	Mins	Balls	6s	4s
P.W. Denning	lbw b Dilley	1	11	6	–	–
P.M. Roebuck	b Dilley	11	29	23	–	2
P.A. Slocombe	c Johnson b Baptiste	20	77	46	–	3
I.V.A. Richards	c Knott b Dilley	51	74	59	–	6
I.T. Botham*	c Johnson b Cowdrey	9	35	29	–	1
N.F.M. Popplewell	c Cowdrey b Dilley	35	89	83	–	2
J.W. Lloyds	lbw b Jarvis	10	37	23	–	1
V.J. Marks	c Benson b Cowdrey	29	37	27	1	2
J. Garner	run out (Cowdrey)	4	6	3	–	–
C.H. Dredge	not out	3	2	2	–	–
T. Gard†	did not bat					
Extras	(B 1, LB 17, W 2)	20				
	(50 overs, 205 minutes)	**193-9**				

Kent		Runs	Mins	Balls	6s	4s
M.R. Benson	c Lloyds b Garner	0	2	3	–	–
G.W. Johnson	b Marks	27	76	53	–	1
C.J. Tavaré*	c Roebuck b Marks	39	85	80	–	5
D.G. Aslett	st Gard b Richards	14	28	39	–	–
C.S. Cowdrey	st Gard b Marks	0	1	3	–	–
E.A.E. Baptiste	b Botham	16	36	27	–	1
A.P.E. Knott†	c Roebuck b Dredge	17	33	22	1	1
R.M. Ellison	b Garner	21	39	26	1	2
G.R. Dilley	b Botham	19	22	16	–	2
D.L. Underwood	not out	5	12	9	–	–
K.B.S. Jarvis	c Botham b Dredge	3	8	6	–	–
Extras	(B 6, LB 1, NB 1)	8				
	(47.1 overs, 180 minutes)	**169**				

Kent	O	M	R	W
Dilley	10	1	29	4
Ellison	10	1	35	0
Jarvis	10	0	43	1
Baptiste	10	1	37	1
Cowdrey	10	2	29	2

Somerset	O	M	R	W
Garner	9	2	15	2
Botham	10	0	29	2
Dredge	8.1	0	50	2
Popplewell	1	0	9	0
Marks	10	0	30	3
Richards	9	1	28	1

Fall of Wickets

Wkt	S	K
1st	10	0
2nd	20	60
3rd	89	73
4th	95	73
5th	112	89
6th	146	112
7th	176	126
8th	190	160
9th	193	162
10th		169

*Captain †Wicket-keeper

John Player League

Yorkshire were reigning County Champions when the John Player League was established, in 1969. Justly proud of their status, they rather looked down on the new competition, much as the gourmet does on junk food. They cared little in those years that they were always also-rans. Now, 14 years later, they were grateful to win the title in a season in which they experienced the humiliation of finishing last in the County Championship. Their last success in any competition was winning the Gillette Cup in 1969.

Ironically, the central figures in the feud within Yorkshire's ranks, Ray Illingworth, the captain and manager, and Geoff Boycott, were also among the principal architects of Yorkshire's latest triumph, and their supporters hoped that the win would act as a balm on old wounds.

There was a thrilling finish to the race for the title, with at least four counties in with a chance until only three rounds of matches remained. They were Yorkshire, Sussex, the holders, who had suffered badly from injuries in mid-season, Somerset, and Kent, both past champions.

At that stage, on the last Sunday of August, Somerset met Kent in a crucial tie at Taunton and beat them decisively by 6 wickets, despite a rousing century for Kent by Derek Aslett. The fixture clashed with a Test match, and Kent were without Tavaré as well as the injured Dilley. Somerset were also missing Botham, but Viv Richards made 86 off only 50 balls, and Kent's title hopes were snuffed out. So also were Sussex's chances of retaining the title when they were beaten by Hampshire at Southampton.

The leaders, but by only two points, were Yorkshire. If they remained on top that day it was thanks to the heroism of Bill Athey. On the eve of their Bradford tie with Derbyshire, he was involved in a road accident and suffered severe bruising over a large area of his chest. When, next day, Yorkshire set out to reply to a Derbyshire total of 168, Athey, going in first with Boycott, faced one ball and was so overcome with pain that he was forced to retire. But when Yorkshire found themselves in the alarming position of 131 for 7 with only five overs to go, Athey, gritting his teeth, resumed his innings and with three lofted fours in an over from Mortensen, narrowed the gap which Simon Dennis then closed with a mighty six.

Still, they had only a slender chance of taking the title, for their last match was against Essex, who were fancied to beat them, while Somerset's opponents were two counties from the lower reaches of the table, Worcestershire and Warwickshire.

While Yorkshire rested on the penultimate Sunday, Worcestershire destroyed Somerset on a slow, turning pitch at New Road. Curiously, the bowler who caused Somerset's agony, which immediately followed the joys of winning the NatWest final the day before, was a young expatriate Yorkshireman, Richard Illingworth.

The weather ultimately determined the championship, for Yorkshire's game with Essex was rained off, giving them two points for an abandoned match. Somerset, playing at home, duly accounted for Warwickshire and finished level on points with Yorkshire. The tie-breaker of more 'away wins' was applied, and Yorkshire, in this instance, were superior by two matches.

Final Table

		P	W	L	T	NR	Pts	6s	4w
1	YORKSHIRE (16)	16	10	3	0	3	46	28	3
2	Somerset (9)	16	10	3	0	3	46	32	3
3	Kent (4)	16	8	3	0	5	42	16	4
4	Sussex (1)	16	9	5	0	2	40	33	1
5	Hampshire (5)	16	9	6	0	1	38	45	3
6	Derbyshire (12)	16	7	5	0	4	36	22	2
	Essex (5)	16	7	5	0	4	36	36	1
8	Lancashire (10)	16	5	5	1	5	32	32	1
	Middlesex (2)	16	7	7	0	2	32	40	3
10	Glamorgan (10)	16	6	8	0	2	28	24	3
11	Leicestershire (3)	16	4	7	0	5	26	16	2
	Surrey (12)	16	4	7	0	5	26	32	1
	Worcestershire (15)	16	4	7	3	2	26	25	3
14	Gloucestershire (14)	16	4	8	0	4	24	22	2
15	Northamptonshire (8)	16	5	10	0	1	22	28	3
	Nottinghamshire (5)	16	4	9	1	2	22	22	4
	Warwickshire (17)	16	4	9	1	2	22	37	2

Yorkshire won the competition by achieving more away wins (5) than Somerset (3), a ruling applicable to the first four places only.
1982 final positions are shown in brackets.

Winners

1969	Lancashire	1974	Leicestershire	1979	Somerset
1970	Lancashire	1975	Hampshire	1980	Warwickshire
1971	Worcestershire	1976	Kent	1981	Essex
1972	Kent	1977	Leicestershire	1982	Sussex
1973	Kent	1978	Hampshire	1983	Yorkshire

1983 Awards and Distribution of Prize Money

£13,000 and League Trophy to champions - YORKSHIRE
£6,500 to runners-up - Somerset
£3,250 to third-placing - Kent
£1,750 to fourth-placing - Sussex
£275 to winner of each match (shared in event of 'no results' and ties)
£350 to the batsman hitting most sixes in the season: C.G. Greenidge (Hampshire) - 17
£350 to the bowler taking four or more wickets most times in the season: J.G. Thomas (Glamorgan) - 3
£250 to the batsman scoring the fastest 50 in a match televised on BBC2: T.A. Lloyd (Warwickshire) - 38 balls v Northamptonshire at Luton on June 19.

Second XI County Championship and Under-25s

Leicestershire won the First-Class Counties Second XI Championship in 1983 for the first time. Now only Derbyshire and Somerset have not won the competition, which was inaugurated in 1959 and has seen the honours spread evenly – 12 different champions in the last 12 years.

There were some fine individual performances during the season, with six batsmen hitting double centuries and six bowlers taking eight or more wickets in an innings. The highest score was P. Robinson's 233 for Yorkshire against Kent. And the best bowling figures were 9 for 43, by Dallas Moir for Derbyshire against Northants.

Leicestershire also won the Warwick Under-25 one-day competition. They won five of their six group matches (the other was a 'no result') and beat Derbyshire in the semi-finals. In a thrilling final, they beat Worcestershire on the last ball, thanks largely to a courageous 88 not out by Tim Boon.

Second XI Championship 1983: Final Table

	P	W	L	D	Bonus points Batting	Bonus points Bowling	Total points	Avge
1 LEICESTERSHIRE (10)	10	6	1	3	35	30	161	16.10
2 Yorkshire (14)	11	5	1	5	29	39	148	13.45
3 Surrey (7)	13	5	3	5	35	40	155	11.92
4 Kent (3)	11	4	4	3	27	35	126	11.45
5 Sussex (16)	11	3	1	7	39	35	122	11.09
6 Lancashire (2)	18	5	3	10	47	56	183	10.16
7 Warwickshire (6)	17	4	5	8	48	52	164	9.64
8 Worcestershire (1)	9	2	0	7	25	20	77	8.56
9 Northamptonshire (13)	12	2	5	5	33	36	101	8.41
10 Glamorgan (17)	13	2	3	8	38	34	104	8.00
11 Essex (12)	12	2	1	9	31	30	93	7.75
12 Nottinghamshire (11)	13	2	3	8	27	37	96	7.38
13 Hampshire (5)	11	1	2	8	25	34	75	6.81
14 Derbyshire (9)	9	1	3	5	17	25	58	6.44
15 Middlesex (4)	11	1	5	5	25	22	63	5.72
16 Gloucestershire (8)	7	0	3	4	13	21	34	4.85
17 Somerset (14)	10	0	2	8	16	25	41	4.10

1982 final positions are shown in brackets.

Warwick Under-25 Competition (Edgbaston, August 21, 40 overs)
Worcestershire 198-8 (G. Matthews 54; D. Wenlock 3-35); Leicestershire 198-5 (T. Boon 88 not). Leicestershire won, having lost fewer wickets.

Minor Counties Championship

The Minor Counties enjoyed the benefits of sponsorship last season, from the United Friendly Insurance Company (the championship) and English Industrial Estates, who provided the cash for a new knock-out competition. The UFI County Championship introduced a fresh format. The teams were divided into two divisions, with the teams in each division playing each other once in two-innings matches over two days. The same system will operate next season, but with the venues reversed.

In a one-day play-off for the Championship between the top team from each division, Herts beat Bucks with just two balls to spare, the match being reduced from 55 to 35 overs because of heavy overnight rain.

Some of the rounds of the knock-out competition were also affected by rain, with matches decided on the toss of a coin. Bedfordshire won two matches, including a semi-final, in this way. But their luck ran out in the final, against Cheshire (whose single Championship win, incidentally, was one more than Beds had been able to muster).

United Friendly Insurance County Championship: Final Tables

Eastern Division	P	W	L	1st inngs W	T	L	NR	Pts	Western Division	P	W	L	1st inngs W	T	L	NR	Pts
1 HERTS*	9	4	1†	1	-	3	-	49	1 BUCKS*	9	6	2	-	-	1	-	61
2 N'land*	9	3	-	5	-	-	1	47	2 Somerset II	9	4	2†	-	1	2	-	47
3 Durham*	9	2	1†	3	-	2	1	36	3 Devon*	9	3	1	4	-	1	-	43
4 Norfolk*	9	2	1	4	-	2	-	34	4 Oxon*	9	3	2	2	-	2	-	38
5 Suffolk*	9	2	3†	3	-	1	-	33	5 Shrops*	9	2	3†	2	-	2	-	31
6 Cumberland*	9	2	2	2	-	2	1	30	6 Berks*	9	2	2	2	-	3	-	29
7 Staffs*	9	2	1	1	-	5	-	28	7 Wilts*	9	2	2	2	-	3	-	29
8 Cambs	9	2	4†	1	-	2	-	28	8 Cheshire	9	1	1	5	1	1	-	28
9 Lincs	9	1	3†	2	-	3	-	22	9 Dorset	9	1	5‡	1	-	2	-	19
10 Beds	9	-	4†	1	-	3	1	11	10 Cornwall	9	1	5	1	-	2	-	15

Points: 10 for win, 3 for first innings lead in match drawn or lost, 2 for first innings tie in match drawn, 1 for match drawn but behind on first innings points (all first innings points for scores at 55 overs), and 2 for 'no result'.
*Qualified for 1984 NatWest Bank Trophy. †Denotes first innings points in 1 match lost. ‡Denotes tie on first innings in 2 matches lost.

Leading UFI Averages

Batting	I	NO	HS	Runs	Avge	Bowling	O	M	R	W	Avge
Mudassar Nazar	12	5	134*	583	83.28	D.R. Parry	149	52	338	24	14.08
R.E. Hayward	16	5	108	853	77.54	S.E. Blott	146.2	38	434	27	16.07
G.R.J. Roope	13	6	79	541	77.28	P.J. Lewington	332	117	741	46	16.10
L. Baichan	17	7	108*	727	72.70	K. Arnold	204	42	590	36	16.38
R.C. Cooper	9	1	137	519	64.87	C. Rutterford	236.4	62	576	34	16.94
Wasim Raja	11	3	115*	478	59.75	J.A. Sutton	164	50	393	23	17.08

English Industrial Estates Knock-out Competition
Final: At Macclesfield, September 24. CHESHIRE beat BEDS by 36 runs (50 overs). Cheshire 228-6 (Tansley 83, Tipton 67); Beds 192 (Daniels 70). Man of the Match: Ian Tansley.

Bucks v Herts, UFI Championship Play-off

Hertfordshire won by 2 wickets
Played at Worcester, September 18 (35 overs)
Toss: Bucks. Umpires: C.L. Head and C. Smith.
Man of the Match: T.S. Smith (adj. B.L. D'Oliveira).

Buckinghamshire

M.E. Milton	lbw b Garofall	34
M.E. Gear	lbw b Hailey	49
R.E. Hayward	not out	60
N.G. Hames	c Osman b Collins	19
K.I. Hodgson	run out	3
D.E. Smith*	not out	11
R.G. Humphrey†	did not bat	
P.J. Newport	,,	
M. Jean-Jacques	,,	
A.W. Lyon	,,	
C.A. Connor	,,	
Extras		14
(35 overs)		190-4

Hertfordshire

W.M. Osman	b Newport	33
N.P.G. Wright	b Connor	7
F.E. Collyer*†	c Newport b Hodgson	29
S. Dean	c Milton b Newport	10
T.S. Smith	not out	59
J.D. Carr	c Humphrey b Newport	0
C. Thomas	c Humphrey b Hodgson	0
A.R. Garofall	b Jean-Jacques	32
B.G. Collins	b Jean-Jacques	0
D. Surridge	not out	0
R.J. Hailey	did not bat	
Extras		21
(34.4 overs)		191-8

Hertfordshire	O	M	R	W
Surridge	7	1	41	0
Collins	7	1	39	1
Garofall	7	1	18	1
Smith	7	1	37	0
Hailey	7	1	41	1

Buckinghamshire	O	M	R	W
Jean-Jacques	7	1	32	2
Connor	7	0	24	1
Newport	7	0	34	3
Hodgson	7	1	25	2
Milton	6.4	0	55	0

Fall of Wickets

Wkt	B	H
1st	82	25
2nd	104	54
3rd	147	86
4th	164	95
5th		95
6th		97
7th		176
8th		176
9th		
10th		

*Captain †Wicket-keeper

Village and Club Cricket

In the sunshine of the last weekend of August, it was the turn of club cricketers to take the field at Lord's in the finals of their two championships – the William Younger Cup for the senior sides and the Whitbread Trophy for the villages. Each event, to the accompaniment of vociferous support, was won by a club playing at 'Headquarters' for the first time.

William Younger Cup (45 overs). Lord's, August 27; Hastings and St Leonards Priory won toss.
Shrewsbury: 191-9 (S.C. Gale 53, I.J.F. Hutchinson 36, J. Foster 22; R.B. Burnett 3-38, R.S.F. Burnett 3-48); *Hastings and St Leonards Priory:* 189 (44.5 overs; T.D. Booth Jones 85, A.C. Booth Jones 23, I. Gillespie 22, K. Turk 21; R.T. Tudor 5-41, D. Williamson 3-33). *Shrewsbury won by 2 runs.*

Shrewsbury, in a thrilling final over, took the Younger Cup in its inaugural year. After putting Shrewsbury in to bat and restricting them to 191 for 9, Hastings and St Leonards Priory, for whom Tim Booth Jones made 85, needed 3 runs to win, with 3 wickets in hand at the start of their 45th over. Richard Tudor, with the aid of two brilliant catches by young Ian Hutchinson, took the wickets without conceding a run, and, against nearly all probabilities, Shrewsbury had won. The winners received £1,000, the runners-up £600, and the competition was organized by the National Cricket Association.

Whitbread Village Championship Trophy (40 overs). Lord's, August 28. Quarndon won toss.
Troon: 155-6 (B. Carter 55 not, J. Spry 23, I. Williams 22 not; R. Taylor 3-31, F. Butcher 2-21); *Quarndon:* 157-2 (39.2 overs; D. Hibberd 53 not, I. Farmer 38 not, S.A. Underwood 36; S. Kitchen 2-27). *Quarndon won by 8 wickets.*

The Whitbread Village Trophy final on Sunday proved equally tense, with Quarndon of Derbyshire beating three-times champions Troon of Cornwall by 8 wickets as bank clerk David Hibberd swept the first two balls of the final over to the long-leg boundary. This made his unbroken stand for the third wicket with Rolls-Royce engineer Ian Farmer worth 104 and Hibberd man of the match.

Batting first, Troon mustered 155 for 6 wickets against determined fielders who held their catches. Particularly pleasing to those surfeited of medium-pace defensive bowling were slow left-arm spinners P.C. Ralph Taylor and Frank Butcher, operating in attacking partnership from Pavilion and Nursery ends. The winners received £500, the runners-up £250, and the competition was organized by *The Cricketer*.

(Statistics by John Fogg)

Schools Cricket

Although the schools' season ended in a blaze of sunshine, persistent rain ruined most of May, and in a number of cases at least half of the fixtures were cancelled or abandoned.

Nevertheless, much good cricket was played, and for some schools 1983 was a memorable year. Among these were Shrewsbury, unbeaten in all matches, with 13 wins and 4 draws; Brighton, who played 11 games against other schools and won 10, the other being rained off in the early stages; Bradfield, who beat Eton, Winchester, Wellington, Charterhouse, and three others and drew the remaining two contests against rival schools; and Durham, with 7 victories, 6 draws, and 1 defeat.

Harrow went through the term without loss, but gained only two wins against schools. Eton did better in terms of victories (four), and their only defeat was by Bradfield. Winchester had 9 successes in 18 fixtures to complete their best record since 1959.

Notable triumphs at the end-of-term festivals were recorded by Aldenham, Ampleforth, Brighton, Hurstpierpoint, Shrewsbury, and Solihull, each of whom won all three matches.

Batsmen again took most of the honours at the major schools, led by N.J. Lenham (Brighton), who scored 981 runs (average 81), J.R. Ansell of Epsom (944 at 78), P. Bent of R.G.S., Worcester (929), J.P. Stephenson of Felsted (885), M.A. Roseberry of Durham, who was just 16 (827), and J.R. Prentis of Eastbourne (826).

R.V. Henderson (Pocklington), C.S. Mays (Lancing), and A. Byers (Colfe's) completed the all-rounder's double of 500 runs and 50 wickets, while Roseberry was very nearly there with 48 victims.

The MCC Schools XI selected after the trials to play the National Association of Young Cricketers was:

J.P. Stephenson (Felsted)
R.M. Pepper (Dover GS)
M. Whitmore (Lutterworth GS)
N.J. Lenham (Brighton)
P.A. Redfarn* (Cambridge College of Art & Tech.)
A. Fordham (Bedford Modern)
R.J.P. Burton (Shrewsbury)
W. Smith (Colston's, Bristol)
K. Medlycott (Wandsworth)
J.M. Robinson† (Solihull)
J.N. Whitehouse (Sir William Turner's, Redcar).

*Captain. †Wicket-keeper.

Young Australians Tour

The Australian Young Cricketers were a happy band, enjoying victory and crediting 'the better side' when defeated, which was only three times. They won the three-match 'Test' series 2-1, losing the third. They also lost the second of two one-day internationals, and at Fenners were beaten (by 1 wicket) by the National Association of Young Cricketers. Their defeats were in their last three matches. Before that they had won eight and drawn three on a tour blessed by beautiful weather.

The Australians' strength was already evident by the time they won the first one-day international at Lord's. Their fast bowlers, Craig McDermott and Greg Connors, bowled straight and to a full length. Tony Dodemaide was clearly a talented all-rounder, and the youngest member of the side, Darrin Ramshaw, a sound and, as it proved, consistent batsman.

In the first Test, which began at Trent Bridge next day, Young England, captained by Hugh Morris of Glamorgan, bowled the tourists out for 137 and earned a small first innings lead. But in the second innings the Australian captain Mark Veletta made a fine 86, and England, needing 253, were never in sight of victory. Dodemaide, as in the first innings, took four wickets, and Australia won by 84 runs. For the second Test, at Scarborough, England made three changes. But they scored only 183, of which Lenham and Johnson made 72 and 50, respectively. Dodemaide, swinging the ball late, took 6 for 54. Australia built up a lead of 114 (Ramshaw 82, Djura 45, Veletta 42), but England batted resolutely through the third day and left them needing 166. Australia soon made these to win handsomely by 6 wickets.

England had lost the series, but when the team for the final Test at Chelmsford was chosen they had found a promising new batsman to bring in. Ashley Metcalfe had just made 122 on his County Championship debut for Yorkshire. Metcalfe's 54 was the foundation of the 109 which he put on for the first wicket with Johnson, who retired ill, and the left-handed Hugh Morris. England were all out for 190. Then off-spinner Peter Such took 7 wickets for 72, and despite a sterling 100 by Craig Bradley, the Australian lead was only 43. Wicket-keeper Steven Rhodes, with Pick and Such, made 166 for the last two wickets, and Australia needing 300 to win were beaten by 67 runs.

A pleasant aspect of the series was the unhesitating acceptance by both sides of umpiring decisions.

The Australian touring party: M.R. Veletta (capt, W. Australia), C.E. Bradley (vice-capt, S. Australia); B. Djura (wicket-keeper), M. England, A.J. Knight, B.E. McNamara (NSW), H.V. Hammelmann, I.A. Healy, C.J. McDermott (Queensland), G.T. Connors, A.I.C. Dodemaide, D.P. Tindale (Victoria), S.A. Henderson, B. Mulder, D.J. Ramshaw (W. Australia); Manager, George Murray; assistant manager and coach, Bob Bitmead (Victoria); scorer Alan W. Walsh (Canberra).

The following represented Young England: H. Morris (capt, Glam, 5 matches), N.H. Fairbrother (Lancs, 5), S.J. Rhodes (wicket-keeper, Yorks, 5), G.D. Rose (Middx, 5), R.A. Pick (Notts, 5), P.M. Such (Notts, 4), P. Johnson (Notts, 3), J.E. Morris (Derbys, 4), N.J. Lenham (Sussex, 3), G.V. Palmer (Somerset, 3), P.A. Smith (Warwicks, 3), G.R. Cowdrey (Kent, 2), P.J. Prichard (Essex, 2), P.W. Jarvis (Yorks, 2 before injury). Appeared in one match: R.F. Bailey (Northants), K.T. Medlycott (MCC Young Pros), A. Golding (Essex), A.A. Metcalfe (Yorks).

Women's Cricket

Sadly, the interference of politics in sport hit women's cricket cruelly at the beginning of 1983. The England Women's Cricket team, who had practised, trained, and saved money for six months up to February 1983, were prevented from undertaking their three-week tour of the West Indies because five of the party had been to South Africa four years previously on a completely private cricket holiday, entirely at each individual's own expense.

This tour would have been Jan Southgate's first as England captain, so the Sussex opening bat was deprived of the opportunity of leading her country in the three Tests and three one-day internationals; the England party were barred from entry to the Caribbean by the various island governments, who were funding the tour for the Caribbean Women's Cricket Federation.

England, who were sponsored by Jack Hayward, the British-born Bahamas-based millionaire who has long been a patron of English women's cricket, then offered the team an unofficial visit to the Bahamas to play matches against visiting men's sides – but once again when the visit became known to the Bahamas government, the team were banned.

Eventually, as a small consolation, the team were sponsored by Monarch Airlines and European Ferries on a week's visit to the La Manga Country Club, southern Spain, where the England women inaugurated the newly built cricket Oval, playing matches against a Cricket Writers XI captained by Don Wilson, the ex-Yorkshire and England player, now the MCC head coach.

So a season of domestic cricket followed, with selectors attending various selected trial matches and all the county matches, to choose players for further trials followed by winter practice and coaching in preparation for a six-week tour by the New Zealand Women's Cricket team of this country in the summer of 1984. The tour includes three three-day Tests, scheduled for Headingley, Worcester, and Canterbury, with three one-day internationals at Leicester, Bristol, and Hove, plus a full programme of county matches from mid-June to the end of July.

Rachael Flint, the former England captain, who was recalled to the England squad for the West Indies tour-that-never-was when Shirley Hodges (Sussex) stood down through illness, took a team of England women cricketers to New York in October 1983. This was a fully sponsored weekend visit to play a one-day international at Mt Vernon Stadium, NY, against a West Indies XI that ironically included several of the players whom England would have faced had their winter tour gone ahead. In a match reduced by rain from 55 to 25 overs, England kept the West Indians to 74-8, and won by 10 wickets. Jan Southgate (31) and Janette Brittin (38) made the runs in 16.1 overs.

Three of England's players – Jan Southgate, Janette Brittin (Surrey), and Jackie Court (Middlesex) – each scored three centuries in the season. Southgate's 128 not out at Hastings was her third successive century in two weeks in July; Court's 123 not out in the National Club KO Final led

Vagabonds, Hertfordshire, to their first title.

Clare Eveson, the 17-year-old Kent bowler, took a match total of 8 for 79 in her first senior England trial match at Hastings in July.

Match Results and Highlights

Warwick Trial Weekend (May 29, 30, rain affected):

J. Southgate's XI 87-8 dec. (C. Hodges 35; C. Barrs 3-15); J. Brittin's XI 42-7 (E. Wulcko 3-8, C. Hodges 3-23). *Drawn.*

C. Watmough's XI 90-5 dec. (J. Edney 38); J. Court's XI 54-3 (W. Watson 30 not). *Drawn.*

J. Brittin's XI 118-9 dec. (J. Brittin 27; J. Court 3-17); J. Court's XI 89-9 (P. Lovell 27; R. Heggs 3-29). *Drawn.*

J. Southgate's XI 106 (R. Flint 53, J. Southgate 27; P. Weeks 4-14, G. McConway 3-8); C. Watmough's XI 83-9 (C. Watmough 32; C. Hodges 3-17). *Drawn.*

Guildford CC Trial Match (June 12):

An England XI 121-7 (48 overs, 3-hr limit, innings closed; M. Lear 58, Jane Powell 33; S. Potter 2-25, R. Heggs 2-26); The Rest 122-4 (39 overs; E. Bakewell 46, J. Court 41). *The Rest won by 6 wickets.*

Hastings CCG Three-Day Trial Match (July 22, 23, 24):

The Rest 231-8 dec. (J. Brittin 77, M. Lear 49, W. Watson 39; C. Eveson 5-26) and 220-7 dec. (J. Brittin 54, M. Lear 49, S. Potter 45; C. Eveson 3-53, C. Hodges 2-12); An England XI 259-6 dec. (J. Southgate 128 not, J. Edney 39, Jane Powell 32) and 177-9 (J. Edney 71, Jane Powell 40; H. Stother 3-33, J. Brittin 3-46). *Drawn.*

Brintons CC, Kidderminster Trial Match (September 10):

Young England 151-2 dec. (L. Cooke 67, J. Brittin 39); Junior England 99-8 (D. Cardall 37 not; J. Stockdale 4-14). *Drawn.*

Mitchells & Butlers CC, Edgbaston Trial Match (September 11):

An England XI v Young England. No play.

Middlesex WCA Golden Jubilee Invitation County Championship Final (Ibis CC, Chiswick, August 28):

West Midlands 169-2 (50 overs; J. Meiring 68, R. Flint 53 not); Middlesex 124 (43.1 overs; M. Taylor 31; W. Williams 3-16, M. Weaver 3-34). *West Midlands won by 45 runs.*

National Club KO Final (Bat & Ball Ground, Gravesend, September 4):

Vagabonds, Herts, 231-4 (40 overs; J. Court 123 not); Somerset Wanderers, Bath, 109-7 (J. Wainwright 3-25). *Vagabonds won by 122 runs.*

Extras

Test Career Averages

The following individual career averages and records include all official Test matches played before September 1, 1983. A dagger (†) indicates a left-handed batsman.

Key to bowling categories:

RF = right-arm fast
RFM = right-arm fast-medium
RM = right-arm medium
LF = left-arm fast
LFM = left-arm fast-medium
LM = left-arm medium
OB = right-arm slow off-breaks
LB = right-arm slow leg-breaks
SLA = left-arm slow leg-breaks

Australia

Batting and Fielding	M	I	NO	HS	R	Avge	100	50	Ct	St
T.M. Alderman	16	21	11	12*	51	5.10	-	-	16	-
A.R. Border†	51	91	16	162	3539	47.18	9	21	58	-
R.J. Bright	16	27	5	33	303	13.77	-	-	8	-
G.S. Chappell	82	145	18	247*	6746	53.11	22	31	114	-
J. Dyson	27	52	7	127*	1282	28.48	2	5	10	-
T.G. Hogan	1	-	-	-	-	-	-	-	1	-
R.M. Hogg	26	41	7	36	272	8.00	-	-	5	-
D.W. Hookes†	14	24	2	143*	923	41.95	1	7	6	-
K.J. Hughes	56	100	6	213	3744	39.82	8	19	40	-
B.M. Laird	21	40	2	92	1341	35.28	-	11	16	-
G.F. Lawson	13	22	4	57*	245	13.61	-	2	3	-
D.K. Lillee	65	86	22	73*	874	13.65	-	1	21	-
R.W. Marsh†	91	144	11	132	3558	26.75	3	16	322	12
C.G. Rackemann	1	1	0	4	4	4.00	-	-	1	-
G.M. Ritchie	3	6	1	106*	205	41.00	1	-	1	-
P.R. Sleep	4	8	0	64	114	14.25	-	1	-	-
J.R. Thomson	49	69	16	49	641	12.09	-	-	19	-
K.C. Wessels†	5	9	0	162	527	58.55	2	1	8	-
G.M. Wood	42	81	5	126	2554	33.60	7	11	32	-
R.D. Woolley	1	-	-	-	-	-	-	-	5	-
G.N. Yallop†	33	62	3	172	2199	37.27	6	8	17	-
B. Yardley	33	54	4	74	978	19.56	-	4	31	-

Bowling	Type	Balls	R	W	Avge	Best	5w/I	10w/M
T.M. Alderman	RFM	4111	1890	66	28.63	6-135	4	-
A.R. Border	SLA	1408	513	15	34.20	3-20	-	-
R.J. Bright	SLA	3598	1343	37	36.29	7-87	3	1
G.S. Chappell	RM	4943	1758	47	37.40	5-61	1	-
T.G. Hogan	SLA	218	116	6	19.33	5-66	1	-
R.M. Hogg	RFM	5387	2277	94	24.22	6-74	5	2
D.W. Hookes	SLA	78	35	0	-	-	-	-
K.J. Hughes	LB	85	28	0	-	-	-	-
B.M. Laird	OB	18	12	0	-	-	-	-
G.F. Lawson	RF	2981	1403	59	23.77	7-81	5	1
D.K. Lillee	RFM	17084	7860	335	23.46	7-83	22	7
R.W. Marsh	OB	60	51	0	-	-	-	-
C.G. Rackemann	RFM	200	96	2	48.00	2-61	-	-
P.R. Sleep	LB	589	381	3	127.00	1-16	-	-
J.R. Thomson	RF	10199	5326	197	27.03	6-46	8	-
G.N. Yallop	LM	192	116	1	116.00	1-21	-	-
B. Yardley	OB	8909	3986	126	31.63	7-98	6	1

England

Batting and Fielding	M	I	NO	HS	R	Avge	100	50	Ct	St
I.T. Botham	63	100	3	208	3548	36.57	12	14	72	-
G. Cook	7	13	0	66	203	15.61	-	2	9	-
N.G.B. Cook	2	4	0	26	51	12.75	-	-	3	-
N.G. Cowans	8	14	2	36	90	7.50	-	-	3	-
G.R. Dilley†	17	27	7	56	328	16.40	-	2	5	-
P.R. Downton	4	7	1	26*	59	9.83	-	-	8	-
P.H. Edmonds	23	28	6	64	430	19.54	-	2	23	-
N.A. Foster	1	2	0	10	13	6.50	-	-	1	-
G. Fowler†	6	12	0	105	436	36.33	1	3	2	-
M.W. Gatting	24	42	3	81	918	23.53	-	7	21	-
D.I. Gower†	53	93	8	200*	3742	44.02	7	19	34	-
E.E. Hemmings	5	10	1	95	198	22.00	-	1	4	-
A.J. Lamb	15	29	3	137*	1061	40.80	3	5	16	-
V.J. Marks	2	4	1	12*	25	8.33	-	-	-	-
G. Miller	32	47	4	98*	1171	27.23	-	7	15	-
D.R. Pringle	7	11	2	47*	166	18.44	-	-	-	-
D.W. Randall	40	68	5	174	2073	32.90	5	11	28	-
C.L. Smith	2	4	0	43	78	19.50	-	-	2	-
C.J. Tavaré	26	48	1	149	1620	34.46	2	12	17	-
R.W. Taylor	51	74	12	97	1073	17.30	-	3	155	7
R.G.D. Willis	83	117	51	28*	775	11.74	-	-	37	-

Bowling	Type	Balls	R	W	Avge	Best	5w/I	10w/M
I.T. Botham	RFM	14725	6876	277	24.82	8-34	20	4
G. Cook	SLA	42	27	0	-	-	-	-
N.G.B. Cook	SLA	812	275	17	16.17	5-35	2	-
N.G. Cowans	RF	1392	843	23	36.65	6-77	1	-
G.R. Dilley	RF	2908	1453	45	32.28	4-24	-	-
P.H. Edmonds	SLA	5220	1733	59	29.37	7-66	2	-
N.A. Foster	RFM	168	75	1	75.00	1-35	-	-
M.W. Gatting	RM	134	52	0	-	-	-	-
D.I. Gower	OB	12	2	1	2.00	1-1	-	-
E.E. Hemmings	OB	1468	558	12	46.50	3-68	-	-
A.J. Lamb	RM	6	0	0	-	-	-	-
V.J. Marks	OB	300	109	4	27.25	3-78	-	-
G. Miller	OB	4981	1717	59	29.10	5-44	1	-
D.R. Pringle	RM	1091	495	11	45.00	2-16	-	-
D.W. Randall	RM	16	3	0	-	-	-	-
C.L. Smith	OB	72	31	2	15.50	2-31	-	-
C.J. Tavaré	RM	12	11	0	-	-	-	-
R.W. Taylor	RM	12	6	0	-	-	-	-
R.G.D. Willis	RF	16042	7471	305	24.49	8-43	16	-

West Indies

Batting and Fielding	M	I	NO	HS	R	Avge	100	50	Ct	St
S.F.A.F. Bacchus	19	30	0	250	782	26.06	1	3	17	-
W.W. Daniel	5	5	2	11	29	9.66	-	-	2	-
W.W. Davis	1	1	0	14	14	14.00	-	-	1	-
P.J. Dujon	8	12	2	110	486	48.60	1	1	27	1
J. Garner	32	40	6	60	424	12.47	-	1	26	-
H.A. Gomes†	27	40	2	126	1596	42.00	5	8	7	-
C.G. Greenidge	41	70	5	154*	2962	45.56	6	22	43	-
D.L. Haynes	29	45	2	184	1764	41.02	4	9	17	-
M.A. Holding	36	49	8	58*	461	11.24	-	2	12	-
C.H. Lloyd†	90	149	10	242*	6238	44.87	16	32	68	-
A.L. Logie	5	6	0	130	167	27.83	1	-	1	-
M.D. Marshall	17	22	2	45	200	10.00	-	-	7	-
I.V.A. Richards	52	80	4	291	4411	58.03	14	19	56	-
A.M.E. Roberts	45	60	10	54	694	13.88	-	2	9	-

Bowling	Type	Balls	R	W	Avge	Best	5w/I	10w/M
S.F.A.F. Bacchus	RM	6	3	0	-	-	-	-
W.W. Daniel	RF	788	381	15	25.40	4-53	-	-
W.W. Davis	RF	312	175	4	43.75	2-54	-	-
J.Garner	RFM	7326	2861	131	21.83	6-56	2	-
H.A. Gomes	RM/OB	1248	469	8	58.62	2-20	-	-
C.G. Greenidge	RM	26	4	0	-	-	-	-
D.L. Haynes	RM/LB	18	8	1	8.00	1-2	-	-
M.A. Holding	RF	8134	3696	151	24.47	8-92	10	2
C.H. Lloyd	RM	1716	622	10	62.20	2-13	-	-
M.D. Marshall	RF	3265	1578	55	28.69	5-37	1	-
I.V.A. Richards	RM/OB	2140	790	14	56.42	2-19	-	-
A.M.E. Roberts	RFM	10801	5026	197	25.51	7-54	11	2

New Zealand

Batting and Fielding	M	I	NO	HS	R	Avge	100	50	Ct	St
J.G. Bracewell	8	13	2	28	85	7.72	-	-	6	-
B.L. Cairns	32	51	7	52	739	16.79	-	1	23	-
E.J. Chatfield	10	14	7	13*	60	8.57	-	-	-	-
J.V. Coney	24	42	6	84	1146	31.83	-	10	28	-
J.J. Crowe	4	7	0	36	81	11.57	-	-	3	-
M.D. Crowe	7	12	0	46	183	15.25	-	-	8	-
B.A. Edgar†	24	43	2	161	1481	36.12	3	8	13	-
T.J. Franklin	1	2	0	7	9	4.50	-	-	-	-
E.J. Gray	2	4	0	17	38	9.50	-	-	-	-
R.J. Hadlee†	44	77	11	103	1601	24.25	1	8	22	-
G.P. Howarth	34	62	5	147	2014	35.33	6	8	22	-
W.K. Lees	21	37	4	152	778	23.57	1	1	52	7
I.D.S. Smith	9	13	3	20	108	10.80	-	-	29	-
M.C. Snedden†	9	10	2	32	120	15.00	-	-	2	-
G.M. Turner	41	73	6	259	2991	44.64	7	14	42	-
J.G. Wright†	25	44	1	141	1233	28.67	2	5	12	-

Bowling	Type	Balls	R	W	Avge	Best	5w/I	10w/M
J.G. Bracewell	OB	1575	654	21	31.14	5-75	1	-
B.L. Cairns	RM	8005	3096	97	31.91	7-74	5	1
E.J. Chatfield	RFM	2447	1073	29	37.00	5-95	1	-
J.V. Coney	RM	1515	485	15	32.33	3-28	-	-
M.D. Crowe	RFM	153	72	2	36.00	2-35	-	-
E.J. Gray	SLA	288	128	4	32.00	3-73	-	-
R.J. Hadlee	RFM	11355	5164	200	25.82	7-23	15	3
G.P. Howarth	OB	518	236	3	78.66	1-13	-	-
W.K. Lees	RM	5	4	0	-	-	-	-
M.C. Snedden	RFM	1530	690	23	30.00	3-21	-	-
G.M. Turner	OB	12	5	0	-	-	-	-
J.G. Wright	RM	6	2	0	-	-	-	-

India

Batting and Fielding	M	I	NO	HS	R	Avge	100	50	Ct	St
M. Amarnath	37	64	5	120	2648	44.88	7	16	32	-
Arun Lal	4	7	0	63	164	23.42	-	2	5	-
D.R. Doshi†	32	37	10	20	129	4.77	-	-	10	-
A.D. Gaekwad	26	46	3	102	1289	29.97	1	7	8	-
S.M. Gavaskar	90	158	12	221	7625	52.22	27	33	80	-
Kapil Dev	53	77	8	126*	2253	32.65	3	12	19	-
S.M.H. Kirmani	69	99	14	101*	2100	24.70	1	10	128	32
Madan Lal	31	49	12	55*	762	20.59	-	3	14	-
Maninder Singh†	8	9	2	12*	30	4.28	-	-	1	-
S.M. Patil	20	33	4	174	1254	43.24	3	7	8	-
B.S. Sandhu	7	9	3	71	206	34.33	-	2	1	-
T.A. Sekhar	2	1	1	0*	0	-	-	-	-	-
R.J. Shastri	19	27	5	128	669	30.40	2	2	8	-
R. Shukla	1	-	-	-	-	-	-	-	-	-
L. Sivaramakrishnan	1	1	0	17	17	17.00	-	-	-	-
K. Srikkanth	6	9	0	65	147	16.33	-	1	2	-
D.B. Vengsarkar	63	103	10	157*	3484	37.46	6	20	44	-
S. Venkataraghavan	55	74	12	64	737	11.88	-	2	44	-
G.R. Viswanath	91	155	10	222	6080	41.93	14	35	63	-
Yashpal Sharma	33	53	11	140	1650	39.28	2	9	13	-

Bowling	Type	Balls	R	W	Avge	Best	5w/I	10w/M
M. Amarnath	RM	2988	1476	26	56.76	4-63	-	-
Arun Lal	RM	7	6	0	-	-	-	-
D.R. Doshi	SLA	9202	3450	113	30.53	6-102	5	-
A.D. Gaekwad	OB	118	83	0	-	-	-	-
S.M. Gavaskar	RM	322	173	1	173.00	1-34	-	-
Kapil Dev	RFM	11572	6082	206	29.52	8-85	15	1
S.M.H. Kirmani	-	1	0	0	-	-	-	-
Madan Lal	RFM	5032	2365	64	36.95	5-23	4	-
Maninder Singh	SLA	1407	636	5	127.20	2-90	-	-
S.M. Patil	RM	633	238	9	26.44	2-28	-	-
B.S. Sandhu	RMF	876	479	9	53.22	3-87	-	-
T.A. Sekhar	RMF	204	129	0	-	-	-	-
R.J. Shastri	SLA	4309	1662	42	39.57	5-125	1	-
R. Shukla	LB	294	152	2	76.00	2-82	-	-
L. Sivaramakrishnan	LB	150	95	0	-	-	-	-
K. Srikkanth	RM	36	10	0	-	-	-	-
D.B. Vengsarkar	RM	29	17	0	-	-	-	-
S. Venkataraghavan	OB	14582	5530	155	35.67	8-72	3	1
G.R. Viswanath	LB	70	46	1	46.00	1-11	-	-
Yashpal Sharma	RM	24	7	1	7.00	1-6	-	-

Pakistan

Batting and Fielding	M	I	NO	HS	R	Avge	100	50	Ct	St
Abdul Qadir	19	22	4	38	255	14.16	–	–	6	–
Haroon Rashid	23	36	1	153	1217	34.77	3	5	16	–
Imran Khan	49	73	11	123	1853	29.88	2	5	16	–
Iqbal Qasim†	36	41	12	56	269	9.27	–	1	27	–
Jalal Uddin	3	2	2	1*	1	–	–	–	–	–
Javed Miandad	52	83	14	280*	3992	57.85	10	21	48	1
Majid Khan	63	106	5	167	3931	38.92	8	19	70	–
Mansoor Akhtar	13	22	3	111	484	25.47	1	2	7	–
Mohsin Khan	22	35	4	200	1516	48.90	4	5	18	–
Mudassar Nazar	35	54	5	231	2138	43.63	6	9	23	–
Salim Malik	8	8	1	107	261	37.28	2	–	9	–
Sarfraz Nawaz	49	62	9	55	827	15.60	–	3	25	–
Sikander Bakht	26	35	12	22*	146	6.34	–	–	7	–
Tahir Naqqash	10	11	3	57	182	22.75	–	1	1	–
Wasim Bari	73	102	24	85	1259	16.14	–	5	175	26
Wasim Raja†	45	74	12	117*	2321	37.43	2	16	12	–
Zaheer Abbas	58	94	7	274	4073	46.81	11	14	31	–

Bowling	Type	Balls	R	W	Avge	Best	5w/I	10w/M
Abdul Qadir	LB	5003	2197	65	33.80	7-142	2	1
Haroon Rashid	RM	8	3	0	–	–	–	–
Imran Khan	RF	12552	5318	232	22.92	8-58	16	4
Iqbal Qasim	SLA	9294	3426	115	29.79	7-49	4	2
Jalal Uddin	RFM	516	244	7	34.85	3-77	–	–
Javed Miandad	LB	1368	634	17	37.29	3-74	–	–
Majid Khan	OB	3584	1456	27	53.92	4-45	–	–
Mohsin Khan	LB	14	6	0	–	–	–	–
Mudassar Nazar	RM	2015	839	25	33.56	6-32	1	–
Sarfraz Nawaz	RFM	12028	5020	155	32.38	9-86	4	1
Sikander Bakht	RFM	4870	2411	67	35.98	8-69	3	1
Tahir Naqqash	RFM	1740	910	23	39.56	5-40	1	–
Wasim Bari	RM	8	2	0	–	–	–	–
Wasim Raja	LB	3091	1425	39	36.53	4-68	–	–
Zaheer Abbas	OB	104	34	0	–	–	–	–

Sri Lanka

Batting and Fielding	M	I	NO	HS	R	Avge	100	50	Ct	St
R.G. de Alwis	2	4	0	9	15	3.75	-	-	1	-
A.L.F. de Mel	6	12	2	34	154	15.40	-	-	5	-
D.S. de Silva	8	16	2	61	364	26.00	-	2	3	-
G.R.A. de Silva†	4	7	2	14	41	8.20	-	-	-	-
R.L. Dias	6	12	0	109	543	45.25	1	5	3	-
E.R.N.S. Fernando	3	6	0	46	73	12.16	-	-	-	-
Y. Goonasekera†	2	4	0	23	48	12.00	-	-	6	-
H.M. Goonatillake	5	10	2	56	177	22.12	-	1	10	3
R.P.W. Guneratne	1	2	2	0*	0	-	-	-	-	-
S. Jeganathan	2	4	0	8	19	4.75	-	-	-	-
V.B. John	2	4	2	8*	11	5.50	-	-	1	-
R.S. Madugalle	8	16	1	91*	431	28.73	-	3	5	-
L.R.D. Mendis	6	12	0	105	450	37.50	2	2	4	-
A.N. Ranasinghe	2	4	0	77	88	22.00	-	1	-	-
A. Ranatunga†	5	10	0	90	266	26.60	-	2	1	-
R.J. Ratnayake	3	6	0	30	58	9.66	-	-	1	-
J.R. Ratnayeke†	5	10	2	29*	102	12.75	-	-	-	-
S.A.R. Silva	1	2	0	8	8	4.00	-	-	2	-
B. Warnapura	4	8	0	38	96	12.00	-	-	2	-
M. de S. Wettimuny	2	4	0	17	28	7.00	-	-	2	-
S. Wettimuny	7	14	1	157	514	39.53	1	3	3	-

Bowling	Type	Balls	R	W	Avge	Best	5w/I	10w/M
A.L.F. de Mel	RFM	1293	905	25	36.20	5-68	1	-
D.S. de Silva	LB	2008	969	27	35.88	5-59	1	-
G.R.A. de Silva	SLA	962	385	7	55.00	2-38	-	-
R.P.W. Guneratne	LB	102	84	0	-	-	-	-
S. Jeganathan	SLA	30	12	0	-	-	-	-
V.B. John	RFM	272	143	8	17.87	5-60	1	-
A.N. Ranasinghe	LM	114	69	1	69.00	1-23	-	-
A. Ranatunga	RM	120	84	1	84.00	1-72	-	-
R.J. Ratnayake	RFM	588	360	7	51.42	4-81	-	-
J.R. Ratnayeke	RFM	761	450	9	50.00	3-93	-	-
B. Warnapura	RM	90	46	0	-	-	-	-
S. Wettimuny	RM	12	21	0	-	-	-	-

Guide to Newcomers

Register of New Players 1983

The following players made their first appearances in English first-class cricket during the 1983 season. Three of them (W.P. Fowler of Derbyshire, D.A. Banks of Worcestershire, and A.A. Metcalfe of Yorkshire) had appeared in limited-overs matches for their counties in 1982. Players marked with a dagger (†) had already made their debuts in first-class cricket overseas.

Key to categories:

RH	Right-handed batsman	LFM	Left-arm fast-medium
LH	Left-handed batsman	LM	Left-arm medium
RF	Right-arm fast	OB	Right-arm slow off-breaks
RFM	Right-arm fast-medium	LB	Right-arm slow leg-breaks
RM	Right-arm medium	SLA	Left-arm slow leg-breaks
LF	Left-arm fast	WK	Wicket-keeper

Surname	Given Names	Birthdate	Place of Birth	Bat	Ball
Derbyshire					
Fowler†	William Peter	13 Mar 59	St Helens, Lancashire	RH	SLA
Mortensen	Ole Henrek	29 Jan 58	Vejle, Jutland, Denmark	RH	RFM
Essex					
Golding	Andrew Kenneth	5 Oct 63	Colchester, Essex	RH	SLA
Hughes†	Mervyn Gregory	23 Nov 61	Euroa, Victoria, Australia	RH	RFM
Glamorgan					
Derrick	John	15 Jan 63	Cwmaman, Glamorgan	RH	RM
Gloucestershire					
Tracy†	Sean Robert	7 Jun 63	Auckland, New Zealand	RH	RFM
Hampshire					
None					
Kent					
Masters	Kevin David	19 May 61	Chatham, Kent	LH	RFM
Lancashire					
Chadwick	Mark Robert	9 Feb 63	Rochdale, Lancashire	RH	RM
Nasir Zaidi	Syed Mohammad	25 Mar 61	Karachi, Pakistan	RH	LB
Stanworth	John	30 Sep 60	Oldham, Lancashire	RH	WK
Leicestershire					
Addison	James Paul	14 Nov 65	Leek, Staffordshire	RH	SLA
Ferris†	George John Fitzgerald	18 Oct 64	Urlings Village, Antigua	RH	RF
Whitaker	John James	5 May 62	Skipton, Yorkshire	RH	OB
Middlesex					
Carr	John Donald	15 Jun 63	St John's Wood, London NW8	RH	OB
Sykes	James Frederick ('Jamie')	30 Dec 65	Shoreditch, London N1	RH	OB
Northamptonshire					
Carse†	James Alexander	13 Dec 58	Salisbury, Southern Rhodesia	RH	RFM
Lines	Steven John	16 Mar 63	Luton, Bedfordshire	RH	RM
Olley	Martin William Charles	27 Nov 63	Romford, Essex	RH	WK
Walker	Alan	7 Jul 62	Emley, Yorkshire	LH	RFM
Nottinghamshire					
Pick	Robert Andrew ('Andy')	19 Nov 63	Nottingham	LH	RFM
Somerset					
Booth	Stephen Charles	30 Oct 63	Leeds, Yorkshire	RH	SLA
Wyatt	Julian George	19 Jun 63	Paulton, Somerset	RH	RM

Register of New Players (contd)

Surname	Given Names	Birthdate	Place of Birth	Bat	Ball
Surrey					
Feltham	Mark Andrew	26 Jun 63	Wandsworth, London SW15	RH	RFM
Waterman	Peter Andrew	26 Mar 61	Hendon, Middlesex	RH	RFM
Sussex					
Reeve	Dermot Alexander	2 Apr 63	Hong Kong	RH	RFM
Standing	David Kevin	21 Oct 63	Brighton, Sussex	RH	OB
Warwickshire					
Lord	Gordon John	25 Apr 61	Birmingham, Warwickshire	LH	SLA
Thorne	David Anthony	12 Dec 64	Coventry, Warwickshire	RH	LM
Worcestershire					
Banks	David Andrew	11 Jan 61	Pensnett, Staffordshire	RH	RM
Moores	Peter	18 Dec 62	Macclesfield, Cheshire	RH	WK
Watkins	Stephen George	23 Mar 59	Hereford, Herefordshire	RH	RM
Yorkshire					
Fletcher	Stuart David	8 Jun 64	Keighley, Yorkshire	RH	RFM
Metcalfe	Ashley Anthony	25 Dec 63	Horsforth, Yorkshire	RH	OB
Swallow	Ian Geoffrey	18 Dec 62	Barnsley, Yorkshire	RH	OB
Cambridge University					
Cotterell	Thomas Archbold ('Archie')	12 May 63	Middlesex Hosp., London W1	RH	SLA
Hewitt	Steven Guy Paul	6 Apr 63	Radcliffe, Lancashire	RH	WK
Roebuck	Paul Gerrard Peter	13 Oct 63	Bath, Somerset	LH	RFM
Oxford University					
Carr	(see Middlesex)				
Cullinan†	Mark Ronald	3 Apr 57	Johannesburg, South Africa	RH	WK
Franks	Jonathan Guy	23 Sep 62	Stamford, Lincolnshire	RH	-
Gibaut	Russel Philip	5 Mar 63	St Saviour, Jersey	RH	RM
Harrison	Dominic Stephen	15 Jan 63	Tittensor, Staffordshire	RH	WK
Heseltine	Phillip John	21 Jun 60	Skipton, Yorkshire	RH	RM/OB
Petchey	Michael David	16 Dec 58	London	RH	RM
Smail	Alastair Harold Kurt	3 Jul 64	Kingston upon Thames	RH	LM
Turnbull	Jonathan Richard	13 Nov 62	Northwood, Middlesex	RH	RM

The following players made their first appearances in county cricket during 1983, but in limited-overs matches only. They have still to make their debuts in first-class cricket.

Surname		Birthdate	Place of Birth	Bat	Ball
Hampshire					
Hardy	Jonathan James Ean	2 Oct 60	Nakuru, Kenya	LH	-
Middlesex					
Rose	Graham David	12 Apr 64	Tottenham, London N17	RH	RM

Newcomers Record in English First-Class Cricket

Batting/Fielding		M	I	NO	HS	R	Avge	100	50	Ct	St
Derbyshire	W.P. Fowler	17	26	2	91	591	24.62	-	5	8	-
	O.H. Mortensen	18	23	15	14*	76	9.50	-	-	5	-
Essex	A.K. Golding	1	2	2	6*	8	-	-	-	-	-
	M.G. Hughes	1	2	0	10	10	5.00	-	-	-	-
Glamorgan	J. Derrick	5	5	3	24*	52	26.00	-	-	3	-
Gloucestershire	S.R. Tracy†	3	3	0	4	4	1.33	-	-	-	-
Kent	K.D. Masters	2	4	0	1	1	0.25	-	-	2	-
Lancashire	M.R. Chadwick	1	2	0	1	2	1.00	-	-	1	-
	Nasir Zaidi	13	16	6	51	215	21.50	-	1	9	-
	J. Stanworth	3	6	2	31*	90	22.50	-	-	2	-
Leicestershire	J.P. Addison	1	2	-	51	67	33.50	-	1	-	-
	G.J.F. Ferris	13	12	4	11	38	4.75	-	-	1	-
	J.J. Whitaker	10	16	4	56*	305	25.41	-	1	4	-
Middlesex	J.D. Carr‡	9	10	4	18	67	11.16	-	-	5	-
	J.F. Sykes	1	1	0	4	4	4.00	-	-	-	-
Northamptonshire	J.A. Carse	11	10	8	36*	129	64.50	-	-	-	-
	S.J. Lines	1	1	0	29	29	29.00	-	-	1	-
	M.W.C. Olley	1	1	0	8	8	8.00	-	-	3	-
	A. Walker	6	4	3	7*	18	18.00	-	-	3	-
Nottinghamshire	R.A. Pick	6	8	2	25*	84	14.00	-	-	-	-
Somerset	S.C. Booth	10	12	5	9	24	3.42	-	-	6	-
	J.G. Wyatt	6	12	2	82*	352	35.20	-	3	1	-
Surrey	M.A. Feltham	1	-	-	-	-	-	-	-	-	-
	P.A. Waterman	2	2	1	6*	6	6.00	-	-	-	-
Sussex	D.A. Reeve	17	20	5	42*	192	12.80	-	-	7	-
	D.K. Standing	4	8	3	60	240	48.00	-	2	2	-
Warwickshire	G.J. Lord	3	3	0	61	91	30.33	-	1	1	-
	D.A. Thorne	5	7	3	23*	62	15.50	-	-	3	-
Worcestershire	D.A. Banks	7	13	1	100	363	30.25	1	1	3	-
	P. Moores	7	11	1	30	154	15.40	-	-	11	2
	S.G. Watkins	1	2	0	77	105	52.50	-	1	-	-
Yorkshire	S.D. Fletcher	3	4	2	12	14	7.00	-	-	-	-
	A.A. Metcalfe	1	2	0	122	129	64.50	1	-	1	-
	I.G. Swallow	2	3	2	11*	19	19.00	-	-	1	-
Cambridge U	T.A. Cotterell	10	12	3	22	81	9.00	-	-	2	-
	S.G.P. Hewitt	6	7	2	6	9	1.80	-	-	6	1
	P.G.P. Roebuck	5	7	3	31*	82	20.50	-	-	1	-
Oxford U	M.R. Cullinan	8	8	2	27	55	9.16	-	-	14	-
	J.G. Franks	5	7	0	29	98	14.00	-	-	2	-
	R.P. Gibaut	2	2	0	7	7	3.50	-	-	-	-
	D.S. Harrison	1	2	0	8	9	4.50	-	-	-	-
	P.J. Heseltine	6	10	1	40	176	19.55	-	-	5	-
	M.D. Petchey	6	6	0	18	21	3.50	-	-	3	-
	A.H.K. Smail	6	6	1	13*	24	4.80	-	-	1	-
	J.R. Turnbull	7	7	4	5*	5	1.66	-	-	6	-

*Not out. †Includes 2 matches for New Zealanders. ‡Includes 6 matches for Oxford U.

206 EXTRAS/GUIDE TO NEWCOMERS

Bowling		O	M	R	W	Avge	Best	5w/I	10w/M
Derbyshire	W.P. Fowler	60	13	214	2	107.00	1-26	-	-
	O.H. Mortensen	518.3	108	1605	66	24.31	6-27	3	1
Essex	A.K. Golding	28	3	97	2	48.50	1-44	-	-
	M.G. Hughes	31.2	2	162	6	27.00	4-71	-	-
Glamorgan	J. Derrick	8	1	31	0	-	-	-	-
Gloucestershire	S.R. Tracy†	54.1	10	170	10	17.00	5-29	1	-
Kent	K.D. Masters	33	4	121	2	60.50	2-26	-	-
Lancashire	Nasir Zaidi	191.3	58	530	16	33.12	3-27	-	-
Leicestershire	G.J.F. Ferris	360	74	1205	53	22.73	7-42	3	1
	J.J. Whitaker	10	2	88	0	-	-	-	-
Middlesex	J.D. Carr‡	170	49	476	9	52.88	2-59	-	-
	J.F. Sykes	21	6	54	1	54.00	1-32	-	-
Northamptonshire	J.A. Carse	238.5	50	722	22	32.81	5-43	1	-
	A. Walker	165.4	30	578	22	26.27	4-61	-	-
Nottinghamshire	R.A. Pick	134.4	16	500	7	71.42	2-50	-	-
Somerset	S.C. Booth	296.2	85	849	21	40.42	4.26	-	-
Surrey	M.A. Feltham	18	5	44	2	22.00	1-19	-	-
	P.A. Waterman	39	7	151	1	151.00	1-64	-	-
Sussex	D.A. Reeve	472.1	131	1233	42	29.35	4-15	-	-
	D.K. Standing	4.3	0	32	0	-	-	-	-
Warwickshire	G.J. Lord	8	3	12	0	-	-	-	-
	D.A. Thorne	45	5	189	2	94.50	1-21	-	-
Yorkshire	S.D. Fletcher	55.4	7	186	8	23.25	4-71	-	-
	A.A. Metcalfe	2	0	6	0	-	-	-	-
	I.G. Swallow	29.4	8	82	2	41.00	1-15	-	-
Cambridge U	T.A. Cotterell	273	67	758	17	44.58	5-89	1	-
	R.G.P. Roebuck	75.5	17	269	6	44.83	2-44	-	-
Oxford U	M.D. Petchey	206.2	36	804	12	67.00	2-70	-	-
	A.H.K. Smail	70	18	222	5	44.40	3-49	-	-
	J.R. Turnbull	130	34	424	12	35.33	4-51	-	-

You're in safe hands with Cornhill Insurance.

Ask your broker about Cornhill's competitive range of insurances — for your car, your house, your life, and your business.

Cornhill Insurance Group, 32 Cornhill, London EC3V 3LJ.

 Cornhill Insurance Test Series

CORNHILL INSURANCE GROUP – SPONSOR OF ENGLISH TEST CRICKET

Obituary 1982-83

Never a year passes but the wide world of cricket loses many a well-remembered figure from the past. From the end of the 1982 English season to the end of the '83, the roll comprises eight Test cricketers of varied opportunity, four well-esteemed county captains, several other men prominent in the English first-class game, along with certain well-known administrators and umpires.

The majority, though not all, played most of their cricket between the wars and were therefore within my watching experience. First in fame was *Alan Melville* (72), the personification of elegance at the crease and the highly respected leader in turn of Oxford, Sussex, Transvaal, and South Africa. Who can argue with the stringing-together of four successive Test hundreds?

Bryan Valentine (75) was as cheerful and popular a cricketer as ever pulled on a boot, a wristy attacking bat of top quality, and a Kent captain who might have led his country but for the war. *Alfred Bakewell* (74) of Northants was within reach of the highest honours when, after opening the England innings in six Tests, his career was cut off in a motor smash. *Jack MacBryan*, a pillar of Somerset's batting, and at the age of 90 the oldest England cricketer, carried to the grave the ultimate frustration of being prevented by rain from getting an innings in his only Test.

Jack Badcock (68), though a spectacular disappointment in Tests on Australia's 1938 tour of England, was a big scorer in his own country, both for his native Tasmania and then for South Australia. *Arthur Liddicut* (91), a Victorian all-rounder who lived into his nineties, was always in the 1920s a possible for Australia without quite getting there. *H.C. Nitschke* (76), of South Australia, known as 'Slinger', a left-handed bat of belligerent inclinations, was luckier in being twice chosen for Tests; even more fortunate possibly to have bred a racehorse named Dayana, which in turn won the Derbies of four States in 1972 and the Perth Cup to boot.

Of the county captains other than the two mentioned, *Arthur Richardson* (76) brought off a pleasant surprise when in 1936 he 'broke the ring' and led Derbyshire to the Championship. Their neighbours, Notts, enjoyed for four early post-war summers the robust leadership of *Willy Sime* (74), better known previously as a Rugby footballer and latterly as a QC and county court judge.

Another whom war deprived of opportunity in his prime was the upright Surrey all-rounder *Jack Parker* (69), who was chosen to go with MCC on the cancelled Indian tour of 1940. *Walter Luckes* (81) was for many years Somerset's staunch wicket-keeper – and there were few better. *John Eggar* (66), as befitted a Winchester disciple of H.S. Altham, was a devoted schoolmaster, who in the holidays gave a welcome strengthening to the Derbyshire batting. *Derrick de Saram* (70) was in a different category from most, an Oxford batsman of high pedigree whose return to his native Ceylon meant in those days – though not in modern Sri Lanka – oblivion from the world scene.

Lastly among the established players come R.O. Talbot (79) of New Zealand, and *Gerald Innes* (50) of South Africa, both of whom went on Test tours without having the luck to be chosen for a Test match. *Arthur Coy* (80), as President of the South African Cricket Association, pleaded his country's cause fervently but in vain in the years after South Africa, by resigning from the Commonwealth, automatically barred itself from the ICC. *R.P. Mehra* (65) had a more fortunate role, as President of the Indian Board in the 1970s, when his country had come to maturity as a Test-playing nation. *George Newman* (78), a fine player in his youth, gave his energies at Lord's over many years as President of Middlesex and on the Committee of MCC.

George Hele (91) was Australia's premier umpire throughout the 1930s, and in particular during the Bodyline cataclysm. *Cortez Jordan* (61) stood successfully in many West Indies Tests and had the moral courage in their own island to no-ball Charlie Griffith for throwing. It was the first time he had been called. *Laurie Gray* (67) figured briefly as a Test umpire, but is better remembered as a Middlesex fast bowler.

All the above had run something like their allotted span, but we should spare a thought for the parents of the 17-year-old Yorkshireman, *Neil Lloyd*, who before his sudden death had already had time to show his rare promise both for the England Young Cricketers and his county 2nd XI. RIP.

E.W. Swanton

Career Details (b – born; d – died; F-c – first-class career)

BADCOCK, Clayvel Lindsay ('Jack'); b Exton, Tasmania, 10 Apr 1914; d Exton 13 Dec 82. Tasmania, South Australia, and Australia. F-c (1929-30 to 1940-41): 7371 runs (51.54), 26 hundreds.

BAKEWELL, Alfred Harry ('Fred'); b Walsall, Staffs, 2 Nov 1908; d Bournemouth 22 Jan 83. Northants and England. F-c (1928-36): 14,570 runs (33.98), 31 hundreds; 22 wkts (57.77); 267 ct.

DE SARAM, Frederick Cecil ('Derrick'); b Colombo, Ceylon, Sep 1912; d Colombo 11 Apr 83. Herts (1933-35), Oxford U. (Blue 1934 and 1935), and Ceylon.

EGGAR, John Drennan; b Nowshera, NWFP, India, 1 Dec 1916; d Hinton St George, Somerset, 3 May 83. Oxford U. (Blue 1938), Hants (1938), and Derbys (1946-54). F-c (1938-54): 1847 runs (31.85), 4 hundreds; 1 wkt (193.00).

EMERY, Raymond William George; b Auckland, New Zealand, 28 Mar 1915; d Auckland Dec 82. Auckland, Canterbury, and New Zealand. F-c (1936-37 to 1953-54): 1177 runs (29.42), 3 hundreds; 22 wkts (34.27).

GRAY, Lawrence Herbert; b Tottenham, London, 16 Dec 1915; d Langdon Hills, Essex, 3 Jan 83. Middlesex. F-c umpire 1953-70 (2 Tests, 1955 and 1963). F-c (1934-51): 901 runs (7.38); 637 wkts (25.14).

HALL, Derek; b Creswell, Derbys, 21 Feb 1932; d San Jose, California, USA, 13 Mar 83. Derbys. F-c (1955-58): 43 runs (3.31); 48 wkts (28.88).

INNES, Gerald Alfred Skerten; b Plumstead, C.P., South Africa, 16 Nov 1931; d Cape Town 19 Jul 82. W. Province and Transvaal. Toured Australia and New Zealand 1952-53. F-c (1950-51 to 1964-65): 4003 runs (33.63), 7 hundreds; 16 wkts (45.50).

JAMES, Ronald Victor; b Paddington, Sydney, Australia, 23 May 1920; d Auburn, NSW, 28 Apr 83. NSW and S. Australia. F-c (1938-39 to 1950-51): 2582 runs (40.34), 4 hundreds; 1 wkt (199.00).

JARRETT, Harold Harvey; b Johannesburg, South Africa, 23 Sep 1907; d Newport, Mon., 17 Mar 83. Warwicks (1932-33) and Glamorgan (1938). F-c (1932-38): 228 runs (15.20); 51 wkts (32.35).

LIDDICUT, Arthur Edward; b Fitzroy, Melbourne, Australia, 17 Oct 1891; d Parkdale, Melbourne, 8 Apr 83. Victoria. Toured New Zealand 1920-21 (Australians) and 1924-25 (Victoria). F-c (1911-12 to 1932-33): 2503 runs (31.28), 3 hundreds; 133 wkts (27.56).
LUCKES, Walter Thomas; b London, 1 Jan 1901; d Bridgwater, Somerset, 27 Oct 82. Somerset. F-c (1924-29): 5640 runs (16.02), 1 hundred; 586 ct, 241 st.
MacBRYAN, John Crawford William ('Jack'); b Box, Wilts, 22 Jul 1892; d London 14 Jul 83. Cambridge U. (Blue 1920), Somerset, and England. F-c (1911-36): 10,322 runs (29.50), 18 hundreds.
MEHRA, Ram Prakash; b Lahore, India, 16 Mar 1917; d New Delhi 7 Mar 83. N. India (1934-35 to 1951-52) and Delhi. President of Board of Control for Cricket in India 1975-77. F-c 1934-35 to 1953-54): 1202 runs (30.82). Scored 209* v Maharashtra in 1940-41.
MELVILLE, Alan; b Carnarvon, C.P., South Africa, 19 May 1910; d Kruger Park, Transvaal, Apr 83. Oxford U. (Blue 1930-31-32-33, captain 1931 and 1932), Sussex (1932-36 – captain 1934 and 1935), Transvaal, and South Africa. Scored four hundreds in consecutive Test innings (1938-39 and 1947). F-c (1928-29 to 1948-49): 10,598 runs (37.85), 25 hundreds; 132 wkts (29.99); 156 ct.
NEWMAN, George Christopher; b London 26 Apr 1904; d Braintree, Essex, 13 Oct 82. Oxford U. (Blue 1926 and 1927) and Middlesex. F-c (1926-36): 2742 runs (25.87), 3 hundreds; 17 wkts (39.41).
NICHOLLS, Charles Omer; b Freeman's Reach, Windsor, NSW, 5 Dec 1901; d Jan 83. NSW. F-c (1925-26 to 1928-29): 369 runs (21.70), 1 hundred; 37 wkts (37.51).
NITSCHKE, Holmesdale Carl ('Slinger' or 'Jack'); b Adelaide, Australia, 14 Apr 1906, d Adelaide 29 Sep 82. S. Australia and Australia. F-c (1929-30 to 1934-35): 3320 runs (42.03), 9 hundreds.
PARKER, John Frederick ('Jack'); b Battersea, London, 23 Apr 1913; d Bromley, Kent, 26 Jan 83. Surrey. F-c (1932-52): 14,272 runs (31.58), 20 hundreds; 543 wkts (28.87); 331 ct.
RICHARDSON, Arthur Walker; b Quarndon, Derbys, 4 Mar 1907; d Ednaston 29 Jul 83. Derbys. F-c (1928-36): 3982 runs (19.05).
SIME, William Arnold (Judge W.A. Sime, CMG, MBE, QC); b Wepener, OFS, South Africa, 8 Feb 1909; d Wymeswold, Leics, 5 May 83. Beds and Notts. F-c (1929-50): 2473 runs (20.44), 1 hundred; 49 wkts (46.94).
SWAMY, V. Narain; b in India 23 May 1924; d Dehradun, India, 1 May 83. Services and India. F-c (1951-52 to 1958-59): 201 runs (14.35); 68 wkts (22.16).
TALBOT, Ronald Osman; b Christchurch, New Zealand, 26 Nov 1903; d Auckland 5 Jan 83. Canterbury and Otago. Toured England 1931. F-c (1922-23 to 1935-36): 1946 runs (24.63), 3 hundreds; 54 wkts (37.14).
VALENTINE, Bryan Herbert; b Blackheath, Kent, 17 Jan 1908; d 2 Feb 83. Cambridge U. (Blue 1929), Kent, and England. F-c (1927-50): 18,306 runs (30.15), 35 hundreds; 27 wkts (41.29); 309 ct.
WATKINS, Bert Thomas Lewis; b Gloucester 25 Jun 1902; d Badminton, Glos 1983. Gloucestershire. F-c (1932-38): 211 runs (6.03); 35 ct, 18 st.
WILLIAMS, Richard Harry; b Brockmoor, Staffs, 23 Apr 1901; d Stourbridge, Worcs, Dec 82. Worcestershire. F-c (1923-32): 713 runs (11.14).

Their Record in Tests

Batting/Fielding	M	I	NO	HS	R	Avge	100	50	Ct	St
C.L. Badcock (Aus)	7	12	1	118	160	14.54	1	–	3	–
A.H. Bakewell (Eng)	6	9	0	107	409	45.44	1	3	3	–
R.W.G. Emery (NZ)	2	4	0	28	46	11.50	–	–	–	–
J.C.W. MacBryan (Eng)	1	–	–	–	–	–	–	–	–	–
A. Melville (SA)	11	19	2	189	894	52.58	4	3	8	–
H.C. Nitschke (Aus)†	2	2	0	47	53	26.50	–	–	3	–
V.N. Swamy (Ind)	1	–	–	–	–	–	–	–	–	–
B.H. Valentine (Eng)	7	9	2	136	454	64.85	2	1	2	–

†left-handed batsman

Bowling	Type	Balls	R	W	Avge	Best	5w/I	10w/M
A.H. Bakewell (Eng)	RM	18	8	0	–	–	–	–
R.W.G. Emery (NZ)	RM	46	52	2	26.00	2-52	–	–
V.N. Swamy (Ind)	RFM	108	45	0	–	–	–	–

Looking forward

England on Tour 1983-84

England's Tour Party

	Age	Caps
Bob Willis, captain (Warwicks)	34	83
David Gower, vice-capt. (Leics)	26	53
Ian Botham (Somerset)	28	63
Nick Cook (Leics)	27	2
Norman Cowans (Middlesex)	22	8
Graham Dilley (Kent)	24	17
Neil Foster (Essex)	21	1
Graeme Fowler (Lancs)	26	6
Mike Gatting (Middlesex)	26	24
Allan Lamb (Northants)	29	15
Vic Marks (Somerset)	28	2
Derek Randall (Notts)	32	40
Chris Smith (Hants)	25	2
Chris Tavaré (Kent)	29	26
Bob Taylor (Derbyshire)	42	51

Tour Manager: A.C. Smith (Warwicks). Assistant Manager: N. Gifford (Warwicks). Physiotherapist: Bernard Thomas. Scorer: Geoffrey Saulez.

Tour Itinerary

In Fiji
- January 2 — One-day match
- 3 — One-day match

In New Zealand
- January 7-9 — Auckland
- 11-13 — Central District (Palmerston North)
- 14-16 — Northern District (Hamilton)
- 20-24 — NEW ZEALAND (Wellington), First Test
- 27-29 — Otago (Dunedin)
- 30 — Otago Invitation XI (Alexandra)
- February 3-7 — NEW ZEALAND (Christchurch), Second Test
- 10-15 — NEW ZEALAND (Auckland), Third Test
- 18 — New Zealand (Christchurch), one-day international
- 22 — New Zealand (Wellington), one-day international
- 25 — New Zealand (Auckland), one-day international

In Pakistan
- March 2 — Pakistan (Karachi), one-day international
- 4 — Pakistan (Lahore), one-day international
- 7-12 — PAKISTAN (Karachi), First Test
- 15-20 — PAKISTAN (Faisalabad), Second Test
- 23-28 — PAKISTAN (Lahore), Third Test

The 1984 Season

The 1984 season in England will depart slightly from the norm, in that after a full Test series against West Indies, England will play their first home Test match against Sri Lanka. This will be at Lord's over the August Bank Holiday week-end, and will not follow the pattern of Nottingham last season, when Sunday play meant that the Bank Holiday fell on the fifth day.

Habits differ throughout the country, and Nottinghamshire doubtless had good reason for wishing to play on Sunday – when in the event only about 4,000 were present. But in most parts, the public is probably not attuned to turning out on a Sunday morning for a whole day's cricket. A family outing to a John Player match for four and a half hours on a Sunday afternoon is a different matter.

It is only two and a half years since West Indies were playing the last of 11 scheduled Test matches in 10 months against England. As most of their side play for English counties, it would be overdoing it to say that they were awaited with the same excitement as was the great George Headley, whose visits in the 1930s were six years apart, or the 'three Ws', Ramadhin, and Valentine, who came in 1950 and not again until 1957.

But the huge population of West Indian origin now in England provides a ready market, and the economic advantages of frequent tours are undoubted. May this visit pass as peacefully as possible. Discussions have already been necessary to clarify the counties' freedom to pick whom they wish against the tourists, and there are usually different outlooks on such subjects as the over-rate and bouncers. Attempts to increase the former and reduce the latter are sometimes seen as dark plots to undermine West Indies' fast-bowling strength.

In theory, West Indies should be in the throes of reconstruction and slightly less formidable than in recent years. Some of their fast bowlers have been at the top for a long time. But as England are in even more prolonged throes with their bowling, and in their captain have a fast bowler even more venerable, that may not prove very significant.

Only twice since World War II have England won a home series against West Indies – in 1957 in the heyday of Peter May, and in 1969 when England under Illingworth defeated West Indies under Sobers. Indeed they have not won one Test match against West Indies in England since 1969, though in the same period Australia, not always with very good sides, have beaten West Indies nine times at home.

It is not hard to put up a reason for this singular disparity. West Indian pitches nowadays are more akin to English pitches in pace and bounce than they are to Australian. And many West Indian cricketers, some permanently resident in England, are so familiar with English conditions through playing here on youth tours and for the counties that they are as much at home as their opponents.

Michael Melford

Fixtures 1984

Duration of Matches (*including play on Sunday)

Cornhill Tests	5 days	NatWest Bank Trophy	1 day
County Championship	3 days	Benson & Hedges Cup	1 day
Tourist matches	3 days or as stated	John Player League	1 day
University matches	3 days	Other matches	as stated

APRIL 18, WEDNESDAY
Cambridge Univ v Leicestershire

APRIL 21, SATURDAY
Cambridge Univ v Essex
Oxford Univ v Nottinghamshire

APRIL 25, WEDNESDAY
MCC v Essex (Lord's)
Cambridge Univ v Hampshire
Oxford Univ v Glamorgan

APRIL 28, SATURDAY
County Championship
Derbyshire v Leicestershire
Gloucestershire v Kent*
Hampshire v Essex
Middlesex v Glamorgan
Nottinghamshire v Surrey
Somerset v Yorkshire*
Warwickshire v Northamptonshire
Worcestershire v Sussex*

Other match
Oxford Univ v Lancashire

MAY 2, WEDNESDAY
County Championship
Kent v Essex
Lancashire v Derbyshire
Nottinghamshire v Leicestershire
Surrey v Northamptonshire
Worcestershire v Glamorgan

Other matches
Cambridge Univ v Sussex
Oxford Univ v Somerset

MAY 5, SATURDAY
Benson & Hedges Cup
Essex v Gloucestershire
Glamorgan v Somerset
Hampshire v Combined Universities
Middlesex v Kent
Northamptonshire v Scotland
Nottinghamshire v Worcestershire
Yorkshire v Leicestershire
Minor Counties v Lancashire

County Championship
Warwickshire v Surrey

MAY 6, SUNDAY
John Player League
Essex v Nottinghamshire
Glamorgan v Gloucestershire
Hampshire v Sussex
Leicestershire v Derbyshire
Middlesex v Kent
Warwickshire v Surrey
Yorkshire v Worcestershire

MAY 9, WEDNESDAY
County Championship
Derbyshire v Glamorgan
Hampshire v Gloucestershire
Lancashire v Kent
Leicestershire v Worcestershire
Northamptonshire v Essex
Sussex v Surrey
Yorkshire v Nottinghamshire

Other matches
Cambridge Univ v Warwickshire
Oxford Univ v Middlesex

MAY 12, SATURDAY
Benson & Hedges Cup
Gloucestershire v Hampshire
Kent v Glamorgan
Lancashire v Nottinghamshire
Leicestershire v Warwickshire
Somerset v Sussex
Worcestershire v Derbyshire
Scotland v Yorkshire
Combined Universities v Surrey

MAY 13, SUNDAY
John Player League
Lancashire v Northamptonshire
Middlesex v Essex
Somerset v Hampshire
Surrey v Glamorgan
Worcestershire v Nottinghamshire

MAY 15, TUESDAY
Benson & Hedges Cup
Derbyshire v Nottinghamshire
Essex v Surrey
Gloucestershire v Combined Universities
Kent v Somerset
Leicestershire v Northamptonshire
Middlesex v Sussex
Warwickshire v Yorkshire
Worcestershire v Minor Counties

LOOKING FORWARD/FIXTURES 1984

MAY 17, THURSDAY
Benson & Hedges Cup
Lancashire v Worcestershire
Northamptonshire v Warwickshire
Somerset v Middlesex
Surrey v Hampshire
Sussex v Glamorgan
Scotland v Leicestershire
Minor Counties v Derbyshire
Combined Universities v Essex

MAY 19, SATURDAY
Benson & Hedges Cup
Derbyshire v Lancashire
Glamorgan v Middlesex
Hampshire v Essex
Nottinghamshire v Minor Counties
Surrey v Gloucestershire
Sussex v Kent
Warwickshire v Scotland
Yorkshire v Northamptonshire
County Championship
Leicestershire v Somerset
Tourist match
Worcestershire v West Indies*

MAY 20, SUNDAY
John Player League
Derbyshire v Lancashire
Glamorgan v Middlesex
Kent v Surrey
Leicestershire v Somerset
Northamptonshire v Warwickshire
Sussex v Gloucestershire
Yorkshire v Nottinghamshire

MAY 23, WEDNESDAY
County Championship
Derbyshire v Surrey
Essex v Nottinghamshire
Glamorgan v Gloucestershire
Middlesex v Northamptonshire
Sussex v Hampshire
Warwickshire v Lancashire
Worcestershire v Leicestershire
Tourist match
Somerset v West Indies

MAY 26, SATURDAY
County Championship
Derbyshire v Nottinghamshire
Essex v Surrey
Kent v Hampshire
Leicestershire v Northamptonshire
Middlesex v Sussex
Somerset v Gloucestershire
Warwickshire v Worcestershire
Yorkshire v Lancashire*

Tourist match
Glamorgan v West Indies*

MAY 27, SUNDAY
John Player League
Essex v Surrey
Gloucestershire v Somerset
Leicestershire v Sussex
Middlesex v Northamptonshire
Nottinghamshire v Derbyshire
Warwickshire v Worcestershire

MAY 29, TUESDAY
Tourist match
Lancashire v West Indies (one day)

MAY 30, WEDNESDAY
County Championship
Hampshire v Somerset
Kent v Middlesex
Northamptonshire v Lancashire
Surrey v Glamorgan
Warwickshire v Nottinghamshire
Worcestershire v Essex
Yorkshire v Sussex
Other match
Oxford Univ v Gloucestershire

MAY 31, THURSDAY
First One-day International
England v West Indies (Old Trafford)

JUNE 2, SATURDAY
Second One-day International
England v West Indies (Trent Bridge)
County Championship
Derbyshire v Middlesex
Glamorgan v Worcestershire
Hampshire v Nottinghamshire
Kent v Gloucestershire
Lancashire v Surrey
Leicestershire v Essex
Sussex v Northamptonshire
Yorkshire v Somerset
Other match
Ireland v MCC*

JUNE 3, SUNDAY
John Player League
Derbyshire v Middlesex
Hampshire v Nottinghamshire
Kent v Gloucestershire
Lancashire v Surrey
Leicestershire v Essex
Sussex v Northamptonshire
Worcestershire v Glamorgan
Yorkshire v Somerset

LOOKING FORWARD/FIXTURES 1984

JUNE 4, MONDAY
Third One-day International
England v West Indies (Lord's)

JUNE 6, WEDNESDAY
Benson & Hedges Cup
Quarter-Finals

JUNE 7, THURSDAY
Tourist match
Comb Universities v West Indies (two days)

JUNE 9, SATURDAY
County Championship
Essex v Warwickshire
Gloucestershire v Derbyshire
Kent v Yorkshire
Lancashire v Sussex
Nottinghamshire v Glamorgan
Somerset v Middlesex
Surrey v Leicestershire
Worcestershire v Hampshire
Tourist match
Northamptonshire v West Indies*

JUNE 10, SUNDAY
John Player League
Essex v Warwickshire
Gloucestershire v Derbyshire
Kent v Yorkshire
Lancashire v Sussex
Nottinghamshire v Glamorgan
Somerset v Middlesex
Surrey v Leicestershire
Worcestershire v Hampshire

JUNE 13, WEDNESDAY
County Championship
Essex v Derbyshire
Gloucestershire v Worcestershire
Hampshire v Yorkshire
Kent v Sussex
Leicestershire v Warwickshire
Middlesex v Surrey
Somerset v Lancashire
Other match
Glamorgan v Cambridge Univ

JUNE 14, THURSDAY
First Cornhill Test
ENGLAND v WEST INDIES (Edgbaston)

JUNE 16, SATURDAY
County Championship
Essex v Northamptonshire
Glamorgan v Lancashire
Hampshire v Leicestershire
Middlesex v Warwickshire
Nottinghamshire v Gloucestershire
Surrey v Sussex
Yorkshire v Derbyshire
Other matches
Cambridge Univ v Worcestershire
Oxford Univ v Kent

JUNE 17, SUNDAY
John Player League
Derbyshire v Yorkshire
Essex v Northamptonshire
Glamorgan v Lancashire
Hampshire v Leicestershire
Middlesex v Warwickshire
Nottinghamshire v Gloucestershire
Somerset v Kent
Surrey v Sussex

JUNE 20, WEDNESDAY
Benson & Hedges Cup
Semi-Finals
Other match
Tilcon Trophy (Harrogate, 3 days)

JUNE 21, THURSDAY
Tourist match
Ireland v West Indies (two days)

JUNE 23, SATURDAY
County Championship
Derbyshire v Kent
Gloucestershire v Hampshire
Lancashire v Worcestershire
Leicestershire v Nottinghamshire
Northamptonshire v Yorkshire
Surrey v Middlesex
Sussex v Glamorgan
Warwickshire v Somerset
Tourist match
Essex v West Indies*

JUNE 24, SUNDAY
John Player League
Derbyshire v Kent
Gloucestershire v Hampshire
Lancashire v Worcestershire
Leicestershire v Nottinghamshire
Northamptonshire v Yorkshire
Surrey v Middlesex
Sussex v Glamorgan
Warwickshire v Somerset

LOOKING FORWARD/FIXTURES 1984

JUNE 27, WEDNESDAY

County Championship
Derbyshire v Essex
Glamorgan v Middlesex
Hampshire v Sussex
Lancashire v Gloucestershire
Northamptonshire v Warwickshire
Nottinghamshire v Yorkshire
Somerset v Leicestershire
Worcestershire v Kent

Other match
Surrey v Cambridge Univ

JUNE 28, THURSDAY

Second Cornhill Test
ENGLAND v WEST INDIES (Lord's)

JUNE 30, SATURDAY

County Championship
Glamorgan v Leicestershire
Lancashire v Middlesex
Northamptonshire v Somerset
Surrey v Hampshire
Sussex v Kent
Warwickshire v Gloucestershire
Worcestershire v Derbyshire
Yorkshire v Essex

Other match
Nottinghamshire v Cambridge Univ

JULY 1, SUNDAY

John Player League
Glamorgan v Leicestershire
Lancashire v Middlesex
Northamptonshire v Somerset
Surrey v Hampshire
Sussex v Kent
Warwickshire v Gloucestershire
Worcestershire v Derbyshire
Yorkshire v Essex

JULY 4, WEDNESDAY

NatWest Bank Trophy (First Round)
Cumberland v Derbyshire
Durham v Northamptonshire
Essex v Scotland
Glamorgan v Nottinghamshire
Hertfordshire v Somerset
Kent v Berkshire
Lancashire v Buckinghamshire
Norfolk v Hampshire
Northumberland v Middlesex
Shropshire v Yorkshire
Staffordshire v Gloucestershire
Surrey v Ireland
Sussex v Devon
Warwickshire v Oxfordshire
Wiltshire v Leicestershire
Worcestershire v Suffolk

Other match
Oxford Univ v Cambridge Univ (Lord's)

JULY 5, THURSDAY

League Cricket Conference v W. Indies (2 days)

JULY 7, SATURDAY

County Championship
Derbyshire v Warwickshire
Essex v Glamorgan
Kent v Lancashire
Middlesex v Worcestershire
Northamptonshire v Surrey
Nottinghamshire v Sussex
Somerset v Hampshire
Yorkshire v Gloucestershire

Tourist match
Leicestershire v West Indies*

JULY 8, SUNDAY

John Player League
Derbyshire v Warwickshire
Essex v Glamorgan
Kent v Lancashire
Middlesex v Worcestershire
Northamptonshire v Surrey
Nottinghamshire v Sussex
Yorkshire v Gloucestershire

JULY 11, WEDNESDAY

County Championship
Essex v Lancashire
Glamorgan v Yorkshire
Hampshire v Northamptonshire
Kent v Derbyshire
Leicestershire v Sussex
Middlesex v Gloucestershire
Nottinghamshire v Somerset
Worcestershire v Warwickshire

JULY 12, THURSDAY

Third Cornhill Test
ENGLAND v WEST INDIES (Headingley)

JULY 14, SATURDAY

County Championship
Glamorgan v Somerset
Gloucestershire v Essex
Hampshire v Lancashire
Middlesex v Yorkshire
Northamptonshire v Kent
Nottinghamshire v Worcestershire
Surrey v Derbyshire
Warwickshire v Sussex

218 LOOKING FORWARD/FIXTURES 1984

JULY 15, SUNDAY
John Player League
Glamorgan v Somerset
Gloucestershire v Essex
Hampshire v Lancashire
Middlesex v Yorkshire
Northamptonshire v Kent
Surrey v Derbyshire
Warwickshire v Sussex
Worcestershire v Leicestershire
Other match
Ireland v Wales

JULY 18, WEDNESDAY
NatWest Bank Trophy (Second Round)
Durham or Northants v Worcs or Suffolk
Essex or Scotland v Surrey or Ireland
Glamorgan or Notts v Northumberland or Middx
Norfolk or Hants v Kent or Berks
Staffs or Gloucs v Lancs or Bucks
Sussex or Devon v Herts or Somerset
Warwicks or Oxon v Shrops or Yorks
Wilts or Leics v Cumberland or Derbys
Tourist match
Minor Counties Cricket Association v West Indies

JULY 21, SATURDAY
Benson & Hedges Cup
Final (Lord's)
Tourist match
Derbyshire (or Warwicks, depending on B&H final) v West Indies*

JULY 22, SUNDAY
John Player League
Hampshire v Yorkshire
Kent v Essex
Leicestershire v Gloucestershire
Nottinghamshire v Northamptonshire
Somerset v Lancashire
Worcestershire v Sussex

JULY 25, WEDNESDAY
County Championship
Derbyshire v Lancashire
Gloucestershire v Leicestershire
Northamptonshire v Middlesex
Somerset v Glamorgan
Surrey v Kent
Warwickshire v Hampshire
Yorkshire v Worcestershire
Tourist match
Nottinghamshire v Sri Lanka

JULY 26, THURSDAY
Fourth Cornhill Test
ENGLAND v WEST INDIES (Old Trafford)

JULY 28, SATURDAY
County Championship
Essex v Worcestershire
Glamorgan v Derbyshire
Gloucestershire v Northamptonshire
Middlesex v Hampshire
Nottinghamshire v Lancashire
Sussex v Somerset
Warwickshire v Kent
Yorkshire v Leicestershire
Tourist match
Surrey v Sri Lanka*

JULY 29, SUNDAY
John Player League
Essex v Worcestershire
Glamorgan v Derbyshire
Gloucestershire v Northamptonshire
Middlesex v Hampshire
Nottinghamshire v Lancashire
Sussex v Somerset
Warwickshire v Kent
Yorkshire v Leicestershire

AUGUST 1, WEDNESDAY
NatWest Bank Trophy
Quarter-Finals
Tourist Match
Notts (if free) v West Indies

AUGUST 4, SATURDAY
County Championship
Hampshire v Warwickshire
Kent v Leicestershire
Lancashire v Yorkshire
Northamptonshire v Derbyshire
Somerset v Surrey
Sussex v Essex
Worcestershire v Nottinghamshire
Tourist matches
Middlesex v West Indies*
Gloucestershire v Sri Lanka*

AUGUST 5, SUNDAY
John Player League
Hampshire v Warwickshire
Kent v Leicestershire
Lancashire v Yorkshire
Northamptonshire v Derbyshire
Somerset v Surrey
Sussex v Essex

LOOKING FORWARD/FIXTURES 1984

Other matches
Warwick Under-25 semi-finals (one day)
(or Sunday, 12 August)
Gloucs v Worcs (Friendly)

AUGUST 8, WEDNESDAY
County Championship
Gloucestershire v Glamorgan
Kent v Surrey
Lancashire v Northamptonshire
Leicestershire v Yorkshire
Middlesex v Essex
Nottinghamshire v Derbyshire
Somerset v Worcestershire
Sussex v Warwickshire

Tourist match
Hampshire v Sri Lanka

AUGUST 9, THURSDAY
Fifth Cornhill Test
ENGLAND v WEST INDIES (The Oval)

AUGUST 11, SATURDAY
County Championship
Derbyshire v Sussex
Essex v Somerset
Glamorgan v Hampshire
Gloucestershire v Surrey
Leicestershire v Lancashire
Middlesex v Nottinghamshire
Northamptonshire v Worcestershire
Yorkshire v Warwickshire

Tourist match
Kent v Sri Lanka*

AUGUST 12, SUNDAY
John Player League
Derbyshire v Sussex
Essex v Somerset
Glamorgan v Hampshire
Gloucestershire v Surrey
Leicestershire v Lancashire
Middlesex v Nottinghamshire
Northamptonshire v Worcestershire
Yorkshire v Warwickshire

Other matches
Warwick Under-25 semi-finals (one day)
(If not played on Sunday, 5 August)

AUGUST 15, WEDNESDAY
NatWest Bank Trophy
Semi-Finals

AUGUST 18, SATURDAY
County Championship
Essex v Hampshire
Glamorgan v Northamptonshire
Kent v Nottinghamshire
Lancashire v Warwickshire
Leicestershire v Middlesex
Somerset v Derbyshire
Surrey v Yorkshire
Worcestershire v Gloucestershire

Tourist match
Sussex v Sri Lanka*

AUGUST 19, SUNDAY
John Player League
Essex v Hampshire
Glamorgan v Northamptonshire
Kent v Nottinghamshire
Lancashire v Warwickshire
Leicestershire v Middlesex
Somerset v Derbyshire
Surrey v Yorkshire
Worcestershire v Gloucestershire

Other match
Warwick Under-25 Final (one-day)

AUGUST 22, WEDNESDAY
County Championship
Derbyshire v Yorkshire
Essex v Kent
Hampshire v Middlesex
Lancashire v Nottinghamshire
Leicestershire v Gloucestershire
Northamptonshire v Sussex
Surrey v Somerset
Warwickshire v Glamorgan

Other match
Scotland v Ireland

AUGUST 23, THURSDAY
Cornhill Test Match
ENGLAND v SRI LANKA (Lord's)

AUGUST 25, SATURDAY
County Championship
Gloucestershire v Lancashire
Hampshire v Kent
Northamptonshire v Leicestershire
Nottinghamshire v Warwickshire
Surrey v Essex
Sussex v Middlesex
Worcestershire v Somerset
Yorkshire v Glamorgan

LOOKING FORWARD/FIXTURES 1984

AUGUST 26, SUNDAY

John Player League
Gloucestershire v Lancashire
Hampshire v Kent
Northamptonshire v Leicestershire
Nottinghamshire v Warwickshire
Somerset v Worcestershire
Sussex v Middlesex
Yorkshire v Glamorgan

AUGUST 29, WEDNESDAY

County Championship
Essex v Middlesex
Glamorgan v Surrey
Nottinghamshire v Northamptonshire
Somerset v Kent
Sussex v Gloucestershire

Tourist match
Warwickshire v Sri Lanka

Other match
Derbys v Yorks (Scarborough, one-day, ASDA Cricket Challenge)

AUGUST 30, THURSDAY

Hants v Lancs (Scarborough, one-day ASDA Cricket Challenge)

AUGUST 31, FRIDAY

ASDA Final (Scarborough, one-day)

SEPTEMBER 1, SATURDAY

NatWest Bank Trophy
Final (Lord's)

SEPTEMBER 2, SUNDAY

John Player League
Derbyshire v Essex
Hampshire v Northamptonshire
Nottinghamshire v Surrey
Warwickshire v Glamorgan
Worcestershire v Kent

Tourist match
D.B. Close's International XI v Sri Lanka
(Scarborough, 3 days)

SEPTEMBER 5, WEDNESDAY

County Championship
Glamorgan v Warwickshire
Gloucestershire v Somerset
Leicestershire v Derbyshire
Middlesex v Kent
Sussex v Nottinghamshire
Worcestershire v Northamptonshire
Yorkshire v Hampshire

SEPTEMBER 8, SATURDAY

County Championship
Derbyshire v Hampshire
Gloucestershire v Middlesex
Kent v Glamorgan
Lancashire v Essex
Somerset v Nottinghamshire
Surrey v Worcestershire
Sussex v Yorkshire
Warwickshire v Leicestershire

SEPTEMBER 9, SUNDAY

John Player League
Derbyshire v Hampshire
Gloucestershire v Middlesex
Kent v Glamorgan
Lancashire v Essex
Somerset v Nottinghamshire
Surrey v Worcestershire
Sussex v Yorkshire
Warwickshire v Leicestershire

Fixtures are the copyright of the Test and County Cricket Board 1984.